The People's Network

AMERICAN BUSINESS,
POLITICS, AND SOCIETY

Series editors
Andrew Wender Cohen, Richard R. John,
Pamela Walker Laird, Mark H. Rose,
and Elizabeth Tandy Shermer

Books in the series American Business, Politics, and Society explore the relationships over time between governmental institutions and the creation and performance of markets, firms, and industries large and small. The central theme of this series is that politics, law, and public policy—understood broadly to embrace not only lawmaking but also the structuring presence of governmental institutions—has been fundamental to the evolution of American business from the colonial era to the present. The series aims to explore, in particular, developments that have enduring consequences.

A complete list of books in the series
is available from the publisher.

The People's Network

The Political Economy of the Telephone in the Gilded Age

Robert MacDougall

PENN

UNIVERSITY OF PENNSYLVANIA PRESS

PHILADELPHIA

Published by
University of Pennsylvania Press
Philadelphia, Pennsylvania 19104-4112
www.upenn.edu/pennpress

Printed in the United States of America on acid-free paper
10 9 8 7 6 5 4 3 2 1

Library of Congress Cataloging-in-Publication Data

MacDougall, Robert.
The people's network : the political economy of the telephone in the Gilded Age / Robert MacDougall.—1st ed.
p. cm.—(American business, politics, and society)
Includes bibliographical references and index.
ISBN 978-0-8122-4569-1 (hardcover : alk. paper)
1. Telephone—United States—History—20th century. 2. Telephone—Canada—History—20th century. 3. Telephone companies—United States—History—20th century. 4. Telephone companies—Canada—History—20th century. 5. Telephone—Government policy—United States—History—20th century. 6. Telephone—Government policy—Canada—History—20th century. 7. American Telephone and Telegraph Company—History. 8. Bell Canada—History. I. Title. II. Series: American business, politics, and society.
TK6023.M25 2013
384.60973′09041—dc23

2013031255

This story should appeal especially to those who have good red American blood in their veins. It is the story of a magnificent fight that was won against overwhelming odds. It is the story of a smug coterie of "Boston gentlemen" of the immaculate type, put to flight by a few sturdy men out of the West. It is the story of a low, scheming campaign of greed that was turned into a rout by a fine, sentimental, American citizenship. . . . It is the story of at least one trust that was "busted." It is a story that, while dealing with the details of an industrial war, will interest even the women, for it is full of good, clean, honest fighting, of the deeds of men who stood shoulder to shoulder under the Stars and Stripes, and, in the name of American freedom and independence, lined up against the most complete and relentless, and successful monopoly of the times—and beat it to a pulp.

—Paul Latzke, *A Fight with an Octopus*, 1906

Contents

Introduction. A Fight with an Octopus 1

Chapter 1. All Telephones Are Local 19

Chapter 2. Visions of Telephony 61

Chapter 3. Unnatural Monopoly 92

Chapter 4. The Independent Alternative 132

Chapter 5. The Politics of Scale 174

Chapter 6. The System Gospel 227

Conclusion. Return to Middletown 259

Notes 271

Index 321

Acknowledgments 331

Introduction

A Fight with an Octopus

In 1906, on the thirtieth anniversary of the telephone's invention, an entrepreneurial author named Paul Latzke published a history of the device called *A Fight with an Octopus.*[1] This was not the story of the telephone that most of us think we know. In Latzke's version of events, Alexander Graham Bell was a fraud. He had not invented the telephone in 1876, as almost everyone believed. Instead, Latzke charged, Bell had swindled the telephone's true inventor, who might have been his rival Elisha Gray, or a Pennsylvania mechanic named Daniel Drawbaugh, or any one of several other contenders. But Alexander Graham Bell was not the villain of Latzke's tale. The real villain was the cluster of corporations organized in his name —the nation-spanning system Latzke called the Bell octopus. For twenty years, Latzke wrote, the Bell octopus had "fastened a gouging monopoly on the necks of the American people."[2] It bribed the press, corrupted government, and manipulated the courts. It charged exorbitant rates, keeping telephones out of all but the wealthiest offices and homes. It refused to serve small towns and rural areas. It grew rich under the shield of fraudulent patents and strangled the growth of a revolutionary new technology.

But then, Latzke said, the people rose up against the octopus. Bell's original patents on the telephone expired in 1894. The Bell companies tried to extend their monopoly with new patents, but the courts struck these down. And when Bell's patents expired, Latzke said, a new era in the telephone's history was born. Enterprising Americans who resented Bell's rates and haughty attitudes started their own companies. Tens of thousands of telephone systems were created in the years immediately after 1894, competing with Bell in hundreds of American cities, and bringing the telephone to thousands of smaller towns and villages that the old monopoly did not serve. The coming of competition, Latzke argued, triggered the mass diffusion of telephone service in America. Prices dropped, access spread, and use of the device grew explosively. The number of telephones in the United States shot from the thousands to the millions in only a few short years.

The heroes of Latzke's fable were the "sturdy citizens who risked their fortunes and their careers in the cause of American Industrial Independence." They called themselves the independent telephone movement. These independents were at once idealists and opportunists, activists and entrepreneurs. They spoke of "giving telephony back to the people," and they saw no contradictions between their goals of smashing the Bell monopoly, serving the cause of democracy, and getting rich. When Latzke published *A Fight with an Octopus* in 1906, the independent movement was nearing its zenith in terms of political influence and market share. After little more than a decade, the independents controlled more than half of the six million telephones in the United States. In parts of the Midwest, independent telephones outnumbered Bell telephones by a factor of five to one, and Bell's regional operating companies were teetering on the brink of bankruptcy, looking for ways to withdraw entirely from the field. "The people," Latzke cheered, had beaten the octopus "to a pulp."[3]

A Fight with an Octopus was hardly reliable history. Latzke was a speculator in telephone stocks and bonds, so his fortune rose and fell with the fortunes of the independent telephone movement. Friends of the Bell companies called Latzke's book "miserable" and "disreputable," a "tissue of falsehoods and slanderous misrepresentations."[4] And if *A Fight with an Octopus* was bad history, as prediction it proved weaker still. In 1906, the independent movement had bloodied the Bell octopus, but the trust was far from busted. Even as Latzke wrote, Bell's parent company was changing hands and direction. In the years to come, the Bell interests would regroup and reorganize, ultimately defeating independent competition and emerging stronger than ever from the battle. A decade after Latzke's book, the independent telephone companies were nearly finished as any kind of coherent movement, though individual independents still remained. By the 1920s, what had come to be called the "Bell System" controlled more than 80 percent of the telephone industry. Its master, the American Telephone and Telegraph Company, was the largest and wealthiest corporation in the world.

Yet Latzke did get one thing right. There was once a fierce battle between Bell and the independents, an "industrial war" which has almost entirely been forgotten. The fighting in this war was not as good, clean, or honest as Latzke claimed, but the stakes were high and the outcome uncertain. What is more, the fight for access to the telephone was not limited to competition between Bell and its independent rivals. It involved a tug-of-war between telephone companies and their own customers, and disputes among different kinds of customers, both as individuals and in groups. The struggle involved different branches and levels of government, as they wrestled for authority over the new industry and medium. The fight for the telephone was also evident between different parts of the Bell System, a term that belies real divisions among the Bell companies at this time. And of course it was fought outside the United States, in every country that adopted the telephone, with different outcomes on different political terrain. This book is about all those struggles in two nations—the United States and Canada—and how they built the communication infrastructure we have today. These fights were at once commercial, political, and cultural. They were also part of a broader debate, much bigger than the telephone, over the social and economic transformations of the age.

How did we come to forget these battles? In part, the blame must fall on historians and the existing literature on the history of the telephone. That history has been kind to AT&T, because AT&T wrote it. Unlike many corporations, the American Telephone and Telegraph Company took an enduring interest in its past. Between the consolidation of the Bell System in the 1910s and its breakup in the 1980s, AT&T personnel wrote or commissioned hundreds of books, pamphlets, and films about the history of the telephone.[5] These works portrayed AT&T's rise to wealth and power as the stately and inevitable unfolding of a benevolent monopoly. They dismissed competition as an error or aberration; the independents appeared as comic villains or not at all.[6] AT&T also shaped its own historical image by preserving millions of documents and artifacts in an astounding set of corporate archives. The AT&T Archives and Historical Collections have been an immense boon to historians. Yet they have also bent the history of the telephone toward AT&T's point of view.[7] Even scholars who are critical of the Bell monopoly have depended on these archives. As a result, their work can be almost as AT&T-centric as the corporate histories they challenge. Of course there are exceptions, but on the whole, historical literature has more often effaced than explored the political, commercial, and cultural struggles of the telephone's early days.[8]

But there is more behind this erasure than a simple gap in the literature. The history of technology has a curious way of disappearing from our memories. When a device or medium like the telephone is new, it is almost impossible not to notice it and remark on it. But as that device becomes more familiar, it recedes from our attention. In particular, we cease to notice the choices made in constructing that device. In inventing and deploying any technological system, people make countless decisions. A patent is granted to one inventor and not another. A wire is built here and not there. Some of these decisions are of little note, but others serve concrete political, economic, and cultural interests. There are winners and losers in the history of any new technology. But once that technology is no longer new, those choices and outcomes are typically forgotten. The device or medium, along all with the social and political structures that surround it, comes to seem natural and inevitable. Nowhere is this truer than in the history of the telephone. Few devices are more ubiquitous or familiar. We have a hard time remembering how anyone got along without the telephone, or imagining that it could have taken a different form.

There is a forgotten history of the telephone that lies outside the American Telephone and Telegraph Company. This history can be found in the trade journals and publications that surrounded and promoted the independent telephone movement. It can be found in the surviving records of AT&T's independent rivals, and in the archives of the regional Bell operating companies, which had their own histories and interests until AT&T brought them all to heel. It can be found in the archives of town and city governments that struggled to regulate the new technology. It can be found in the diverging paths taken by the telephone industry in different regions, in Canada as well as the United States. This alternative history can even be found in actual, physical networks. The telephones, poles, and wires of a century ago are historical sources in their own right, both evidence and artifacts of Latzke's forgotten fight.[9]

The entrepreneurs of the independent movement—men like Indiana's Henry Barnhart, Nebraska's Frank Woods, and New York's John Wright—were in this fight for profit, but they were also animated by their vision of "a telephone for the people." They believed, or at least professed to believe, that the new medium had a civic mission to fulfill. They argued strenuously that communication networks ought to be owned and operated by the people who lived in the communities they served. They saw the telephone as a democratizing force, a weapon against monopoly capital, and an instrument for defending the autonomy of small communities and regions. Advocates of the people's telephone argued that "local" did not equal "backward," that prosperity and progress did not inevitably require centralization, and that there were good reasons to be wary of the new nation-spanning corporations and their power.

Such ideas were hardly unique to the independent telephone movement. These ideas could be heard from many quarters, including at least one of Bell Telephone's founders, and they predated the arrival of independent competition by several years. Indeed, they descended from a civic understanding of communication that went back to the American Revolution if not before—the belief that free and open communications were a basic ingredient of democracy.[10] But the call for a people's telephone had more specific resonance in the last decades of the nineteenth century and the first decades of the twentieth. Questions of corporate size, regional autonomy, and monopoly power were never more salient to American politics than in these years. In the historical moment at which the telephone appeared, debates about the new technology could not escape becoming debates about monopoly and antimonopoly; these two opposing poles exerted a magnetic pull on the politics and technology of the day. Competing telephone networks were seen as articulations of dueling political philosophies. Enlist the telephone in the service of monopoly, and you might build something resembling the Bell System. Enlist the telephone in the service of antimonopoly, and you have the people's telephone.

This book describes the contests between rival visions of the telephone in the United States and Canada, exploring the interplay of political economy, business strategy, and social practice in the construction of North American telecommunications. Comparing two nations helps illuminate the role of context and contingency in shaping final outcomes. In particular, the comparison reveals that the political environments of different regions encouraged certain appeals or arguments while discouraging others. These arguments found expression in competing visions of telephony—like the populist-inflected vision of a people's telephone, which took hold in the American Midwest but never found the same purchase in Central Canada—and were ultimately embodied in the actual networks that different regions built. Thus, political and cultural debates took physical form in the poles and wires of competing telephone systems.

The argument of this book is not that history could have been different—although it could have been. In different regions, and under different regulatory structures, Americans and Canadians constructed very different sorts of networks. Outcomes often appeared natural or inevitable in retrospect, but they were not. Nor is it the argument of this book that history *should* have been different. Readers will discern that I am sympathetic, on the whole, to the people's telephone idea. But I am less interested in advocating for either side of a battle fought one hundred years ago than I am in understanding that battle and its outcome. The argument of this book is that history *was* different: the history of the telephone was altogether more contentious, dramatic, and significant than the story we think we know. The forgotten fight for the telephone—and by this I mean not only competition between Bell and the midwestern independents, but also broader debates in both Canada and the United States over the meaning, use, and organization of telephony—was more than just a commercial skirmish. It was a turning point in the history of communications and information networks. The implications of that moment were bigger than the telephone. For it was not only the telephone that became ubiquitous yet invisible; it was the whole corporate order constructed in those years. The story told in this book did not turn out as Paul Latzke must have hoped, but it was indeed "full of dramatic interest." I hope it appeals to those who have "good red American blood in their veins," and even to some that do not.[11]

The Incorporation of North America and the Politics of Scale

The octopus, the spider, the hydra—historians find these images of large corporations strewn across the culture of the late nineteenth and early twentieth century like the bones of dinosaurs long extinct. Why were Americans of this era so inclined to portray big business in this manner? Any large corporation might be imagined by its enemies as a monstrous, ravenous beast. But the specificity of these images suggests a particular anxiety. The grasping tentacles of the octopus are what made it a powerful symbol, as are the long limbs of the spider and the ensnaring strands of its web. These were visual metaphors for new technological networks—railroad tracks, oil pipelines, telephone and telegraph wires—that sprawled across geographic space. How often were the railroads, telephone and telegraph companies, and oil trusts depicted as monsters stretched across maps or globes? The octopus and the spider were not caricatures of corporate size alone. They were nightmares of reach: vivid depictions of local and individual autonomy being threatened by forces from afar.[12]

Few features of late nineteenth-century life seemed more novel or remarkable to observers than the new technologies of reach. In the decades

Figure 1. The midwestern independents portrayed their Bell rival as an octopus, stretching its tentacles across the plains. "The Octopus Releasing Its Grasp," *Telephony*, April 1907, 235.

after the Civil War, railroads linked the far-flung corners of North America. A transcontinental telegraph was completed in 1861, providing theoretically instantaneous communication from coast to coast. And the telephone, born in the centennial year of 1876, grew to augment, rival, and eventually eclipse its older sibling, connecting almost every home and life to international networks of communication and exchange.[13]

These networks were the nerves and arteries of a new economic order. When it emerged from the Civil War as the nation's dominant telegraph network, the Western Union Telegraph Company became the first truly national corporation in the United States. At once creation, agent, and symbol of the new interdependence, Western Union's nation-spanning wires made new kinds of business organization possible. First organized as local and regional undertakings, the railroads used the telegraph to expand their reach over great distance, amassing armies of employees and building thousands of miles of track. New managerial hierarchies were devised to oversee the growing complexity and geographic scope of these corporations, and new financial systems were created to raise the large amounts of capital railroad construction required. Other industries followed in these tracks. The investment mechanisms that provided funds for railroad construction and consolidation in the 1870s and 1880s bankrolled an extraordinary wave of corporate mergers in the decades that followed. In the five years from 1898 to 1902, over two thousand American companies were absorbed into roughly 150 larger firms. Big business, "big" in both an organizational and a geographic sense, had arrived.[14]

Words like modernization and consolidation are unavoidable in business history, but such terms are too bloodless to capture the turmoil of the so-called Gilded Age.[15] Consider a few synchronicities from the year of the telephone's invention. Think of them as scenes from the incorporation of America. The day that Alexander Graham Bell demonstrated his telephone at the 1876 Centennial Exhibition in Philadelphia was the very same day that a force of Lakota and Cheyenne defeated George Armstrong Custer and the Seventh U.S. Cavalry at the Battle of Little Big Horn. We rarely associate Custer's last stand with American business history, but the Seventh Cavalry was in the Black Hills only to protect the Northern Pacific Railroad; Custer himself was on the railroad's payroll and a stakeholder in several mining ventures in the region.[16] The following winter, while Bell toured the country promoting his new invention, the Western Union Telegraph Company and its news-gathering partner the Western Associated Press played a key role in promoting the so-called Compromise of 1877, removing federal troops from the South and effectively ending Reconstruction.[17] And a week after the Bell Telephone Company was founded in July 1877, railroad workers in West Virginia launched what became the United States' first national strike. News of the strike flashed along telephone and telegraph lines, igniting uprisings of sympathetic workers as far afield as Texas and California, while President Rutherford Hayes used the same wires to monitor and ultimately quash the strikes. Thousands were wounded and over one hundred killed in bloody clashes between striking laborers and the troops dispatched to put them down.[18]

From the Civil War to the Indian wars, from class struggle to cutthroat competition, the incorporation of America was an unruly and often violent process. In the words of muckraking journalist Ida Tarbell, the late nineteenth century "dripped with blood."[19] North of the border, the consolidation of British North America into Canada is widely held to have been more peaceful, but conflict and upheaval were hardly unknown. 1876 and 1877 were also years of explosive violence between workers and capitalists in the Maritime Provinces of New Brunswick and Nova Scotia. On the other side of the continent, the railroad and telegraph were instrumental in both provoking and putting down the Northwest Rebellion of Louis Riel and his Métis and Native followers in 1885.[20] The violent spasms of the late nineteenth century make barely a ripple in the history of the telephone as it has traditionally been written. And the telephone's history is rarely connected to these broader struggles. Yet this was the milieu in which the telephone was invented and deployed. The history of the wire and the incorporation of North America were inextricably intertwined.

One of the nineteenth century's great clichés was that the rail and wire would "annihilate" space and time. The violence of that phrase is rarely remarked on. Why were time and space to be "annihilated," rather than simply transcended or transformed?[21] The pace of change in this era was exhilarating and at the same time wrenching and alarming to many Americans. Each advance in communication technology gave new powers to its users yet compounded the ability of distant people and events to affect those users' lives. As society and economy became more obviously interdependent, it proved harder to imagine individual people or communities as the solitary masters of their fates. The causes of conditions and events seemed to move further away and become more difficult to trace. Local sources of meaning and order such as the family or the parish were, in one historian's vivid words, "drained of causal potency," becoming "merely the final links in long chains of causation that stretched off into a murky distance."[22] Towns and villages that could once be imagined as stable, homogenous "island communities" feared absorption into national and even international networks. Historians have raised questions about how isolated nineteenth-century communities really were.[23] But perceptions of shrinking distance and autonomy were genuine, and the fears they roused were real. The small seemed threatened by the big, the local vulnerable to the national, in every part of American life.

How big is big? How near is far? Where do the boundaries of the local lie? Scale itself is cultural and political. Our experiences and representations of space, scale, and distance are not simply natural or given but are constructed by human choices and institutions.[24] The technological and organizational changes of the late nineteenth century destabilized understandings of distance. They created a new politics of scale where the meaning of these concepts would be contested and redefined. Virtually all the political and economic battles surrounding the construction of nineteenth-century railroads were at some level about the organization and production of space. Turn-of-the-century Americans were less divided on the legitimacy of big business than on what big business might do to distance, and what it might do to the autonomy of their island communities.[25] The incorporation of America provoked a host of vigorous political responses, among them agrarian populism, urban progressivism, and municipal home rule. All these movements were, in various ways, attempts to grapple with what it meant to live in a more networked nation and a smaller, more interdependent world.

Many of these movements flowed into and out of the political tradition known broadly as antimonopolism.[26] Antimonopolism was not a single movement, but a language of resistance to the growing concentration of economic and political power. Prosperous merchants, prairie populists, and labor activists all learned to speak this language. Their concerns and programs varied, but most who marched under the banner of antimonopoly mistrusted the rapid rise of giant corporations and a single financial market centered in New York. They argued for decentralized alternatives to the new economic order, for regionally oriented rather than nationally oriented economies, and for public policies geared to sustaining competition rather than enabling monopoly.

Because these paths were not taken, it has been common for historians, sympathetic or otherwise, to see antimonopoly movements as antimodern, backward-looking opponents of progress or technological change.[27] This is an unfortunate distortion. Antimonopolists were not reactionaries but reformers. They believed in change, but charted in a different direction than their corporate opponents. Far from fearing or rejecting technologies like the railroad, telegraph, and telephone, many antimonopolists embraced them as central to their plans. Antimonopolists called for greater regulation of the railroads and for a government takeover of the telegraph. They sought rate structures and reforms that would put these technologies in service to smaller firms and more regional commerce.[28] In the same way, municipal politicians, independent telephone promoters, and others enlisted the telephone in the defense of regional autonomy, against the consolidation with which communication technologies are generally associated. The struggle between the antimonopoly movement and its opponents was, in other words, an argument about space and scale. What was the proper scale of political power and economic life? And the space-bending networks of the telephone, like those of the railroad and the telegraph before them, would be central to this fight.

General Kemper's Two Telephones

In 1929, the sociologists Robert and Helen Lynd published *Middletown*, their classic study of life in one ordinary American city. The Lynds began their book with a catalog of technological changes that had arrived in the lifetime of one Middletown resident, born in 1839. "Within the lifetime of this one man," the Lynds claimed, the people of Middletown had progressed from lives unchanged since "the time of Homer" to a world of telephones, radios, airplanes, and automobiles.[29]

Though not identified in the Lynds' book, "Middletown" was in fact Muncie, Indiana, and the elderly resident was a retired doctor named General William Harrison Kemper. Named for General William Henry Harrison, Kemper was not a general; "General" was his first name. Twenty years before the Lynds' arrival, Kemper had written his own history of Muncie and the surrounding county. In it, he linked the technological advances cited by the Lynds to broader transformations in political economy, economic geography, and social structure. "The history of a county like Delaware abounds with proofs that individualism is yielding to social interdependence," Kemper wrote: "The world, whether our scope of view be a county, state or nation, is coming to be all of a piece. Once every little community could live by itself, make its own clothes, wagons, tools, and all the articles necessary for its existence. But with the coming of the railroad, telegraph, telephone, etc., closer relations were established and communities and states became dependent upon each other. There is no isolation now."[30]

The trajectory Kemper described, from "isolation" to "social interdependence," is today one of our central paradigms for understanding American history in the half century following the Civil War. Historians chronicling this era have spoken of "the response to industrialism," "the search for order," and "the incorporation of America."[31] Most agree that a crucial development of this period was the rise of nation-spanning corporations and a corresponding eclipse of smaller groups and firms. Various historians have attributed this expansion in scale of social and economic life to industrialization, to the visible hand of managerial capitalism, and to the rise of a nationally minded middle class. But when Kemper reached for an explanation for the sweeping changes through which he had lived, he found it first in the technological triumvirate of railroad, telegraph, and telephone.

Two telephones sat in General Kemper's parlor as he composed his thoughts on electrical communication and social change. Kemper knew that the changes he and Muncie had witnessed were much bigger than the two telephones sitting by his desk; yet he also believed that those two telephones were crucial to their outcome. "Electrical communication," Kemper wrote in 1908, was the "greatest vital issue" facing the United States.[32] But why did Kemper have *two* telephones? What difference did that make? Kemper was at that time one of a few hundred Muncie residents who paid two bills and kept two telephones in his home. One of these telephones was operated by the Bell-affiliated Central Union Telephone Company and connected Kemper to its lines and those of several other Bell companies, which by 1908 linked more than four million telephones from New York to Colorado. Kemper's other telephone was part of a much smaller network, of about fifteen hundred telephones, built by the local Delaware and Madison County Telephone Company and completely separate from the Bell lines. This hometown independent offered a few unreliable regional links, but its strength lay in intensive local coverage, connecting Kemper to his patients in the farms and tiny villages of Muncie's rural hinterland.

Each of these networks represented a different understanding of the telephone and its role. One, the still-emerging Bell System, symbolized and promoted nationwide connection and integration. The other, Muncie's hometown independent, stood for locally oriented networks and local control of commerce and communication. Independent leaders and promoters asked why "foreign" corporations—that is, companies based in far-off places like Boston or New York—should be allowed to take money from midwestern consumers. In return, Bell and AT&T executives sang the praises of consolidation and intercommunication, and they encouraged their customers to see themselves as part of an integrated national economy. Thus, the competition between Bell and its independent rivals became a referendum on the organizational transformation of the age. Choosing between these two networks was fraught with personal and political significance, as Kemper understood.

Two Cities and Two Nations

A contemporary of General Kemper's, living in Kingston, Ontario, Canada, shared some of the Indiana doctor's convictions about electrical communication and its import. George Monro Grant, the principal of Queen's University at Kingston, described his own young country as an "archipelago" of island settlements in an "ocean" of wilderness. In 1872, Grant accompanied a coast-to-coast expedition surveying a route for the Canadian Pacific Railway. He became a lifelong promoter of Canadian confederation and of those technological systems, like the railroad and telegraph, that might strengthen the British Empire and Canada's place within it. "How much nearer to the core of the Empire may not Canada be considered," Grant asked, "with the means of instantaneous telegraphic communications extended to every part of the Dominion?" Plagued by anxieties about distance and disunity, Canadians like Grant were, if anything, even more enthralled by the promise of rails and wires than their American neighbors.[33]

Both Canadians and Americans claim credit for the telephone through the inventor Alexander Graham Bell. Bell was actually born in Scotland but moved to Canada as a young man and crossed back and forth between the United States and Canada throughout his life. He made his first telephone call in Boston, Massachusetts, in March 1876, and in Brantford, Ontario, later that year, his first "long distance" call (over a distance of about eight miles).[34] In both countries, the telephone industry would be dominated to varying degrees by a network of companies organized around Alexander Bell's original patents. Though ostensibly autonomous, the Bell Telephone Company of Canada was deeply dependent on American Bell, and later AT&T, for capital, equipment, direction, and personnel.[35]

Living in large nations in which state-building and commerce involved communication across great distances, both Americans and Canadians took a special interest in devices like the telephone. Living in young countries with distinct sectional tensions, both Americans and Canadians grappled with issues of regional versus national identity, and of local versus centralized economic and political power. And living under federal systems with multiple levels of government, both Americans and Canadians had to decide where to locate authority over the telephone. In doing all these things, Canadians and Americans faced the question of just what the new technology was and what it was for.

The telephone developed differently in each country. Indeed, the telephone industries that developed in the United States and Canada were different from each other and from those in every other nation. In almost every other part of the world, the telephone began as or soon became a national, government-run monopoly, often under the aegis of the national postal service. In the United States, the industry remained in private hands, excepting one year of government control during World War I. With the rise of the independents in the 1890s and 1900s, Americans saw telephone competition on a scale seen nowhere else in the world. Canadians also left the telephone in private hands, at least in its early years. Regulatory differences between the two countries made the Bell monopoly in Central Canada far more secure than in the American Midwest. Elsewhere in Canada, the Bell interests did not fare as well. They suffered from their failure to serve French Canadians in Quebec and lost several of the western provinces to an uprising of prairie populism. A patchwork of regional monopolies—some private, some public, some mixed—emerged in Canada and nowhere else.

Most histories of the telephone tell national stories. Based as they are on documents from the archives of AT&T or Bell Canada, they generally accept a single firm and a centrally controlled national network as their basic unit of study.[36] As useful as these histories have been, they reproduce a picture of change from the top down and the center out, beginning at the first Bell headquarters in Boston or at Bell Canada in Montreal. This book uses a transnational and comparative approach to trace the history of the telephone. My approach is transnational because the history of the telephone in Canada and the United States is in many ways one story, linked by border-crossing people, capital, and wires. But my approach is also comparative, as I contrast national and regional cases to shed light on each.[37] Systematic comparison of Canadian and American history is surprisingly rare. Historians in the United States are rarely well informed about the history of Canada; while Canadian historians are marginally more knowledgeable about the United States, they are prone to stock generalizations and the narcissism of minor differences. There is little reason for this to be so. Because of their proximity and deep similarity, each country offers a test case for all manner of comparative questions about the development of the other. Certainly, the different paths taken by the telephone in the two countries, and in different regions within each country, beg for comparative explanation.[38]

This book begins with case studies of two small cities—Kemper's Muncie, Indiana, and Grant's Kingston, Ontario—and then steps back to tell a larger tale. The first chapter steps out of strict chronological order to tell the story of the telephone in Kingston and Muncie from the 1870s to the 1910s. The second chapter returns to the 1870s, and from there the narrative is roughly chronological, though the scene does shift from place to place. Readers seeking a straight chronological narrative with no spoilers may skip ahead to Chapter 2. But I begin with local case studies because the first telephone systems *were* local. They were local networks, providing only local service, largely built with local capital by local entrepreneurs. Like Robert and Helen Lynd, I make no strong claims for the universality of Muncie's experience, or of Kingston's.[39] The point is not that every city in the United States made the same choices as Muncie, or that every city in Canada built a telephone network like Kingston's. On the contrary, the case studies are meant to demonstrate a variety of options and thus the importance of local choices in shaping the telephone's birth.[40]

That said, Muncie and Kingston do each demonstrate a pattern in the development of the telephone. These patterns were not national but regional.[41] In the farmland of eastern Indiana, Muncie lay near the heart of the independent telephone movement and midwestern opposition to Bell. Its dueling telephone networks and the raucous, egalitarian culture of telephone use they spawned were typical of hundreds of towns and cities across the American Midwest. Kingston's experience was similarly typical of Central Canada. Its story of private monopoly, thwarted municipal regulation, and a more genteel, less expansive, telephone culture exemplifies the experience of the technology in much of Ontario and Quebec.

Sketched in this way, these stories seem to dovetail with stereotypes about acquisitive, entrepreneurial Americans and placid, deferential Canadians. But we should be wary of explanations that ascribe concrete differences in commercial or political development to vague notions about national character. If we say that Canada and the United States are different because Canadians and Americans are different, we have not said very much.[42] We come closer to a causal explanation of these differences when we compare the strength of independent competition in the midwestern United States to its relative weakness in Canada. Clearly, competition shaped the development of the telephone in Indiana just as monopoly shaped it in Ontario. But why did competition thrive in one region while it languished in another?

The real story is political. Political choices, and the underlying jurisdictional differences that made these choices possible, are what launched the paths of telephone development in Muncie, in Kingston, and in hundreds of other communities in both countries. Almost from the invention of the telephone in 1876, local governments in the American Midwest took an active interest in the device. Before the advent of competition in the 1890s, and long before the emergence of state and federal regulation in the 1900s, midwestern town and city councils encouraged the construction of locally owned telephone systems, levied taxes on out-of-state telephone companies, and actively regulated telephone rates and the placement of poles and wires. In Central Canada, by contrast, local governments wanted to take a stronger hand in the telephone industry but had little power to do so.

These early developments had significant consequences for the future of the telephone. Independent competition thrived in the 1900s and 1910s in the very towns and cities where municipal government had been actively involved in the telephone industry since the 1870s and 1880s. Even where competition did not emerge, municipal pressure forced reluctant telephone companies into offering wider and cheaper access, greater interconnection between town and farm, and more permissive protocols of telephone use. In towns and cities without municipal engagement, competition withered or was blocked, and the idea of a people's telephone never took hold.

These trajectories highlight the power of political structures and public policies to shape business strategy, technological development, and even culture and ideas. The populism of the independent telephone movement was encouraged and rewarded by the regional political economy of the American Midwest but thwarted by corresponding political structures in Central Canada and the northeastern United States. In Ontario, the political environment pushed Bell Canada into posing as, and to some extent becoming, an agent of national unity. Business strategies and commercial outcomes were channeled by the structures of the state—and the states, provinces, and municipalities too.[43] So too were rhetoric and political culture. When physical telephone networks, the structure of the telephone industry, and ideas about the telephone were brought into harmony with existing political structures, the results would seem inevitable—not the outcome of a contested political process, but the natural evolution of the technology. But what was "natural" and "inevitable" differed from place to place. Impressions of inevitability concealed the differences political environments had made.

To say that things could have been otherwise is not to say that all outcomes were equally likely. To highlight the role played by the independent telephone movement in shaping North America's communication networks is not to deny the formidable power and ingenuity of that movement's opponents at AT&T. The triumph of powerful and moneyed actors often looks predetermined, especially in retrospect. But that is an argument for the significance of politics and power, not against it.

The comparative aspect of this history is ironic in the end. In Canada, the telephone was framed as a national undertaking and an instrument of Canadian unity. Yet Bell Canada did not create a single national system. The patchwork telephone network that had emerged in Canada by the 1910s was both symbolic and symptomatic of the country's decentralized federalism and its distinctly regional identities and economies. In the United States, on the other hand, the telephone was enlisted by independent entrepreneurs, municipal politicians, and others in the fight to preserve local and regional autonomy. By the 1920s, the independents were finished as a political and commercial force, but they had transformed the telephone and indeed their foes at Bell and AT&T. This fight, and the political conditions that made it possible, set American telephony on a different path than in any other nation. AT&T did not imitate the independents so much as outflank them, but it did learn from them, and in the crucible of the telephone struggles, it forged a powerful defense of big business and consolidation that would be applied well beyond the telephone field. No American company did more than AT&T in the 1910s and 1920s to legitimize the new nation-spanning corporation, or to sell Americans on the desirability and inevitability of national integration through commerce.

Debates and contests over the telephone returned again and again to issues Kemper, Grant, and Latzke had raised—questions of independence, interconnection, and scale. These were not simply arguments about the way the telephone or the telephone industry should be organized. These were arguments about the way the country ought to be organized, and about the ways that commerce and information should flow. These debates shaped technical and commercial choices made by network builders—where to construct telephone lines, how to charge for service, and so on. In this way, ideas and attitudes about scale and distance were wired into competing telephone systems. The dueling networks of turn-of-the-century telephony came to embody, in their very technology, dueling arguments about the proper scale of social and economic life. Great and abstract struggles—large corporations against small firms, national markets against local ones, and even more existential questions about national, regional, and local identities—were fought by proxy over the telephone and its wires.

Chapter 1

All Telephones Are Local

"They have been with us a long time. They will outlast the elms." So begins "Telephone Poles," a poem by the author John Updike. The novelty of a poem about telephone poles underscores Updike's reflection on their everyday invisibility. "Our eyes . . . run through them," he writes. "They blend along small-town streets / Like a race of giants that have faded into mere mythology." This is even truer today than when "Telephone Poles" was published in 1963. Our communication infrastructure is ubiquitous but unseen. Underground cables and satellite links render some parts of the network literally invisible, but telephone poles and wires still stand along many highways and residential streets. Our eyes simply run through them. Through reliability and familiarity, the physicality of our communication networks, and the choices we made in building them, have faded from our view. "Yet they are ours," Updike continues, noting marks on the poles made by linemen's cleats and spikes set at intervals for human legs to climb. "We made them." His poem is a succinct statement of what historians call the social construction of technology. Our tools and systems are ours. For good or ill, we made them. To rescue their history from mythology, we must open our eyes to the built environment around us, to see our marks on it and the marks it has made on us. We might begin with that utterly prosaic, nearly invisible construction, the common telephone pole.[1]

In December 1880, the newly chartered Bell Telephone Company of Canada erected three utility poles on the Rue de Buade, a short but busy thoroughfare in the oldest part of Quebec City. The streets of Old Quebec are famously narrow; at its skinniest point, the cobblestoned Rue de Buade was only thirty-two feet wide. To leave room for carriage traffic, one of the three poles was set directly in the middle of a footpath beside the street. That pole obstructed the front door of a local newspaper, the *Quebec Daily*

Telegraph. This made an enemy of the paper's publisher, James Carrel, who launched a crusade against the Bell Telephone Company and its invasive poles. Through the spring and summer of 1881, Carrel wrote blistering editorials attacking Bell Canada's "abominable aggressions," the "useless . . . extravagance" of its product, and the "intolerable grievance" of its "unsightly and obstructive telephone masts."[2] Ultimately, Carrel's fight brought the legal status of the telephone before the courts, Quebec's provincial legislature, the Canadian Parliament in Ottawa, and the Judicial Committee of the Privy Council in London. The decisions made by these bodies would set the telephone industry in Canada on a very different trajectory than the industry in the United States. In the end, Carrel lost the war against his wooden nemesis. But it cannot be said that he met its arrival lying down.

Carrel was not alone in his indignation. Newspapers and magazines in the 1880s called utility poles eyesores and traffic hazards, "outrages that in almost any European city would lead to revolution and bloodshed."[3] Sometimes municipal governments ordered their fire departments to chop down offending poles. Sometimes company linemen perched atop those poles to prevent firemen from chopping. Vigilantes tore wires down by night, and company workmen snuck out to erect new lines under cover of darkness. Farmers charged that telephone and telegraph wires were poisoning their crops and altering the weather.[4] During a smallpox epidemic in Quebec in 1885, rumors spread that the disease was transmitted by telephone lines, and an angry mob attacked the Montreal exchange.[5]

It is difficult to appreciate the intensity of feeling that a telephone pole could once provoke. We can hardly imagine a time when poles and wires were controversial, even frightening, harbingers of change. Yet in the late nineteenth century, the physical presence of the new communication networks was far harder to ignore. Before the 1890s, almost all telephone and telegraph lines ran above ground, and every private telephone required its own separate wire. In cities like New York and Chicago, downtown utility poles stood up to ninety feet tall—two or three times the height of an average pole today—and thousands of wires blackened the sky. Cartoons from the era show forests of poles and crossbars blocking city streets, and pedestrians entangled as if in a spider's web. Of course these images exaggerate, but like James Carrel's fulminations, they help us recapture the subjective experience of this new technology at a time when it was anything but invisible.

Telephone poles and wires became sites of conflict for municipal governments, telephone companies, and the publics that both claimed to serve.

Figure 2. Telephone and telegraph poles and wires were far from invisible in the 1880s and 1890s. In cities like New York and Chicago, utility poles stood up to ninety feet tall, and thousands of wires blackened the sky. This cartoon appeared in *Harper's Weekly* in 1881 with an article entitled "The Tyranny of Monopolies." The image was "not greatly exaggerated," claimed the magazine. *Harper's Weekly*, 14 May 1881, 312–315.

One particular pole blocking a footpath in Quebec City forced Canadians to debate whether telephone networks were essentially local, regional, or national in character. They reached a different position on this question than many of their counterparts in the United States. I will return to that story in a few pages, and to the difference that it made. But my larger point is that every telephone pole rooted the new technology to a specific place, and thus every pole was a potential site of political maneuver and cultural debate. All telephone poles are local. To begin a history of telecommunication with a prosaic wooden pole is to insist on a story that is both physical and political, rooted in city streets and local choices.

Histories of the telephone often begin with Alexander Graham Bell tinkering in his Boston garret, then chronicle the growth of the company that took his name. We imagine a single telephone network spreading outward across the country. But this is not how the telephone grew. In the 1870s and 1880s, Americans and Canadians built hundreds of entirely separate telephone systems in hundreds of cities and towns. These little systems were local undertakings, providing only short-distance service. They were franchised by municipal governments and operated by local firms. Long-distance calling, state and federal regulation, and a united Bell System all lay in the future. A tumultuous history of political and commercial struggle preceded the state and federal regulation of the telephone industry in the 1900s, but the invisibility of municipal politics, like the invisibility of utility poles, has kept it from our view.[6]

This chapter tells the story of the telephone in two ordinary communities—Muncie, Indiana, and Kingston, Ontario—from the 1870s to the 1910s. The following chapters return to the 1870s and then move chronologically through the broader story of the telephone in both the United States and Canada. But I begin with the history of the telephone as experienced in Kingston and Muncie in order to illustrate the importance of local politics, and the politics of localism, in the construction of the telephone. This history may end with a single, continent-spanning network, but it did not begin that way. For some, that was never the goal.

Middletown and Centreville

The sociologists Robert and Helen Lynd came to Muncie, Indiana, in 1924, Helen Lynd recalled, "precisely because there was nothing exceptional about it."[7] John D. Rockefeller's Institute of Social and Religious Research had commissioned the Lynds to find and study one truly representative American community. They chose Muncie, a modest midwestern city fifty miles northeast of Indianapolis, and renamed it "Middletown." Kingston, Ontario, had no Lynds to make it famous, but Kingston in the late nineteenth and early twentieth centuries was at least as representative of Canada as Muncie was of the United States. Canadian scholars and marketers have indeed regarded Kingston as a microcosm of its larger society, and it offers a plausible Canadian Middletown—call it "Centreville."[8]

Muncie sits on flat Indiana farmland; Kingston's hinterland is gnarled by the rocky hills of the Canadian Shield. Kingston's proudest buildings are gray limestone; Muncie's are red brick. But beyond superficial differences, the two cities were, in the Lynds' day, much the same. At the start of the twentieth century, each contained about twenty thousand people. (Kingston is considerably larger than Muncie today.) Each had a handful of churches, a stately courthouse, and a town hall. Each had the same wooden-frame houses for the working-class majority, and the same middle-class professionals clustered around a small university. In each, a handful of wealthy families owned the mills and factories and principal stores. The great majority of residents were white, Protestant, and native born.[9] Each city was governed by a mayor and an elected city council, and in each city, considerable informal power was held by a handful of prosperous business elites. Both cities boasted fledgling industries—Muncie made glass jars and steel wire, Kingston textiles and pianos—but their economies were chiefly local and agricultural in orientation. Both were trading centers for farmers in surrounding counties, and the day was not far gone in either town when swine and cattle roamed the downtown streets. In all these ways, Muncie and Kingston looked much like each other, and like dozens of other cities in Central Canada and the midwestern United States.[10]

In September 1877, the first telephones in the state of Indiana made their debut at the state fair. Two wooden transmitters were connected at opposite corners of the fairgrounds, and Hoosier farmers lined up to shout, sing, and whistle to their friends along the wire. The demonstration was sponsored by a pair of local coal merchants, who ran advertisements in the local newspapers for weeks, urging Indiana fairgoers to "See and Hear the Wonder!"[11] Also in September 1877, the telephone was introduced to the city of Kingston, but in a rather different setting. A select group of leading citizens gathered for a piano recital in the parlor of one of Kingston's grandest homes. The tinkling of the piano was transmitted by telephone from the other side of town. This demonstration was arranged by the Reverend Thomas Henderson, a former Kingston resident and a family friend of Alexander Graham Bell. Press coverage was modest, and attendance by invitation only. The mayor, certain business leaders, and a handful of clergymen were there.[12]

So Indiana met the telephone on the grounds of the state fair, while Kingston made its introduction behind oak panels and lace curtains. One telephone was hawked to farmers and fairgoers like a carnival attraction; the other was introduced into polite society like a debutante, vetted by old connections and family friends. The technology was identical; indeed, the first telephone switchboards in each city were manufactured by the same

Indianapolis firm. But its reception was different in each locale. Choices that Muncie and Kingston would make about the telephone, and other choices imposed on them, would shape the development of the new medium and the contests over its control.

In Muncie and across the American Midwest, local businesses and politicians pushed vigorously for hometown control of telephony. After Alexander Graham Bell's original patents on the telephone expired in 1894, and another key patent was overturned by the courts, the Bell interests in the Midwest and elsewhere faced decades of aggressive competition from thousands of small, locally oriented telephone systems. But this independent telephone movement did not begin with the end of the Bell patents. It grew out of earlier clashes in the 1880s between the telephone industry and local governments and would have been impossible without the active involvement of mayors, city councils, and Main Street business elites. In Kingston, by contrast, local interests made less effort and had far less success in asserting control over the telephone's development. The Bell patents in Canada were actually overturned in 1885, a decade earlier than in the United States, but independent competition in Ontario never approached the size or intensity seen in Indiana or the rest of the Midwest. In almost all of Central Canada's urban centers, the Bell Telephone Company of Canada maintained its monopoly on the industry and to some extent the meaning of the telephone.

Telephones spread faster and further in Indiana than Ontario. In Muncie and the rest of the Midwest, middle-class and even working-class citizens became telephone users and subscribers long before their counterparts in Kingston and in Central Canada generally. And midwestern telephone networks spread from towns and cities into rural areas sooner and with more success than in Canada or elsewhere in the United States. With these diverging patterns of growth, distinctly different cultures of telephone use emerged. The telephone culture of Muncie and the Midwest was far friendlier to social and indeed frivolous uses of the telephone, like gossiping, singing and banjo playing, or eavesdropping on party lines. The telephone culture of Kingston and Central Canada was more inclined to restrict such practices, defining the telephone first and foremost as a tool for business, something serious and genteel. These distinctions were reflected and reinforced by different billing structures but also represented social and cultural choices about which kinds of speech and interconnection were worthwhile and which were not.

The most important difference shaping the development of the telephone in Muncie and Kingston was the involvement and relative power of each city's municipal government. In Muncie and the Midwest, local government was an active participant in constructing the city's telephone system, regulating services and rates, encouraging local ownership, and levying taxes and fees. In Central Canada, by contrast, local government played little role in building or regulating the new networks. There were legal reasons for this difference, and they turned on the question of the network's local nature. Were telephone networks local, regional, or national projects? What level of government had authority over a technology whose wires seemed to annihilate distance while its poles were rooted in local space? Governments, corporations, courts, and consumers debated these questions in the early days of the telephone and came to different answers in different regions. The choices they made set the politics and culture of telecommunication on divergent paths.

Poles and Politics

In September 1882, Connecticut telephone executive Morris Tyler reported to his colleagues on the state of telephone legislation across the United States. The action and the danger, from Tyler's perspective, was clearly at the local level. "Municipal or local legislation has been more abundant and . . . much more onerous or threatening to the business than any State action," he said. There was no federal legislation regarding the telephone, and the amount of state legislation was, Tyler thought, "astonishingly small." But municipal activity was, he observed, both frequent and severe. Tyler also highlighted the regional character of this activism. "This tendency [toward municipal regulation] has appeared more clearly West than East," Tyler said. "In New England there has not been much of it. . . . The further west we go, the worse this becomes."[13]

Municipal governments in Indiana—still part of the West to a Connecticut Yankee in 1882—were active in telephony from the industry's start. Before the first telephone exchange in Indianapolis began operations in 1879, the city council there reviewed applications and passed individual ordinances permitting or prohibiting each private telephone line. In December 1878, the council voted against allowing the newly formed Indiana District Telephone Company to construct an exchange in Indianapolis.

Only after the city's fire board drafted a detailed ordinance regarding the placement of poles and lines could the company begin operations.[14]

Smaller cities like Muncie were no less active. Muncie's first telephone company was in some ways a creation of local government, conceived when Lloyd Wilcoxon, a prosperous miller and sometime city council member, formed the Muncie Bell Telephone Company with his son Charles and son-in-law Milton Long. In February 1880, Muncie's city council gave Wilcoxon and Long permission to offer telephone service in the city. That ordinance established the municipal character of the telephone industry and set a precedent for active control over the telephone by city government. The city council asserted its authority over the location of all telephone poles and wires, retaining the right to move them or remove them "in any manner, at any time."[15] The city council also reserved the right to grant any other telephone company the use of Muncie Bell's poles and wires. Bell engineers later insisted it would be impossible to grant rival companies the use of their lines in this way, but the ordinance remained on Muncie's books until 1890. Such a bylaw seemed to invite competition; whatever capital Muncie Bell invested in building its network did not necessarily have to pose a barrier to the entry of other firms. Muncie's city council apparently intended to regulate Muncie Bell indirectly through the hidden hand of competition. Muncie Bell was a private company, but Wilcoxon's ties to the city council and the fact that city government was at once the telephone company's patron and its most important customer make it hard to draw sharp lines between the producers, the regulators, and the users of the telephone in its early days.

What is clear is that the network was local in orientation. The name of the Muncie Bell Telephone Company announced two things. It said that Wilcoxon and Long had chosen to use Alexander Graham Bell's telephone over its rivals. In 1880, Bell's monopoly on telephone patents was still in considerable doubt, and competing models were available. The name Muncie Bell also highlighted the local origins and identity of the firm. It was not a subsidiary of the American Bell Telephone Company of Boston, but an independent undertaking, which secured local patent rights and leased telephones from the Boston firm. This pattern was repeated by hundreds of communities across the country. There was no unified Bell System at this time, only an archipelago of local franchises and competing patent rights. The Boston company was still a small operation in 1880, with a valuable invention on its hands but not much capital or personnel. It relied on entrepreneurs like Wilcoxon, who leased the local rights to Bell's patents and invested their own money to construct, promote, and operate telephone systems in each of their hometowns.[16]

Wilcoxon and Long bought a switchboard from the Gilliland Electric Company of Indianapolis, installed it in a room above Long's hardware store, and engaged a friend's teenage daughter to operate the board for five dollars a week.[17] The exchange began service in March 1880. Though the network was modest, connecting only thirty-seven telephones, the new technology was immediately the talk of the town.[18] The *Muncie Daily News* boasted of its new telephone on the front page and exhorted citizens to visit and try the device. "The telephone exchange had 225 calls yesterday," the *News* reported after a few days of service. "The little talking machine is destined to be a great institution." The *News* kept the telephone on its front page for a month, reporting on new installations, ribbing one city lawyer who took a dislike to the device, and even describing dreams Muncie residents had about the telephone. "People in Muncie are doing an unusually great amount of talking," the paper was proud to report.[19]

Kingston, Ontario's, early encounters with the telephone were quieter than Muncie's, less breathless and more reserved. Certainly, the city's leading newspaper managed to contain its excitement. "The telephone has become a most useful instrument in other cities," allowed the *Daily British Whig* in 1881, "and its value has been appreciated by a few who have already experimented with it here."[20] No flurry of wire-stringing followed Thomas Henderson's virtual piano recital in 1877. No local firms sprang up to market the telephone in Kingston. Why they did not is not clear. Kingston had detractors who called it "Sleepy Hollow," a slow-moving place where people were stuck in their ways.[21] But few Ontario cities showed much more initiative than Kingston in adopting the telephone. The reasons for Kingston's sluggishness relative to Muncie were probably more structural than cultural. Generally speaking, the Canadian economy was less robust than the American economy at this time. Corporations were harder to create and more strictly regulated in Canada than in the United States.[22]

Kingston's first exchange, built a year later than Muncie's, was not a local undertaking in the same manner as Muncie Bell's. The Kingston exchange was established and owned from the start by the Bell Telephone Company of Canada. Direction for Kingston's first telephone office came from Montreal, with money and equipment from Boston. Kingston's local manager and linemen were dispatched from Toronto. Only the young women at the switchboard were local employees.[23] And while Muncie's municipal government asserted its authority over the telephone before the city's first exchange was even built, the Kingston city council took no action on any telephone issue until November 1883, after the city's system had been in operation for over two years. Unlike Muncie's 1880 ordinance, Kingston's first telephone bylaw did not purport to authorize the existence of the Bell exchange. The city claimed no power over the placement of Bell's telephone poles, and no authority to make Bell carry the wires of other companies.[24]

In other ways, however, Kingston's telephone exchange was no less local than Muncie's. It connected 107 telephones in 1881, all well within the city limits. At a time when the upper limit of audible telephone transmission was between twenty and forty miles, all telephone networks were in a sense local affairs. Kingston's first "long distance" call was to nearby Belleville in 1883. As late as 1886, Muncie's long-distance network consisted of a single circuit to Union City, Indiana, thirty miles away.[25] Even when long-distance lines arrived, they were not fully integrated with local telephone systems. The transmitters in most early telephones were not powerful enough to make long-distance calls. To use long-distance lines, many subscribers had to go in person to a local office, just as they might to post a letter or send a telegraph. Until at least the early 1900s, long-distance telephoning remained a luxury and an abstraction. In time, telephone cables would span the continent and the globe. But the telephone network as most Americans and Canadians first experienced it reached only across town.

Though the first telephone exchanges in Indiana were established by local firms, consolidation of these companies into larger units moved control of the industry out of smaller towns and cities and ultimately out of the state. In the spring of 1883, Wilcoxon and Long sold their Muncie Bell franchise to the Midland Telephone Company of Chicago. In July of that year, Midland merged with two other midwestern firms to form the Central Union Telephone Company. Based in Chicago, with many of its shareholders in New York, Central Union eventually consolidated all the Bell licenses in a territory spanning most of Indiana, Illinois, and Ohio.[26] The creation of Central Union was part of a nationwide pattern of consolidation that replaced the early multiplicity of tiny companies with a few dozen state and regional monopolies.[27] Boston's American Bell went along with these consolidations "in the interest of convenient and economical management," but its leaders worried that the trend should not be encouraged if it moved ownership of telephone companies outside of the territories they served. "It has always been our policy to keep local capital and influence interested in the business," said American Bell's annual report for 1882.[28]

This consolidation of local exchanges raised concerns in Indiana and elsewhere about giving out-of-state companies the power to operate on local streets. Americans in the 1880s still used the word "foreign" to describe businesses based in other states or even neighboring cities. Such firms remained a rarity right up to the turn of the century, and local businesses and governments regarded them with suspicion. One opponent of the Bell interests in Ohio asked rhetorically—assuming a negative answer was a given—whether Cleveland residents would ever permit "a Massachusetts Company" to supply them with water, gas, or electricity.[29] The crisis of legitimacy that big businesses faced in late nineteenth-and early twentieth-century America had as much to do with their geographic reach as with their growing size.

But the centralization of the telephone industry in the 1880s should not be overstated. What began as an archipelago of hundreds of local companies was by the end of the decade still an archipelago of dozens. This was by no means the unified Bell System of the middle twentieth century. Almost every telephone system in the country remained wholly local in its outlook and reach. The parent company in Boston controlled Alexander Graham Bell's key telephone patents, but little else. Operational decisions and most technical innovation were left to local management. In 1891, the president, the general manager, and the chief electrician of Cumberland Telephone and Telegraph, a Bell affiliate serving southern Indiana as well as several southern states, traveled from their Nashville home to New York, New England, and Quebec to study the state of the telephone art. "The only thing learned on that trip was that all were groping in the dark," Cumberland's president James Caldwell recalled. "The parent company, the American Bell Telephone Company, was struggling to maintain its patents. . . . As to how to build the system, what prices to make for service, how to induce the public to take hold of and make use of the implement, and how to induce capital to come into the scheme, no one offered any sort of sensible suggestion. I realized that all of those questions were for us to work out for ourselves."[30]

The Bell operating companies focused on large urban markets in the 1880s, ignoring demand for telephone service in rural areas and smaller towns. In 1886, there were more than seven thousand American towns with populations under ten thousand; Bell companies had established exchanges in just over five hundred.[31] Between 1886 and 1895, the proportion of telephones in small towns and rural areas only decreased as Bell's urban networks grew. Half of Bell's telephones in 1895 were in cities of more than fifty thousand people, while the 71 percent of the American population living in small towns and rural areas had access to only 6 percent of Bell's phones. Small-town business groups and local governments petitioned the Bell operating companies for service but were often refused. Others were more than willing to serve this unmet demand.

When a community was denied telephone service by the Bell affiliate in their region, local entrepreneurs sometimes tried to build their own exchange. Often they began by finding competing telephone patents, of which there were no shortage. Some smaller towns seemed to have established telephone service without legal authority at all. The electrical trade journals of the era regularly announced the formation of non-Bell telephone companies in communities around the country like Noblesville, Indiana; Big Timber, Montana; and Waterville, Maine. But the trade press also announced scores of injunctions, confiscations, and closures, as Bell lawyers sued these little systems for patent infringement. Between 1878 and 1894, the Bell interests filed over six hundred patent infringement lawsuits. Some of these competitors were well-financed enterprises posing an actual threat to Bell's business; some were simply farmers stringing up wire from kitchen to barn for their own private use. Still others were flimsy stock-promotion schemes. To Bell's Boston owners, they were all illegal "wildcats," in violation of the company's patent rights.

It is hard to know exactly how many telephone companies operated outside of the Bell umbrella in this period. Bell's patent monopoly was tight but not airtight. Pennsylvania became fertile ground for wildcat systems in 1883 and 1884, when courts temporarily suspended patent litigation in the state. A showdown over rate regulation in Indiana, described below, inspired the creation of several short-lived wildcats there. A 1902 census of electrical industries counted seventy-four independent telephone systems operating in that year that claimed to have been established before Bell's patent monopoly was broken in 1894. How these systems escaped patent litigation is not clear, but they do seem to have been off the beaten path, at least as far as Boston was concerned. None of the former wildcats extant in 1902 were in New England. The state with the largest number of such systems was West Virginia, with eight, followed by Texas and Arkansas, each with five. According to one history of the independent telephone movement, perhaps not wholly reliable, an illegal exchange operated for years in San Francisco's Chinatown, connecting all the principal Chinese merchants, warehouses, and docks. Only when Pacific Bell's non-Chinese subscribers began switching to the cheaper system did Bell executives discover the secret network right under their noses.[32]

Poles and wires became a site of regular conflict between a gradually centralizing telephone industry and defenders of local control. The physical footprint of the network was one aspect of the new medium that all city residents encountered—not only the small fraction of residents that were telephone subscribers. Poles and wires were regarded as unsightly and dangerous. And they provided a target close at hand for local governments seeking leverage against companies based in distant cities and states. Municipal governments passed innumerable ordinances regarding pole placement, height, condition, and even color. In December 1889, a New York City electrician told the *New York Times* that of twenty thousand telephone poles in the city, it was "safe to say that 15,000 of them violate some regulation or rule and must therefore be removed."[33]

The most drastic answer to the problem of poles and wires was to remove them entirely. Several large cities did try to force all telephone, telegraph, and electric companies to bury their wires underground. Chicago's city council passed an ordinance requiring this move in 1881, though the Chicago Telephone Company fought desperately against it and held up the ordinance in court for years. Similar legislation was enacted by the New York state legislature in 1884 and considered in Pittsburgh, Philadelphia, and Indianapolis.[34] Telephone company managers balked at these laws, insisting that underground lines were technologically unfeasible. It would take years of municipal pressure before telephone companies began replacing their urban wires with underground cable. A major blizzard in 1888, which brought down hundreds of poles in New York and across the northeast, helped many cities force recalcitrant companies to bury their lines. So too did a series of accidental electrocutions in 1888 and 1889. In one gruesome case, the body of an electrocuted Western Union lineman was suspended in the wires above a Manhattan street corner for nearly an hour; the *New York Times* described "blue flames" crackling from his mouth and nostrils and "a great pool of blood" dripping on the horrified crowd below. A city official who witnessed this spectacle pledged his determination to have all overhead wires "come down at once."[35] City by city, block by block, municipal governments pressed the fight for their streets and skies. Even today, one can guess at the clout of a city government, or the property value of an urban neighborhood, by whether poles and wires remain part of its skyline or are invisibly underground.

Lawmakers in smaller cities and towns also tried to control the poles and wires on their streets. As Morris Tyler observed in 1882, such activity was most frequent and aggressive in the Midwest and the West. In 1890, Muncie passed a "civic beautification" law that ordered the removal of all telephone poles from the downtown sections of its Main and Walnut Streets. What each member of the council knew was that Central Union's local switching office was located at the corner of Main and Walnut, so every telephone wire in the city had to pass along one of those two streets. After months of negotiating, Central Union convinced the city council to amend its ordinance, but only after agreeing to supply free telephone service to the mayor, the fire chief, and every schoolhouse in the city.[36]

This pattern of negotiation and manipulation was repeated in communities all over the Midwest, as local governments secured political points and often outright payoffs by decrying the nuisance of poles and wires. The Bell affiliates called such tactics blackmail. "Regulation, as practiced in this country, appears to be nothing more nor less than a hold up game," complained Cumberland Telephone's James Caldwell.[37] He and his fellow managers did not believe that bylaws regulating poles and wires had anything to do with civic beautification or even public safety. "In almost all cases," Morris Tyler said, pole ordinances were simply "attempts to get more or less out of the companies."[38]

Raising revenue was indeed a large part of late nineteenth-century urban politics and a critical issue underlying the era's municipal reforms. State constitutions and electoral politics limited the money available to municipal government. Rapid urban growth and ever-increasing demand for city services drove local governments to seek new revenue anywhere they could find it. Unpopular foreign monopolies, based out of city or out of state, were an obvious choice.[39] Yet, while neither Central Union nor the Muncie city council could deny financial motives, there was more at stake in their confrontations than simply dollars and cents. Whether they knew it or not, city and company were fighting over control of a new industry and over the shape of the infrastructure through which other commerce would be channeled. Municipal governments found themselves sharply limited in the ways they could control an outside company like Central

Union or American Bell. They had difficulty controlling telephone prices, and they could not overturn Bell's patent monopoly. So they seized what powers they did have—sovereignty over their own streets, sidewalks, and skies—and leveraged those for every advantage they could exact.

These contests played differently in Canada. Central Canadian cities also clashed with telephone companies over the placement and upkeep of their poles, but they proved to have much less power in these fights than their midwestern counterparts. Even the most modest regulations proved nearly impossible for municipal governments to enforce. It remained an open question in Canada whether Bell was required to submit to municipal regulation at all. The reason for these doubts was Bell Canada's federal charter, granted by Parliament in 1880, and a crucial amendment to that charter in 1882 declaring the company "a work for the general advantage of Canada." This phrase came from the British North America Act of 1867, which delineates the separate powers of Canada's federal and provincial governments. The British North America Act gives the federal government the power to bring any local enterprise under exclusive federal jurisdiction by declaring it a work for the general advantage of the nation. Bell Canada's original charter granted the company permission to operate telephone systems in all parts of the country. But exactly what authority this conveyed in provincial and municipal jurisdictions was not clear, so the company petitioned Ottawa for the general advantage declaration in 1882.[40]

Bell Canada's petition was a result of the company's dispute with publisher James Carrel over telephone poles in Quebec. Unable to get satisfaction from Quebec City's municipal government, Carrel filed a private criminal suit against Sigismund Mohr, the Bell manager for the province of Quebec. Mohr was arrested and convicted of obstructing the Queen's highway. Bell Canada appealed the decision, insisting that its federal charter gave it the authority to erect poles and wires without municipal permission. But Quebec's superior court upheld Mohr's conviction, occasioning much crowing in the pages of Carrel's *Daily Telegraph*.[41]

The case turned on the politics of Canadian federalism but also, significantly, on the local character of the telephone at this time. Antoine-Aimé Dorion, the chief justice of Quebec, had been a leading opponent of Confederation in 1867 and remained a staunch defender of Quebec's provincial autonomy. Quebec City's telephone system was, Dorion ruled, "purely of a local character and intended to serve local purposes, having no pretension to connect provinces or even to cross navigable rivers." This meant that the telephone fell under the authority of Quebec's provincial government, not the federal government in Ottawa, and so Dorion deemed Bell Canada's federal charter invalid. The fact that Bell Canada also operated telephone systems in Ontario and other provinces was, Dorion said, of no account. Telephone wires did not connect cities across provincial boundaries and so the individual systems remained "absolutely local." Ottawa did not have the power, he ruled, to authorize Bell Canada to erect poles on Quebec streets.[42]

Carrel congratulated himself on this victory, yet the pole outside his office remained. As soon as Dorion's decision was handed down, Bell Canada petitioned the federal government to change its charter, declaring the telephone a work for the benefit of the whole country and thus insulating the company against municipal and provincial authority. Covering its bases, Bell Canada also asked the provincial governments of Quebec, Ontario, and Manitoba for legislation reaffirming its authority to erect poles and wires without municipal consent. As in Quebec, discussions in Ottawa turned on whether telephone systems were local enterprises or something larger. "Telephone companies are purely local undertakings, as a rule, and intended for carrying on local business," argued one senator. But Bell's sponsors assured Parliament that the company intended to extend telephone service into rural districts and to build long-distance lines between provinces. The company received its declaration, effectively reversing Dorion's decision, without a great deal of debate.[43]

The effect of this amendment was to severely limit the power of Canadian municipalities over Bell Canada's affairs. The telephone company did not need and did not need to seek municipal permission before erecting poles or stringing wires. Canadian town and city councils soon found they had little leverage over Bell's activities and little recourse when unhappy with its actions. The City of Toronto tested Bell's immunity to municipal regulation in the years that followed. In 1900, the city ordered its engineers to prevent Bell Canada from erecting poles without a permit. That case ultimately went to the Judicial Committee of the Privy Council in London, then Canada's highest court of appeal. It ruled in Bell Canada's favor in 1904, affirming that Bell's federal charter and the general advantage clause placed the company's activities beyond municipal or provincial jurisdiction.[44]

One testament to the significance of Bell's general advantage amendment was the queue of private utility promoters—railways, gas, and electric companies—that petitioned Ottawa for a similar declaration in the 1890s and 1900s.[45] Another was the relative ease with which Bell Canada weathered the end of its patent monopoly in 1885 and marginalized telephone competition in Ontario and much of Quebec. Bell effectively substituted the general advantage clause for its lost patent protection. Bell's federal charter also shaped political understandings of the telephone in Canada in a way that went unrecognized in 1882. The first telephone networks in the United States and particularly the Midwest were seen as local enterprises. As such, they fell under municipal control. Only after long-distance lines spread to connect distant cities would American state governments contemplate telephone regulation. And only as a truly national long-distance network emerged did the federal government of the United States take an active interest in the telephone field. In Canada, by contrast, the telephone was deemed a national undertaking and a creation of the federal parliament years before interprovincial or even intercity calling was possible.

Rate Regulation in Indiana

Though midwestern cities had more authority over the telephone than their central Canadian counterparts, that power was far from complete. The limits of municipal authority over the telephone were revealed by a series of contests in the 1880s between the growing Bell companies and the cities they served. Regulatory instruments from different levels of government—municipal franchises, state legislation, and the federal patent system—were enlisted on both sides of this fight. But the real drive to regulate the new industry and to maintain local control of the telephone came from municipal officials and from the Main Street businessmen of midwestern cities and towns.

In 1885, legislators in Indiana, Illinois, Massachusetts, Ohio, New Jersey, and New York all debated bills to limit or reduce telephone rates. The only state to pass such a law, however, was Indiana, and the fight that followed there became a test case for telephone regulation around the country. It also illustrated the crucial role of municipal activism in the early telephone industry in the Midwest.[46] In April 1885, the Indiana state legislature, then controlled by the Democratic Party, passed a law fixing three dollars per month as the maximum rate companies could charge for telephone service in the state.[47] The sponsor of this legislation was state representative Samuel

Williams, a Democrat with ties to the Knights of Labor and Henry George's single tax movement. Williams gained considerable notoriety and the nickname "Telephone Sam," from his involvement in this fight. He would later help to draft the Omaha Platform of the People's Party, and was the Populist candidate for vice president in 1908.[48]

Executives from the two Bell affiliates operating in Indiana, Chicago's Central Union and Nashville's Cumberland Telephone and Telegraph, denounced Williams's bill as blackmail cooked up by rival telephone promoters from outside the state. But the timing of the bill and the preceding history of conflict between Central Union and the city of Indianapolis make it clear that the impetus for rate regulation was municipal in its origin. Efforts to exact revenue from the telephone company were not separated in city politics from efforts to regulate telephone service or rates. Councilmen questioned the legitimacy of the company's prices and sought to control them. Complaints about the quality of telephone service and arguments about telephone poles routinely triggered, or were used to justify, new taxes and fees. In this way, consumer protection and municipal graft went hand in hand. In 1881, the Indianapolis city council had drafted and debated an ordinance requiring telephone and telegraph companies to pay the city 5 percent of their gross receipts. After city attorneys advised the council that they had authority to tax tangible property but not revenues, that ordinance was revised to charge companies two dollars per year for each pole they erected on Indianapolis streets.[49] In 1884, the Indianapolis Common Council voted to charge the Central Union Telephone Company an additional five dollars per telephone per year. City aldermen, fearing the company would simply pass the charge on to its customers, struck down the ordinance.[50]

Central Union was deeply unpopular among its customers in Indianapolis. "The best portion of the business community" in Indiana "were ready to take this corporation by the throat," admitted Chicago telephone executive Charles Norman Fay.[51] In December 1882, the Indianapolis city council had declared that Central Union was "unreasonably extorting unjust demands."[52] In January 1884, after lobbying by local business leaders and the city's Democratic paper, the *Indianapolis Daily Sentinel*, aldermen passed a resolution stating that Central Union "does not give satisfaction to its patrons," and that "great complaint is made by the public on account of the delay and annoyances arising from such inadequate service." The board asked their judiciary committee to determine what political remedy could be devised for this state of affairs.[53]

The first remedy proposed by the committee was competition. In the spring and summer of 1884, Indianapolis granted telephone franchises to three different companies, with the intent that they should compete against Central Union in the city. Similar franchises were granted to competing companies in smaller Indiana towns and cities, like Richmond and Samuel Williams's own Vincennes. But legal action from American Bell in Boston, which still held exclusive patent rights to Alexander Graham Bell's invention, prevented any of these companies from actually beginning operations.[54]

The next remedy considered by the city was direct regulation of Central Union's rates. In August 1884, the Indianapolis city council proposed but did not pass an ordinance to regulate telephone rates, setting three dollars per month as the maximum charge for residential service and five dollars per month for business service.[55] In January 1885, the council took up the rate regulation proposal as General Ordinance No. 1, its first order of business for the year. But a city assessor warned the council that, short of repealing Central Union's franchise altogether, the municipal government did not have the legal right to regulate the company's prices. Such regulation would, he thought, require state legislation. Nine days after the Indianapolis city council debated General Ordinance No. 1, Samuel Williams proposed his bill to limit telephone rates in the Indiana state legislature.[56]

Indiana legislators approved the Williams bill by a vote of sixty-six to nine.[57] The new law was hailed in Indianapolis and around the state as a blow for local control of Indiana's business affairs. "Corporations, monopolies, and capitalists must be taught that they cannot control the affairs of this city," said Indianapolis alderman Calvin Rooker. "We had better be without telephone service for the next twelve months . . . than to let this corporation go any further in its wild and mad career." Bell company executives immediately challenged the law, denying both its wisdom and its constitutionality. "Why should the telephone business be regulated as to price more than other industries?" asked American Bell president William Forbes. "Sound public policy is surely against the regulation of the price of any class of commodities by law."[58]

In February 1886, the Supreme Court of Indiana upheld the constitutionality of the rate law.[59] After consultation with American Bell, Central Union's management announced that they would shut down any telephone exchanges that could not be operated profitably under the new rates. Cumberland Telephone and Telegraph terminated all its operations in Indiana, leaving the southern portion of the state entirely without telephones. This was not the outcome Indiana legislators had been expecting. It was widely believed that telephone prices were grossly inflated—in particular, by the royalties Cumberland and Central Union paid to American Bell in Boston—and that the Bell interests would quickly capitulate to the new law or allow local telephone companies to take their place. "We will not be lacking for friends or telephones," the *Daily Sentinel* promised.[60] (The city's Republican paper, the *Indianapolis Journal*, opposed rate regulation.) But with similar regulation pending in New York, Massachusetts, and Ohio—all states more populous than Indiana and more important to American Bell's balance sheets—the Bell interests deemed it imperative to fight. Central Union executives expressed regret for the inconvenience these actions would cause but insisted their company was "helpless to give relief."[61]

Indianapolis was the main battleground in the fracas that followed. Though Central Union threatened to disconnect every telephone in the state, in fact it kept open many of its small town exchanges, like Muncie's, though it changed their billing structure, charging subscribers five cents per call rather than a flat rate for unlimited monthly service. But Indianapolis was the state's largest and most profitable market, and the place where Central Union chose to fight regulation head on. While the rate law had been passed by the Indiana state legislature, the Indianapolis city council remained Central Union's real antagonist in this fight. The state legislature sat only from January to April, and only every other year. It passed the Williams bill on the very last day of its 1885 session and was not sitting when the state supreme court upheld the law or when the contest between city and company reached its boiling point in the spring and summer of 1886. Municipal government was the stage on which this drama played out.

Central Union began disconnecting its Indianapolis subscribers in April 1886. By the middle of that month, more than 250 telephones had been removed—about one-quarter of the city's phones. At that point, the company stopped disconnecting telephones, arguing that it could not remove any more until its contracts with individual subscribers expired in June or July. It continued to charge these subscribers rates in excess of the mandated three dollars per month. The city council declared this a violation of the new state law and voted unanimously to revoke Central Union's municipal charter. On 16 April, Indianapolis ordered the company to remove all its poles and wires from the city within fourteen days.[62]

Figure 3. Linemen (one wearing leg braces for pole climbing), installers (with telephones), and other employees stand before a forest of poles and wires on the roof of the Central Union Telephone Company's Indianapolis exchange, about 1888. Between 1885 and 1889, the state of Indiana tried to regulate telephone rates, setting a maximum charge of five dollars per month. Central Union fought the law, and Indianapolis was the key battleground in the showdown that followed. Courtesy of AT&T Archives and Historical Center, San Antonio, Texas.

Tempers rose and the fight grew increasingly chaotic. At large "indignation meetings," city officials and the public gathered to denounce the telephone company and demand its immediate capitulation to state law.[63] At the same time, other telephone subscribers petitioned the city council to leave their phones in operation, offering to pay double the legal rates if necessary. While the Indianapolis board of aldermen delayed the city council's order to chop down Central Union's poles, the council invited applications from any other parties willing to provide telephone service at the prescribed rate. Several companies from inside and outside the state announced their willingness to try. Central Union, however, promised to prosecute any companies that infringed on its patent rights. "The Bell has not permitted any company to operate anywhere undisturbed," observed the *Indianapolis Journal*. It warned entrepreneurs petitioning for a franchise from the city council that all such a charter would earn them was "the right to be sued."[64]

The *Journal*'s warning proved correct. As Central Union closed down exchanges in the state, a few Indiana towns installed new systems from the Cushman Telephone Company, a Chicago-based manufacturer organized around the patent claims of one Sylvanus D. Cushman, who claimed to have invented a working telephone twenty-five years before Alexander Graham Bell. The Bell companies scoffed at such claims and were quick to sue for patent infringement anywhere Cushman telephones were installed. In South Bend, Elkhart, and tiny La Porte, Indiana, Central Union and American Bell sued not only the Cushman Company but dozens of individual subscribers using its telephones. By the end of 1888, federal courts shut down all the Cushman exchanges in Indiana. In the La Porte case, a judge reputedly ordered all Cushman telephones in the village be shipped back to Chicago and burned.[65]

That resolution still lay in the future on 23 April 1886, when the Indianapolis city council held a special meeting on the telephone controversy. Central Union president George Phillips attended the meeting to request more time from the city, but "perceiving the temper of the body towards his corporation," as the *New York Times* put it, Phillips withdrew his request. The city council voted to grant a new telephone franchise to a syndicate of local businessmen calling themselves the Citizens Cooperative Telephone Company. The council's special telephone committee believed the Citizens instruments were different enough from the Bell telephone to withstand Central Union's inevitable patent challenge. The city council hedged its bets, however, by requiring the new telephone company to provide access to its poles and wires to any other company that sought to compete with it. Such a restriction, the Citizens Cooperative complained, made their new ordinance practically worthless, and they declined to accept the franchise they had just been given. "The result of tonight's action is to leave the situation more muddied and unsatisfactory than ever," declared the *Times*.[66]

The chaos of the situation in Indianapolis reflected a more general confusion over which level of government had authority over the telephone, and what regulatory devices they might use to control it. The city of Indianapolis had provoked the fight with Central Union and was the most active body in prosecuting it. But the city's franchise power was a blunt instrument. Short of chopping down poles—a threat the city made repeatedly yet never carried out—the municipal government found it had few ways to coerce a truly recalcitrant monopoly. The state legislature, for its part, had the authority to limit telephone rates but found it had no power to make a telephone company operate at those rates if it did not wish to do so.

Events at the federal level ultimately tipped the balance of power in Bell's favor. In March 1888, the U.S. Supreme Court ruled for American Bell on a cluster of patent cases, ending an eight-year legal battle and dismissing several of the most persistent challenges to the Bell patents (see Chapter 3). With this decision, the security of American Bell's patent monopoly appeared assured, and whatever leverage Indianapolis might have held over Central Union evaporated. Also, in the elections of November 1888, Indiana Republican Benjamin Harrison won the White House and state Republicans rode his coattails to control of the Indiana legislature. In February 1889, the Indiana statehouse repealed the 1885 telephone law with little fanfare or debate. Central Union immediately resumed telephone service in Indianapolis at a new rate of seven dollars per month.[67] American Bell's patents, enforced at the federal level, seemed to have trumped state legislation and municipal bylaws. This pattern was repeated in numerous industries in the late nineteenth century, making the federal courts and patents a key bulwark of national corporate power.[68]

The Bell interests had won a considerable victory. They maintained their monopoly, defeated regulation in Indiana, and discouraged similar laws in other states. Legislators in Ohio and Iowa postponed pending telephone legislation immediately after the stalemate in Indiana. Similar bills were defeated in New York, Massachusetts, and Illinois. Yet the failure of rate regulation in Indiana does not seem to have discouraged municipal action toward the telephone. If anything, municipal governments in Indiana were more active in telephone matters after the rate law was repealed. The Indianapolis city council had learned a great deal about telephone technology during the fight over telephone rates. And the Bell companies had made no new friends in the state. Above all, the experience confirmed for many Hoosiers the dangers of out-of-state monopolies and the importance of local control.

The Bell Monopoly in Central Canada

Despite differences in outlook and regulation, the telephone networks of Muncie and Kingston looked roughly similar after ten years of telephone service. Central Union's subscriber rolls in Muncie had dwindled during the showdown over telephone rates, but by 1891, the Muncie exchange had connected 120 telephones—roughly one telephone for every hundred people in the city. Bell Canada's growth in Kingston was more steady, and by 1891 the Kingston exchange had connected 370 telephones—one for every fifty people.[69]

Who used the telephone first? Newspapers, telegraph offices, and banks, all in the business of moving or trading information, had quickly adopted the telephone. So had coal dealers and millers of flour and feed, businesses that commonly maintained downtown sales offices separate from their mills and warehouses. Doctors and druggists took to the telephone quickly for emergency use. Undertakers and livery stables were early adopters too. In 1891, more than two-thirds of the telephones in each city were installed in workplaces rather than homes.[70]

Differences between adoption patterns in Kingston and Muncie were idiosyncratic. Fewer than a tenth of Muncie's attorneys had telephones in 1891, compared with more than two-thirds of lawyers in Kingston. It is hard to explain this difference, although it is true that Muncie's city prosecutor, J. E. Mellett, was for unclear reasons hostile to the telephone. He told the *Muncie News* that he was "bitterly opposed to permitting ladies to talk or in any manner connect themselves" with the telephone.[71] Kingston had its own influential resister in George Monro Grant. Though an important promoter of the imperial telegraph, Grant took an aversion to the telephone and, as the principal of Queen's University, prevented the school from installing any telephones until after his death in 1902.[72]

The development of the telephone in Kingston and Muncie diverged far more dramatically in the 1890s, after the end of Bell's patent monopoly and the explosive growth of competing telephone systems in the American Midwest. To beleaguered executives at Central Union, it may have seemed that independent competition had sprung up out of nowhere. But the roots of telephone competition in the Midwest, and the reasons for its relative weakness in Central Canada and elsewhere, lay in the struggles of the 1880s and the profoundly local politics of early telephony.

The importance of the patent monopoly to the thinking and strategy of American Bell in the 1880s and early 1890s can hardly be overstated. American Bell president William Forbes predicted in 1886 that just one decision against the patent would "flood the country" with competing telephone systems.[73] Yet when Bell's Canadian telephone patents were overturned by a court challenge in 1885, this decision did not produce in Canada the great wave of competition Forbes had predicted, or anything like the actual competition that eventually swept the American Midwest.

In order to promote domestic manufacturing, Canadian law required that all patented products be manufactured in Canada. In 1884, the Toronto Telephone Manufacturing Company challenged Bell Canada's patent on the telephone, showing that Bell imported much of its equipment from Western Electric in Chicago, rather than manufacturing it at home. On 26 January 1885, Canada's commissioner of patents stunned Bell's directors by siding with the small Toronto firm and nullifying Bell Canada's exclusive right to the telephone.[74]

Bell's friends and foes on both sides of the border watched the end of patent protection in Canada with great interest. Most predicted a substantial drop in telephone prices. Many expected the flood of competing companies that Forbes had foreseen for the United States. "Canada may become an inviting field," declared the *New York Times*. "The telephonic art might enjoy that legitimate development which has been suppressed by the greedy Bell monopoly in the United States."[75] Some believed the overturning of Bell's patents was only a prelude to more radical government action. Bell Canada's president, Charles Fleetford Sise, speculated that the patent commissioner had been ordered by his government to nullify Bell's patents in preparation for public takeover of the telephone.[76]

New telephone companies began appearing in Canada almost immediately after 1885. Bell Canada ceded some parts of the country to other companies, but when competing systems were organized in its lucrative urban markets, its response was swift and aggressive. "We occupy the field, we are entitled to it, and propose to hold it," growled Sise. He urged his local managers to "meet the enemy with a united front," and to "completely kill it."[77] In April 1888, the Federal Telephone Company, backed by owners of the Canadian Pacific Railway, received government permission to offer a competing telephone service in Montreal, the site of Bell Canada's headquarters and Canada's largest city. Bell Canada cut its prices in Montreal by one-third. After a two-year price war, Federal Telephone's investors surrendered, selling their system to Bell Canada in 1891.[78]

In smaller cities, Bell Canada hit its competition even harder. In both Dundas and Peterborough, Ontario, the company offered telephone service for free until its smaller rivals were driven out of business. Accused of unfair dealing, Sise told a parliamentary investigating committee, "I do not know that anybody in Peterborough ever objected."[79] In Winnipeg, Manitoba, where public resentment of the company ran high, Bell Canada secretly sponsored a dummy firm to underprice and undermine both the competition and the original Bell exchange. No dummy himself, Sise named this fake competitor the People's Telephone Company. When Bell's real competition collapsed, the charade was revealed and the counterfeit firm absorbed by the old Bell Canada exchange. Its customers were charged the old Bell prices.[80]

An agent of Sise named William Scott became infamous among independent telephone men and municipal politicians in Canada for the ruthless business tactics he described as "war to the knife." These included price slashing, political lobbying, inflammatory public statements, and legal obstructions. Many suspected Scott of setting fire to the municipally owned telephone exchange in Fort William, Ontario, in 1903. In 1904, he demanded a government audit of the exchange, knowing that most of its records had been consumed in the fire. "It is his special duty to smooth over . . . difficulties," Charles Sise told parliamentarians in 1905. "He is a diplomatist, then?" scoffed one of Sise's examiners. "I do not always approve of his diplomacy," Sise admitted.[81]

Bell Canada's confrontations with municipal and independent competition were sometimes dramatic. But in most central Canadian cities, Bell was able to preempt competition before it even began by negotiating exclusive franchises with town and city governments. In exchange for rate rebates and sometimes a small percentage of Bell's net receipts, municipal governments in Ontario and Quebec gave Bell Canada the exclusive right to offer telephone service in their communities. Bell also secured agreements with all the major railways in Canada—the Canadian Pacific, the Grand Trunk, and a dozen more—for exclusive rights to place telephones in railway stations and to construct telephone lines along railroad rights of way. This arsenal of agreements, Charles Sise said, was sufficient to "stop competition in embryo." The competition agreed. F. Page Wilson, secretary of the Canadian Independent Telephone Association, called the municipal and railroad contracts "the Bell's strongest point in Canada" and "the greatest need of the Independent movement."[82] By 1905, Bell Canada had secured exclusive franchises with thirty-six towns and cities in Central Canada. By 1910, it had negotiated over seventy, preserving or restoring its monopoly in every major urban market in Ontario and Quebec.[83]

The contract Bell signed with Kingston in 1892 was typical. It gave the company exclusive rights to the telephone business in Kingston for seven years in return for four hundred dollars per year. This was agreeable to Bell Canada. Four hundred dollars represented about 5 percent of the company's gross annual revenues in Kingston. The company paid the same proportion for an exclusive franchise in Toronto; in many smaller cities it bought its monopoly for only a few free telephones. Besides the four hundred dollars, Bell Canada made Kingston few concessions. The company promised not to raise its rates, but only until it deemed it necessary to modernize Kingston's lines. Bell agreed to observe city bylaws on the placement and painting of telephone poles but was careful to stipulate that this was a voluntary concession on its part. The company never admitted in principle that it was bound to municipal bylaws.[84]

Municipal politicians agreed to these contracts without enthusiasm because they had no other leverage with Bell Canada. Kingston's interactions with Bell Canada in the 1890s and 1900s demonstrate the city's lack of power in dealing with the company. In 1899, just as Kingston's 1892 contract with Bell Canada was coming up for renewal, the Ontario Court of Appeal made a controversial decision regarding the property taxes paid by Ontario utilities. Poles, wires, rails, and cables were to be appraised not as capital investments, but at what their value would be if taken apart and sold as lumber or scrap iron. This drastically reduced the property taxes owed to Ontario municipalities by telephone and telegraph companies, power companies, and street railways.[85] When Kingston's mayor Edward Ryan joined a delegation of mayors from fourteen Ontario cities to lobby the provincial government against the change, Bell Canada's district superintendent threatened not to renew its agreement with the city and to stop offering telephone service in Kingston altogether. The mayors' delegation was unsuccessful in the end. Bell Canada kept its tax cut and Kingston kept its phones. But the dispute demonstrates the telephone company's willingness and ability to bully Ontario's municipal governments.[86]

When the Kingston-Bell contract came up for its second renewal a few years later, municipal politics and the telephone company's machinations once again threatened the deal. Kingston's city council negotiated a new agreement with the telephone company in August 1903, and Bell's local manager submitted it to his superiors in Montreal.[87] But two weeks after ratifying this agreement, Kingston's city solicitor Donald McIntyre attended a meeting of the Ontario Municipal Association, a lobby group for the province's local governments. Among a variety of other proclamations, this session of the Municipal Association passed a resolution that local governments deserved full control over telephone rates and the placing of poles and wires. "It would be still better in the public interest," the resolution continued, if municipalities owned and controlled their own telephone systems, and the federal government operated all long-distance lines.[88]

The resolution was simply a petition to the federal government and carried no legal weight. But Bell Canada took any talk of government-controlled telephony seriously. A week after the Ontario Municipal Association meeting, the new Kingston-Bell agreement was returned to Kingston unsigned, with a note from Charles Sise. "I regret the position taken by the Council is such that we cannot execute the proposed agreement," Sise wrote. He would not sign the new contract, and the company would not spend the $80,000 it had earmarked to modernize the Kingston exchange and move its downtown wires underground.[89] Talks broke down, and the city's day-to-day relationship with the company deteriorated. A minor quarrel over the proper painting of telephone poles turned into a year-long feud. Only after Kingston dropped its support of the Ontario Municipal Association's resolution, sixteen months after the dispute began, would the telephone company sign a new franchise agreement and begin the work of burying its wires.[90]

In Canada after 1885, it was such municipal "agreements," not federally enforced patents, that preserved Bell's monopoly on the telephone. Independent telephony in Central Canada remained largely restricted to remote and rural areas. After 1894, the coming of serious competition in the United States inspired a modest second wave of Canadian independents, but this remained a marginal movement, largely relegated to the small towns and rural areas that Bell Canada did not wish to serve.[91] In sharp contrast to the growth of competition in the American Midwest, in only a handful of Canadian locales did direct competition between telephone systems occur. In exchange for granting exclusive franchises and blocking the development of independent competition, cities like Kingston gained a few financial concessions from Bell Canada and some ability to negotiate the placement of poles and wires in their streets. But they had little power over the telephone monopoly and found themselves on the losing end of nearly every conflict over the telephone and its growth.[92]

Competition in the American Midwest

Alexander Graham Bell's original patents on the telephone in the United States expired in 1893 and 1894. This did not necessarily mean the end of American Bell's monopoly; the company held about nine hundred other patents on telephone technology and expected to be shielded from competition for decades to come. In December 1894, however, a government lawsuit instigated by a midwestern telephone manufacturer voided another crucial patent, and the legal edifice of American Bell's monopoly began to crumble.[93] Within a year, dozens of new companies were manufacturing telephone equipment, and over one hundred American towns and cities had begun constructing independent telephone systems—that is, systems with no legal connection to American Bell. The Bell interests continued to litigate against their competitors, but the courts were increasingly unenthusiastic about precluding new entrants to the field. By 1897, about a quarter of American cities with a population of five thousand or more had competing telephone systems. By 1902, more than half of American cities had two or more competing telephone companies. The independents reached their zenith in 1907, at least in terms of market share, when they controlled more than half of the six million telephones then operating in the United States.[94]

The independent movement grew most rapidly in the Midwest, both in the industrial cities around the Great Lakes and the agricultural regions beyond them. In 1907, more than half of the independent telephones in the country could be found in seven states: Indiana, Illinois, Iowa, Kansas, Missouri, Ohio, and Pennsylvania. Indiana, site of the battle over rate regulation, had more independent telephone companies in the 1890s than any other state. According to the 1902 electrical census, a dozen commercial independents had been established in Indiana by the end of 1894, with twenty more established in 1895, and more than 120 before the turn of the century. Bell's midwestern affiliates were soon greatly outnumbered by their independent rivals. In Indiana, three-quarters of all telephones in 1907 belonged to independent firms. Eighty-four percent of Iowa's telephones belonged to the independents in that year, along with more than 80 percent of the telephones in Kansas and more than 60 percent of the phones in Ohio.[95]

Competition in the midwestern United States dwarfed anything seen in Canada. Even the most generous estimates place the number of independent telephones in Canada between eighteen and twenty thousand at this time—less than 10 percent of the nation's total.[96] Per capita, there were fifteen times as many independent telephones in the United States as in Canada. Writing from Montreal in 1895, Charles Sise urged his American colleagues to follow Bell Canada's example in securing exclusive contracts with the municipalities they served.[97] Some Bell operating companies in New England and the northeast negotiated such contracts, but with no equivalent to Canada's "general advantage" clause, midwestern towns and cities had much less reason to agree to such deals. They preferred to franchise local companies to compete with the "foreign" Bell affiliate and let a combination of competition and municipal regulation restore control over the telephone network to their communities.

Independent telephony was the child of municipal government. Few American cities established municipally owned telephone systems, but the independent movement grew directly out of conflicts between the Bell operating companies and local government in the patent monopoly years. The ties between city councils and independent entrepreneurs were often close, close enough that Bell agents were not wrong to make charges of collusion. Every town or city independent owed its existence to a municipal franchise. These franchises shaped, and often constrained, the movement's growth. Many independent telephone systems were bound by their franchise to maximum price limits or minimum subscriber levels. Some were permitted to sell or issue stock only to residents of the communities they served. Especially in the early years of the movement, independent telephony could be seen as municipal politics by other means.[98]

"The businessmen of this city will receive the information of competition with delight," declared the *Muncie News* in 1895.[99] In 1896, Muncie's city council voted unanimously to authorize a second telephone system in the city. The new franchise did not initially go to a local firm. Instead, the city council gave the right to establish competing telephone service to W. J. Kurtz, an electrical manufacturer from New York. Still, Muncie welcomed the enterprise. Lafayette, Elkhart, and Fort Wayne, Indiana, were already constructing their own independent networks, and Muncie's boosters did not intend to be left behind.[100]

Things did not go as planned. Kurtz promised to have one hundred telephones in operation by early 1897, but at the end of 1896, no poles had been erected and no telephones installed. In January 1897, the city council appointed a committee to investigate the matter, but Kurtz and company were gone for good, leaving behind some bad debts, a snarl of wires, and an unsightly wooden tower at the edge of town. The *Muncie News* noted dryly, "There is one thing about the new telephone company that commends itself to the people—it does not require so many poles as other companies."[101]

Kurtz' disappearance did not sour Muncie's business leaders on telephone competition, but it did reaffirm the city council's bias against entrusting the telephone business to outsiders. In March 1897, the city transferred Kurtz' franchise to the Muncie Electric Company, a privately owned power utility and an established local firm. The terms of the agreement were similar to Muncie's ordinance for Central Union—discounted rates for city offices, the placement of poles and wires to be approved by the city engineer—with one significant exception. Muncie Electric pledged to charge less than half of what Central Union was asking for telephone service, and this was written into its ordinance by law. "Phones will be cheap," promised a headline in the *News*. The ordinance restricted telephone rates to fifty cents per week for business users and twenty-five cents per week for residential phones.[102]

The local firm made progress where outsiders had not. By May 1897, one hundred telephones were in operation, with fifteen to twenty-five new telephones being added every day. The new company's superintendent told Muncie newspapers that he had six hundred subscribers waiting for telephones and two operators making preparations for steady work.[103] Muncie Electric and Central Union were immediately engaged in a contest for subscribers. As many had predicted, Central Union lowered its rates in Muncie, though it did not match the prices of its rival. Central Union also switched back to charging a flat rate for unlimited local service, abandoning the five cents per call charge the company had instituted under the Indiana rate law in 1887. With lower rates and aggressive marketing, both telephone systems in Muncie grew rapidly. In 1894, Muncie had fewer than three hundred telephones. By 1898, after only a year and a half of direct competition, Muncie Electric and Central Union each had connected more than double that amount.

Muncie Electric's telephone system was soon suffering the pains of its rapid success. Its poles and wires were erected quickly and cheaply, and before long they needed expensive repairs. An exchange built to handle two hundred subscribers was serving six hundred within a year. And the low rates the company had pledged to charge proved unsustainable after the system reached a certain size. This proved to be a common pattern for many midwestern independents, especially those with fixed rates in their municipal franchise: a few years of explosive growth, and then a financial crisis as their unit costs grew and their physical facilities reached their limit. Companies that were able to negotiate new rates at this point generally survived; companies that were not generally did not.[104]

In the summer of 1899, Muncie Electric sold its telephone system to David Allen of Frankfort, Indiana. This loss of local control, even to a fellow Hoosier, aroused suspicions in Muncie. The *Muncie News* declared that Allen was an agent of the "Bell Trust" and predicted the end of the independent company. Allen denied the accusation but did little to improve the Muncie exchange. Service deteriorated and customers deserted the company. By the end of the year, only 375 subscribers remained—almost half of the network gone in a matter of months. In December 1899, Allen sold the Muncie exchange to Central Union for nine thousand dollars. The independent system was dismantled, and its remaining subscribers switched over to Central Union telephones and lines.[105]

Yet Muncie's business leaders had not given up on telephone competition. "There is a large number of people in the city who want a second exchange," reported the *Muncie Herald* after a year under Central Union's monopoly.[106] In November 1901, a group of Muncie businessmen known as the Commercial Club met to discuss the telephone situation. They resolved to petition Central Union for better service and lower rates. When that failed to achieve results, the club resolved to establish an independent exchange.[107] In December 1901, the city council voted nine to one in favor of a new telephone franchise for two local businessmen, William Hitchcock and George Beers.[108]

The new Delaware and Madison County Telephone Company began service in February 1903. Unlike Muncie Electric, the Delaware and Madison Company was not tied by its franchise to fixed rates. Still, it remained cheaper than Central Union. Freed from rate control, and backed by Muncie's Commercial Club, Delaware and Madison proved a more durable competitor than Muncie Electric. By 1907, the new independent had roughly fifteen hundred subscribers in Muncie to Central Union's twenty-five hundred. It was even stronger in the smaller towns and villages surrounding Muncie. In 1907, Delaware and Madison had a network of almost three thousand telephones in Anderson, Indiana, a majority of the telephones in that city.[109]

None of the regional Bell companies suffered more from competition than Central Union, in the midwestern heartland of independent competition. By 1907, Central Union had not seen a dollar of profit for twelve straight years.[110] In March of that year, the besieged Bell affiliate begged independents in Indiana and Ohio for a truce. Central Union's managers offered to abandon their local exchanges in many Indiana and Ohio cities and to merge with the independents in others, effectively ending direct competition in both states. In return, they asked that the independents leave them their monopoly over long-distance lines. Independent telephone associations in Indiana and Ohio, believing their foe to be on the ropes, rejected the proposal with some glee.[111]

Americans in the early twentieth century often echoed American Bell's William Forbes in describing the rapid rise of independent competition as a "flood," an "eruption," or an "explosion"—metaphors suggesting that the movement was born suddenly and out of nowhere when Bell's patents expired in 1894. It may have seemed that way at the time, but the local history of the telephone in the Midwest demonstrates that independent competition in the 1890s and after grew out of struggles between municipal regulators and the Bell monopoly in the 1880s. In Central Canada, where the balance of power was more strongly tilted in Bell's favor, the independent movement never really took hold.

Two Cultures of Telephone Use

In the spring of 1905, the Canadian Parliament organized a special commission to investigate the telephone industry in Canada. After two months of hearings and testimony, the acting chair of the commission posed a glaring question to his colleagues. "What I cannot understand," said Adam Zimmerman, "is why the people in the United States find so much more use for the telephone than they do in Canada. There must be some reason for it." In the state of Indiana, Zimmerman noted, there was by 1905 one telephone for every twelve people. In Zimmerman's own province of Ontario, there was only one telephone for every ninety people—and populous, prosperous Ontario was well ahead of most Canadian provinces in this regard.[112]

But those figures told only part of the story. As Zimmerman's question suggested, the difference between telephone systems in Indiana and Ontario was not only one of numbers. Midwestern Americans seemed to make more use of, and find more uses for, the telephone than their central Canadian cousins. A close look at turn-of-the-century Muncie and Kingston shows that the shape of the telephone network, and the character of its use, was different in each locale.

Wealthy citizens in both countries were able to afford telephone service before their less affluent neighbors. Yet in Muncie and across the Midwest, middle- and even working-class Americans became telephone subscribers long before their counterparts in Kingston and Central Canada. The percentage of Muncie residents with telephones in their homes was nearly double that of Kingston residents in 1900, and more than triple in 1910. In 1911, wealthy professionals made up less than 3 percent of Kingston's working public, but accounted for over 20 percent of the city's residential telephones. In Muncie, the professional class was also overrepresented on the Bell network but not nearly as much; professionals owned 9 percent of the city's telephones. By that time, over 35 percent of the Bell telephones in Muncie belonged to farmers, tradesmen, and unskilled laborers—a group that accounted for only 13 percent of Kingston's residential telephones. So, in both Muncie and Kingston, there were subscribers like Muncie's George Ball or Kingston's James Richardson, wealthy and important business leaders. But Muncie's telephone books also listed subscribers like Martha Haisley, the widow of a grinder at the ironworks; Wick Adams, a black stable worker; and laborers like John Catlin and George Main. The telephone began as a privilege of the rich in both cities but spread much sooner in Muncie into humbler middle- and working-class homes.[113]

In fact, these figures, which are based only on Bell or Central Union telephones, probably understate the more egalitarian character of telephony in Muncie. Subscriber data is not available for Muncie's independent telephone systems. During the era of telephone competition, the more expensive Bell networks were associated with a wealthier class of subscribers. If directories for the cheaper independent systems were also available, the proportion of working-class telephone users in Muncie would almost certainly be higher than given above. This would make the contrast between Muncie and Kingston, where there was no independent system, only more striking.

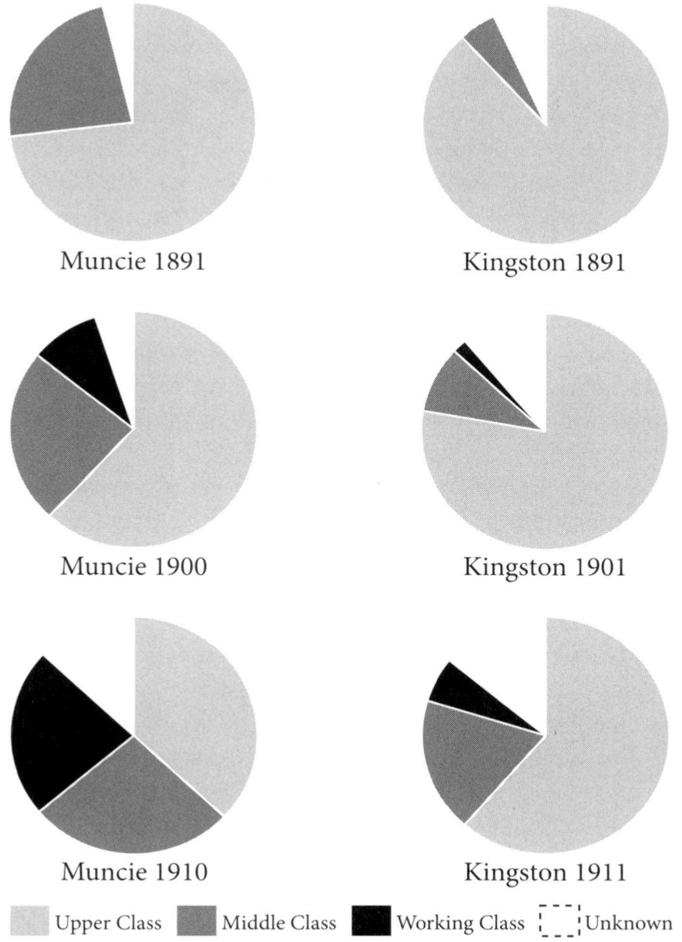

Figure 4. Socioeconomic Status of Telephone Subscribers in Muncie and Kingston
The charts here show only residential telephones (not public or workplace phones) and only telephones attached to the Bell affiliate in each city. A detailed picture of early telephone subscribers was developed by cross-referencing telephone directories with census data and other sources. Annual street directories provided occupations of most subscribers; these were used as approximate indicators of socioeconomic class.

Telephones were installed in different spaces at different times. Most early telephones were installed in offices and workplaces rather than in private homes. But telephones moved from the office to the home more than a decade sooner in Muncie than in Kingston. Telephone use also spread from towns and cities into rural areas more quickly and with more success in the American Midwest than in Canada or indeed in any other part of the United States. The number of women with telephone service in their own name was higher in Muncie than in Kingston, and while it is difficult to track telephone use by nonsubscribers, telephones seem to have been used more commonly by women, children, and servants in the Midwest than in Central Canada. Certainly, there was more discussion of use by nonsubscribers, and less hostility expressed to them, in midwestern newspapers and industry trade journals than in their Canadian equivalents.

The kinds of spaces where telephones appeared in each city give another sense of the diverging character of telephony in Central Canada and the Midwest. In Muncie at the turn of the century, telephones could be found in several saloons, stables, and barber shops. In Kingston before 1900, the telephone remained largely a privilege of business offices and wealthy homes. Midwestern cities also had more public telephones than Canadian cities, which provided service to many who could not afford a private telephone in their home. Public telephones, as well as semipublic phones installed in working-class boardinghouses or flats, were pioneered by Bell operating companies in San Francisco and Chicago.[114] Such innovations helped popularize the telephone in the largest cities in the United States, just as independent competition lowered prices and broadened access in and around smaller cities and towns.

The differences that puzzled Zimmerman extended beyond the shape and size of telephone networks. Indiana and Ontario were by the turn of the century developing different telephone cultures. From the beginning, the character of the new technology was shaped by the ideas and assumptions of telephone companies, consumers, and regulators about who and what the new technology was for. Commercial and cultural choices became deeply intertwined. In regions where the Bell companies had a free hand—in places like Central Canada and the northeastern United States, where there was little significant competition or municipal agitation against the Bell interests—many instituted "measured service." Under measured-service plans, customers paid a lower monthly rate for telephone service, or even no monthly rate at all, but were charged five or ten cents for each call they made. In the Midwest and also on the West Coast, where Bell faced independent competition and more active municipal regulation, measured service proved unpopular with consumers, and the Bell companies were often forced to offer flat rates for unlimited local calls. This issue provoked a bitter confrontation between Central Union and the Muncie city council in 1887, during the brief period of rate regulation in Indiana. When Central Union instituted measured service in Muncie at five cents a call, the city voted to revoke its franchise. Their threat to remove Central Union's poles and wires was never carried out, but upon the arrival of independent competition in Muncie, the Bell company was forced to reinstitute a flat monthly rate.[115]

Measured service and flat-rate billing structures reflected and encouraged two distinct cultures of telephone use. Where individual calls were free, telephone users embraced social and many argued frivolous uses of the telephone. They gossiped, courted one another, and sang or played music over the lines.[116] Flat rates were preferred by many urban businessmen—heavy telephone users who had an obvious financial stake in the question—but also by many small-town and rural telephone users who opted for flat monthly rates even when measured service would have saved them money. Clearly, they valued a diverse range of telephone practices and preferred not having to meter their sociability. The Bell companies would try for decades to shift from flat to measured rates, and to convince consumers that this shift was in their own economic interest. But this was an uphill battle, and measured service never entirely prevailed.[117] In 1917, to cite just one example, a telephone manager in Whiteland, Indiana, petitioned the state's new public service commission for permission to move from flat rates to measured service, saying that "unending gossip" was tying up his wires. According to the telephone trade press, "the whole countryside turned out" in support of flat rates and gossip, and the state commissioners ruled they could do nothing.[118]

Technical differences also shaped telephone protocols and practices. Automatic or dial telephones, favored by independent companies long before Bell, made prank phone calls possible. Party lines enabled eavesdropping, a universally acknowledged and widely accepted part of small-town and rural telephone culture. One survey done in 1945 found that more than half of rural customers questioned had no objection to "listening in" by others on their line.[119] Of course such behavior could happen anywhere—no doubt Kingstonians gossiped on their telephones too. But Muncie and similar midwestern communities developed a far more boisterous, casual, and communal culture of telephone use than their cousins to the north. They did not name this culture, though many remarked on it. We might label these practices and protocols with the name so often adopted by independent telephone companies in these years: the people's telephone.

In Kingston and Central Canada, a countervailing culture of telephone use proved more influential. Adherents of this measured telephone culture, both inside and outside the Bell companies, attempted to restrict many practices of small-town, flat-rate telephone use. Charging by the call made economic sense. In the days of human operators, it cost real time and money to connect each call. But measured service had cultural repercussions too. Kingstonians and others like them were more likely than midwesterners to regard the telephone as a sober, serious tool for business. They paid higher prices for a higher quality of service. They appreciated the assistance of the Bell operator, a surrogate servant connected to their offices and households by the wire.[120] Energy and capital that Muncie's dueling systems put into new construction could be spent by Bell Canada in Kingston on maintenance and repairs. Supporters of this more formal telephone culture demanded higher standards of privacy and etiquette on their telephones and deplored the idea of eavesdropping or "useless" calls. Some actively tried to keep women, children, and the lower classes off the lines. Wired into the commercial and technical choices of both communities were all manner of assumptions about the value and appropriateness of different social connections and different kinds of speech.

This contrast between Muncie and Kingston should not be overdrawn. The two countervailing cultures of telephone use were not exclusively contained by any regional, national, or company boundaries. They grew up side by side, in tension and in conversation with each other. Each community and each telephone system across the continent might show a proportion of both cultures at any given time. Yet on the whole, the telephone did look different in Kingston than in Muncie. These differences might be traced to the very first impressions made at a genteel piano recital and on the muddy grounds of a midwestern state fair. But they were sustained and enhanced year after year by municipal politics, commercial practices, and the cultural protocols both produced.

Others wrestled with Adam Zimmerman's question. The Canadian independent F. Page Wilson looked wistfully at the success of independent telephone systems in the midwestern United States and pressed his colleagues to explain: "There is no reason on earth why the province of Ontario should not have just as many telephones to the square mile as, say, the state of Indiana. Conditions are just as good; the density of population about the same; the intelligence and enterprise of its inhabitants by no means inferior. Why, then, are we . . . unable to show similarly splendid results?"[121]

The *Canadian Engineer*, a trade journal eager for American-style competition in Canada, blamed the Canadian public for their "craven fear" of "the Hello Giant." "Promoters have found a certain lack of moral courage on the part of users," the journal charged, "to whom the appeal to public spirit and patriotism has seemed in vain."[122] But AT&T vice president Frank Pickernell assured parliamentarians: "It is not that the farmers in Ohio and Indiana are so much better and more vigorous than they are in Canada." Rather, he said, the Midwest was plagued by "men with peddler's wagons" who traveled the backcountry "drumming up" hostility to Bell and hawking telephones like patent medicines.[123] American independents scoffed at this explanation. "He must have been joking," said J. B. Ware, the general manager of the Citizens Telephone Company of Grand Rapids, Michigan. "Until I read Mr. Pickernell's testimony, I never heard of a peddler's wagon passing through the state selling telephones as sewing machines are sold."[124]

It is tempting to ascribe the differences detailed above—the rapid spread of the telephone in one region, along with a more raucous and egalitarian culture of telephone use—to the presence of independent competition in the Midwest and its relative absence in Central Canada. There is no doubt that competition served to lower the cost of telephone service, speed its growth, and shape its use. Yet this only presents further questions. Why did competition emerge in one region and monopoly in the other? How can the experiences of other regions, or variations within these regions, be explained? Chicago, for example, was the home of many independent telephone manufacturers, and the heart of the territory where independent telephony saw its greatest success. Chicago was also the country's second largest urban market, and the Bell interests fought fiercely to protect their monopoly there. The independents, to their great frustration, were never able to capture Chicago for the cause. One independent firm, the Illinois Telegraph and Telephone Company, did operate in Chicago for a few years, but it was hampered by the terms of its municipal franchise—among other stipulations, it could not disturb the pavement of Chicago's streets—and never overcame the commanding lead of the Chicago Telephone Company, Bell's operating company there. Chicago Telephone executives were innovative and aggressive in bringing telephones to the masses, and even without serious competition, the telephone spread more quickly there than in northeastern cities like Boston or New York.[125]

What made Chicago different? The deeper variable was as obvious, and as easy to overlook, as telephone poles. The action and inaction of municipal governments in the 1880s and 1890s played a decisive role in the development of the telephone industry in each locale. The midwestern communities in which local government became actively involved in regulating the telephone industry were generally the same communities where independent competition thrived. And even where lively competition did not emerge, those towns with early and active municipal engagement constructed telephone systems and cultures more like Muncie's—that is, with wider, earlier access to telephone service and a less genteel culture of telephone use. In towns and cities without such active municipal involvement, systems and cultures like Kingston's were more common—with a better quality of equipment and transmission but more expensive service and less penetration as a social medium.

In Chicago, as in Muncie and across the Midwest, local government was an active participant in constructing the telephone, regulating services and rates, encouraging local ownership, and levying taxes and fees. Chicago was the first major American city to make telephone companies bury their wires underground, a move Chicago Telephone's Charles Fay called "brutal treatment," and "an act of injustice and spoliation."[126] The city council constantly pressured the company to improve its service and lower its rates—or to buy off its lawmakers with bribes. This was of course extortion, a time-honored tradition in Chicago politics as elsewhere, but such extortion ironically became an engine of innovation. Municipal interference pushed Bell's Chicago affiliate to expand its network and improve its service in much the same way that competition drove innovation in many smaller cities and towns.[127]

In Central Canada, by contrast, Bell faced neither vigorous competition nor strong municipal pressure. Local governments had little power to shape the telephone industry and nothing with which to threaten the incumbent firm. By defining the telephone as a national rather than local undertaking, Bell Canada's federal charter effectively immunized the company from municipal authority. Exclusive franchise agreements did the rest, blocking competition in most urban markets and relegating Canadian independents to rural areas and tiny hamlets. Secure in its monopoly, Bell Canada let its urban exchanges grow at a more stately pace. On the carefully tended Canadian networks, the more boisterous and unruly culture of the people's telephone did not thrive.

These patterns were repeated in other regions. In New England, the home of American Bell, there was little municipal agitation around the telephone, as Morris Tyler had observed in 1882. Independent competition never took hold there, and by 1900 telephony in New England looked not unlike telephony in Central Canada. California and the Pacific Northwest, by contrast, resembled the Midwest more than not. Though independent competition on the West Coast did not quite reach the levels it did in states like Iowa or Indiana, it was also significant there, as were the activities of municipal governments. Along with the Midwest, the West Coast had by 1907 the highest number of telephones per capita in the country and the highest number of daily calls per telephone—compelling evidence that a mass telephone habit was taking hold.[128]

Clearly, local government played a shaping role in the growth of telephone communication. Pine and cedar tree trunks sunk into city streets embedded the supposedly space-annihilating technology of the telephone into both physical spaces and local political milieus. Midwestern town and city councils were not wealthy or powerful actors. Nor were they technologically sophisticated—though decades of squabbling over the telephone did provide something of an education in the field. And their motives for engaging the telephone company always combined altruism and self-interest. Yet the messy, ground-level realities of municipal politics proved to be among the best defenses of the public interest—sometimes the only such defense—against a would-be Bell monopoly.

"Middletown does not make its own history," wrote one historian of Muncie. "It patiently suffers the history made outside."[129] In the case of the telephone, this was untrue. Alexander Graham Bell may have invented the telephone receiver in 1876, but each city and town had to invent or reinvent the telephone system for itself. The story of early telephony is therefore a story of humble wooden poles and local politicians, of a thousand local exchanges in a thousand average towns. The political economy of the telephone in the Midwest empowered municipal governments to take an active role in shaping the industry and public understandings of the new medium. A vision of the telephone that emphasized the local use and social character of the device took hold. In Central Canada, the telephone quickly became a federal responsibility, and a very different understanding of the new medium was the result. In different regions of each country, different ideas about the telephone took hold. The next chapter returns to Bell, Boston, and the telephone's birth to trace the roots of these competing visions.

Chapter 2

Visions of Telephony

Alexander Graham Bell's original goal was not to transmit speech, but to make it visible. Bell was keenly interested in deafness—his mother, Eliza, and future wife, Mabel, were both deaf—and he considered the education of the deaf his principal purpose in life. By recording sounds in a visible way, Bell hoped to help the deaf understand spoken words. His father, the elocutionist Alexander Melville Bell, had developed a symbolic alphabet that represented the pronunciation of any phoneme with a diagram of the lips, tongue, and palate. He called it "Visible Speech."[1] The younger Bell's experiments with sound were, in his mind, mechanical extensions of his father's work. In 1874, Bell constructed a macabre device to trace sound vibrations on paper using a charcoal pencil and a human cadaver's severed ear. "If we can find the definite shape due to each sound—what an assistance in teaching the deaf," he enthused. Transmitting sound across distance was an afterthought for Bell. "I invented an apparatus by which the vibrations of speech could be seen," he recalled in later years, "and it turned out to be a telephone."[2]

The telephone did make speech visible, just not in the way Bell had imagined. For what is a telephone wire but a visible conduit for human speech? The communications scholar James Carey famously argued that the telegraph separated communication and transportation, making it possible to send messages faster than any person, horse, or train could carry them. The electric telegraph was not really the first device to do this—smoke signals, semaphore flags, and optical telegraphs all transmit intelligence faster than human messengers. But because the electric telegraph drastically increased the speed and distance that messages could travel, it has often been seen as liberating communication from the constraints of geography or the transportation of physical objects.[3] What Carey's formulation neglected was the elaborate and very physical network on which every insubstantial telegraph message relied. In many ways, the telegraph and telephone made communication more physical and material, not less. Telegraph messages were insubstantial flashes of electricity, but the poles and wires that carried them were not. As messages became more immaterial, the networks on which they traveled became expensive installations requiring immense capital investment, regular maintenance, and legal rights of way.

In the late nineteenth century, the most important fact about electrical communication may not have been the separation of communication from transportation, but the marriage of communication to capital. Before intelligence could be converted to electricity and slip the surly bonds of geography and space, wires and poles had to be erected. This demanded deliberation in advance about where the wires would go. And that turned telegraph and telephone construction into a series of debates over intercommunication and interdependence. Who would or should be communicating with whom? As Americans and Canadians built their first telegraph and telephone networks, they were making speech visible, mapping and constructing the channels through which commerce and communication would travel.

There were examples available to guide the way Canadians and Americans spoke and thought about the telephone. Two of the most obvious and influential precedents were the mail and the telegraph. Each had its own organizational legacy. The U.S. Postal Service was by the late nineteenth century a true mass medium, more extensive and accessible than the postal system of any other country, and seen by most Americans as a crucial democratic good. The telegraph, by contrast, was the child and agent of private business. By the 1860s, the Western Union Telegraph Company enjoyed a near monopoly on long-distance telegraphy. It served large businesses and very wealthy individuals, and it made possible an unprecedented private monopoly in the national distribution of news and information. The precedents of the telegraph and the mail pulled ideas about the telephone in different directions, even as the new technology refused to conform exactly to either model.[4]

Debates around the telephone in the 1870s, 1880s, and 1890s often resembled earlier debates about the telegraph and the mails, just as they anticipated later discourse surrounding radio, television, and the Internet. Popular discussion around new media is a predictable genre, with conventions and clichés that have stayed remarkably consistent from the days of Samuel Morse down to our own times. But telephone talk was also rooted in the historical moment at which the technology appeared. The telephone was born in an era of rapid and wrenching economic change. The consolidation of national markets, the growth of continent-spanning corporations, and the turmoil of economic depression and labor unrest all added up to a profound transformation for which communication technology was both a symbol and a cause. Wires and poles could be seen, while abstractions like "the economy," "the market," or "big business" could not. The visible parts of the new networks came to stand for the interdependency they made possible. Plans for the telephone contained arguments about how people ought to be connected, and thus about the proper organization of business, the economy, and society.

This chapter describes three competing visions of telephony—three ways of understanding the technology and its purpose. These three visions and the contests between them would shape the development of telephony for decades to come. Yet all three emerged in the telephone's early days, and each was championed by one of the Bell companies' very first leaders. Gardiner Hubbard, the Bell Telephone Company's first president, was animated by a quasi-populist vision of "a telephone for the people," which found many adherents, though few at Bell. William Forbes, who pushed Hubbard out of his position as president, embraced a far more conservative vision of the telephone. And Theodore Vail, Bell's first general manager and later the founder of the American Telephone and Telegraph Company, articulated a third vision: an ambitious dream of "one big system," a single continent-spanning network uniting telephone and telegraph under one corporation's control.

Each of these visions of the telephone and its purpose suggested different strategies to the Bell companies' first leaders. How should the telephone be marketed, and to whom? Where should telephone lines be built? How much should service cost? But the implications of these questions went well beyond corporate strategy. Debates about where telephone lines should be constructed were, beneath the surface, about who could and ought to speak to whom. Disputes about billing structures were, at another level, about the relative value of different kinds of speech. And arguments about the character and control of the Bell monopoly could not be separated from broader questions about the growing power of big business and the incorporation of America.

Gardiner Hubbard and the People's Telephone

The independent telephone movement that erupted in the midwestern United States after Bell's patents expired in 1894 would be animated by populist rhetoric, with demands on behalf of "the people" for locally controlled networks of cheap and accessible telephones. The independents of the 1890s and early 1900s denounced Bell as an octopus and a greedy trust. They demanded a "telephone for the people," by which they meant a more decentralized industry, with networks oriented toward local and regional service, and billing structures designed to promote middle-class social use.[5] Yet this vision of telephony had been advanced nearly two decades before, in the very lair of the octopus. The idea of a people's telephone, and the policies and priorities it implied, was actually present at the birth of the Bell corporate system, in the person of Gardiner Greene Hubbard.[6]

Gardiner Hubbard was a lawyer and entrepreneur in Cambridge, Massachusetts. He was born into a well-off New England family, but his personal fortunes fluctuated all his life. Although an effective promoter, Hubbard's enthusiasm for a scheme often outran his capital and good sense. He was said to have a "blissful disregard" for money—"an enviable trait to possess, but scarcely a desirable one in a business partner," his colleague Thomas Sanders complained—and was happiest when pursuing a public-spirited municipal scheme.[7] Hubbard was in the vanguard of nineteenth-century urban improvements. He established the first water and gas utilities in Cambridge in 1852, bold ventures at a time when many larger cities still lacked such services. He then lost most of his fortune in failed real estate ventures, and in building a street railway between Cambridge and Boston.[8]

In the 1860s and 1870s, Hubbard appeared on the national scene as a persistent critic of the Western Union Telegraph Company. Western Union was one of America's very first nation-spanning corporate monopolies. Before the Civil War, several telegraph companies jockeyed for dominance in the United States. A "Treaty of Six Nations" in 1857 divided the country into six territories, each to be served by a different telegraph firm. But with the coming of the war, and aided by a close relationship with the Union Army, Western Union broke ranks with the rest of the industry in a bid for national supremacy. By 1866, it had absorbed its major rivals, cementing a near monopoly over long-distance telegraphy in the United States.[9]

Western Union's size, its rapid growth, and its suddenly unchallenged control of an increasingly indispensable technology alarmed many civic-minded Americans, but none so much as Gardiner Hubbard. In magazine articles, pamphlets, and petitions to Congress, Hubbard waged a personal war against the giant firm. The "great evil of the present system," he wrote in 1883, "is the unrestricted and almost despotic power of the Western Union Telegraph Company."[10] Hubbard became a leader in the "postalization" movement, a campaign to create a second telegraph system under the aegis of the U.S. Postal Service. His persistence made him a constant aggravation to the telegraph giant. Between 1866 and 1900, Congress considered more than seventy bills to reform the telegraph industry.[11] Western Union president William Orton is said to have vowed that Hubbard should "never . . . make one dollar if he could help it." Wags dubbed the endless congressional hearings for telegraph reform the "Wm. Orton and Gardiner Hubbard Debating Society."[12]

Hubbard charged Western Union with holding back the development of American telegraphy. "As a telegraph for business, where dispatch is essential and price is of little account, the Western Union is unrivaled," Hubbard wrote in 1883, "but as a telegraph for the people it is a signal failure."[13] In many European countries, control of telegraphy had been given to the post office, and inexpensive telegrams were widely used for social as well as business communication. In Belgium, for example, social and family matters made up 55 percent of telegraph traffic by 1880. Such messages comprised no more than 5 or 6 percent of Western Union's business. Instead, the company focused almost exclusively on the long-distance transmission of business messages: stock prices, buy and sell orders, and instructions from head offices to salesmen in the field. Large businesses were willing to pay high rates for these messages, and Western Union obliged them. But only in dire circumstances would ordinary Americans have cause to send or receive a telegram. According to Orton's successor Norvin Green, less than 1 percent of Americans were customers of the firm.[14]

Yet Western Union, Hubbard argued, was not just ignoring an untapped market. It was thwarting the public good. Accessible and affordable communication ought to be the basic democratic right of all Americans, he said. A "telegraph for the people" would liberate the flow of information, nurture democracy, and strengthen the republic against the machinations of corporate financiers. Hubbard and many like him worried about what a private company could do with monopoly control over the nation's vital circuits of information. Telegraph transmission of stock and commodity prices, information almost as valuable as the commodities themselves, gave the company real influence over farmers, businessmen, and investors. And an exclusive contract with the New York Associated Press gave Western Union immense leverage against any newspaper that dared to criticize it. It was no secret that the Associated Press and Western Union used their power to influence national politics, most famously in the disputed elections of 1876 and 1884.[15] The telegraph monopoly's control over the press was "absolute," Hubbard warned. "It can ally itself—and probably will at no distant day—with kindred monopolies, and aspire to supreme power."[16]

Nineteenth-century reformers saw communication networks as crucial agents of the new economic order and central to any prescription for change.[17] Trade unions and agrarian protest movements like the Knights of Labor and the People's Party often demanded the nationalization of the telegraph.[18] But far less radical groups were also advocates of communication regulation and reform. Business organizations like the New York Board of Trade and Transportation and the Philadelphia-based National Board of Trade lobbied for stronger regulation of the telegraph, especially after 1881, when Western Union fell under control of the notorious speculator Jay Gould. Mistrusting Western Union, particularly Jay Gould's Western Union, was something a broad spectrum of Americans could agree on.[19]

Western Union was the first American company of any kind to forge a national monopoly out of what had previously been a competitive industry. After absorbing the United States Telegraph Company and the American Telegraph Company in 1866, Western Union controlled perhaps 90 percent of the telegraph market in the United States. It was capitalized at over $40 million, operated 2,250 telegraph offices, and owned nearly a hundred thousand miles of working wire.[20] In geographic scope, Western Union dwarfed even the railroads, the largest corporations of the day. More than that, however, Western Union's long-distance telegraph network underwrote and embodied America's economic consolidation. Its wires made physical the lines of communication carrying capital and information. In a way, the telegraph network *was* the economy, or at least served as a vivid proxy for abstractions like the market, interdependence, or big business.

Thus, when Hubbard and others criticized Western Union, they were talking about more than the telegraph. They were raising questions about their country's emerging corporate order. "Intercommunication is the one great cause of consolidation in our country," Hubbard wrote. "The tendency is to heap up enormous wealth and power in a few hands and in large corporations. . . . This accumulation of wealth . . . [is] due in a greater degree to the introduction of steam and the telegraph than to any other causes." Intercommunication was no evil in and of itself, Hubbard argued, but control of that communication belonged by right to the people. A private monopoly over telegraph communication threatened the health and stability of American democracy. "It is in vain to hope that such evils will remedy themselves, or that these corporations will voluntarily surrender any powers they have acquired," Hubbard warned. "The time will come, and that soon . . . when the people will rise in their might and crush these monopolies."[21]

Hubbard, who served as chairman of a federal postal commission in the 1870s, admired the postal service as much as he mistrusted Western Union. "Our Post-office is maintained by the people solely for their benefit, and is better managed, and with more economy, in our country than in any other," he maintained. "The telegraph is run by a private company primarily for the benefit of its shareholders, and is managed with less economy than the Post-office."[22] Hubbard was hardly alone in this view. The nineteenth-century post office was innovative and efficient for its time, and Americans held it in high esteem. By the middle of the century, cheap postage and rising literacy had turned the mail into a true mass medium. The penny-a-pound rate for second-class mail, introduced in 1885, further expanded the use of the postal service and played a key role in sparking the agrarian crusades of the Farmers' Alliances, the Grange, and the People's Party. The idea of the mail as a medium of the people and a basic civic good offered a critical counterpoint to the precedent of the telegraph in the early development of the telephone.[23]

Fate handed Hubbard another way to challenge Western Union in 1874. His daughter Mabel had been permanently deaf since a childhood bout of scarlet fever; in 1873, Mabel Hubbard began taking elocution lessons from a young teacher of the deaf named Alexander Graham Bell. The following year, Bell asked Gardiner Hubbard for permission to court his daughter. He also told him of certain experiments he was conducting on the electrical transmission of sound. Hubbard was lukewarm toward the romance but encouraged Bell's experiments with enthusiasm.[24] Bell's ingenuity offered Hubbard a way to challenge Western Union without government action, and to make a healthy profit as well. After years of effort, Hubbard had not convinced Congress to reform the telegraph industry. How much greater the rewards would be, Hubbard realized, if he could remake the industry without Congress, through a private enterprise of his own.

What Hubbard wanted from Bell was not a telephone. What Hubbard wanted, like everyone else in the industry, was a quadruplex or multiplex telegraph, a device that could transmit four or more messages simultaneously over a single wire. Bell's idea was to construct a "harmonic telegraph" that could send different messages using different musical notes. Hubbard knew that others, including Thomas Edison and Western Union's Elisha Gray, were working along similar lines. Hubbard pressed Bell to complete his work as rapidly as possible—in fact, he convinced his daughter to say she would not marry Bell until he perfected his telegraph.[25] It was Hubbard who filed Bell's first application for a patent on "Improvements in Telegraphy" in February 1876. According to Bell's later testimony, Hubbard did so without Bell's knowledge and in advance of his wishes, so anxious was he that the patent rights not fall into Western Union's hands.[26] It would be another month before Bell and his assistant, Thomas Watson, actually transmitted the human voice by electricity for the very first time, on 10 March 1876. In July 1877, by then convinced of the telephone's commercial and political potential, Hubbard drew up the papers establishing the Bell Telephone Company as an unincorporated partnership between Hubbard, Bell, Watson, and Thomas Sanders, a Salem leather merchant with a deaf son also tutored by Bell. Two days after the company was formed, Mabel Hubbard and Alexander Bell were married in the parlor of the Hubbards' Cambridge home.[27]

Hubbard led the Bell Telephone Company for the next two years. In the choices he made, we can see his determination to make the telephone a "telegraph for the people," an alternative to Western Union and the accumulation of wealth and corporate power it had come to represent. While traveling around the country on behalf of his postal commission, Hubbard carried a pair of telephones to demonstrate in every city he visited. Hubbard encouraged local entrepreneurs to establish their own telephone businesses, leasing Bell equipment in return for an annual commission. Hubbard was an effective promoter, and within a few months of establishing Bell Telephone, he had granted dozens of local and regional licenses. In another year, there were hundreds of tiny telephone fiefdoms like the Muncie Bell Telephone Company of Lloyd Wilcoxon and Milton Long. Growth was rapid and haphazard. The territories Hubbard established varied enormously in size; his arrangements with different agents differed widely in details. The Bell trustees in Boston had little influence over the local firms and affiliates, especially as the telephone spread into the Midwest and beyond. Yet by throwing the business open to local investment in this way, Hubbard made it possible for Bell telephones to spread rapidly across the country, much more quickly than his fledgling company could have managed on its own.[28]

The traditional corporate histories of Bell Telephone, written from the point of view of its descendant AT&T, praise Gardiner Hubbard for his decision to lease, rather than sell, telephones. This decision had a centralizing effect on the industry. It cast the telephone as an ongoing service rather than a discrete product and kept the parent company involved in the distribution and operation of its instruments over time. The same corporate histories present Hubbard's reliance on local investors—a decentralizing decision—as only a temporary expediency made unavoidable by his company's early lack of capital.[29] But local ownership was an essential part of Hubbard's vision for the telephone. As we have seen, he deeply mistrusted the size and influence of Western Union. "Such a power cannot exist without its exerting a pernicious influence on public affairs, and every observant public man has long perceived the demoralizing influence of this powerful, but subtle agency," Hubbard wrote in 1873.[30] In contrast and opposition to Western Union's national monopoly, Hubbard conceived and constructed the telephone industry as a patchwork of local exchanges, each one owned and operated by residents of the areas they served.[31] After rising profits made it possible for Bell to contemplate buying up its affiliates, Hubbard argued vigorously against such a move. In 1884, he warned the new president of American Bell, William Forbes, against taking over the local companies or even trying to operate them "as parts of an entire system." This would be bad business and worse politics, Hubbard insisted. "The Am. Bell cannot operate such companies as economically as parties resident in the locality," he wrote. "Thirty-five percent of the stock of a company *managed by owners* will pay larger dividends than fifty-one percent of the stock of a company managed by *agents*."[32]

In promoting the telephone to consumers, Hubbard cast the device as an answer to the evils of Western Union. His earliest promotional material stressed what he saw as the telephone's chief advantages over the telegraph: it was simple enough to be used by anyone; it required no knowledge of Morse code; and it admitted no third parties, in the form of telegraph clerks or messengers, into private communications. (Hubbard was imagining private lines, with no telephone operators.) The telephone, Hubbard promised, would break Western Union's dangerous monopoly over the transmission of vital information and shift power back toward the people by putting the instruments of communication into every customer's hands.[33]

Hubbard and Alexander Graham Bell were both confident the telephone would be adopted by businesses that already used the telegraph. But they imagined a much larger destiny for their invention than the business market alone. Bell and Hubbard predicted the installation of telephones in homes as well as business offices, where they imagined "a flood of uses" to which they might be put.[34] Hubbard set the price for telephones in the home at half the price of telephones in the workplace and strove to keep costs within reach of the middle-class Americans that Western Union so conspicuously ignored. He questioned the importance of long-distance communications, as epitomized by Western Union's transcontinental lines, and stressed instead the need instead for affordable short-distance connections, within cities or between neighboring towns. And in sharp contrast to Western Union's telegraph, which measured charges by the word, Hubbard encouraged active use of the telephone by offering unlimited local service for a flat monthly fee. (Alexander Graham Bell had assumed that telephone users would pay by the minute.)[35] In all these ways, Hubbard sought to make the telephone a true "telegraph for the people," a replacement for, and rebuke to, Western Union's expensive wires.

Hubbard's populism and his long-term influence on the Bell companies should not be overstated. His alleged disregard for money was never complete. Neither socialist nor saint, in all his enterprises Hubbard combined a civic spirit with the cheerful pursuit of private gain. And Hubbard's vision of a telegraph or telephone for the people hardly encompassed all the people. The most likely customers for the telephone, Hubbard believed, were upper- and middle-class Americans in urban areas. Few thought otherwise in the 1870s and early 1880s. The price of telephone service was still out of reach for working-class Americans and would remain so for some time. Finally, Hubbard's time at the helm of Bell Telephone was short, and his early influence was soon countered by other views. Less than two years after forming the Bell Telephone Company, Hubbard, Sanders, and Alexander Graham Bell would all be removed from its executive committee, forced by their shortage of capital to sell control of the company to wealthy new investors with a very different understanding of the telephone and its future.

That said, Gardiner Hubbard set several important precedents for the future of the telephone. He imagined and did much to construct the

American telephone industry as a decentralized network of local and regional systems, each owned and operated by residents of the territories they served. He tried to make the telephone affordable to middle-class, if not working-class, Americans, and he introduced a billing structure that encouraged social and casual use. Finally, Hubbard articulated a strong vision of the telephone as a democratic good, an instrument of opposition to Western Union and the corporate order it was coming to represent. By the mid-1880s, the company Hubbard founded would reject most of these aspirations. But Hubbard's vision lingered at many of the regional Bell operating companies and would erupt a decade later in the independent telephone movement and its gospel of a people's telephone.

William Forbes and the Bostonians

During Gardiner Hubbard's two-year tenure as president, the Bell Telephone Company remained desperately short of cash. Even before the business began, Hubbard owed a considerable sum of money to his own father-in-law; when he began leasing telephones, the cost of equipment and promotion rapidly devoured his and Thomas Sanders's reserves.[36] The company's need for capital became even more critical in December 1877, when Western Union established its own telephone business with instruments developed by Thomas Edison and Elisha Gray. The Bell partnership suddenly faced two expensive battles with a wealthy and determined rival—one on the streets for subscribers, and one in court to protect Alexander Graham Bell's patents. Sanders tried to convince Hubbard to sell out to Western Union, which he feared would otherwise "crush" both men "by fair means or foul." But Hubbard refused any settlement that would leave the telephone in Western Union's control. Sanders told Hubbard sternly in February 1878: "Absolute bankruptcy of the whole concern must result if we do not procure money from some source."[37]

On the verge of ruin, Hubbard and Sanders found a sort of salvation in a group of Boston investors organized by the railroad executive William Hathaway Forbes. The upright Forbes was considerably higher born and better connected than either Hubbard or Sanders. He used his connections, and his reputation for financial probity, to attract capital for the fledgling telephone business from some of the wealthiest, most important families in New England. In February 1879, Bell Telephone was reorganized as the

National Bell Telephone Company, with a new capital investment of $850,000. This intervention saved Bell, Hubbard, and Sanders from insolvency, but the price of the rescue was control of their company and its patents. Within a month, the new circle of investors pushed Hubbard out of the president's chair and elected Forbes in his place.[38]

"The people will rise in their might and crush these monopolies," Gardiner Hubbard had prophesied after the panic of 1873.[39] It was not always clear whether Hubbard imagined this uprising with anticipation or dread. But the men who replaced him on Bell's board of directors left no doubts about which side of the class struggle they were on. Known colloquially as "the Forbes group," they were men of money and aristocratic mien, conservative Boston Brahmins with no sympathy for populist unrest.

Bell's new president was the son-in-law of Ralph Waldo Emerson and the son of railroad tycoon John Murray Forbes. "Forbes represented the East—the East of the East—with its conservative stability and its regard for tradition and social and financial standing," declared a company history from 1923.[40] William Forbes made his name and multiplied his fortune by resuscitating, and when necessary amputating, the unprofitable lines in his father's railroad empire. He was politically active as an opponent of the labor movement and similar causes. Forbes fought the unionization of railway workers and efforts to regulate the railroads by farmers in western and midwestern states. He published a biweekly circular defending the gold standard against currency reforms and raised substantial sums for "sound money" Republicans.[41] Like most of his social circle, Forbes was a particular foe of Benjamin Franklin Butler, a congressman and former Civil War general who, after moving back and forth between the Democrats and Republicans, became the standard-bearer for the Greenback-Labor and Anti-Monopoly Parties—even as he worked and lobbied for financier Jay Gould. Butler's 1882 election as governor of Massachusetts, in the face of bitter opposition from Boston's elite, convinced Forbes that "communism is nearer the control of affairs than we have believed."[42] Butler returned the compliment, lumping Bell Telephone in with Western Union and the railroad conglomerates as notorious enemies of the people. "The great instruments by which commerce is carried on are transportation, money, and the transmission of intelligence," read Butler's platform as the Anti-Monopoly candidate for president in 1884. "They are now mercilessly controlled by giant monopolies, to the impoverishment of labor, and the crushing out of healthful competition, and the destruction of business security." Butler sponsored legislation to foster competition in telegraphy and championed government regulation of the telephone and telegraph industries.[43]

So William Forbes, no less than Gardiner Hubbard, was engaged in the great political debates of his day. And like Hubbard, the policies Forbes pursued at the head of the Bell company reflected his understanding of the telephone and the larger transformations of which it was a part. But Forbes's sympathies and inclinations were very different than those of his predecessor. Hubbard, inspired by the post office, considered Bell to be a "quasi-public" corporation. Forbes, influenced by the railroad and telegraph industries, firmly rejected such claims. His Bell Telephone was a private firm, responsible only to its investors. "The time has come to put the company's affairs on a business footing," Forbes lectured Alexander Graham Bell on the day he assumed the presidency.[44] Bell's new owners thought little of the way Gardiner Hubbard had run the company. They did not share his belief in an untapped middle-class market for the telephone, or his dedication to the many entrepreneurs operating Bell's local and regional affiliates. And Hubbard's vision of telephony as a tonic for democracy left them entirely unmoved.

While Hubbard had hoped to make the telephone a telegraph for the people, the Forbes group preferred to concentrate on the wealthiest segment of the market. The telephone, as Forbes and his colleagues saw it, did not belong to the people. It was not meant to be an answer to monopoly or a new mass medium. It was simply a tool of commerce, a modest refinement of the telegraph, most useful for well-to-do men much like themselves. "The telephone is peculiar in this," said Charles Fay, vice president and general manager of Bell's Chicago affiliate, in 1887. "It is patronized almost entirely by the plutocrats of the country; its merchants, bankers, professional men, managers of great corporations, and the like; in a word, by the richest, best educated and most conservative class." The Bostonians might not have put the matter so bluntly, but their prices and private remarks suggest that they did not disagree.[45]

Under Forbes's direction, National Bell pursued the monopolist's traditional strategy of maximizing profit through high prices and limited supply. The Boston company pushed rate increases onto its local licensees, setting prices that only the wealthiest users would bear. If this meant slower growth of the network, it did not trouble the Bostonians. "I am opposed to low rates unless made necessary by competition," said one Bell executive in 1883, expressing the general consensus within Forbes's firm. "Cheaper service will simply multiply the nuisance of wires and poles . . . without materially improving profits."[46] In an era of reckless speculation and competition, John Murray Forbes's railroad enterprise had been marked by its cautious, conservative rate of expansion. Unenthralled by growth for the sake of growth, the elder Forbes had often clashed with midwestern railroad boosters eager for new construction.[47] His son brought the same approach to the telephone industry.

What predisposed the Boston bankers to understand and frame the telephone as they did? To some degree, the Bostonians' cautious approach was a reaction to immediate conditions. Investing $850,000 in the telephone was a considerable risk in 1879. The technology was untested and the market unproven. And Bell Telephone spent its early years in what Forbes called "a struggle for existence," desperately short of capital, its patents under attack.[48] Bell's new owners understandably tried to protect their investments and secure as much profit as possible in a fairly short term. The company could easily have gone bankrupt. Its crucial patents were in real danger of being overturned. The technology itself might have failed in some unforeseen but irrevocable way. All these uncertainties encouraged caution. Thus, the Bostonians kept rates high and limited the construction of new telephone exchanges. They avoided debt and privileged short-term profits over long-term expansion. Such conservative policies would persist at Bell long after the perils of the early 1880s had passed.

The Bostonians were also influenced by their belief in the diseconomy of growth and scale. By the late nineteenth century, economy of scale—the expectation that large enterprises could produce goods more cheaply than small ones—was widely recognized as the chief engine making big business big. "Increasing business and decreasing rates have come to be almost axiomatic," said Bell counsel George Anderson in 1906.[49] Economies of scale were invoked to explain the unprecedented growth of American corporations and to justify the mergers and combinations of the day. But Bell's owners discovered to their dismay that economies of scale did not apply to the telephone. In fact, it cost more per subscriber to serve a large telephone exchange than a small one. This is simply a mathematical property of networks. Consider a tiny system connecting three telephones. There are six potential connections the operator may be asked to make: A may call B or C, B may call A or C, C may call A or B. But if just one phone is added to this network, there are suddenly twelve potential connections between the four subscribers. Add a fifth subscriber and there are twenty possible connections, a sixth and there are thirty. As the number of telephones in any community grew, the number of potential connections and the amount of actual telephone traffic grew far more rapidly than revenue from new subscribers. Switchboards became increasingly complex, as did the work required to operate them. As a result of these diseconomies of scale, providing telephone service in large cities soon cost three to four times what it cost in smaller communities.[50]

Bell executives had great difficulty in convincing their customers of this principle. "We do not take any stock in the point you make that the more telephones you have, the more it costs you," said the leader of an angry group of Bell subscribers in Rochester in 1886. "It is too profound. So different from the usual course of business, that we cannot see it."[51] But for Bell under the Bostonians, the diseconomy of scale was the true natural law—in George Anderson's words, "unexpected, unperceived, and yet absolutely inevitable." One Bell manager estimated that for every one hundred new subscribers, he would have to raise his rates by five dollars per year. Another said that, "so far as he could see, all he had to do was get enough subscribers and the company would go broke."[52] The high cost of growth seemed to demand regular hikes in the cost of telephone service and provided a compelling reason not to rapidly expand the network.

Forbes and his colleagues were also influenced in their vision of telephony by the precedent of the telegraph and the policies of Western Union. Gardiner Hubbard considered the telegraph giant dangerous to democracy, but National Bell's new owners could hardly ignore the company's tremendous success. Many of the managers and engineers they brought on board had considerable experience in the telegraph industry. It was easy to see the telephone as an adjunct to the telegraph, and it seemed logical for the Forbes group to look to Western Union as they considered how to promote and exploit the telephone.

Western Union in the 1880s remained the rich man's mail. Telegrams were expensive and were used almost exclusively by large businesses and the very wealthy. Western Union executives did not apologize for their high rates or their focus on an elite clientele. The company's leaders flatly denied that the telegraph would, should, or even could become a medium of popular communication. Norvin Green, who succeeded William Orton as president of Western Union in 1880, said that telegraphy would always remain "an adjunct of commerce and speculation." Even if a telegram were as cheap as a postage stamp, Green declared, less than one in ten Americans would choose the telegraph over the mail. The rest, he insisted, had no need or even desire for instant communication.[53]

Bell's Boston owners adopted a similar view of the telephone. When they imagined the potential market for telephone service, they imagined themselves. In their minds, the telephone's natural users were affluent businessmen working in urban offices, to whom rapid communication would have tangible fiscal rewards. They were men of means, who could afford to pay over a hundred dollars per year for service at a time when that represented more than a quarter of the average worker's annual wage.[54] Bell executives did not believe they were keeping telephone service from people who truly desired or deserved it. "The telephone, like the telegraph . . . is only upon extraordinary occasions used or needed by the poor," declared the outspoken Charles Fay in 1886. "It is . . . depended upon, and should be liberally paid for by, the capitalist, mercantile and manufacturing classes. This talk about oppressing the people is the merest rot."[55]

An immediate effect of the shift from Hubbard's expansive quasi-populism to the conservative policies of Forbes and the Bostonians can be seen in the industry's slowing growth. In Gardiner Hubbard's last year as president, Bell licensees installed seventeen thousand new telephones, tripling the size of their networks. The following year, Bell under William Forbes leased only five thousand new telephones, growth of less than 20 percent. In future years, the system's rate of expansion slowed even further, in both absolute and relative terms.[56]

More dramatic proof of the changes at Bell Telephone came in November 1879, when Forbes signed a contract with Western Union, ending competition and the patent battle between the two firms. Both Hubbard and Alexander Graham Bell were alarmed by the Bostonians' willingness to parley with their foe, but they had little influence on the company's new owners.[57] Indeed, such an accommodation was one of the first orders of business for Forbes and his colleagues when they acquired National Bell. They did not share Hubbard's hostility to the telegraph monopoly, and they had little interest in waging an expensive crusade against the giant firm. Western Union's leaders, preoccupied with fighting a takeover bid by Jay Gould, also proved willing to settle. Forbes and Western Union president Norvin Green signed their truce on 10 November 1879.[58]

This agreement inaugurated an era of partnership between the two companies. National Bell dropped its patent infringement suit against Western Union, and Western Union gave Bell its own patents on telephone improvements in exchange for 20 percent of the gross earnings on all telephones leased in the United States until the patents expired in 1894.[59] More broadly, Western Union agreed to acknowledge Alexander Graham Bell as the sole inventor of the telephone and withdrew from the telephone industry in exchange for a promise to cooperate with the telegraph, rather than compete, in the transmission of long-distance messages.

"It was predicted in the early days of the telephone that it would become a serious rival to the telegraph," observed the *New York Times* in 1886. "The result has been directly the reverse." In his truce with Western Union, Forbes agreed not to develop long-distance transmission of "general business messages, market quotations, or news for sale or publication." This was, of course, the heart of the telegraph business, and just the sort of communication that Gardiner Hubbard had hoped to free from Western Union's control. After 1879, Bell ordered its managers to transmit any telegraph messages they received by telephone to Western Union, effectively turning all local telephone networks into a feeder system for the telegraph giant. Forbes also promised not to provide telephone service to any companies in competition with Western Union—an explicit endorsement of the telegraph monopoly. "Without a dollar of expenditure on the part of the telegraph companies, their field of operations has been enormously increased" by the telephone, the *Times* concluded, "with the result of correspondingly increasing their business." The Bostonians' telephone was not the telegraph's rival, but its servant.[60]

Observers hailed the Bell contract with Western Union as a victory for both sides and the salvation of the fledgling firm. National Bell shares, selling for fifty dollars in March 1879, surged to nearly one thousand dollars per share the day after the agreement was signed. In March 1880, National Bell was reincorporated as the American Bell Telephone Company, with a capitalization of $7,350,000, more than eight times the worth of National Bell just thirteen months before. The next year, American Bell's net earnings were over $500,000; in 1882 they were nearly $1 million.[61] The Western Union contract made the fortunes of Bell's investors, including Alexander Graham Bell and even Gardiner Hubbard, who never gave up his shares.[62] But it was a repudiation of Hubbard's civic-minded vision of a telegraph for the people, and it cast the telephone as a junior partner in the new corporate order that Western Union had come to represent.

For more than two decades, the same close-knit circle of Boston investors would control American Bell, and through its patents, dominate the telephone industry in the United States and Canada. The continuity of their tenure was remarkable. In 1899, American Bell had thirteen directors; over half of these men had been on the board since at least 1887, and five of the thirteen had been there since American Bell's creation in 1881.[63] Like many of New England's business elite, Forbes and his colleagues saw themselves as guardians of order, steady hands on the tiller aiming to sail between the Goulds and Butlers of the world—the evils of rapacious speculation on one side and wild-eyed socialism on the other.[64] This narrative of order and stability was their answer to Hubbard's vision of a people's telephone. American Bell's owners never had complete command over the other Bell companies, nor could they control the ways that those outside their company used or imagined the telephone. But they exerted a powerful force on its development and imprinted their cautious, conservative vision on the North American telephone industry for years to come.

Theodore Vail and the Bell Operating Companies

There was another vision of the telephone emerging in the early 1880s—a third narrative of the technology's meaning and future that would shape the industry profoundly in years to come. This was the dream of "one big system": a single, continent-spanning telephone network, controlled by one corporation, connecting every subscriber in the nation and perhaps even the world. The man most associated with the idea of a unified Bell System was present in the industry almost from the start. But his dream of consolidation remained idiosyncratic at this time, not embraced by the Boston owners of American Bell, and actively resisted by the decentralized federation of operating companies that made up the nineteenth-century telephone business.

Theodore Newton Vail was Bell Telephone's first general manager, hired by Gardiner Hubbard in 1878. He would leave the industry in 1889 after quarrels with Bell's directors and return only in 1907, after the Bostonians had been overthrown. A big man with a big ego and big ideas, Vail casts a large shadow on the history of the telephone. The Bell System he is credited with building became so famous in the twentieth century for its uniformity and homogeneity that it has been common for historians and others to project that unity back onto the industry's nineteenth-century past. Vail himself was prone to do so, claiming after his return to Bell in the 1900s that the company had been following his ideas and policies all along.[65]

Little evidence from the 1880s or 1890s supports this assertion. Even before the arrival of independent competition, the nineteenth-century telephone business was less unified or centralized than it has often been portrayed. The real work of building and running telephone networks around the country was done by local companies that were organizationally distinct from American Bell: first the dozens of Bell-affiliated operating companies that leased the right to use Bell's patents, and later the thousands of independent companies that challenged them. In large cities and in tiny hamlets, both Bell and independent operating companies faced the street-level challenges of telephony, and their innovations built the industry. American Bell did own stock in several affiliated operating companies, particularly in large markets like New York and Chicago, but these companies still remained organizationally distinct. And many more of the Bell operating companies were the product of local capital and enterprise alone. Relations between American Bell and its affiliates could be fractious. Many operating company managers resented the fees charged by the Bostonians and resisted efforts to meddle in their work. They would fight to retain their autonomy—a battle it took Theodore Vail some thirty years to win.[66]

Vail was only thirty-three years old when he joined the Bell companies, but his whole working life had been a romance with large communication systems. An electrical current ran in Vail's family. His second cousin Alfred Vail was Samuel Morse's partner in developing the telegraph, and family tradition held that Alfred Vail was the real inventor of the code that bore his colleague's name.[67] Theodore Vail learned that code, and how to operate the telegraph, as a teenage drug store clerk in Morristown, Ohio. He worked as an operator for Western Union, and later as a mail clerk on the Union Pacific Railroad. In 1873, Vail joined the head offices of the U.S. Postal Service in Washington, where he made a name for himself by streamlining and reforming the railway mail.[68] He and others worked to restructure the post office to mirror the organization of the country's railway networks, effectively merging the two systems to achieve maximum efficiency for long-distance communication. "It was the kind of work he loved," wrote Vail's biographer Albert Paine. "He thought of nothing else, talked of nothing else, studied the maps and postal guides far into the night."[69]

Vail's passion and guiding principle was the idea of system. System was a word to conjure with in this era. For the engineers and entrepreneurs of

Vail's generation, transportation and communication systems like the railroad and telegraph were powerful symbols of the age. More than just technical achievements, they seemed to point toward the future of human organization. These technological systems seemed to offer arguments for the ideal of system itself—for the standardization of procedures, the consolidation of ownership, and the centralization of control. "A railway, like a vast machine, the wheels of which are all connected with each other . . . requires a certain harmony, [and] cannot be worked by a number of independent agents," declared one 1850 treatise on the economy of railways. "The organization of a railway requires unity of direction and harmony of movement, which can only be attained by the combination of the entire carrying business with the general administration of the road."[70] Vail would echo this language all his life.

Gardiner Hubbard met Vail in the 1870s while working for his congressional postal committee. Hubbard sold the younger man on the telephone's bright future and hired him away from the postal service in 1878. Paine's biography of Vail describes one of Vail's associates saying, "Hubbard tried to sell *me* some of that stock . . . I'm sorry he got hold of a nice young man like Vail."[71] Vail was soon regarded inside and outside Bell as the company's most active and ambitious executive; Hubbard called him "a thousand horsepower steam engine." When Vail left his position as general manager of American Bell in 1885, the trade journal *Electrical World* said he had been "either the originator or the prime mover in nearly every enterprise fostered by that corporation."[72]

Though the three men had different ways of seeing and framing their industry, Vail's talents were highly regarded by both Gardiner Hubbard and William Forbes. Perhaps Vail's experience with both the U.S. Postal Service and Western Union prepared him for mediating between Hubbard's civic-minded vision of telephony and Forbes's profit-centered emulation of the telegraph giant. But Vail was beholden to neither mail nor telegraph as a model for the telephone. He was less interested in politics than either Forbes or Hubbard, and not inclined to regard the telephone as any kind of intervention in the politics of the day. If Forbes and Hubbard had anything in common, it was that both men saw the telephone as a means to some end. For Vail, the telephone network was an end in itself. What interested him most was neither profit nor the people, but rather the organization and expansion of the system.

In constant contact between the Boston company and its regional affiliates, Vail worked to centralize the industry's corporate structure and perfect the efficiency of both its technical and human systems. Vail became, among other things, Bell's most influential champion of the long-distance telephone. It was he who convinced Forbes not to trade away rights to the long-distance market in his negotiations with Western Union in 1879.[73] And Vail was almost certainly the first person at Bell to articulate a dream of uniting all the nation's telephone exchanges in "one great big general system." That vision became the central theme of his long and spectacular career. "The Bell System was founded on the broad lines of 'One System, One Policy, Universal Service,'" Vail would declare in 1910. This meant, he said, "the idea that no aggregation of isolated independent systems, not under common control . . . could give the public the service that the interdependent, intercommunicating, universal system could give." Although that slogan appeared only in 1908, Vail claimed then that the idea was not new. "In fact," he said, "the theory was evolved and developed before the business, and the business has been developed on that theory."[74]

But this version of history would have been a great surprise to the owners and managers of the many Bell operating companies. The operating companies valued their independence from American Bell and resisted attempts by the parent firm to control or direct their operations. "The American Bell Telephone Company does not own a dollar of stock in our company," insisted James Caldwell, president of the Cumberland Telephone and Telegraph Company, in 1885. Nearly twenty years later, the Nashville-based company still boasted that it remained "controlled by Southern men, financed with Southern money, and its affairs directed by Southern brains."[75] Southern sentiment obviously played a part in Cumberland's independence, but similar statements could be heard at operating companies around the country. Men like Morris Tyler, the first president of the Southern New England Telephone Company, and Charles Fay, vice president and general manager of the Chicago Telephone Company, remained equally unmoved by Vail's paeans to centralization or common control. They were nobody's subordinates and bridled at efforts to make them otherwise.

In 1880, the Bell operating companies formed their own trade group, the National Telephone Exchange Association. The NTEA became a key forum for the circulation of technical and organizational innovations in the industry, and a counterweight to efforts by Vail and others to centralize authority at American Bell. In many ways, the NTEA, and not American Bell, was the real center of the American telephone industry at this time. The operating company managers were often at odds with American Bell, and they took a variety of positions on the questions that divided Gardiner Hubbard and William Forbes. In the 1880s, few of these managers embraced Hubbard's vision of the telephone as a popular medium. They moved toward this vision only after the overturning of Bell's patent monopoly and the coming of independent competition. But most did, like Hubbard, favor flat rates over measured service (in part because they were much easier to administer) and a decentralized telephone industry, owned and operated by local entrepreneurs.

Vail's enthusiasm for long-distance telephony was a regular area of contention with the Bell operating company managers. They were in the business of providing short-distance service, and they perceived that in Vail's mind, long-distance interconnection and the surrender of regional autonomy went hand in hand. "The connection of many towns together . . . made it of importance to bring as large areas as possible under one management," Vail wrote in 1883.[76] The local and regional Bell managers were not so sure. Many were reluctant to commit to either the expense of long lines or the centralization of management such interconnection was said to require. "His ambition was to be recognized as the wire king of the world," James Caldwell said of Vail, "and with that in view he began making plans to bring under his control all the telephone companies in this country."[77] When Vail proselytized for long distance, the operating companies always asked the same question: "Will it pay?" The answer was not clear. The technology needed for long-distance transmission remained uncertain in the 1880s and 1890s, as did the public's desire for it. Though "fondly regarded" by "some," long-distance service had "always been a source of actual loss to the company," Morris Tyler declared in 1885. Caldwell and Tyler's fellow managers scoffed at the sort of pronouncements on the bright future of long distance to which Vail was given: "It was almost suggested that the life of the average American would be incomplete were he to omit from his daily routine the pleasure of telephoning to his friends in Japan," said one.[78]

Vail also clashed with William Forbes and the rest of American Bell's directors. He agreed with some of the Bostonians' strategies for the telephone but strongly disagreed with others. He shared their belief in keeping rates high to ensure high quality service and was comfortable with their focus on businessmen as the principal market for the telephone. But Vail fought with Bell's executive committee in the 1880s over their short-term perspective and conservative fiscal policies. The Boston circle did not share his expansive ambitions for the telephone and echoed the doubts of local management about the profitability of long distance. Vail's inclination was always to pump profits back into the network with new construction and the improvement of existing lines; the risk-averse Bostonians preferred to collect their dividends right away. For all his managerial acumen, Vail often resembled Gardiner Hubbard in his incautious way with money. "His habit of lavish expenditure . . . was more than a habit it seems, it was a natural trait," testified an old friend.[79]

In Vail's first five years at American Bell, the company's licensees enrolled 117,000 new subscribers, a rapid increase of about 35 percent per year. Around 1884, demand for new telephones seemed to slide. Vail saw this dip as temporary, part of a general "dullness" in the economy that year. Others disagreed. "The telephone business has passed through its 'booming' stage, and . . . the pendulum is now at the other end of its swing," declared *Electrical Review*. Some felt Vail's "anxiety to obtain subscribers" had been too great. Many were inclined to think the market had reached saturation. With one telephone in use for every 385 Americans, and roughly one per 150 residents in cities like Boston and Chicago, perhaps the country had all the telephones it required.[80]

The downturn in the industry weakened Vail's position at Bell and fortified those who preached frugality and restraint. Telephone stock prices sagged, and money for expansion or improvement was scarce. The Bostonians' answer was higher rates and more rigid economies. "The establishment of systems in small towns was probably pushed too rapidly," said William Forbes in 1885. He pledged a tighter rein on company finances—in other words, on Vail—and a pause in building new exchanges. At an annual meeting of American Bell shareholders in May of that year, Forbes agreed to investor demands that new construction be "reduced to the lowest figure, with a view to resuming dividends at an early date." Only eight thousand telephones would be installed in that year, a relative increase of just 5 percent. The number of telephone exchanges in the country actually declined from 906 in January 1884 to 747 in January 1886. Some were simply consolidated into larger exchanges, but others were deemed unprofitable and shut down. But the company's shareholders were well taken care of.

American Bell paid dividends of sixteen dollars per share—a dollar per share increase over the previous year.[81]

The slump also damaged Vail's dreams for long distance. In March 1884, the Southern New England Telephone Company completed construction of a two-hundred-mile-long line from Boston to New York City. It was then the longest telephone line in existence, and a personal triumph for Vail. But doubters, many Bell investors among them, dubbed it "Vail's Folly." The cost of building and maintaining the line was higher than anticipated, and demand for long-distance calling proved scant. In September and October 1884, for example, only nineteen calls were made on the line, and the company's earnings from it totaled less than ten dollars. The economic downturn made such a folly seem particularly extravagant. In May 1885, the New England Company announced it was abandoning the line.[82]

Vail's vision suffered another blow in May 1885, when the Massachusetts state legislature rejected American Bell's request to increase its capitalization from $10 million to $30 million. Vail had hoped to put this money toward constructing a truly national long-distance network. But Massachusetts law required legislative approval for any increase in capital of companies chartered in the state. "The American Bell desires to connect every system in the United States . . . so that direct telephoning may be accomplished to all parts of the country," company attorneys told the legislature. "What objection can there be to this?" State legislators, however, felt American Bell was already large enough, and, like many of Vail's employers and colleagues, they doubted whether long-distance telephony was widely desired or even possible.[83]

Vail admitted to a "growing dissatisfaction" with his position at American Bell at this time, and especially with his employers' refusal to sacrifice immediate dividends for long-term goals.[84] His quarrels with American Bell's general counsel, the attorney John Elbridge Hudson, were particularly intense. By many accounts, especially those written by admirers of Vail, Hudson was a haughty aristocrat who seldom smiled, a pious Brahmin given to drafting memos in ancient Greek. He is said to have told the board of directors that there was not enough room in the company for both himself and Vail, and that a choice between them would have to be made. Hudson was not wrong about that—he and Vail epitomized two incompatible views of the telephone and its future.[85] In the wake of the Massachusetts decision, the Bostonians' renewed fiscal conservatism, and the abandonment of the Boston-New York line, Vail resigned his position as general manager of American Bell in the summer of 1885. John Hudson took his place.

After some negotiation, the Bostonians did convince Vail to stay on as president of the Metropolitan Telephone and Telegraph Company, American Bell's crucial New York licensee. Vail's price for taking this job was permission and capital to establish a brand new company—a fully owned subsidiary of American Bell called the American Telephone and Telegraph Company.[86] Freed from the close supervision of his conservative superiors in Boston and the strictures of Massachusetts law, Vail was better able to articulate his expansive aspirations for the telephone. The new subsidiary was dedicated entirely to the development of a long-distance telephone network. Although the company was initially capitalized at only $100,000, the permissive laws of New York State set no limit on its ultimate size. "If it is to grow into a large Company," Vail told his new staff, "we shall want unlimited rights."[87] AT&T's founding charter, drafted by Vail and his lieutenant Edward Hall, is worth quoting at length. Obviously a document like this is written to be expansive. Still, Vail's ambitions were remarkable for this time:

> The lines of this association . . . will connect one or more points in each and every city, town or place in the State of New York with one or more points in each and every other city, town or place in said state, and in each and every other of the United States, and in Canada and Mexico; and each and every other of said cities, towns and places is to be connected with each and every other city, town or place . . . and also by cable and other appropriate means with the rest of the known world.[88]

The name of the new company suggested one more goal. Vail ultimately hoped to unify all wire communications in America—both telephone and telegraph—under one company's control. The 1879 contract with Western Union had partitioned the communication industry, with Bell agreeing to stay out of the telegraph business and Western Union giving up its designs on the telephone. But Vail had convinced William Forbes and the Bostonians not to trade away their rights to long-distance communication in that contract, and as early as 1879 or 1880, Vail later claimed, he had been looking forward to "the ultimate absorption of the telegraph business" as a means to providing universal long-distance communication.[89]

Vail's AT&T took over the abandoned Boston–New York line and began constructing another long-distance line from New York to Philadelphia. Completed in April 1886, this new line used a metallic circuit of doubled copper wires, a great improvement over the single iron wire used by most local exchanges. The quality of transmission was unprecedented, better than most local calls, and the line was hailed in the press as an astonishing achievement.[90] But Vail was soon reminded of the distance between his priorities and those of his colleagues. For technical reasons, the Bell licensees in Philadelphia and New York were not ready to connect their local systems to the new long-distance line; nor were they enthusiastic about spending the money to do so. And despite its ambitious prospectus, AT&T in the 1880s had no authority over the operating companies. Vail could not force the Bell affiliates to accommodate his plans—not yet. The Philadelphia company in particular did not show "any disposition . . . to cooperate," reported Edward Hall, and "the purpose for which the line was intended [was] practically defeated."[91]

Vail may have left Boston in 1885, but he had not escaped the Bostonians' conservative vision of the telephone. And with Vail in New York, there was nobody back in Boston to challenge the Brahmin philosophies. As AT&T's earnings fell short of expectations, Vail grew further apart from the owners of American Bell on the one side and the operating company managers on the other. After William Forbes retired from the presidency of American Bell in 1887, Vail's isolation was complete. Vail had once considered himself Forbes's natural successor, but after a brief interregnum, the Bostonians chose Vail's old foe John Hudson to head the parent company. Calling his position at Bell "embarrassing and unpleasant," Theodore Vail resigned from AT&T in 1887 and from Metropolitan Telephone and Telegraph in 1889, leaving the industry entirely. He believed at the time it would be for good.[92]

Boston on the St. Lawrence

Nowhere was the imprint of the Bostonians' conservative policies deeper or longer lasting than on the Bell Telephone Company of Canada. American Bell's Boston investors organized the creation of Bell Canada in 1880. At first, Alexander Graham Bell and his father had hoped to sell the rights to the telephone in Canada to a Canadian firm. The obvious bidders were

Canada's two leading telegraph companies, the Montreal Telegraph Company and the Dominion Telegraph of Toronto. But Montreal Telegraph was a close ally of Western Union, and the Dominion was associated with financier Jay Gould. Neither Hubbard nor the Bells wanted any patent rights to fall into the hands of such rivals, so Alexander Bell Sr. and Jr. arranged to sell the Canadian patents to Forbes and American Bell.[93] Based in Montreal, Bell Canada was officially independent of American Bell, with its own patents, its own directors, and its own corporate charter from the government of Canada. But in truth, Bell Canada had closer ties to Boston than many of the Bell operating companies in the United States. American Bell owned about one-third of Bell Canada's voting stock in 1885 and held four positions on its eight-member board of directors. Bell Canada relied heavily on American Bell for capital and equipment and conferred with Boston on policy and rates.[94]

American Bell's man in Montreal was Charles Fleetford Sise. Though raised in New England, Sise had sided with the South in the American Civil War. He fought at the Battle of Shiloh, was a shipping agent for the Confederacy, and became the personal secretary of Confederate president Jefferson Davis from 1861 to 1863. After the war, these ties to the Confederacy limited Sise's prospects in Boston but proved no particular liability in Montreal. Sise led Bell Canada from 1880 until 1915, and his sons and protégés held significant positions in the company for decades thereafter.[95]

It is difficult to measure the autonomy of Bell Canada under Charles Sise because, in contrast to many American operating company managers, his policies and philosophies were so closely aligned with the Bostonians. Handpicked for his post by William Forbes, Sise was a staunch supporter of American Bell's conservative policies. Bell Canada under Sise favored high prices and slow expansion. It encouraged business uses of the telephone over social uses, and it developed urban telephone networks rather than rural or long-distance lines. The most egregious example of Bell Canada's conservatism in these years was its willful neglect of French Canadian customers. Though headquartered in the French-speaking province of Quebec, Bell Canada conducted all of its operations in English and was, like most of Montreal's large business enterprises, dominated by English-speaking executives and employees. Bell Canada directed most of its efforts in Montreal to serving the Anglophone business community and made almost no effort to market telephones to the less affluent but far more numerous Francophone majority. "The French do not, and except to a very limited extent will not, adopt the telephone," Sise concluded less than a month after his arrival in Montreal.[96]

This remained the company's position for decades. Well after Montreal's electric utility and Quebec's major railroads had adopted bilingual reforms, Bell Canada continued to operate entirely in English.[97] In 1904, a Bell Canada executive wrote to AT&T saying, "the very large proportion of French speaking people here . . . it seems to us, could never be induced to use the telephone even at extremely low rates."[98] French Canadians complained bitterly that Bell Canada was not welcoming to them, that Bell operators did not speak French, and that Bell would deal with its customers only in English. "We cannot get an answer in French from the telephone," complained the newspaper *Le Nationaliste* in 1907. "We cannot call in French . . . without being insulted by some low improvised clerk."[99] Sise's hasty dismissal of the Francophone market became a self-fulfilling prophecy.

Even after Bell's patent monopoly ended, and competition and political threats drove the Bell companies in the United States away from the conservative strategies of the Boston years, Bell Canada did not significantly change its course. When the Canadian government nullified Bell's patents in January 1885, the Bostonians took a direct role in shaping Bell Canada's response. Charles Sise kept in close contact with Boston throughout the affair, remarking to one friend that he was "merely the mouthpiece of the Am[erican] Bell in the matter."[100] Less than a week after the patent commissioner's decision, Theodore Vail and John Hudson met with Sise and his colleagues in Montreal. Company legend celebrates the advice Vail offered at this meeting. "Build long distance lines at once," he is said to have said. "But they will not pay," protested the Canadians. "I did not say they would, but they will unify and save your business," Vail allegedly replied. But the story is apocryphal and does not have the ring of truth.[101] Soon after returning to Boston, Vail wrote Sise to inform him that American Bell would not subsidize new long-distance lines in Canada unless they could be shown to "greatly strengthen existing exchanges, or unless there is a very profitable field unoccupied."[102] And even if Vail really did advise the Canadians to build long-distance lines in 1885, Bell Canada's policies after that date owed far more to John Hudson's conservative instincts than to any of Vail's expansive schemes. The company did not embark on any ambitious construction projects after 1885. In fact, its growth slowed considerably and remained steady but very conservative for the next twenty years. Nor did Bell Canada lower its regular prices in the face of competition, as many had predicted it would have to. In certain markets, as the previous chapter discussed, the company did offer lower rates and sometimes even free service in order to eliminate a local competitor, but these were temporary measures. There was no move to reduce Bell Canada's regular rates and certainly no push to bring the telephone to the masses.[103]

Sise and the Bostonians seem to have decided that they did not have the political or financial capital to maintain a monopoly over the entire country of Canada. They chose instead to focus on the market they considered most profitable—wealthy customers in the populous urban centers of Ontario and Quebec. Bell Canada sold its fledgling network on Prince Edward Island in 1885, and its holdings in British Columbia in 1889. In the Atlantic provinces of Nova Scotia and New Brunswick, the company tried for a few years to retain its larger urban exchanges, ceding only the less profitable rural territories to local interests. But by 1888, Bell Canada had sold all of its operations in the East.[104] These cessions left the company in control of the telephone in Manitoba, Ontario, and Quebec.[105] There, Bell Canada made clear its plans to retain a complete monopoly over urban markets.

These concessions may or may not have sat well with Theodore Vail. In just a few months, he would be drafting his charter for the American Telephone and Telegraph Company, with its ambitious talk of uniting "every city, town or place" in the United States, Canada, and "the rest of the known world."[106] But Sise's decisions were all entirely in keeping with the strategies of the parent company in Boston, still protected by its patents there.

Many Bells

Hubbard's marginalization and Vail's departure left conservative visions of the telephone unchallenged at American Bell. The effects of the Brahmin philosophy on the telephone in the 1880s and early 1890s are easy to see. Between 1885, the year Vail left Boston, and 1894, the end of Bell's patent monopoly, the total number of telephones in the United States grew steadily but very slowly, with an average growth in subscribers of only 6 percent per year. The Bostonians kept their shareholders happy. During the patent monopoly years, American Bell earned an average annual return on investment of 46 percent—lucrative profits, especially in an era of financial panic and general deflation—and paid out $26 million in dividends.[107]

The telephone did not become an instrument of the people. By 1893, there were only 266,000 telephones in the entire United States, or approximately one telephone for every 250 people. In a period of general deflation, in which consumer prices declined by 20 percent and commodity prices by nearly one-third, telephone rates only went up. In 1893, a year of telephone service cost between $60 and $150 in most cities and could cost as much as $200 in Chicago or New York. Ordinary Americans and Canadians would not be lining up for telephone service at these prices; the average worker earned just $450 per year in 1893.[108] Even a doctor or lawyer making ten times that amount would have to think twice before installing a telephone in his home. Geography also kept telephone service out of many Americans' reach. Half of the country's telephones in 1893 were located in the nation's largest cities, home to less than a fifth of the American population.[109] And the telephone remained primarily a business tool. Roughly four out of five were installed in offices and other workplaces, rather than ordinary homes.[110]

There was, as we have seen, no unified Bell System in the 1880s or 1890s, at least not outside the mind of Theodore Vail. There were many Bells: American Bell in Boston, American Telephone and Telegraph in New York, and dozens of operating companies around the country, not to mention Bell Canada in Montreal. And there were at least as many ways to imagine the telephone and its future as there were companies with Bell in their name. But the three traditions represented by Gardiner Hubbard, William Forbes, and Theodore Vail exerted powerful influences in decades to come. Hubbard's hopeful vision of a telephone for the people, Forbes's conservative understanding of the same technology, and Vail's ambitious dream of one big system were all present at or near the birth of the many Bells. These ideas would shape and define the battles over the telephone for many years thereafter.

One thing that Forbes and Hubbard both seemed to understand was that ideas about the telephone were inescapably political. They involved arguments about monopoly and competition, about national and local commerce, and about the proper scale of business and social life. Such arguments were waged within the Bell companies from the telephone's earliest days. But these debates were never contained within those walls, and they would not be settled there. Which understandings of telephony won—and would in retrospect come to seem natural or inevitable—was not to be determined by the Bell companies alone, but also by telephone users, competing firms, city councils, state legislatures, and federal courts. The next chapter turns to those venues and debates.

Chapter 3

Unnatural Monopoly

At least in theory, the Bell interests on both sides of the border enjoyed a monopoly over the telephone for most of its early years. American Bell and Bell Canada owned exclusive patents on key parts of telephone technology and used these patents to maintain commercial control of their industry. To a more limited extent, they were also able to shape popular understandings of the telephone and its use. Yet none of these monopolies—under the law, in the marketplace, or out in the broader culture—was ever total or secure. The Bell companies struggled with their own subscribers over the proper use and cost of the telephone. They fought endless legal battles to protect their patents. And when rival manufacturers finally succeeded in overturning those patents—in Canada in 1885, in the United States in 1894—the Bell interests faced a potential onslaught of independent competition. With the end of Bell's patent monopolies, battles boiled over that had been simmering for years: a commercial struggle for control of the telephone industry, a political struggle over telephone regulation, and a cultural struggle about what the telephone meant and what it should become. Yet in different regions and different regulatory environments, these contests had rather different outcomes.

Debates around the telephone in the 1880s and 1890s involved repeated claims about the natural or inherent qualities of the new device. Bell's owners and allies, for instance, declared the telephone a natural monopoly. Many of Bell's foes called such a monopoly illegitimate and unsustainable, declaring competition the natural state of affairs. Of course, the novelty of the telephone made it impossible for Americans or Canadians to know what, if anything, was truly natural—what aspects of the new technology must be fixed and what aspects might be changed. But that did not stop them from trying, or from ascribing policy choices to presumed technological and economic imperatives.

The economic theory of the era did little to solve these riddles. In 1887, economist Henry Carter Adams defined any industry enjoying economies of scale as a "natural monopoly." If a large enterprise could produce goods or services more cheaply than a small one, the argument went, monopoly must be the inevitable result.[1] Yet by the time Adams wrote, it was clear that the telephone industry did not automatically enjoy such economies. The opposite was often true.[2] Another argument held that the telephone was a natural monopoly because only a monopolistic system could connect every telephone to every other, avoiding the duplication and inconvenience of dual service—the state of affairs illustrated by General Kemper's two telephones. But this argument did not indicate whether that system must take the form of one big national (or international) monopoly or a patchwork of interconnected regional and local monopolies, each supreme in its own territory. Nor did it contemplate the interconnection of competing telephone networks—the system Americans and Canadians have today.

What no one acknowledged was that neither competition nor monopoly in the telephone industry could ever be natural. Both had to be constructed; both were outcomes of a contested process that, in a different political environment, could (and did) turn out differently. In the American Midwest, the Bell interests faced decades of fierce competition from independent systems. But rise of the midwestern independents was neither automatic nor inevitable. Independent telephony was a quasi-municipal movement, constructed by the franchise-granting power of local governments. In Central Canada, by contrast, the Bell interests weathered the loss of their patents with little difficulty. Bell's Canadian monopoly was not created by the workings of a free market or by any inherent logic of the technology. It was the child of Bell Canada's generous federal charter, upheld by court decisions and buttressed by dozens of exclusive municipal franchises.

Political environments drove outcomes, not only by influencing business strategy and handicapping commercial fights, but also by shaping rhetoric and ideas. In different regions, regulatory arrangements encouraged different kinds of arguments. The rhetoric of the people's telephone took hold in the American Midwest not because of some innate populism that stopped at the 49th Parallel, but because the political economy of the telephone in those regions was hospitable to populist appeals. Municipal governments there had the means and the motive to play an active role in the telephone industry, and Bell's enemies quickly learned to speak a language aldermen and city councilors liked to hear. In Central Canada, the municipalities were only bit players, marginalized from the start by Bell's charter and other laws. The venues that mattered most in Ontario—Parliament and the courts—rewarded declarations of Canadian nationalism, not populism. Its American origins notwithstanding, Bell Canada quickly learned to play its appointed role. By the middle of the twentieth century's first decade, the telephone industries in Canada and the United States, and in various regions within each country, had taken strikingly different paths. Yet in each region, a discourse of naturalness or inevitability concealed the differences political economy had made.

"Telephone Subscribers as Knights of Labor"

It is tempting to see the clashes between Bell managers and their customers in the telephone's early days as a story of consumer agency and empowerment: the Bell monopoly began with a narrow, conservative vision of the telephone, but plucky consumers appropriated the technology and used it in innovative ways. Ordinary people, especially women and rural telephone users, were instrumental in inventing the social uses of the telephone and imposing them on stodgy captains of industry.[3] This narrative is appealing and contains some truth, but we should not overestimate the power that individual consumers had to shape policy at American Bell or Bell Canada. Patent monopolies and conservative mindsets rendered the Bostonians fairly impervious to individual demands. Organized political pressure, boycotts over rates and rate structures, challenges to the Bell patents and municipally enabled competition after those patents expired, and the threat of further regulation or even nationalization: these were the ways consumers and citizens could shape the telephone industry. To understand the development of the telephone in this era, and in particular the decline of the conservative policies and philosophies favored by the Bostonians, we must look beyond individual consumers to consider more organized collective and commercial actions.

Urban businessmen were the first market the Bell companies sought for the telephone, and the first group to adopt the telephone in large numbers. American Bell fought for their business but also their allegiance to the Boston vision of telephony. Yet this does not mean that relations between the Bell companies and their business users always ran smoothly. Indeed, Bell managers and their early customers were wired together in a relationship of surprisingly intense hostility. "The Bell Company has had a monopoly more profitable and more controlling—and more generally hated—than any ever given by any patent," warned company lawyer James Storrow in 1891. And the contempt was often mutual.[4]

As early as 1881, businessmen in New York City complained of unfair rates and poor service in the country's largest and most expensive telephone exchange. State commissioner E. G. Blackford told the *New York Times* that the Bell companies in New York "showed an almost total indifference to the interests of its patrons, and generally turned a deaf ear to their complaints." When New York City's Metropolitan Telephone and Telegraph raised its rates for telephone service, the indignant commissioner threatened to call a protest meeting of all the subscribers in the city. That this could even be contemplated was a measure of how exclusive the telephone network remained. New York City in 1881 had roughly twenty-seven hundred telephone subscribers, or one telephone for every 450 residents of the city.[5]

Chicago Telephone's Charles Fay gave candid voice to his view of such protests in an 1887 speech entitled "Telephone Subscribers as Knights of Labor." "Nine men out of ten in every community are antagonistic to the Telephone Company which serves them," Fay declared. Such men might imagine themselves to be "conservative men of property," Fay said, but their "ignorance and prejudice" against the telephone company, which he judged "the greatest and the most beneficent of all the Monopolies," revealed them to be "socialists" under the skin. This was, of course, no compliment. "Beneath the mask of the brilliant editor or the conservative financier," Fay continued, lurked "the ignorant, vicious, unreasoning Knight of Labor."[6]

To men like Fay or William Forbes, the Knights of Labor were the most feared and detested labor union in the country. Fay's contemptuous characterization of his own customers suggests again how the politics of telephony were colored by the larger conflicts of the day. In the 1880s, most disputes between the owners and users of the telephone were, after all, quarrels between groups of wealthy businessmen whose politics were probably not so very different. Yet these were years of economic chaos and unrest, and on both sides of the telephone struggle, violent metaphors of class warfare were always close at hand.

Telephone price hikes in 1885 and 1886 provoked protests and boycotts of Bell service around the country. In cities like Schenectady, New York, and Concord, Massachusetts, thousands of subscribers removed their telephones. In some communities, service had to be discontinued altogether. A well-organized boycott in Rochester, New York, shut down telephone service in that city for eighteen months before the Bell affiliate there capitulated to subscriber demands. Upper-class subscribers called these actions "telephone strikes," even though many of them probably deplored the real strikes convulsing America in those years. Wealthy telephone users denounced the evils of the Bell monopoly and professed their solidarity with "the people."[7]

These boycotts mirrored thousands of consumer and labor boycotts that more working-class Americans launched in this decade against street railways, newspapers, and every kind of manufacturing firm. Labor unions—the Knights of Labor in particular—embraced boycotts as a tactic in the early 1880s. For a few years, the boycott was deemed a more effective and important weapon in the hands of labor than the strike. The New York Bureau of Labor reported more than thirteen hundred union-led boycotts in that state between 1885 and 1892. New York judges called such tactics "wicked" and "insolent," a threat to the underpinnings of economic order, and moved to define labor boycotts as a form of criminal conspiracy or extortion. In 1886, over one hundred labor organizers in New York City were indicted on such charges. It is unlikely that any well-to-do telephone subscribers would ever have faced prosecution for this offence. Indeed, judges who ruled on boycott cases took pains to single out tactics used by labor (pickets, street demonstrations, and so on) while ignoring the techniques of boycott led by business or professional groups.[8] Still, such decisions technically made criminals of hundreds of businessmen in Rochester and across the state.

The telephone users that Charles Fay disparaged as pseudo-socialist Knights of Labor found a spokesman in Gardiner Hubbard, father of the people's telephone idea. Still a stockholder in American Bell, though without any influence in its operations, Hubbard knew that the company was enjoying more than healthy profits even in the dull times of the mid-1880s. Given such prosperity, he asked, how could the company justify another hike of its rates? In a series of angry letters, Hubbard lectured William Forbes on Bell's responsibilities to the people. "The American Bell is not an ordinary manufacturing company, it is to a certain extent a quasi-public corporation," Hubbard wrote. "It cannot like an ordinary manufacturing company carry on its business simply with a view to the largest profit to its stockholders, but is bound to consider the rights of the public."[9] This was, of course, the critique Hubbard had leveled at Western Union for years. Now he assailed what had once been his own company with the same complaints and warned darkly of the day the American people might rise up against the outrages of monopoly.

Forbes and his colleagues scoffed at the notion that their customers' complaints amounted to any kind of popular uprising. "All this fuss is over a matter of perhaps ten dollars a year apiece to the very wealthiest and most extravagant class in the community," said Charles Fay. "Far from oppressing the people, as the newspapers say, [the telephone] does not reach the people at all."[10] Fay had a point. The telephone users who organized against American Bell in the 1880s were hardly the proletariat. Yet they echoed Gardiner Hubbard in calling for a "people's telephone" and wrapped their complaints about service and rates in the garb of democratic resistance to monopoly. In so doing, they employed a long American tradition of invoking "the people" to press for reform without evoking specific class interests.[11]

If there was less at stake in the struggles between Bell and its customers than a genuine revolution, there was nevertheless more at issue than Fay's ten dollars a year. Consider the Rochester telephone boycott. After Indiana's attempt to regulate telephone rates, the eighteen-month Rochester strike was perhaps the decade's longest and most bitter standoff over control of the new technology. Like several shorter boycotts elsewhere, the Rochester strike was not precipitated by an increase in the cost of telephone service, but by a change in the way subscribers were to be billed. In October 1886, the Bell Telephone Company of Buffalo announced its plan to move Rochester subscribers from the flat-rate billing structure championed by Gardiner Hubbard to the kind of measured service preferred by William Forbes and Theodore Vail. Under the old flat-rate system, telephone subscribers in Rochester paid sixty dollars a year for unlimited local service. Under the new system, subscribers would pay fifty dollars a year for their first five hundred calls and six cents per call thereafter.[12]

This seemingly modest change, Rochester's *Democrat and Chronicle* reported, "had the effect of a dynamite bomb on the city."[13] Three hundred Rochester businessmen—a quarter of the city's twelve hundred telephone subscribers—formed an organization to fight the move to measured service. Echoing the language of Gardiner Hubbard, they called themselves the People's Telephone Association. As in Muncie and the Midwest, agitation against the telephone monopoly combined public protest, private enterprise, city government, and local pride. A group of local businessmen quickly formed the Citizens Mutual Telephone Company of Rochester in hopes of constructing a competing telephone system. Rochester's city government got in on the action too, voting to revoke Bell's franchise and ordering it to remove its poles from city streets. Both of the city's newspapers supported the People's Telephone Association, one calling Bell "the most greedy business concern in the western hemisphere," and the other urging state legislation to "crush the monopoly."[14] At noon on 20 November 1886, the city's central switchboard fell silent as about a thousand Rochester subscribers voluntarily disconnected their telephones.

The author of the unpopular measured service plan was Edward Hall, general manager of the Buffalo Bell company. Hall was one of the first Bell managers to promote measured rates—indeed, Bell executives often called measured service "the Buffalo system." In the years ahead, he would become an important vice president at AT&T and a key ally of Theodore Vail. When protest erupted against measured rates in Rochester, Hall placidly informed the People's Telephone Association that they had misunderstood the benefits of his plan. Measured rates would improve the quality of telephone service by discouraging needless calls, he said, and would decrease the cost of service for all but the heaviest users. Privately, Hall told his superiors in Boston that Rochester subscribers were "simply being 'worked' by people who are interested in developing some opposition scheme." He predicted a quick end to the boycott as Rochester's businessmen came to see the wisdom and economy of buying telephone service by the call.[15]

Yet the boycott did not end quickly. And if the Rochester papers can be believed, support for the telephone strike remained nearly unanimous, both among the heavy telephone users who stood to lose money under Hall's plan as well as many users who did not. When Charles Fay gave his speech comparing unruly telephone customers to labor movement radicals, the Rochester telephone strike was in its eleventh month with no end in sight. Fay marveled at the obstinacy of the strikers in Rochester and elsewhere. Heavy telephone users, he said, had duped the rest of the city's subscribers into supporting the strike against their own self-interest.[16] If this was so, Rochester's heavy users had duped their fellow subscribers very well. The boycott would last a year and a half. In that time, Rochester's striking subscribers rejected all offers to lower prices while maintaining measured service. Their one non-negotiable condition for ending the boycott was the restoration of flat rates.

In the end, it was Hall's company that capitulated. The key factor resolving the standoff was the intersection of state and municipal politics with corporate strategy and consumer activism. In response to the Rochester boycott, and to rising complaints about telephone prices in New York City, the state legislature launched a formal investigation into the industry in April 1887. Fearing a rate law similar to the one that had just passed in Indiana, Theodore Vail ordered Hall to reach a settlement. Staring down rate regulation in Indianapolis was one thing; the Bell companies could not countenance such a law in New York City. In late 1887, Hall dropped his measured service plan and, in May 1888, instituted a new flat rate of $64 per year for business subscribers. Though the cost of telephone service had increased across the board, the flat-rate principle had been preserved. The People's Telephone Association declared this a great victory.[17]

Men like Hall and Fay shook their heads at the failure of subscribers to understand their own best interests. Flat rates worked to the economic benefit of heavy telephone users and the cost of everyone else. Why didn't the majority of telephone users embrace measured service? But Hall and Fay had misunderstood the nature of their opposition. Consumers do not always behave rationally in strict economic terms. The Rochester telephone strike and others like it were less about the price of telephone service than about control of the device. Arguments about flat rates and measured service were rooted in this issue. Given a choice, telephone users preferred flat rates for unlimited calling, even when this meant paying more than they would for service by the call. Telephone users wanted to make calls, including "needless" or "frivolous" ones, without cost or guilt. And even though they did not technically own the telephones in their offices and homes, they felt entitled to control of these devices. A poll conducted in Buffalo, where measured service was born, found only sixteen respondents in favor of that system, versus four hundred against. Bell's representatives disputed the objectivity of this poll, but in the years to come its findings were borne out again and again, as telephone consumers rejected measured service in almost every place it was introduced. Only in the largest urban markets would measured service gain wide acceptance before 1900, and this happened only after key innovations like coin-operated and outgoing-call-only telephones had been introduced.[18] "Every attempt to charge strictly by measure [has] been fought by political means," Charles Fay wrote in 1912—"a very pretty illustration," he thought, "of the public indifference to principle."[19]

The Bell companies fought similar clashes with merchants like druggists, grocers, and hotel proprietors, who often gave customers free use of the telephones in hotels and stores. Bell executives called nonsubscribers who borrowed telephones in this way "dead heads" or "pirates." Edward Hall claimed in 1886 that dead heading accounted for between 25 and 35 percent of all telephone traffic.[20] But when the Bell companies tried to extinguish such practices, their business customers fought back. In 1891, for example, three hundred Baltimore pharmacists signed a pledge to remove their telephones if the company instituted extra charges for the use of phones by nonsubscribers. Similar threats were made in New York, New Jersey, and Pennsylvania. In 1907, when the Cumberland Telephone and Telegraph Company tried to enforce its rules against letting nonsubscribers borrow the telephone, irate users in Nashville cut down their own lines.[21]

As Hall's ideas spread, the Bell operating companies became increasingly aggressive in fighting "the dead head evil."[22] In 1902, when grocers in Indianapolis voted to boycott the Central Union Telephone Company over the issue of nonsubscriber charges, the Bell affiliate threatened tit-for-tat retaliation by opening its own grocery stores in the city, where the telephone company proposed to sell meat and produce so cheaply as to bankrupt the grocers. Similar tactics had allegedly been used to answer a grocer's boycott in Omaha.[23] The outcome of Central Union's foray into grocery retail is not recorded, but that such tactics were entertained at all illustrates the company's combative attitude toward its own customers.

As in the fights over flat rates, for Bell's opponents these contests were less about money than about who controlled the telephones in their offices and stores. Bell managers sometimes allowed shopkeepers to charge a fee for telephone use and share that revenue with the telephone company. In Buffalo, Hall reported, some druggists and grocers earned fifty to a hundred dollars a year in this way. But other merchants rejected these offers, saying they would only make them "servants" of a "gigantic monopoly." Once again, Bell's customers and critics reached for the language of antimonopoly and the people's telephone when defending their right to unmetered use of the device. "Every manly druggist should throw out the pay station," said a circular printed in 1894 by Brooklyn pharmacist Thomas France. "Every citizen who is not willing to become a slave should teach this company that it is a servant of the people and not its master."[24]

Urban businessmen were a key constituency of users, perhaps the key constituency, in shaping telephony in the 1880s and 1890s. They used the telephone more than any other group, and they had political and economic clout that others did not have. Most crucially, they organized, in both private-commercial and public-political forms. Organized business users won some of their battles with the Bell companies and lost others. In the long run, many of these disputes led to city hall, where they would be settled through the use of municipal franchise agreements—or by bribes to city politicians. Bell managers called this extortion. But it was only through these untidy tactics that consumers could achieve any leverage over the telephone company while American Bell's patent monopoly remained.[25]

Patent Battles

"It is certain," said William Forbes in 1886, "that one decision by the United States Court invalidating our patent would be enough to flood the country with competing companies."[26] Between Forbes's truce with Western Union in 1879 and the expiration of Alexander Graham Bell's American telephone patents in 1894, Bell under the Bostonians theoretically enjoyed exclusive patent rights to the telephone in the United States.[27] But as the commercial value of the telephone became clear, imitations poured into the market and a parade of tinkerers and engineers came forth to challenge Alexander Graham Bell's priority as inventor of the telephone. "Every day brings forth someone who claims to antedate Bell in the domain of telephone invention," observed *Electrical World* in 1884. "If the telephone litigation is not settled before long, there will very soon be more 'great and only' telephone inventors in the country than there are Charlie Rosses."[28] American Bell had to fight constantly to defend its patent claims. Between 1879 and 1894, the company filed over six hundred suits for patent infringement against unauthorized manufacturers of telephone equipment, non-Bell operating companies, and even individual telephone subscribers. By 1886, Bell had spent over $1 million in legal fees defending its monopoly. Alexander Graham Bell, though no longer directly involved in the company or any kind of telephone research, spent years in court as the company's star witness.[29]

The economic and technological ferment of late nineteenth-century America produced many legal struggles over patents and invention. Epic battles of litigation were waged over the cash register, the sewing machine, driven wells, baking soda, and barbed wire. But the most notorious and expensive patent battle of the century was the fight for control of the telephone. Popular history casts these contests as quarrels between individual inventors. Yet the fights around the telephone patent were only superficially about who invented what. Patents are ultimately instruments of market power, and the struggle over Bell's patents in the 1880s and 1890s was a protracted contest between commercial and political interests in which both inventions and inventors were merely pieces on the legal chessboard.[30] At stake was control of the industry and the nation's communication infrastructure. Who actually deserved credit for inventing the telephone was almost beside the point.

Bound up in these legal battles were debates about federal, state, and municipal authority; monopoly and antimonopoly; and the legitimacy of the new nation-spanning corporations. Patent law was one area where federal authority trumped state and municipal power, and patents were an important foundation of national incorporation. Without a federal patent, there was really no reason the same company had to control the telephone in New York, Boston, San Francisco, and Muncie. Patents were also lightning rods for antimonopoly sentiment. Many Americans, including farmers in the South and West but also middling business interests everywhere, saw the U.S. Patent Office as a tool of big industry and greedy "patent sharks" and resented legal barriers that increased the prices of useful items like sewing machines or barbed wire. That resentment was only fed by a trend in the jurisprudence of the 1870s and 1880s toward more generous interpretation of patents and more stringent penalties for infringers. In 1854, the U.S. Supreme Court had taken a very narrow view of Samuel Morse's telegraph patent, opening the field to widespread imitation and innovation and offering an influential precedent against the broad interpretation of patent claims. But by the 1880s, federal judges were far friendlier to patent holders. While antimonopoly sentiment roiled at the state and local level, the patent system and the courts that enforced it became key defenders of national corporate power.[31]

Bell's first patent battle, against Western Union, has received the lion's share of historical attention. It pit the fledgling telephone company against the telegraph giant and led to the pivotal 1879 agreement between the two firms. Elisha Gray, the scientist who developed Western Union's telephone, had more evidence in his favor than any of Bell's later challengers. Gray had been working along the same lines as Alexander Graham Bell and even filed a caveat with the U.S. Patent Office on the very same day that Bell applied for his first patent.[32] There have always been questions about the competing claims filed by Bell and Gray on 14 February 1876—their timing, what they covered, and what each man knew of the other's work. In every generation since, investigators have rediscovered evidence suggesting that Bell, or perhaps Gardiner Hubbard, could have seen Gray's patent application and borrowed ideas from his work.[33] Certainly, the inventors knew of each other's efforts, and irregularities in the nineteenth-century patent office were hardly unknown. But Gray's chief backer, Western Union, agreed to forfeit his claims to the invention in exchange for 20 percent of Bell's earnings on the telephone for the duration of the patent—about $7 million over the next fifteen years. It was this agreement, not skullduggery in the patent office, that made Alexander Graham Bell the "great and only" inventor of the telephone. Indeed, the idea that the telephone network, in all its complexity, could be said to have had just one inventor is in many ways a fiction of the decade's legal decisions and a century of Bell public relations since.[34] "Strictly speaking, the telephone was not invented," declared one of Bell's opponents in later years. "Like Topsy, it simply grew."[35]

To nineteenth-century observers, the most dramatic challenge to Bell's patents did not come from the mighty Western Union but from a village mechanic in rural Pennsylvania. In the spring of 1880, an eccentric tinkerer named Daniel Drawbaugh came forward to declare that he had invented the telephone at least five years before Alexander Graham Bell. Drawbaugh was an inveterate self-promoter, styling himself "one of the greatest inventive geniuses of this age."[36] His workshop at Eberly's Mills, Pennsylvania, was crowded with odd inventions and contraptions, including an improved flush toilet and a faucet for dispensing molasses. Drawbaugh produced an "electrical talking machine"—a crude but working telephone—which he said he had constructed in or around 1871. In 1880, Drawbaugh made contact with Washington patent attorney Lysander Hill and, through him, a group of investors in New York, Washington, and Cincinnati eager to enter the telephone field. Drawbaugh filed for a patent on his talking machine in July 1880, and his backers incorporated themselves as—naturally—the People's Telephone Company.[37]

In October 1880, American Bell sued Drawbaugh and the People's Telephone Company for patent infringement. Bell's lawyers expected a quick victory. "We consider them to be absolutely without chance of success," Chauncey Smith and James Storrow advised William Forbes. "It is absurd to suppose that practical telephones existed . . . for ten years before anybody published the fact."[38] But the People's Telephone Company would not go away. They dragged out the evidence-gathering phase of the trial for over three years and produced nearly two hundred witnesses to testify that they had seen Drawbaugh's telephone and heard people speak through it in the early 1870s. By 1884, the case had generated over eight thousand pages of testimony and cost American Bell more than $500,000.[39]

To the Bostonians, Drawbaugh's challenge had no legal or technical merit—certainly less than that of Elisha Gray. Forbes called the case "pure blackmail."[40] Drawbaugh had no written evidence of his work, nor could he remember exactly when or how he had come up with his invention. When asked why he did not patent or publicize his invention in the early 1870s, Drawbaugh said that poverty had prevented him from doing so—a claim Bell's lawyers rapidly dismantled. Many of his witnesses changed their stories under cross-examination; only forty-nine were prepared to swear that they had actually heard Drawbaugh's telephone speak before 1876. Yet the Drawbaugh case lasted longer, cost more money, and received more publicity than any other of Bell's six hundred patent suits. By the time it reached the U.S. Supreme Court in 1887, the press was calling it the most important patent case in American history.[41]

What the People's Telephone Company had going for it was not technological merit but political and cultural appeal, built on both the unpopularity of the Bell monopoly and Daniel Drawbaugh's peculiar charms. Drawbaugh was a colorful character with bristly whiskers and a backcountry drawl. In court against American Bell's Yankee lawyers, he seemed to epitomize the common man set upon by Eastern monopoly. Reporters contrasted his rustic manner of speaking with the perfect diction of elocutionist Alexander Graham Bell. They eagerly described Drawbaugh's homely contraptions of tin cans and teacups, and their ridicule by Bell's platoon of electricians and engineers. Even the name of the case—*American Bell v. People's Telephone*—plucked populist sympathies. The Drawbaugh suit seemed to pit monopoly against the people, the city against the heartland, wealth and power against honest toil.[42]

Of course, a penniless mechanic could hardly have afforded years of litigation against a multimillion-dollar corporation. But Drawbaugh's backers had deep pockets, and shares in the People's Telephone Company sold briskly. According to the *New York Times*, its investors soon included "Governors of States, members of Congress, and millionaires."[43] These investors hoped to invade the telephone business in competition with American Bell. They secured Drawbaugh the services of several celebrated attorneys, and it was their efforts and money that kept the case alive. Yet somehow Drawbaugh's backers managed to maintain a low profile. Perhaps, as Bell's aggrieved defenders charged, the People's Telephone Company had some special influence with the press.[44] Or perhaps the common man versus monopoly angle was simply too appealing for reporters to undermine. The language of populism had immense resonance and elasticity in 1880s America.

It may have even served the Bell interests to let Drawbaugh's lawyers play the populist card. American Bell's owners understood the political overtones of the case and worried they would find their way into the courtroom. Forbes warned his lawyers of this, writing to James Storrow in 1884: "Our most serious danger is in the possibility that the Judge may look upon us, as so many do, as a monopoly really hostile to the true interests of the public . . . If he has any taint of grangerism or any political bee in his bonnet he might lean towards taking a broad easy view of the Drawbaugh claims."[45] By "grangerism," Forbes referred to the Order of the Patrons of Husbandry, better known as the Grange, a movement of farmers in the West and Middle West who organized agrarian cooperatives and fought for regulation of monopolistic railroads and grain elevators in the 1870s. Here Forbes indulged in some stereotyping. The Drawbaugh case would indeed turn, at least in part, on the virtues and failings of the Bell monopoly. But it was not only, or even primarily, agrarian radicals who resented Bell policies and rates. "In no part of its history does the Bell Telephone Company appear as a corporation showing the least regard for the people," charged the *New York Times* in 1886. "From the beginning it has plundered the people," by means of "a fraudulent patent . . . stock watering, collusive suits at law, secret alliances with other similar corporations, unjust discrimination, and extortionate rates."[46] The many challengers to Bell's patents pressed the courts to consider not only priority of invention, but also the social and commercial costs of the telephone monopoly. The telephone was "interwoven into the commerce of the country," argued lawyers for the Cushman Telephone Company in a related patent suit, "and it is not for the owner of the patent to say that he can give it or not to the public at his own price, and upon his own terms." Bell's lawyers dismissed this line of argument as a "Kansas populist notion."[47] Kansas populists were not the only Americans unhappy with the Bell monopoly. Yet American Bell saw and framed the issue as one of hot-headed midwestern yokels versus sober East Coast investors.

American Bell had its defenders, but many observers—East Coast businessmen and Kansas farmers alike—hoped that Drawbaugh might win his case and the Bell monopoly be overthrown. When a U.S. circuit court upheld Bell's injunction against the People's Telephone Company in 1885, *Scientific American* lamented the decision. Competition, the magazine argued, was the only way to challenge Bell's "exorbitant" rates.[48] As the Supreme Court deliberated on the Drawbaugh case in 1887, the *New York Times* declared, "if the Bell patent should be annulled, the telephone might soon approach perfection."[49]

In March 1888, the Supreme Court rejected Drawbaugh's final appeal by a narrow vote of four to three.[50] In the wake of this decision, dozens of other patent challenges collapsed. The company's legal monopoly would remain secure until the natural expiration of Alexander Graham Bell's patents in 1893 and 1894. But Bell's legal victory was no political triumph. The public had been treated to an eight-year performance of American Bell versus the people. While the patents had survived, the company's legitimacy was seriously damaged. Whatever conclusions one drew about the paternity of the telephone—and the court's split decision hardly eradicated all doubt in this regard—the trial cast a harsh light on American Bell's monopoly and suggested the breadth of the constituency eager for its demise.

Bell's other patent cases in the 1880s and early 1890s ran along similar lines. The challengers that earned the most publicity always seemed to have some sentimental regional or cultural appeal. Sylvanus Cushman was another country rustic, a lightning-rod salesman from Racine, Wisconsin, who claimed to have invented a telephone in 1851, after hearing the croaking of bullfrogs somehow transmitted on a telegraph wire.[51] Antonio Meucci was an Italian-born machinist in Staten Island who blamed his failure to patent the telephone on an inability to speak English and the prejudices of American investors.[52] The Pan-Electric Telephone Company of Memphis offered barely any pretense of an invention predating Bell's, but it parlayed southern sentiment and a few well-placed allies—including Grover Cleveland's attorney general, Augustus Garland—into another serious challenge to American Bell.[53] In each case, Bell's patents were upheld, but the company was cast as the villain in another drama of plutocrats versus the people: city slickers against country folk, bluebloods against immigrants, or Yankee carpetbaggers against the brave defenders of the South.

The last crucial case of the patent monopoly years concerned a microphone for telephone transmitters developed by the inventor Emile Berliner. In 1891, as the expiration of Alexander Graham Bell's original patents neared, the U.S. Patent Office issued a new patent to American Bell on Berliner's microphone. Berliner had actually applied for this grant back in 1877, but his application sat in the patent office, pending, for fourteen years. The Bell company hired Berliner and bought his rights to the device in 1878. The natural lifespan of a U.S. patent was, at this time, seventeen years from date of issue. Thanks to the patent office's protracted delay, American Bell saw a way to prolong its legal monopoly until 1908 at least.[54]

The tardy arrival of the Berliner patent provoked an outcry from Bell's foes and ultimately a federal lawsuit against the company. Government action was instigated by an electrical engineer named Milo Gifford Kellogg. Kellogg had been superintendent of Chicago's Western Electric Manufacturing Company in the late 1870s. In 1882, American Bell acquired a controlling interest in Western Electric and turned it into the manufacturing arm of the Bell companies. Kellogg stayed on at Western Electric for a few more years, but his relationship with American Bell became unfriendly. He allied with, and invested personally in, several of the Bell operating companies and fought Boston's centralization of financial and operational control. In 1887, Kellogg brought suit against American Bell on behalf of minority shareholders in the Great Southern Telephone and Telegraph Company, charging the Bostonians with bleeding their subsidiary through high royalties and policies designed to serve only the parent company's interests. He threatened similar action on behalf of the Central Union Telephone Company, where he held a seat on the board of directors, but ultimately resigned that position and disposed of his shares.[55]

In March 1892, President Benjamin Harrison appointed an Indiana lawyer named Charles Henry Aldrich to be the U.S. solicitor general. Aldrich had been Milo Kellogg's lawyer during the Great Southern case. As the clock ran down on the old Bell patents, Kellogg persuaded Aldrich to launch an investigation into the legality of the Berliner grant. Kellogg claimed he was acting on behalf of the Bell operating companies, seeking to free them from the usurious rentals charged by American Bell. But Kellogg was also eager to reenter the telephone manufacturing business for himself. A prolific inventor, he held more than one hundred pending patents on telephone equipment and improvements. The Berliner patent, if unchallenged, could have locked him out of the industry for another seventeen years.[56]

In December 1894, the Circuit Court of Massachusetts voided the Berliner patent. No evidence of fraud or collusion was found to explain the fourteen-year delay; the patent office may simply have been waiting for the Drawbaugh case and other claims to be resolved. Nevertheless, the Massachusetts court endorsed the "Kansas populist notion" that the political implications of the case demanded special scrutiny and held American Bell to have "intentionally acquiesced" in the long delay in order to prolong its monopoly.[57] The Supreme Court would overturn this ruling in 1897, restoring the Berliner patent but seriously limiting its scope. Countersuits and appeals would continue for years, but by the time of the decision, Forbes's prophecy had come true. Hundreds of new telephone companies entered the field between 1894 and 1897. (Many of them would buy their equipment from the newly established Kellogg Switchboard and Supply Company.) The independent telephone movement had begun.[58]

Milo Kellogg is not well remembered today, but he succeeded where Drawbaugh, Cushman, and Meucci had failed. We often gloss the legal history of the telephone by saying that American Bell's monopoly ended when Alexander Graham Bell's original patents expired. The implication is that Bell's monopoly died a natural death–yet another claim of naturalness for a process that was always contested and contingent. This robs the independents of credit for their first great victory: breaking American Bell's patent monopoly and opening the door to competition.

The patent fights of the 1880s and early 1890s encouraged Americans to see the telephone as an innovation stolen from its rightful owners. They tied their legal fights with Bell to a kind of referendum on the legitimacy of the patent system, corporate monopoly, and the emerging economic order of the day. These battles fuelled the legend of a people's telephone, cheap and accessible, stolen by a fraudulent monopoly from the honest folk to whom it once belonged. This language was not the creation of hot-headed agrarian radicals. It was the language of Gardiner Hubbard and Milo Kellogg, of well-to-do telephone subscribers in Rochester, New York, and of the well-connected backers of Drawbaugh's People's Telephone Company. The challengers to Bell's patents combined a professed crusade for economic justice with a transparent desire for profit, as many of their successors would do. All this laid the foundation for a more successful and influential revolt against American Bell along populist and commercial lines.

Independent Telephony

"The Bell people worked from the top down and the Independents from the bottom up," declared Harry MacMeal in 1934. "The Bell group organized the larger centers of population first and expanded from them. The Independents began amidst the farms and in the villages."[59] MacMeal had been the editor of the trade journal *Telephony* and an important promoter of the independent movement in its heyday. There was truth to his characterization, but it would be more accurate to say that the independent telephone movement started in the middle, targeting middle-class customers in the medium-sized towns and cities of the Middle West. MacMeal and other partisans celebrated the rural telephone cooperatives that appeared by the thousands in the years right before and after 1900, but the very first wave of independent telephone systems was more urban and commercial. When the Berliner patent was voided at the end of 1894, independent telephone systems were already being constructed in over one hundred American cities: in San Antonio and Austin, Texas; in Salem and Portland, Oregon; in Raleigh, North Carolina, and Richmond, Virginia. The most vigorous activity was in the Midwest, where political opposition to Bell had been strongest. Within a year, independent systems were operating in Detroit, St. Louis, Cleveland, Indianapolis, and dozens of smaller cities and towns.[60]

The independent telephone movement did not appear out of nowhere. The makeup and geography of the first wave of independent telephony make it clear that the movement grew quite directly out of the political and legal battles of the patent monopoly years. The entrepreneurs who established independent exchanges in the 1890s were often former Bell customers unhappy with its policies and rates. Disgruntled Bell subscribers were ubiquitous in the origin stories of independent firms. These men were also the brothers, cousins, neighbors, and backers of those mayors and city councilors who had clashed with Bell in the 1880s over poles and wires. And the manufacturers who built the telephones and switchboards for the new independent systems were, like Milo Kellogg, veterans of the prior decade's patent fights.

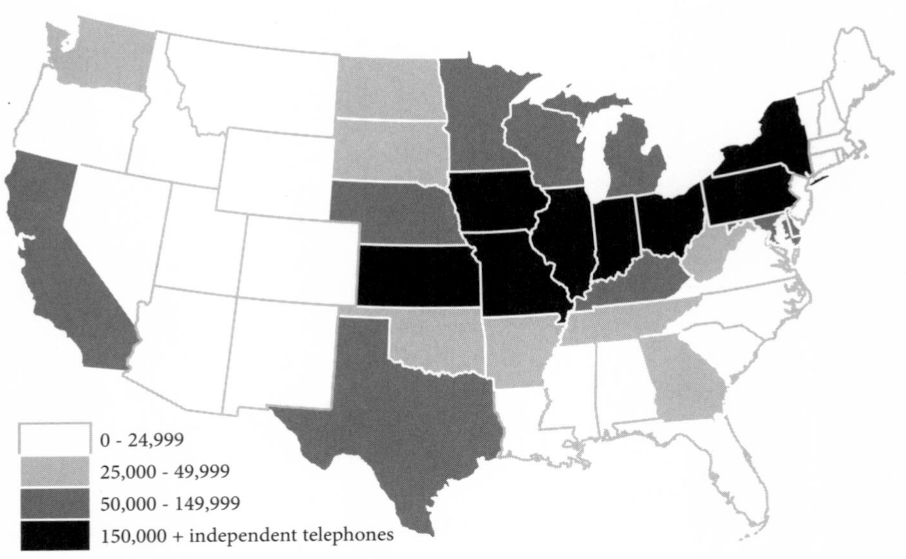

Figure 5. Independent Telephones by State, 1907

Still, the speed of the independents' rise was remarkable. Over one thousand new telephone companies were formed in the United States between 1894 and 1898, and more than two thousand more were operating by 1902. Close on the heels of these commercial independents came the great wave of farmers' mutuals or cooperatives, tiny telephone systems organized not for profit but to supply service in rural areas that Bell and the more urban independents did not serve. The U.S. Census counted 994 of these little systems in 1902—admitting that this was an underestimate—and over seventeen thousand independent telephone cooperatives in 1907. In 1912, the Census Bureau counted commercial and cooperative independents together, reporting over thirty-two thousand active telephone companies outside of Bell's control.[61]

The independents' most dramatic success came in midwestern states like Indiana, Iowa, Michigan, and Wisconsin. This was, as we have seen, where municipal governments had been most active and aggressive in regulating the telephone before 1894, and local government remained a key player in the independent movement and its rise. Competition did not flourish, by contrast, in the urban centers of the Northeast. Bell coverage

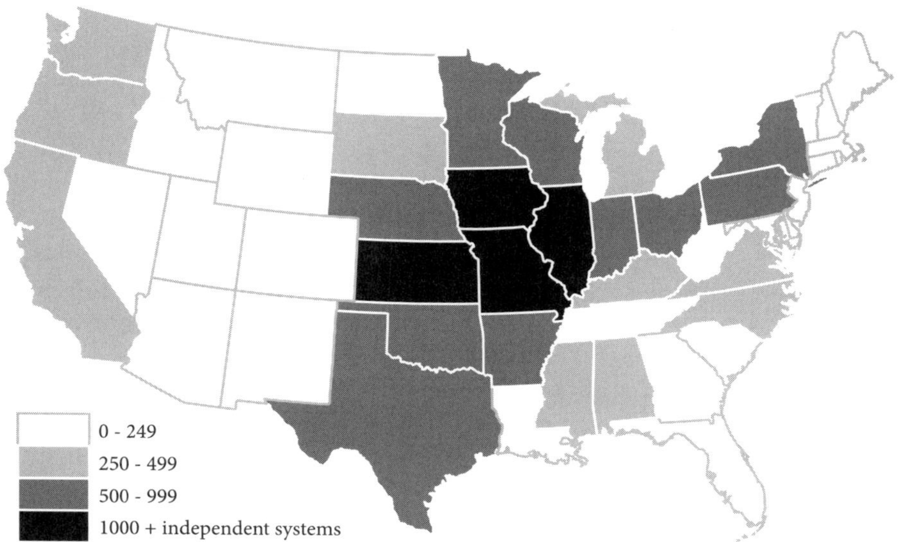

Figure 6. Independent Telephone Systems by State, 1907
The independent movement was most successful in midwestern states like Indiana, Illinois, Iowa, Ohio, and Missouri, the same places where municipal governments had actively and aggressively regulated the telephone during Bell's monopoly years. In 1907, there were more than three thousand independent telephone systems in the state of Iowa alone, each one connecting an average of forty-four telephones. Iowa also had one of the highest numbers of telephones per capita—151 phones per thousand people, more than twice the national average.

of that territory was greater to begin with, and animosity to the Bell companies was weaker there. But again, it was state and municipal politics that defined the geography of independent failure and success. In several northeastern cities, the Bell operating companies secured exclusive franchises akin to those that thwarted competition in Canada. In 1899, Bell's Southern New England Telephone Company secured a remarkable law making it illegal to organize a new telephone company in Connecticut without acquiring a special charter from the state legislature, convincing the state superior court that competition was required by public necessity, and then having 50 percent of the company's capital stock paid for in cash.[62] These sorts of legal hoops made competition in New England and the Northeast all but impossible. In 1907, 98 percent of the telephones in southern New England still belonged to the Bell affiliate there, as did 83 percent of the telephones in New Jersey and 74 percent of the phones in New York.[63]

The independent movement was as much an assault against American Bell's way of thinking as against its market share. In their trade journals, advertisements, convention speeches, pamphlets, broadsides, and even poetry and song, the independents attacked Bell and promoted their own vision of the telephone in a bombastic style. Independent propagandists spoke of "revolution," of "liberating" America from the "tyranny" of the Bell monopoly; they called Bell a "monster" and an "octopus."[64] "It would hardly be possible to find in history . . . any sovereign who governed with a more absolute disregard for all principles and practices of constitutional liberty and business sense, than . . . the Bell octopus," proclaimed Illinois independent E. J. Mock. "No tyranny is so galling," agreed an independent organizer from Iowa. Opposition to Bell, he declared, was "the bounden duty of all who believe in the right, revere justice, and love their fellow men."[65] Independent propagandists angrily attacked the alleged naturalness of Bell's monopoly. "The Bell has tried for years to cram down the misnomer that the telephone business is a natural monopoly. It is a natural fake!" shouted an editorial in the independent journal *Sound Waves*. Bell's monopoly was not natural, they insisted, but profoundly illegitimate, foisted on the people against their will. "The great argument urged by the Bell people is that telephony is a monopoly from the nature of things," said independent A. F. Wilson. "Consider, however, not what is the nature of the telephone, but what is the nature of a monopoly. Can the leopard change his spots, or the Ethiopian his color? Can joint stock monopoly . . . ever yield one single concession except under force?" The independents maintained that in telephony, competition, not monopoly, was the natural and desirable order of things.[66]

Bell's rivals presented themselves, above all, as servants and defenders of the people. In keeping with populist rhetorical tradition, the exact identity of "the people" was never clearly defined, but the independents let there be no doubt about their loyalty to that noble if imprecise abstraction. One cannot count the number of independent systems that named themselves the People's Telephone Company, or some variation on that theme. Citizens and Home Telephone Company were also popular favorites. Indiana independent Charles Norton said that the mission of America's independent companies was "to do the will and bidding of the people," and that the "fundamental principle" for which they fought was "the right of the people to own and operate their own telephone system." His fellow Hoosier A. C. Lindemuth described the independent fight with Bell as a "revolutionary struggle . . . for the recovery of the rights of the people." Paul Latzke cast the battle with Bell as "the War for American Industrial Independence"—a reenactment of the American Revolution in which Boston was not a cradle of liberty but the throne of the tyrant. Iowa's William Crownover called the independent movement "telephony of the people, by the people, for the people." This language was ubiquitous among Bell's enemies, from the patrons of the smallest rural cooperatives to the owners of the largest commercial enterprises. In the diverse ranks of the independent telephone movement, one constant was the language of the people's telephone.[67]

Given the geography and timing of the independent telephone movement, it is tempting to look for direct connections between the people's telephone and the People's Party. There were clear affinities between the independents and the Populists of the 1890s. Both movements attracted a mix of farmers and businessmen, fighting to protect their livelihood as small producers in a changing industrial economy. Successive generations of American historians have depicted the Populists as varyingly utopian and pragmatic, progressive and nostalgic, democratic and intolerant. But the best work on the People's Party recognizes it as part of a larger response to the late nineteenth-century incorporation of America. The Populists were businessmen, yes, but also advocates of an alternative capitalist order, one more open to cooperative and state-based enterprise and more committed to economic opportunity for all classes and sections. Populist orators thundered about the crimes of eastern capital and the plight of beleaguered farmers. They fought, they said, for the farm against the city, for the people against the plutocrats, for the South and West against the Northeast. The People's Party hoped to check the rise of private monopolies and end their concentration of wealth and power. This was the very language the independent telephone movement would employ.[68]

Yet this language was hardly original to the People's Party. When the independents described the telephone as an instrument of democracy, they allied with a long American tradition that sees communication and broad access to information as a basic democratic good. Since the printers and pamphleteers of the Revolution, if not before, Americans have been inclined to see communication and the free transit of ideas as a crucial foundation of liberty and the republic. A related tradition has championed personal ownership of technology in general as a defense against tyranny, as in the constitutional right to bear arms. Belief in the emancipatory potential of technology is an enduring and perhaps particularly American trait.[69]

The Populists' hostility to monopoly was also widely shared. Their rhetoric of the people and the plutocrats had deep historical roots and could be heard in districts where the People's Party would never win a seat. As we have seen, opposition to the Bell monopoly could be found in many corners of the country. It was Gardiner Hubbard of Cambridge, Massachusetts—not exactly a Boston Brahmin, but no Kansas sodbuster either—who first articulated the idea of a telephone for the people, and of telephony as a weapon against corporate monopoly.[70] The language and symbols of populism were broadly accessible and inclusive. Upper-class reformers, urban businessmen, labor activists, and agrarian radicals could all reach for the people's telephone when attacking or critiquing American Bell.

That said, the idea of a people's telephone had more success in some venues than others. This was true of populism in general. For all its sound and fury, the People's Party of the 1890s won elections only in states like Kansas and Nebraska, where the Democratic Party was weak and Populism seemed the only alternative to probusiness Republican rule. In states like Indiana and Iowa, where there was lively competition between Democrats and Republicans, one or both of the older parties (usually the Democrats) generally managed to co-opt Populist issues and political support.[71] The exact geography may have differed—Indiana and Iowa, where the People's Party was stymied, were hotbeds of independent telephony—but the independents' fortunes were similarly driven by the contours of state and municipal politics. The language of the people's telephone could be heard from many quarters, but independent competition only flourished where regulators and policy makers were inclined and empowered to enable it.

The success or failure of independent competition in one place or another would shape ideas about the telephone and about business and politics more broadly. In communities and regions where competition did arise, the arguments of the independents seemed to be confirmed and reinforced. In communities and regions where it did not, the same arguments stumbled. Claims about the naturalness or inevitability of monopoly that seemed quite reasonable in Central Canada or New England came to sound rather dubious in the American Midwest. In this way, the uneven fortunes of the independent telephone movement not only shaped local thinking about the telephone but also ultimately affected debates about competition and monopoly, communication, business, and scale. Populist appeals took hold where the political environment rewarded them and dissipated where the political environment did not. Political economy shaped not only business strategy but also political culture and ideas.

The Competitive Era

American Bell's stock prices tumbled in the immediate wake of the decision voiding Berliner's patent. "There is a widely extended impression that we are on the eve of an era of active production of cheap telephones and of a healthy competition," reported *Western Electrician*. Yet at Bell headquarters in Boston, there were few outward signs of alarm. American Bell's president in 1894 was the aloof John Hudson. His dedication to the conservative strategies of the 1880s—high prices, slow expansion, a focus on urban markets and wealthy business clients—remained complete. American Bell under Hudson took no drastic action on the eve of competition. It made no reduction in the royalties charged to its operating companies, authorized no major expansion of its networks, and anticipated no particular change to the market for the telephone. The Bostonians seemed determined to rely on what had worked in the past: protecting their monopoly through patent infringement suits.[72]

Bell's regional operating companies could not afford such nonchalance. It was they, not the parent company in Boston, who would suffer the brunt of independent competition. The midwestern affiliates were the first and hardest hit. Independent rivals undercut their prices, while American Bell's royalties remained nonnegotiable. "This competition has been largely inspired by promoters, and is based on entirely wrong estimates of the cost of doing the telephone business; but while it lasts, it is, from its ignorance, the more severe," lamented the president of the Central Union Telephone Company in 1896.[73] Casper Yost, manager of the Bell-affiliated Iowa Telephone Company, begged American Bell for capital to improve and expand his network. "What the Iowa Company must have is money, and plenty of it, and at once," Yost told his superiors in Boston. "If your company does not solve the problem, the Iowa Company will go into the hands of a receiver."[74]

Under the pressure of independent competition, Bell's regional executives would abandon many assumptions and strategies of the monopoly years. The decade or so between the arrival of the independents and Theodore Vail's return to AT&T would not be the American telephone industry's most profitable era, but it was one of its most creative and dynamic. Innovation sprang not from the conservative redoubt of American Bell but from the operating companies on the front lines of the struggle, Bell and independent alike.

One of the first old assumptions to be challenged involved the pricing of telephone service and the size of the market for telephone service. In the first years of the competitive era, American Bell held fast to its old idea of a limited market for the telephone. Well into the twentieth century, some Bell executives declared it impossible to bring telephones to everyone and predicted ruin for companies that tried to do so.[75] The independents, by contrast, declared the telephone "a necessity to all." They broke into the market charging considerably less for telephone service than Bell had done to date. In many cities, independent prices were only half or three-quarters of Bell prices. Rural cooperatives asked even less of their subscriber-patrons; after an initial outlay to install the telephone and string the wires, many offered rudimentary but profitable service for as little as five or ten dollars per year. The telephone "has ceased to be a luxury," declared independent partisans. They spoke grandly of bringing a telephone to every farm and household in the country.[76]

In communities with direct competition, the Bell operating companies had little choice but to lower their rates. Even in cities where there was no independent franchise, Bell operators felt pressure to contain their prices lest municipal government authorize a new competitor to enter the field. Lower prices and aggressive marketing revealed, or created, the larger market for telephone service that Gardiner Hubbard had always said would be there. In 1893, the last full year of American Bell's patent monopoly, there were 266,000 telephones in the United States—roughly one for every 250 people. By the turn of the century, there were over one million telephones in the country. By 1907, there would be more than six million—one telephone for every fourteen Americans—and more than half of those six million telephones belonged to Bell's independent rivals.

"It is clearly demonstrated that the masses, in one form or another, will have telephone service," declared Cumberland Telephone's James Caldwell in 1903. Caldwell did not embrace the populist rhetoric of the independents, but his policies turned in their direction, making Cumberland the most progressive Bell affiliate in the South. "I had no maudlin sentiments about a public benefit or philanthropy," Caldwell later wrote, "but I knew that to make money . . . we would have to . . . make [the telephone] a great bargain, at prices that would attract the masses." Companies like Cumberland and Iowa Telephone played catch up in rural areas, building lines into the countryside and courting tiny farmers' networks for connections just as the independents had done. "A short time ago, [the Bell companies] would not look at a farmer, they would not even give him a hearing," jeered Iowa independent William Crownover in 1907. Now, Crownover said, they were "breaking their necks" to get the farmer's business.[77]

While the independents led Bell in bringing telephones to small towns and rural areas, Bell's urban operating companies took the lead in popularizing telephone use in the city. By the turn of the century, a second generation of Bell managers had replaced the more conservative executives of the patent monopoly years. Bell's new big city managers—men like John Sabin in San Francisco, Angus Hibbard in Chicago, and Union Bethell in New York—were innovative and aggressive in meeting or preempting independent competition by bringing telephone service to a mass urban market.[78]

The career of John Sabin illustrates both the innovations made by Bell's urban operating companies in this period and the resistance to such innovation by some at American Bell. Sabin replaced George Ladd as president of the Pacific Telephone and Telegraph Company, also known as Pacific Bell, in 1889. Ladd, originally at Western Union, had always followed the Bostonian strategy of high prices and conservative growth. While protected by Bell's patents, Sabin showed little inclination to change course. When patent protection ended, however, Sabin launched an energetic effort to improve service, lower rates, and popularize the telephone.[79]

Pacific Bell under Sabin invested heavily in new switchboards and systems, including centralized common batteries, to handle more traffic, improve call quality, and reduce the time needed to make connections. Above all, Sabin worked to lower the cost of telephone service and reach a new mass market for urban telephony. In 1895, Pacific Bell started crisscrossing San Francisco with inexpensive party lines that could be shared by as many as ten subscribers at a time. It introduced very cheap "kitchen phones" that could place calls only to one or two other numbers. Sabin created a new Canvassing Department that went door to door in many middle- and working-class neighborhoods that the old Pacific Bell had disdained, signing up thousands of first-time telephone subscribers. In many of these homes, especially in working-class boardinghouses and apartments, the company installed a new kind of coin-operated telephone that became known as the "nickel-in-the-slot." Nickel-in-the-slots were like pay telephones but placed in private or semiprivate residences. Each call cost five cents; those who installed the telephones paid no monthly telephone bill but were obliged to make at least one call per day. In this way, Sabin and like-minded colleagues in Chicago and New York began to bring affordable telephone service, on the pay-as-you-go principle, to the urban masses.[80]

One of Pacific Bell's tactics was less innovative, but also effective in warding off competition. It was revealed in 1907, two years after Sabin's death, that for almost a decade, his company had been paying monthly bribes to San Francisco's mayor, its board of supervisors, and notorious city boss Abe Ruef, in order to keep an independent franchise out of the city. At least nine independent companies attempted to secure telephone franchises in San Francisco between 1893 and 1912, but only two such charters were ever awarded. The first, granted in 1893, came with many regulatory strings attached, and its recipient never successfully began operation. Real competition came to San Francisco only after the earthquake of 1906, when the city granted a franchise to the Home Telephone Company of San Francisco—Home Telephone's A. K. Detweiler having more than matched Pacific Bell's under-the-table contributions to Ruef's "emergency relief" fund. But John Sabin's energetic response to the threat of competition had already transformed telephony in the city. When the Berliner patent was voided in 1894, Pacific Bell connected only forty-five hundred telephones in San Francisco. By 1906, it connected more than fifty thousand.[81]

The Bell affiliates that did not innovate suffered. In Indiana and Illinois, Central Union clung stubbornly to its old policies and predicted ruin for its independent competitors. "Telephone competition is not being developed for the purpose of serving the public," Central Union president W. A. Jackson insisted, but "to blackmail our institution into a purchase or consolidation." Reluctantly admitting that his industry was "in a transition state," Jackson thanked shareholders for their patience in waiving dividends and weakly assured them that "their sacrifices in this respect" were "but temporary." But they were not temporary. Squeezed between the independents and the parent company's rents, Central Union bled money and customers for years, operating at a loss from 1895 until the company's demise in 1913.[82]

A rising star in the Bell companies, John Sabin came from San Francisco to Chicago in 1901 to take charge of both the struggling Central Union and the more profitable Chicago Telephone. Chicago Telephone's Angus Hibbard had already been working to popularize the telephone along similar lines as Sabin: investing heavily in improved switchboard and trunking technology, offering flexible pay-as-you-go plans, and doing whatever it took to stay friendly with city officials. Together, the two were extraordinarily successful in Chicago, breaking the bottleneck of big-city telephony's reverse economy of scale and bringing telephone service to tens of thousands of new customers. Chicago Telephone's growth was even more impressive than what Sabin had accomplished in San Francisco. At the end of patent protection in 1894, the company operated about 1,100 telephones; when Angus Hibbard retired in 1911, it had over 250,000.[83]

Sabin and Hibbard succeeded in keeping serious competition out of the one city the midwestern independents sought above all others. Yet outside Chicago, Sabin had little success in stemming the independent tide. In cities and towns with more serious independent opposition—in Central Union's territory this included Indianapolis, Fort Wayne, Toledo, Columbus, Peoria, Muncie, and dozens more—the nickel-in-the-slot did not catch on. Smaller-city customers were not interested in coin-operated service as long as the independents offered unlimited calling for affordable monthly rates. Sabin's innovations also met some hostility from his own parent company. Bell's chief engineer John Joseph Carty opposed both the nickel-in-the-slot and the ten-party line as a departure from Bell's traditional quality standards, as did Theodore Vail upon his return to AT&T. Sabin's other plan to save Central Union involved taking over "short haul" and "medium haul" traffic, transferring control of all long-distance calls that travelled less than two hundred miles from AT&T to Central Union. But AT&T rejected this proposal. Such a move would have been staunchly opposed by men like Vail or Edward Hall, who were committed to centralizing the entire long-distance industry under one company's control. In the end, it is hard to say whether Sabin's rise was thwarted more by the midwestern independents or by resistance from his superiors in Boston and New York. Either way, he resigned in frustration and returned to California after only two years in the Midwest.[84]

At Chicago Telephone, Angus Hibbard continued the work that he and Sabin had begun. But Sabin's replacement at Central Union promised a return to "conservative management" and closer cooperation with the parent company. A focus on business subscribers was reasserted and the ten-party lines were removed. After four more years of such management, independent telephones in Central Union's territory outnumbered Bell telephones by nearly three to one. In 1907, independents in Indiana and Ohio roundly rejected Central Union's pleas for a truce. When AT&T finally moved to absorb and dismantle its bankrupt affiliate in 1913, Central Union's minority shareholders successfully sued AT&T for mismanaging the firm.[85]

Even the owners of American Bell were eventually pushed away from the conservative strategies and ideas of the patent monopoly years. They were also pushed away from Boston, a move that proved more than symbolic in ending the dominance of the Bostonians. Once again, regional regulatory environments played a key role in shaping both policies and ideas. By the end of the 1890s, American Bell reached the limit of its capitalization under its Massachusetts state charter. Massachusetts law also prevented American Bell from owning more than a 30 percent share of certain subsidiaries, which blocked the company's desire to tighten its control of the regional operating companies. The Bostonians looked around for greener pastures and found them in the corporate-friendly laws of New York State. On the next-to-last day of the nineteenth century, American Bell transferred all of its assets to the New York–based American Telephone and Telegraph Company. The onetime subsidiary thus became the new parent company of the Bell organization, and the system's corporate headquarters moved from Boston to New York.[86]

John Hudson died in 1900 and was replaced as president of the new AT&T by Frederick P. Fish. Of all the Bell organization's leaders, Fish was perhaps the most impressed by the achievements of the independent movement. Like many of his regional managers, Fish had been convinced by the coming of competition and the explosive growth of independent telephony that his predecessors' vision had been too narrow. "It is certain," Fish wrote in 1906, "that the business will develop . . . to an extent much greater than even the most enthusiastic telephone man ventured to expect a few years ago." Fish broke with the old Boston policy of ceding marginal areas to the competition and carefully choosing markets in which to compete. He pressed instead for construction of telephone lines on virtually every front.[87]

The total size of the Bell networks more than tripled under Fish's tenure, from about eight hundred thousand telephones in 1901 to over three million in 1907. But in order to expand at this rate, Fish had to abandon another pillar of the Bostonians' policies—their cautious fiscal management. AT&T under Fish spent hundreds of millions of dollars on construction, taking on heavy debt through aggressive bonds. In 1901, the company had modest debts of about $15 million. By 1906, AT&T's debts totaled $128 million.[88]

Such hunger for capital left the Bostonians vulnerable. In February 1906, a group of New York bankers including the financier John Pierpont Morgan made a bid to take over the entire Bell enterprise, organizing a syndicate to purchase $100 million in AT&T bonds. After several months of boardroom intrigue, the Bostonians' hold over AT&T and its subsidiaries collapsed. In April 1907, the New York investors pushed the last of the Bostonians off AT&T's board of directors and forced their man Frederick Fish to resign. In Fish's place, the New Yorkers installed none other than Theodore Vail.[89]

Watching the defeat of the men who had owned Bell since the 1880s, the independents prematurely declared their own victory. "We have won in this fight," said Indiana's Charles Norton. The battle between competition and monopoly, many independents crowed, was over. The "old water-soaked octopus" had been "beat[en] to a pulp."[90] The independents did not know that 1907 would be their movement's zenith, at least in terms of market share. With Vail's strategic vision, the deep pockets of the New York syndicate, and a board of directors no longer beholden to the failed strategies of the past, AT&T had actually become a far more formidable opponent. The battle for the telephone was hardly over.

What was over was the dominance of the Bostonians and their ideas over the American telephone industry. The telephone had grown far beyond the conservative expectations of John Hudson or William Forbes. Together, the small town independents and the big city Bell operating companies had created and revealed a mass market for telephone service that the Bell parent company once seemed determined to ignore. One might say that innovation in this era moved inward from the periphery to the core—except that the operating companies had always been the real core of the nineteenth-century telephone business.

The telephone industry was radically transformed by competition, the political pressure created by competition's threat, and the technological and commercial innovations that such pressure provoked. However one parses the exact order of causation—did the threat of competition lead to technical innovation, or did innovation ward off the threat of competition?—it cannot be denied that the map of the American telephone industry was redrawn in these years. When Bell's patent monopoly was broken in 1894, there had been only 270,000 telephones in the United States, roughly one for every 250 Americans. More than a third of those telephones were within three hundred miles of Boston. By 1912, there were nearly nine million telephones in the nation, almost one for every ten Americans. Telephones could be found in one-third of urban households and one-third of American farms. The region with the most telephones in 1912 was not the urban Northeast but the independents' Midwest; the state with the highest number of telephones per capita was rural Iowa, boasting one phone for every six residents.[91] The contours and timing of this growth make clear that the popularization of the telephone cannot be attributed to purely economic incentives or to technological change alone. Left to their own devices, there is no telling how long the Bostonians would have clung to their old policies—though the experience of Central Canada will provide some clues. The impetus for change, when it came, was political. Court decisions ended Bell's patent monopoly, and municipal franchises enabled independent competition. For proof of this, we need only look to a region where the political economy was different, and telephony took a different path.

Making Monopoly Natural in Canada

There is one place the Bostonians' understanding of telephony survived long after 1900: Central Canada. While independent competition shattered the Bell monopoly in the American Midwest, Bell Canada's federal charter and municipal franchise deals preserved the company's dominance in Ontario and Quebec. Here again, political economy shaped not only commercial outcomes but rhetoric and even culture. Without the phenomena of serious independent competition, the market for ideas about the telephone never broke open in Canada the way that it did in the United States. The populist gospel of the people's telephone made far fewer converts north of the border. Conservative attitudes abandoned in Boston and New York remained conventional wisdom in Ottawa and Montreal.

While the American Bell interests went through several chief executives and corporate reorganizations between the 1880s and the 1910s, one man led Bell Canada for thirty-five years—the Boston Confederate Charles Sise. As one historian of Bell Canada put it, Sise "built Bell in his image—

authoritarian, severe, and moralistic."[92] If "system" was Theodore Vail's watchword, "service" was Sise's. Long after Bell left Boston, Sise remained deeply committed to the Bostonian strategy of high-quality service for high-quality customers. He saw the telephone as a luxury good priced for an exclusive, discriminating clientele. "Service must come before economy," Sise lectured his subordinates. "I cannot too strongly impress upon you that we cannot attempt to run this service CHEAPLY." While American farmers turned barbed-wire fences into crude party lines and John Sabin and Angus Hibbard covered San Francisco and Chicago with inexpensive nickel-in-the-slot phones, Sise's company resisted any innovations that might dilute the quality of telephone service. "Service with him [Sise] came first," said Kenneth Dunstan, manager of Bell's Toronto exchange. "You'd quickly bring condemnation down on your head if you ever tried to save money for the Company at the expense of good service."[93] The effects of these differing orientations were predictable and obvious. By 1905, there were three times as many telephones per capita in the United States as in Canada. Indeed, there were more telephones in the city of Chicago than in the entire nation to the north.[94]

The difference between Canadian and American telephony was especially pronounced in the countryside. While Bell and the independents competed to connect farmers and rural lines in the American Midwest, Bell Canada studiously ignored the rural market. "It is a waste of time and temper to connect these small lines," Sise told Canada's Parliament in 1905: "If a line is required from Toronto to Montreal to give a service to the business men, to the mercantile community of Montreal and Toronto, and on the other hand the same amount of money is required for farmers' lines that will give little or no return, on any proper business principle anyone would say: Build the long line, and give the service to the greatest number of people to whom it is of the greatest value."[95]

Small town, village, and rural telephone systems were "absolutely neglected and discouraged" in Canada, complained independent telephone expert Francis Dagger. Bell Canada's general manager claimed in response that "not more than 20 percent" of rural Canadians "evinced the slightest desire to have a telephone."[96]

Bell Canada was unapologetic in its orientation to urban and upper-class customers. The telephone remained the servant of the wealthy in turn-of-the-century Canada, and Bell's Canadian executives saw little need to deny it. "Of the 60,000 people in the city [of Ottawa], not more than 1200 have or require the telephone," a Bell Canada circular stated bluntly in 1902.[97] In the first decade of the twentieth century, as both Bell and independent telephone executives in the United States began to speak of "universal" telephone service, Bell Canada continued to market the telephone only to businessmen and the wealthiest of homes. "Telephone service is not universal in its character as are the systems of Waterworks, Gas, Electric Light, or even the Street Railway Service," declared another Bell Canada broadside in 1902. The company maintained that working-class and rural Canadians had no need or wish for its services.[98]

Bell Canada seemed to go out of its way to preserve the upper-class character of its networks. In 1903, the company established summer telephone service in the Beaches, a suburb of Toronto then inhabited by farmers and working-class families but visited by many upper-class Torontonians in the summer months. When summer ended and the wealthy tourists went home, Bell shut down its exchange. Year-round Beaches residents signed petitions requesting telephone service be continued, but Bell Canada did not regard the full-time residents as promising customers. "There are no industries in the place," said Toronto manager Kenneth Dunstan. "As a community, the occupants of the houses are not well off." Grudgingly, Dunstan set the price for continued service in the Beaches at a prohibitive $100 per year—almost twice what the company charged in other parts of Toronto. Only after the character of the Beaches neighborhood had changed did Bell Canada normalize prices and establish year-round service in the area.[99]

The Bell interests were not entirely unopposed in Canada. Municipal politicians continued the fights of the 1880s over poles and wires in their streets. And a modest movement of independent telephone companies emerged in Canada after 1900, hoping to replicate the success of their American cousins. But Bell Canada's federal charter gave it the upper hand in most dealings with municipal government, and exclusive franchise arrangements locked the independents out of most urban markets in Central Canada. Independent telephony north of the border never became more than a pale shadow of the explosive movement in the American Midwest.

In 1900, the city of Toronto ordered its chief engineer to prevent Bell Canada from erecting poles without a permit. A virtual replay of James Carrel's earlier battle with Bell Canada in Quebec ensued. Relations between Toronto and Bell Canada had been rocky since at least 1896, when negotiations to renew Bell's franchise in the city broke down in a dispute over rates. Bell Canada asserted its right to act without municipal interference. In 1901, the city sued the company over the issue, taking its fight to the Judicial Committee of the Privy Council in London—then Canada's highest court of appeal. But the city lost. The Privy Council upheld Bell Canada's federal charter, reaffirming that the 1882 "general advantage of Canada" clause placed Bell's activities beyond municipal jurisdiction.[100] A strikingly similar case came before the U.S. Supreme Court in 1899 but was decided differently. In a dispute with the city of Richmond, Virginia, the Southern Bell Telephone Company argued that it should be exempt from municipal regulation because its operations were governed by the National Telegraph Act. The American courts rejected this argument, insisting that telephone companies remained subject to both municipal regulation and federal law.[101]

As the Toronto lawsuit was just beginning its journey to Ottawa and then to London, Toronto's mayor Oliver Howland received a letter from William Lighthall, mayor of the Montreal suburb of Westmount. "I see you are having trouble with the Bell Telephone Company claiming control of your streets," Lighthall wrote. He proposed forming a lobby group of united municipal governments, a suggestion Howland enthusiastically received.[102] Lighthall would become the energetic center of a movement Canadian historians call "civic populism"—the fight by town and city governments in the early 1900s to win back power and autonomy from private corporations.[103] "No matter how wealthy or powerful the municipality, without organization it is an easy victim for franchise grabbers and large monopolists," Lighthall told the mayor of Kingston in 1906.[104] He exhorted his fellow mayors to band together against "the charter-shark, the grasping monopolist, the legal sneak, and the venal politician."[105]

Under Lighthall's direction, the newly formed Union of Canadian Municipalities became one of Bell Canada's most vocal opponents. But the tactics and proposals of the union revealed its limitations. Mayors and city councils had to organize against companies like Bell Canada precisely because they had no power over such companies on their own. And because municipalities had so little leverage against private utility companies, the union's only real course of action was to lobby provincial and federal governments for aid. Civic populism in Canada was never a mass movement, and it was born out of municipal weakness, not strength.

In 1903, Lighthall's union petitioned the federal government to take over all long-distance telephone and telegraph lines in Canada, and to declare all local telephone systems under municipal jurisdiction. Local exchanges could then be operated directly by city governments or franchised to private companies at the municipality's discretion. The union's plan gained considerable publicity and was soon at the center of Canadian efforts to reform the telephone industry. By 1905, it had been endorsed by 195 Canadian municipalities and counties, plus the powerful merchants associations of Montreal and Toronto, and the farmers of the Dominion Grange. (The American Grange, by contrast, endorsed private competition.)[106]

Bell's opponents in Canada and the United States sometimes recognized each other as kindred spirits, animated by the same anxieties and goals. Francis Dagger, a British-born telephone engineer who helped to draft the telephone plan of the Union of Canadian Municipalities, cultivated close ties with the American independents. He penned articles for American trade journals about Canadian opposition to Bell and spoke regularly at independent conventions in both countries about "the Common Cause."[107] But there were differences between Bell Canada's moderate municipal opponents and the fiery midwestern independents that Dagger's diplomacy could not conceal.

Bell's Canadian foes were more lukewarm in their opposition to Bell and its policies than their American cousins. The one issue of government ownership notwithstanding, the civic populists' plan for telephones in Canada was considerably closer to ideas espoused at Bell than the entrepreneurial populism of the midwestern independents. In their ideas about the telephone's essential nature, Central Canada's mayors and municipal aldermen did not seriously challenge the fundamental tenets of Bell's old Boston ideology.

In contrast to Bell's American opponents, the Union of Canadian Municipalities did not advocate competing telephone systems within cities. "Competition ought to meet us at the border of the municipality," Lighthall told Parliament in 1905. "Local monopolies . . . regulated locally," was the Union's proposal. Private companies could compete for the favor of municipal governments by bidding for exclusive franchises, but there would be no direct competition for subscribers under this plan. Some smaller municipalities, less eager to enter the telephone business than Toronto or Montreal, said the federal government should take over all telephone service, operating both long-distance and local lines. Either way, municipal politicians in Canada showed little desire to import what they saw as the "bedlam" of independent competition in the midwestern United States. Bell Canada vice president Lewis McFarlane told Canadian lawmakers tales of American cities choked by the poles and wires of "four or more" competing systems—though when pressed, he could not name any place with more than two.[108]

Canadians were quick to accept such exaggerations. Though they envied the dynamism of the American economy, most upper-class Canadians in these years saw the United States as turbulent and chaotic—plagued, as one put it, by "the spirit of license, the contempt of authority, [and] negligence in enforcing the laws." "We are free from many of the social cancers which are empoisoning the national life of our neighbours," boasted the *Canadian Methodist Magazine* in 1880. "We have no polygamous Mormondom; no Ku-Klux terrorism; no Oneida communism; no Illinois divorce system; no cruel Indian massacres."[109] Cutthroat competition could easily have been added to this eclectic list of America's social ills. Canadians had little commitment to the ideal of competition, in the telephone or other industries, as an economic and social good. Canada's leading economist, W. J. Ashley, spoke out against "the worry and laceration of spirit, and the vulgarization of business" stemming from unregulated competition. The antitrust tradition was nowhere near as powerful in Canada as in the American Midwest, and Bell's Canadian opponents showed correspondingly little enthusiasm for competition in telephony.[110]

Opposition to Bell in Canada also differed from the American independent movement in its style and its attitudes toward telephone rates and access to the telephone. Though dubbed civic populists, William Lighthall and his fellow mayors did not go in for the raucous rhetoric of the midwestern independents. As loyal British subjects, they were left cold by talk of "revolution" or "war for industrial independence." More importantly, they did not embrace Gardiner Hubbard's vision of a telephone for the people. Certainly, municipal governments in Canada would have liked to lower the cost of telephone service for their constituents. But few promised to make telephones available to all Canadians, or spoke at any length about the democratic purpose of the device. Nor did Canadian mayors or city councils make strenuous efforts to extend the telephone to rural areas. In effect, most accepted Bell Canada's vision of the telephone as a natural monopoly, a tool for urban commerce, and a privilege of the well-to-do.

Bell's Canadian and American opponents also split on the issue of government ownership and regulation. Municipal politicians in Canada supported the regulation of utilities, and many called for outright public ownership. In the United States, although the support of municipal government was critical to their rise, private entrepreneurs—both operating companies and telephone manufacturers—took leadership of the independent telephone movement. The American independents downplayed their indebtedness to local government, effacing the political construction of their success just as Bell effaced the political construction of its monopoly. In the opinion of Philadelphia independent Edward Cooke, competition was "a more potent righter of wrongs and regulator of business than any possible concoction of our legislative bodies." Cooke and his colleagues rarely acknowledged that competition itself had been concocted through thousands of municipal bylaws and franchises.[111]

At base, the Canadians and Americans differed as to the naturalness of telephone monopoly. Lighthall and his fellow mayors came to accept the proposition that telephone service in any given city must naturally be controlled by one entity or firm. Indeed, their whole plan was predicated on it. Municipal politicians in Canada opposed direct competition in telephony within their cities and echoed Bell arguments about its nuisance and inconvenience. While they clamored for authority to regulate the telephone, municipal authorities in Canada often rejected applications from independent companies who sought to compete directly with Bell.[112] In 1903, Canada's Minister of Justice declared that competition among telephone companies was "not only impossible but highly undesirable."[113] This odd wording reflected the common slippage in such debates between descriptive and prescriptive claims. What was deemed undesirable was dubbed impossible. What was seen as desirable was described as natural.

Francis Dagger, close friend to the American independents, did not believe the telephone was a natural monopoly, but he found himself in a distinct minority north of the border.[114] Even Canada's relatively small number of independent entrepreneurs sometimes declared the telephone a natural monopoly. While negotiating the sale of Montreal's Federal Telephone Company to Bell Canada in 1891, an executive at the Federal Company wrote, "It is quite evident that the Public prefers one Company at a fair price to two Companies at low rates."[115] Another chastened independent was Senator Richard Scott, who had tried and failed to establish a competing telephone system in Ottawa. He then became one of Bell Canada's most loyal parliamentary allies. In 1892, Scott told his fellow senators, "A telephone company must necessarily be a monopoly. You cannot have two telephone lines—it is absolutely impracticable. . . . We tried it here in Ottawa . . . it simply meant a mad competition and loss of money on both sides."[116] Anthony Ochs, the organizer of a failed rural system in Hespeler, Ontario, agreed. "We feel very strongly," Ochs said after selling his system to Bell Canada, that telephone service "is in its very nature a monopoly."[117]

Events, in other words, produced theory. Political economy determined commercial outcomes, but these outcomes were then declared to be natural and inevitable. The failure of competition in Canada convinced Bell's defeated rivals and others that the telephone industry was naturally and properly monopolistic. In 1907, Senator Thomas Davis repeated what had become a nearly unanimous sentiment north of the border. "Every reasonable and sensible man knows that you cannot have competition in telephone service," he said. "It is a monopoly in its very nature and you cannot make anything else of it."[118] Yet when Davis spoke, nearly 60 percent of the towns and cities in the United States had just such direct competition. And there were more independent telephones in the state of Iowa alone (also in Illinois or Ohio) than there were telephones in all of Canada, Bell and independent combined.[119] What the Canadian experience proved was "natural," the American experience disproved. But in constructing theories about the telephone, Canadians and Americans looked almost exclusively at conditions close to home.

Never Natural, Never Free

In 1912, a year after the court-ordered breakup of the Standard Oil monopoly and on the eve of federal antitrust action against AT&T, Charles Fay, the former telephone executive who had fulminated in the 1880s against "telephone subscribers as Knights of Labor," published a book entitled *Big Business and Government*. The thrust of this truculent volume was a defense of big business and a critique of government regulation. "Our valiant American people has never stopped running away from Big Business long enough squarely to face and size up its bogy," Fay began. Trusts and monopolies were never as powerful or secure as they appeared. They were almost always vulnerable to competition, and competition, Fay argued, was a far better safeguard of public interest than government regulation could ever be.[120]

In the case of the telephone, Fay made a partial exception to his brief for unfettered competition. "There a few businesses, such as the telephone industry, which are bound in the nature of things to be monopolies," he wrote. This was not due to any economies of scale, he said, but because of the cost and inconvenience of dual service. Yet at the end of his chapter on the telephone, Fay appended a note. "Since writing the foregoing chapter," Fay added, he had read in the papers that a new combination of independent telephone and telegraph companies had declared "open warfare" against Bell and Western Union. "This confirms my main thesis that competition is in general bound to come," Fay said, "but at the same time it rather upsets my prophecy that a natural monopoly will eventuate in the telephone industry. Well, I will let the prophecy stand; and wait with interest to see how the thing works out."[121]

Fay understood that theoretical claims about what was natural or inevitable always risked being disproved by actual events. Yet people were drawn to them nonetheless. At such an uncertain moment in the history of the telephone and indeed the history of North America's economic order, determinist claims had real rhetorical power and appeal. Technology, after all, is artificial. It is constructed by human beings, and what is constructed can always be designed to serve one interest or another. It is political, debatable, and contingent. What is natural, by contrast, has or seems to have the authority of existence. This is the great utility of technological determinism. Decisions about technology are almost always made to promote various social, commercial, or political arrangements, but when such arrangements can be ascribed to technological imperatives, they are removed from the realm of political debate.

Telephone monopoly in Canada was never really "natural"; telephone competition in the Midwest was never truly "free." Both were political outcomes, established and maintained by regulation and litigation. Yet politicians, telephone executives, and the public all colluded in effacing their own choices with the language of determinism. The success of the midwestern independents in the 1890s and 1900s seemed to prove—in that place, and for that time—the rightness and inevitability of competition. The explosive growth of both the Bell and independent systems dealt a fatal blow to conservative understandings of the telephone in the United States.

In Central Canada, by contrast, the persistence of Bell's monopoly seemed to confirm belief that the telephone was naturally a monopoly, and conservative ideas about the telephone's market and meaning survived well into the twentieth century. Even Bell Canada's leading opponents accepted many of the company's assumptions about the proper market for telephony, the shape and scope of telephone networks, and the naturalness of monopoly control.

In Central Canada in years to come, one of Bell's greatest assets was the apparent absence of alternatives to its domination of the telephone industry there. Canadian politicians struggled to find a regulatory framework that might control Bell Canada without contravening any of the "natural" facts so many Canadians had come to accept as true. In the United States, on the other hand, the American Telephone and Telegraph Company and its subsidiaries did fierce battle with the independents on the fields of commerce, politics, and conventional wisdom. Ultimately, AT&T would win many of these battles—battles with the independents and with its own subsidiaries—by forging a new vision of the telephone, a strategy and a public identity more compelling and successful than the old assumptions of the patent monopoly years. First, however, the midwestern independents would have their day.

Chapter 4

The Independent Alternative

In December 1903, an Indiana businessman named Henry Barnhart took the podium at a meeting of the Interstate Independent Telephone Association, an organization of midwestern telephone entrepreneurs. Barnhart was the head of an independent telephone company in the little town of Rochester, Indiana, and president of the National Independent Telephone Association, another of several overlapping organizations in the often chaotic independent movement. "The public no longer tolerates telephone rate extortion," Barnhart congratulated his colleagues. "Our once powerful and still resourceful rival"—nobody needed to be told who he meant—"has been scourged and repudiated into a retreat."[1]

From where Henry Barnhart was standing, this seemed to be true. Barnhart was part of the first wave of entrepreneurs to enter the telephone business after Bell's patent monopoly expired. He incorporated the Rochester Telephone Company in 1895 and began operation in 1896 with one operator and 149 subscribers. A decade later, Barnhart's business was thriving, as were thousands of other small telephone companies across the Midwest. By 1907, there were over two hundred thousand independent telephones operating in Indiana—three times more independent phones than Bell phones. In Iowa and Kansas, independent telephones outnumbered Bell by a factor of four or five to one.[2]

It has been easy to interpret the eventual defeat of the independents as inevitable.[3] But from a comparative point of view, what cries out for explanation is the independents' relative success. Neither Canada, Mexico, Europe, nor any other region of the United States experienced anything like the intensity of telephone competition seen in the American West and Midwest. Nor did any other country or region construct a network quite like the one created there. Between the 1890s and the 1910s, the heyday of truly independent competition, the midwestern independents built telephone networks with less long-distance reach than their Bell rivals but more intensive local and regional coverage, connecting small towns to their hinterlands and Main Street to the farm. They built networks that were in many ways less efficient but in other ways more free, sustaining a lively, communal, and creative telephone culture. And they built an ecosystem of networks that was much less centralized than the emerging Bell System, an argument in wires for an economy and polity that remained locally oriented and controlled.[4]

This chapter describes the independent telephone movement in its heyday, from the 1890s to the 1910s: first the people that made up the movement, and then the networks that they built. My argument throughout is that independent telephony represented a real alternative to the Bell or AT&T monopoly. Talk of a people's telephone was not just empty rhetoric. Political environments shaped political culture and ideas, as we have seen. Those ideas, in turn, shaped the technical and commercial development of the industry. Different pricing structures, differences in technical operation, and the different geographic scales of Bell and independent networks meant that independent telephony really was different, in philosophy and practice. Independent networks embodied different ideas about corporate power, local autonomy, and the scale of economic and social life.

Could the independents have triumphed in the end? That depends on what "triumph" means, and what "in the end" and "could have" mean as well. But the people's telephone was an idea with powerful appeal, and the independents were phenomenally successful in the Midwest for nearly twenty years. The political economy and culture of the region encouraged and rewarded populist rhetoric about a people's telephone. That vision informed the technical choices and business strategies of the independents and shaped the very networks that they built. Taking up the struggle for local control of the telephone begun by municipal governments in the 1880s, the independents enlisted telephone technology in a fight against national integration and consolidation. Could things have been different? I return to that question later. But this chapter argues that things *were* different, for a time.

Who Were the Independents?

When Henry Barnhart stood before the Interstate Independent Telephone Association in 1903, he called for harmony and friendship among members of the independent movement. "Cooperation . . . is facilitated by success, pleasantry, mutual understanding, close acquaintance, and overlooking each other's faults," Barnhart said. A subtext of his remarks was the behavior exhibited at the same banquet one year before, when quarrels between factions of independent telephone men erupted into a drunken food fight. "Buns, loaf sugar, cheese, hard crackers, ice cream and other edibles" were hurled as missiles, and toastmaster J. J. Nate was chased from the hall by "a shower of champagne, squab, tenderloin of beef, fillet of bass, and tomato mayonnaise." Local police were eventually called in to quiet the scene.[5]

Unruly bun tossing was only one symptom of independent telephony's fractious nature. There were by the time of this fracas literally tens of thousands of independent telephone companies in the United States, and their owners never united behind one leader or connected their wires into a single system. Umbrella organizations like the National Telephone Association and the Interstate Independent Telephone Association formed, split, feuded, and reformed. Efforts were occasionally made to standardize equipment or coordinate the exchange of messages, but many independent managers rejected even the mildest forms of centralization. "The *real* independents," according to one Bell observer, saw themselves as strictly local operations and rejected any talk of interconnection.[6] As a movement of mavericks, a network of those suspicious of national networks, independent telephony remained leaderless and decentralized almost by design. To AT&T executives who embraced the gospel of system and standardization, the chaos of the independent movement seemed inexplicable and foolish. But decentralization was independent telephony's raison d'être, and the creative ferment and flexibility to local conditions this allowed were among the movement's key strengths.

To the extent that one can generalize about such a varied, cantankerous group, Henry Barnhart offers a fair portrait of the typical independent entrepreneur. When Barnhart established his own telephone company in 1895, Rochester, Indiana, was a tiny town with a population of about three thousand people. Barnhart was one of Rochester's leading citizens—the owner and editor of the local newspaper, cofounder of a local savings bank, active in local politics and municipal organizations. A populist Democrat, Barnhart won attention from the national party with emphatic editorials attacking Wall Street and supporting the monetization of silver. He feared the centralization of wealth by corporate trusts or combines would strangle competition and corrupt democracy, creating an "economic oligarchy or plutocracy." In 1908, Barnhart was elected to the United States House of Representatives, where he served six terms as a Democratic congressman. He described his politics succinctly: "Whatever William Jennings Bryan thinks, that's me too."[7]

Barnhart owned a large house on Rochester's Main Street and a hundred-acre farm on the outskirts of town. He described himself as a "man of progress," what today we might call an early adopter. Barnhart owned the first phonograph in Rochester, the first bathroom with indoor plumbing, and one of the town's first automobiles, a 1908 Studebaker EMF. A young friend of Barnhart's son Hugh recalled taking a country drive in this car during an election campaign. The elder Barnhart cursed at the farmers blocking the road with horse-drawn carts and buggies, telling the boys he hoped the election would soon be over so he "wouldn't have to stop for 'those voters.'"[8] But when Barnhart stood before his colleagues in the Interstate Telephone Association, he spoke sweetly of harmony and cooperation between Main Street and the farm. "If our farmer friends will stand by us shoulder to shoulder, back to back, and cooperate and help, each with the other, we shall surely win the victory."[9] Such was the duality of the midwestern independent movement. On the stump or at a lectern, Henry Barnhart could hail the yeoman farmer with as much enthusiasm as any populist orator. But behind the wheel of his Studebaker, he sometimes shook a fist at the slow-moving sodbusters blocking his road.

"We represent people of all classes—rich and poor, farmer and artisan, banker and clerk," said Indiana independent Charles Tarte in 1907.[10] The independent telephone movement included conservative Republicans, fusion Democrats, radical Grangers, and representatives of a dozen other political tribes. It contained big men like Adolphus Busch, the millionaire brewer whose fortune helped build the prosperous Kinloch Telephone Company of St. Louis, and little men like William Sennett, a farmhand in Crawfordsville, Indiana, who split his days between managing a fledgling telephone company and tending to his uncle's hogs.[11] The ranks of the independents contained women too, like Leigh Jamison of Claypool, Indiana, whose Whippoorwill Telephone Company boasted 145 patrons in 1915.[12] Like Barnhart, Busch, and Sennett, most independent telephone entrepreneurs had other jobs. In a 1915 Iowa state census, only 6 percent of independent company officers described the telephone business as their primary occupation. Farmers and merchants made up the two largest segments of the movement by far.[13] The independent telephone movement lived, like Henry Barnhart, on and between Main Street and the farm.

Independent systems varied in size and technical sophistication, from tiny rural cooperatives connecting half a dozen farm families to million dollar businesses serving tens of thousands. Some were short-lived speculative schemes. Others were solid and profitable enterprises. Some rustic systems slung their wires from tree to tree or even used barbed-wire fences to carry an electric current. Others built sophisticated communication networks that rivaled anything operated by the Bell companies. Barnhart's Rochester Telephone Company was a fairly typical small-town independent. As of 1909, the company had about seven hundred telephones. Three hundred and seventy-nine were in the town of Rochester proper, the rest in the surrounding area. About 175 rural subscribers were served by multiparty lines. But much smaller and larger systems could be found. The Citizens Telephone Company of Grand Rapids, Michigan connected more than thirty thousand telephones with state-of-the-art metallic circuits and underground wires. In 1904, it became the first large urban system in the country to automate its switchboards, offering dial service decades before most of the Bell licensees.[14]

Refusing to believe that thousands of telephone systems could spontaneously emerge in the heartland, or that Bell policies had so underestimated popular demand for the telephone, some Bell executives engaged in a fruitless search for the true leaders or instigators of the independent movement. Rumors swirled as to which great industrialist was behind the independent phenomenon—J. P. Morgan's name was often heard.[15] Bell agents were dispatched to infiltrate independent meetings, to dig up dirt on independent finances, and to report back to Boston and New York on the secrets of independent success.[16] Conspiracy theorists at Bell decided the independent movement was the creation of telephone equipment manufacturers, who swept up anti-Bell hostility in order to unload their inferior wares. Others blamed unscrupulous speculators and promoters, duping rural hayseeds with wily stock-watering schemes.[17] But independent telephony was never organized under one roof, and any search for its secret masters was bound to fail.

There were of course men who built large fortunes in the independent telephone business. Frank Henry Woods was a Nebraska attorney who entered the telephone business in 1903. When Woods's Lincoln Telephone and Telegraph Company began operations, it offered free service until the day its subscribers exceeded the number served by the existing Bell exchange. That day was not long in coming. By 1912, Woods was able to buy out Bell operations in most of Nebraska; the check he wrote his ex-competitors for $2.3 million was said to be the largest ever to have changed hands in the state.[18] Theodore Gary was a former lightning-rod and insurance salesman who purchased an independent telephone exchange in Macon, Missouri, in 1897. By 1905, Gary owned multiple independents in Missouri and Kansas. The Gary group would ultimately include dozens of telephone operating and manufacturing companies in the United States, Canada, Latin America, and Europe. By the 1930s, they claimed to control 80 percent of the dial-operated telephones outside the United States. After Gary's death in 1952, his company merged with General Telephone to form General Telephone and Electronics, or GTE. In 2000, GTE would merge with Bell Atlantic to form Verizon Communications.[19]

Yet while there were leading independents, there were few unanimously recognized leaders. The movement was too fractious and decentralized for that. Many important independent spokesmen, like Henry Barnhart or Ohio's James Thomas, did not head large systems but only modest small town exchanges. Their views and interests were not identical with bigger independents like Woods or Gary, as a bitter split in the movement after 1910 would make clear (see Chapter 5). Independent promoters and publicists like Paul Latzke, author of *A Fight with an Octopus*, and Harry MacMeal, publisher of the trade journal *Telephony*, enjoyed positions of some influence within the movement. But that influence hardly went unchallenged. Barnhart often complained, for example, that MacMeal was too beholden to the manufacturers who advertised in his pages. Around 1912, rumors even spread that *Telephony* had sold out, accepting money from the Bell octopus in exchange for blunting its editorial attacks.[20]

Telephone manufacturers were an important and necessary part of the independent movement. Western Electric sold its wares only to Bell affiliates; without outside manufacturers of telephones and equipment there could have been no independent telephony. As Bell's patent protection crumbled in the 1890s, dozens of telephone manufacturing companies emerged. By 1901, there were at least eighty or ninety firms supplying telephones, switchboards, and other equipment to the independent field. Most were based in Chicago, home of Western Electric, and many, like Milo Kellogg's Kellogg Switchboard and Supply, were established and staffed by former Western Electric employees. Some of these manufacturers took an active role in organizing and promoting the independent movement. They published manuals or guides to telephony that doubled as catalogs for their products and backed publications that carried their advertising and promoted the independent cause. *Sound Waves*, for many years *Telephony*'s chief competitor as the voice of the independent movement, was originally a house organ for the Swedish-American Telephone Company, another Chicago-based manufacturer. Around 1895, independent manufacturer James Keelyn established the Telephone Protection Association, a legal defense fund for equipment manufacturers facing patent suits from Bell. After 1897, this organization became a general trade group for independent operating companies and manufacturers alike, renamed the National Independent Telephone Association.[21]

But there is little evidence, beyond the assertions of Bell propaganda, that Chicago manufacturers secretly controlled the independent movement, or that they had created opposition to Bell in the first place in order to unload merchandise on gullible yokels across the Midwest. Independent operators certainly scoffed at these charges. Henry Barnhart's correspondence shows that operating companies could lead manufacturers, rather than follow them, toward untapped markets. Barnhart wrote regularly to manufacturing companies in Chicago and elsewhere, warning them that "the rural telephone business is coming like a whirlwind," and urging them to be ready with sturdy, inexpensive telephones. Indeed, Barnhart's interactions with manufacturers like Chicago's Automatic Electric and Stromberg-Carlson of Rochester, New York, could be comically quarrelsome. He constantly berated them for the quality of their equipment and the desultory way they handled his correspondence and told a friend he was more likely to be put out of business by "slippery independent manufacturers" than by Bell. In 1904, he backed an ambitious but ultimately unsuccessful attempt to establish a new manufacturing company owned and controlled by independent telephone operators. Certainly Henry Barnhart would never have agreed that manufacturers were pulling his wires.[22]

The independents' enemies sometimes denied that a unified independent movement existed at all. Bell publicity drew a sharp distinction between the small cooperative systems, called "mutuals" or "farmers' lines," that brought telephones to rural areas Bell did not serve, and the larger commercial independents that entered into direct competition with Bell in its valued urban markets. Bell managers saw the former group as harmless if cantankerous rustics but denounced the latter as trespassers and charlatans. Yet in practice, the division between rural telephone cooperatives and commercial urban enterprises could not be sharply drawn.[23] The U.S. Census gave up on trying to distinguish between the different types of independent system in 1912, finding "no clear line of demarcation" between urban and rural networks or between commercial and mutual endeavors. Clearly there was a gulf between Frank Woods's network of more than two hundred thousand subscribers and the half dozen telephones strung together by the People's Mutual of Bigfoot, Indiana.[24] But a binary distinction between urban-commercial and rural-cooperative systems, or between those that did and those that did not compete with Bell, does not reflect the reality of the independent telephone phenomenon.

For one thing, the distinction between commercial and cooperative independents did not line up with the divide between those systems competing directly with Bell affiliates and those operating in areas the Bell companies did not serve. There were cooperative systems that competed directly with Bell, and commercial systems that did not. And neither of these divides corresponded precisely to the line between urban and rural systems, as if that line could be drawn with any clarity in the small towns and villages of the early twentieth century. The most typical independent system, to the extent that such a thing existed, lay between—and connected—the country and the town.

Nor is it easy to categorize independent systems as wholly commercial or wholly cooperative. As we have seen, the independent movement was a quasi-political creation, born of municipal politics and shaped by the franchise agreements that gave it birth. Independent telephone companies came in all shapes and sizes: purely private systems, privately owned commercial systems, commercial stock companies, mutual stock companies, purely mutual lines. They changed hands rapidly and experimented with a variety of mixed organizations and forms.[25] Many ostensibly cooperative systems issued transferable stock, allowing subscribers to sell their shares without giving up their telephones. Some telephone systems grew from tiny cooperatives into large and profitable businesses.[26] The telephone systems in larger towns and cities were usually more profitable and commercially oriented their rural partners, but there was still considerable variety in their precise orientation toward profit and public service.

What independent systems did have in common was their local ownership and orientation. "The Independent system is composed of local companies, officered, financed, managed and controlled by local citizens, whose interests are identified with those whom they serve," wrote Indiana independent A. C. Lindemuth in 1908. "Telephone service is furnished under different conditions in different parts of the country," began a declaration of general principles issued by the National Independent Telephone Association in 1913. "Thus we favor locally owned telephone systems—this reserves to the people in the locality the right to determine for themselves what kind of telephone service they want."[27] Few independents rejected the profit motive. Even purely cooperative systems were ultimately intended to increase the profit and convenience of the farmers who built and ran them. But almost all independents agreed that revenue should stay in the community that raised it. Independents of all stripes were determined that the telephone would not be one more innovation that took money out of the local economy—like the railroad or the mail order catalog—and sent it to Chicago, Boston, or New York. Most argued that locally owned systems provided better service to their subscribers than systems operated from afar. "It is impossible for companies whose stockholders are not subscribers to give as good service for the same money or at as low rates, as telephone companies who do not operate for profit or who pay the profits back to their subscribers," declared a 1902 manual on rural telephony, echoing the arguments of Gardiner Hubbard twenty years before.[28]

Independent systems were constantly combining and interconnecting. Farmers' mutuals linked their wires to other rural systems in order to expand their range; these in turn connected to larger commercial systems in neighboring villages and towns. Muncie's independent exchange was connected in this way to at least a dozen other systems by 1906. Such interconnections created hybrid telephone networks that mixed for-profit, nonprofit, and not-quite-for-profit organizations. Henry Barnhart's correspondence from this era offers vivid illustration of the density and complexity of interactions between independent telephone companies in the Midwest. Barely a month went by in which Barnhart was not making or removing or negotiating some connection with a neighboring telephone system. Connecting with these systems was not always easy, and relations between Barnhart and his neighbors rarely ran smoothly. In his private correspondence, Barnhart could be combative and cantankerous, giving and expecting no quarter from his "brothers" in the movement. Yet Barnhart needed the farmers' lines just as he needed farmers' votes. So he constantly negotiated such connections, describing them as "a matter of self-protection."[29]

The success of independent telephone companies correlated strongly with the frequency and density of such interconnections, particularly across the town-rural divide. A study of the organizational ecology of independent telephone systems between 1900 and 1917 found clear evidence of symbiosis between different organizational forms. In other words, the more telephone systems operating in a given area, and the more interconnection between different systems and different sorts of systems—town and rural, for-profit and cooperative—the more successful each individual system was likely to be. The midwestern independents would not have been surprised at this conclusion. Companies that made such connections flourished in the competitive era of telephony. Companies that did not rarely survived.[30]

It would be misleading to divide the independent movement into urban and rural, or commercial and cooperative, halves. Hybrid clusters of commercial and cooperative telephone systems—networks of smaller networks—were a characteristic feature and a critical strength of independent telephony in the Midwest.[31] At its strongest points, the independent movement was an alliance between rural farmers and small-town businessmen, an alliance made physical in the interconnection of town and rural networks. The borders between rural and urban America were where the independents found their most profitable niche.

"The independent movement produced a number of competent local leaders, but none of national importance," sniffed an AT&T-sponsored history of the telephone published in 1910.[32] AT&T's boosters misunderstood a central fact about the independent movement. Independent entrepreneurs were almost by definition oriented toward local networks and local questions. Their failure to organize behind one national leader, or to tightly integrate into a single national system, was not just preordained; it was part of the reason for their movement. The roots of independent telephony lay in and around thousands of little communities like Rochester, Indiana, where unmet desire for telephone service or dissatisfaction with Bell inspired people to string their own wires or demand their own telephone systems. Local leaders like Henry Barnhart did their best to mediate between the many sorts of independent firm, but the independent phenomenon was always fragmented, full of disputes and disagreements between companies, manufacturers, and telephone users. Out of that ferment, an alternative telephone system emerged and spread with astonishing speed. Independent telephony could indeed be chaotic and inefficient. Yet it could also be innovative and adaptive, responsive to its customers and local conditions, and surprisingly robust.

Independent Networks in Practice

"The origin and policy of the Independent—that is, the non-Bell—telephone systems are exactly the reverse of the Bell system," independent A. F. Wilson said in 1907. "It is a people's movement, in the truest sense, causing and propelling a social revolution."[33] Bell owners and managers were always scornful of such claims. "It is absurd for either side to claim altruism. . . . Each side is animated by purely selfish motives," wrote one executive for Bell's New England Telephone Company in a moment of aggravated candor. "The people are equally selfish on their side. Isn't it about time to drop the cant that competition is introduced for the benefit of the 'dear people'?"[34] In years to come, the Bell companies would embrace an ideology of public service, and there would be no more admissions from Bell executives about having "purely selfish motives." But this Bostonian's complaint was hardly unjustified.

Were the independents "real" populists? The question misses the point. As we have seen, populist rhetoric was a lingua franca shared by many of Bell's opponents. The propaganda of the independents was undoubtedly self-serving. But if acting out of economic self-interest disqualifies one from genuine populism, than the People's Party were not "real" populists either. What we can say is that the independents were united in embracing the idea of a people's telephone, an idea that thrust the telephone into contemporary debates about competition and monopoly, regionalism and localism, and the legitimacy of corporate power. The stakes of their fight with Bell, the independents insisted, were much higher than simply lowering the cost of telephone service or expanding their market share. The question to be asked, then, is: was this true?

One way to get beyond the sound and fury of independent propaganda, and the Bell propaganda that answered it, is to look more closely at the subject of this battle, telephone networks themselves. How much did telephone service cost? How were rates determined? How well did the telephone work? Where did the wires go? The telephone systems built by the independents differed from Bell's in concrete physical ways. They were not just smaller copies of the Bell System. Nor did they represent a primitive stage in the "natural" evolution of the technology. The independents had different priorities and goals than Bell, and they made different decisions than Bell's executives and engineers. Independent networks themselves make the best case that the idea of a people's telephone was not just empty rhetoric. An alternative organization of the telephone industry was possible, for a time. By reading physical telephone networks as historical sources in their own right, it is possible to identify real differences between Bell and its opponents, and to understand more clearly the stakes of their fight.

Cheaper than Bell, Better than Walking

To consumers in much of the country, the first and most obvious difference between Bell and its challengers was that independent telephones were cheaper. A study conducted in 1913 found that independent companies offered cheaper service than Bell in 90 percent of the 471 exchanges examined—typically between one-half and three-quarters of Bell rates. (A crucial exception was in very large cities, where innovations like the nickel-in-the-slot had changed the game.) In a medium-sized city where the Bell operating company charged a flat rate of fifty dollars per year, the independent might charge thirty. In a smaller town where Bell charged thirty dollars a year, the independent might charge eighteen. Rural cooperatives asked even less of their subscriber-patrons; after an initial outlay to install the telephone and string the wires, many offered rudimentary service for ten dollars per year or less.[35]

How did the independents manage to offer telephone service so cheaply? Local telephone exchanges, the independents demonstrated, did not demand a large initial investment. And as long as it cost less money per subscriber to operate small networks than big ones, modest independent systems benefited from telephony's diseconomies of scale. It is true that the quality of telephone service offered by the independents was often inferior to that offered by American Bell and its subsidiaries. Bell publicity decried "the craze for 'cheap and nasty' telephony" in the Midwest, but the independents demonstrated an untapped market for rudimentary service at lower rates. A 1902 manual on independent telephony encouraged rural entrepreneurs to install equipment of good quality, but of no higher quality than necessary. "As the value of a telephone depends almost entirely upon the number of people that can be reached," the manual suggested, "it is . . .

advisable to use that system which will reach, on account of its low first cost, the greatest number of people and will give service sufficiently good for all practical purposes."[36] One Michigan independent described his no-frills rural telephone as "cheaper than the Bell" but "better than walking." Many independents found room for profit between those two poles.[37]

Bell and independent telephone companies were also financed differently. Independent financing was often precarious. Certainly, the independents had more difficulty attracting capital investment than their Bell rivals, especially in the East. Independent securities were rarely traded on the New York market or backed by the big financial institutions there. Independent securities were risky compared to Bell's blue-chip stocks, and AT&T and its influential backers actively dissuaded investors from supporting independent firms. In 1902, for example, George R. Sheldon, a wealthy member of the New York Stock Exchange, invested a sizable sum in an independent telephone company based in Milwaukee. Sheldon was soon visited by representatives of both J. P. Morgan and Company and the First National Bank, dispatched at the request of AT&T president Frederick Fish. The bankers persuaded Sheldon to withdraw his support, the Milwaukee independent went bust, and AT&T compensated Sheldon for the expenses he had incurred. In 1905, AT&T vice president Frank Pickernell urged executives at Central Union to find some way to block their independent rival in Indianapolis from raising money for maintenance or improvement. When Indianapolis Telephone successfully petitioned city government for permission to raise its rates, Central Union secretly backed a lawsuit opposing the increase.[38]

Unable to raise money in New York, independent entrepreneurs had to attract investors in their own communities or on regional stock exchanges in cities like Cleveland, Minneapolis, and Toledo. "In some respects this has been a wholesome thing," maintained one Indiana independent, "in that it has compelled the Independent companies to look to their own localities for financial assistance; so that each town or city to a large extent holds the securities of its own telephone company." But the truth was that these smaller markets could never generate the kind of capital available to AT&T.[39]

Whether by necessity or design, independent operators spent less on maintaining and replacing their equipment than Bell. Bell publicity called such independents short-sighted and warned subscribers and investors they would suffer from this neglect. "A telephone plant deteriorates rapidly—more rapidly, perhaps, than the mechanical equipment used by any other modern industry," argued a spokesman for Bell's New England Telephone and Telegraph Company. The New England Company set aside one third of its annual revenue for maintenance and depreciation and accused companies that did not of "wildcat financiering."[40] Another Bell pamphlet claimed that Cleveland's Cuyahoga Telephone Company, which it dubbed "the leading independent company in the country," spent only 4 percent of the estimated value of the company's equipment on maintenance in 1902. "No engineer of any reputation will deny that at least eight percent of the cost value of the property is required to properly maintain and perpetuate telephone property—many put it higher," said the pamphlet's anonymous author. "It is quite clear that the [Cuyahoga] plant . . . is not being properly paid for."[41]

The independents tried to defend their practices. "The depreciation of a well constructed telephone plant is very small. Properly taken care of, it does *not* depreciate," claimed Cuyahoga's president, Frederick Dickson. Dickson charged instead that the Bell companies exaggerated the cost of maintenance and depreciation because their plants, built before 1890, were "antiquated and worse than useless." Cuyahoga's modern equipment, he boasted, would not decrease in value for decades, nor was it liable to require expensive repairs. According to Dickson, the only damage the company's equipment had suffered in five years was during a sleet storm in 1900, when Bell telephone poles fell over onto two of the Cuyahoga company's poles and broke them down.[42]

Dickson's boast of invulnerability to the elements was dubious, to say the least. Yet it did not follow that every telephone company had to be financed like AT&T. Many accused the Bell companies of overstating the cost of depreciation and maintenance. New York independent Bert Hubbell called AT&T "unnatural, unwieldy, and unnecessarily extravagant in its methods of operation." He believed the Bell companies forced their subscribers to pay for upgrades and improvements they did not need, and that their large reserves for maintenance and depreciation were simply a way of concealing profits and inflating the price of telephone service. The Bell companies were over-capitalized, the independents insisted, and charged exorbitant rates to keep stockholder dividends high. "In the old days . . . the prices charged were so exorbitant that they amounted to extortion," argued independent George Shanklin. "In order to justify these excess charges the Bell people announced that deterioration in telephone apparatus was so great that the entire system had to be renewed every few years."[43]

There was exaggeration in both the independent's charges of extortion and extravagance at Bell and in Bell's frequent predictions of ruin for independent systems. But together they pointed to genuine differences in strategies and priorities. The Bell companies and the independents had different understandings as to what level of quality was necessary or desirable because they stood for different philosophies about the industry and the technology.

The Difference Flat Rates Made

Billing structures also differed between Bell and the independents. As we have seen, Gardiner Hubbard established the precedent of flat-rate pricing in the industry's earliest years. Flat rates complemented Hubbard's vision of a social role for the telephone and his hostility to the telegraph, which obliged customers to carefully measure their words. A flat rate for service was also the simplest billing structure to oversee. After Hubbard was gone from American Bell, however, most of the Bell operating companies came to embrace the principle of measured service, in which charges increased with the amount of telephone use. The independents, by contrast, cast their lot with flat rates. This seemingly technical distinction had a deep impact on the growth and character of each set of telephone networks.

To champions of measured service, it was more reasonable and logical to charge telephone users by the call than by the month. It was also usually more profitable. When calls were connected by human operators, the marginal cost of each connection was high, especially in large cities where connecting a call involved multiple switchboards and operators. Charging by the call, Bell executives argued, improved service quality by reducing traffic congestion and lowered the price of telephone service for the majority of consumers.[44] In America's largest cities, where the challenges of switching and connecting calls were most acute, it is difficult to see how the telephone could have reached a mass market as rapidly as it did without some form of measured pricing. In 1893, on the eve of the competitive era, Chicago Telephone charged its business subscribers a flat rate of $125 per year for unlimited local calling—prohibitively expensive for many consumers. A metallic circuit suitable for long-distance connections cost $175 per year. By 1901, the average cost of telephone service in Chicago had dropped, according to the company's calculations, to $35 per year. Technological advances and political pressures, including the threat of competition, were crucial elements of this drastic change. But it could not have been realized without moving to the measured service plans devised by Angus Hibbard, John Sabin, and others.[45]

Nevertheless, Americans demonstrated a stubborn preference for flat-rate pricing. Even when measured service would save them money, many consumers opted or stated a preference for flat rates instead. In the 1880s, the issue provoked subscriber boycotts like the telephone strike in Rochester, New York. In the 1890s and 1900s, measured service drove customers in small towns and cities away from Bell exchanges to their independent rivals. Later in the century, regulators responding to public demand would force the Bell System to return to flat rates for local service; flat local rates would be subsidized by AT&T's high profits from long-distance calling.[46] When a Colorado state commission endorsed flat rates for small and medium sized communities in 1914, the reasons given showed the interconnection of economic criteria and cultural considerations in this debate. "Flat rates are justified in smaller districts or cities because the condition of the individual subscribers are approximately alike," read the report. Smaller towns have "no large business houses . . . no great difference between the rich and the poor; distances are short; time is not at a premium; people's ambitions are not strung so high; haste is neither necessary nor known."[47]

The flat-rate bias—a consumer preference for flat rates over usage-based billing, even when the latter is cheaper—is familiar to economists and marketers today. They speak of "insurance effects," in which risk-averse consumers choose a flat rate to avoid unexpected variations in their expenses, and the "taxi meter effect," in which the ticking of a meter, real or perceived, reduces one's enjoyment of a service. And they understand that consumers are sensitive to the location of transactions, and resent having to pay for things that are already "in" their own home.[48] But these phenomena mystified and aggravated Bell executives a century ago.[49]

The independents set themselves apart from their Bell rivals by obliging consumer demand and offering flat rates for unlimited local calling. They had a number of reasons to do so. Flat rates were considerably easier and cheaper to administer. In the smaller towns and cities where the independents were based, network congestion was not so acute. And because many independents used automatic switchboards, in which customers dialed their own calls rather than speaking to an operator, the marginal cost of making each connection was not as high. But what the independents returned to, again and again, was the simple fact that their customers, especially the Main Street businessmen whose capital and custom had launched the independent movement, demanded flat rates. "There is no doubt that a measured service is a mighty good thing—for a monopolist," said the president of the Wisconsin Independent Telephone Association in 1905. "There is more money in it." But, he said, in any market with competition, consumers would demand flat rates and abandon the exchange that did not offer them. "I do not think any of us could compete with the Bell company for a month using measured service."[50]

As we saw in Kingston and Muncie, this difference between Bell and independent billing structures had a significant impact on the use and character of telephone networks. It meant, among other things, that the so-called frivolous uses of the telephone, such as nonbusiness calls to family or friends, were encouraged on most independent systems, and discouraged on most Bell lines. At a deeper level, flat rates and measured service implied a different relationship between consumers, the company, and the telephone itself. Was the telephone in a subscriber's home a device that, once rented and installed, the subscriber could use in any way they wished? Or, were individual telephone calls a service purchased from the operating company, on their terms and at their discretion? The choice between flat rates and measured service, and related debates about the proper and improper uses of the telephone, were always part of a deeper struggle for authority over the network.

The first generation of Bell owners and directors tried to keep a tight rein over telephone use. "The unlimited use of the telephone leads to a vast amount of unnecessary occupation of the wires," American Bell told its subscribers in 1880. "Thus the telephone system is so encumbered with calls which are unnecessary, and largely illegitimate, that the service is greatly impaired."[51] Bell's early managers sought to limit frivolous telephoning, especially undignified activities like courting or gossiping over the telephone, and to control certain groups of users, like women, children, and servants, who were thought to be particular offenders. Charging by the call, Theodore Vail argued at this time, would "cut off all the superfluous business that tends to make the operation of the business so unremunerative." Measured service was not seen in these early days as a way of profiting from casual use of the telephone but as a way of preventing it.[52]

Women were often accused of misusing or overusing the telephone: interrupting their husbands at work with calls about unimportant matters, eavesdropping on their neighbors over rural party lines, or tying up telephone lines with idle gossip and unnecessary chat. Bell managers asked male subscribers to train their wives in proper telephone use, and to monitor the length and frequency of their calls. A barrage of jokes in the trade press about foolish, gossiping women testify to the industry's anxiety and hostility toward female telephone users.[53] The stereotype of women misusing or overusing the telephone spread faster than the technology itself —Mark Twain published a story depicting a nonsensical telephone conversation between two housewives in 1880, before many Americans had even seen the device.[54]

Does the clamor around women's use of the telephone mean that women discovered or invented the social uses of the device? Did they appropriate a technology intended for business communication and recast it for their ends?[55] There is probably some truth to this story. But the fulminations of nineteenth-century executives are not very good evidence that women used the telephone in ways that differed markedly from men. Our portrait of talkative women as the inventors of telephone sociability has been overdrawn, both by hostile Bell executives in the 1880s and 1890s, and by sympathetic historians a century later. Nineteenth-century anxieties about women and the telephone tell us more about attitudes toward speech, gender, and the public sphere than they do about actual telephone practices. Yes, women learned to gossip on the telephone. But so did their husbands, brothers, and sons. When flat rates were available, as they were on most independent systems, both men and women made heavy use of the telephone for nonbusiness purposes. It is probably more accurate to observe that it served Bell executives in the late nineteenth century to cast social uses of the telephone as feminine—as "gossip," "frivolity," and "idle chatter"—and therefore as unnecessary and invalid.[56]

Women were not the only telephone users that measured service was designed to control. AT&T management instructed operators not to connect calls made by children and implored subscribers to control their children's access to the telephone.[57] Servants and other subordinates were also thought to be irresponsible with the device. "Servants and others abuse the service, using the lines for trivial conversations and also holding them at times for half an hour while others are waiting," grumbled Bell Canada president Charles Sise.[58] Male clerks and office underlings were charged with abusing the telephone nearly as often as women. "The most scrupulous office-boy, whose conscience would quiver at the thought of taking a postage stamp, will thoughtlessly visit with all his chums and discuss the baseball news over the telephone," said one Bell executive in 1906.[59]

In the early 1900s, many Bell executives, especially at the more innovative urban operating companies, moved away from these narrow visions of legitimate and illegitimate telephone practices. By 1910, advertisements for New York Telephone and other Bell operating companies actively promoted the social uses of the telephone, often targeting women. Yet in other quarters, the old Bell prejudice against frivolous use of the telephone lingered on for many years. "There is a vast amount of talk over the telephone which serves no useful purpose whatever," complained New England Telephone and Telegraph's George Anderson in 1906.[60] As late as 1928, Walter Gifford, Theodore Vail's successor as president of AT&T, still vividly recalled his company's old hostility to idle talk. "It is really funny when I think back," Gifford told a meeting of Bell advertising executives in that year. "I can remember the time in the business, not so long ago, when we wished people wouldn't talk on the telephone, we wanted to put rate structures in that would stop them because the talk was frivolous." He was quick to add, "I hope most of this will be expunged, for I am not telling this for publication."[61]

If differences between men's and women's telephone practice existed mostly in the minds of male executives and engineers, differences between small town and big city telephone practices were real. Big city residents with measured service plans counted their nickels and chose their calls carefully. Their country cousins were far freer to use the telephone when and how they wished. "The principal use of farm line telephones has been their social use," said Ohio independent George Johnson in 1909. "The telephones are more often and for longer times held for neighborly conversation than for any other purpose."[62] Urban dwellers who visited the country in these years often commented on the ubiquity of the rural telephone and the frequency of its use. A column in *Outlook Magazine*, published in 1902, described the divide: "In a large city there are telephones without number, of course, but the average householder never dreams of having one, and even those who indulge in a telephone of their own have a limit of calls per year, which makes them think twice before using the instrument once." Outside the city, however, the writer found "a telephone in almost every house . . . used without stint and prized to the full." These differences could even be mapped on a national scale. Traffic data on the number of telephone calls per capita or per telephone show that telephone use generally increased from east to west, particularly in regions with independent competition, innovative Bell operating companies, and aggressive municipal regulation. In 1907, Massachusetts residents made an average of ninety-seven telephone calls per person per year. In Connecticut and New Hampshire, that number was eighty-four. But Indiana residents made 182 telephone calls per person per year and Ohio residents 226. On the West Coast, residents of Washington State made 317 telephone calls per person per year, and California residents 261. The region with the least telephones and the lowest telephone use was the South; South Carolina residents made just thirty-five calls per person per year. "Nowhere has the use of the telephone become more widespread than . . . the farming communities of the Western States of America," declared *Cassier's Magazine* in 1907. "It must be acknowledged," concluded *Outlook*'s columnist, "that they do these things better in the progressive provinces than in the arrogant but backward metropolis."[63]

Measured service could lower the cost of access to the telephone, especially in large cities where the marginal cost of each new connection was high. But flat rates encouraged heavy use of the telephone by those who had one, and a wider variety of uses. A flat-rate system encouraged innovation. It let subscribers experiment with their telephones, generating new uses and practices for the network. Some of the innovations of early telephone users are familiar to us. Others have been forgotten. Decades before the rise of radio broadcasting, "telephone newspapers" were established in small communities across the West and Midwest. At a set time every day or evening, the telephone would ring, and an operator or subscriber would report the news, farm prices, and local doings to everyone on a multiparty line. Some newspaper publishers initially opposed this practice but later found these brief reports increased demand for the printed paper. In Indiana and Michigan, rural postmasters experimented with opening letters requiring quick delivery and reading them to their intended recipients over the telephone. The U.S. Department of Agriculture began distributing daily weather reports by telephone in 1904. An estimated one million farms received these reports in 1908. Librarians answered research inquiries over the telephone, an innovation *Telephony* credited to Mrs. D. E. Allen, a village librarian in Downs, Kansas. Some midwestern political conventions transmitted speeches by telephone to farmers in surrounding areas; in 1907, *Telephony* reported, Senator Albert Beveridge delivered a speech entitled "The Nation's Peril" over the wires from Chicago to Indianapolis.[64]

The most characteristic innovations of flat-rate telephone culture were social uses. Youngsters courted and oldsters gossiped. Ministers delivered sermons over the telephone, even performing weddings and funerals, and schoolteachers taught lessons to scattered rural pupils. Neighbors and operators were asked to keep an ear on sleeping babies. "Your friends are always in your parlor—if you have an Independent Telephone," read one advertisement in an Iowa newspaper. "A telephone at your bedside dispels loneliness, and enables you to pass many pleasant hours in talking with your friends," read another.[65] Telephone musicales, in which friends and neighbors met on the lines to sing and play musical instruments—violins, banjos, French harps, pianos—became a popular rural pastime. *Cassier's Magazine* declared these virtual concerts "much more satisfactory than a phonograph," although flat-rate telephone subscribers also played and listened to phonograph records over the wires. Large telephone parties connected dozens of families at a time on several multiparty lines. "Imagine an evening like this in the town or city," remarked a North Carolina newspaper in 1910. "Here, 'Central' is not a person to be sworn at but serves as a social arbiter and distributes rare joys each evening to hundreds, for miles around."[66]

Other innovations were less welcome but accepted and even indulged as part of the culture of small town and rural telephone use. Eavesdropping, also known as "rubbering," was rampant on rural party lines. Though each subscriber on a multiparty line could be summoned with a distinctive pattern of long and short rings, there was nothing preventing his or her neighbors on the line from picking up their own receiver to listen in—or to butt into the conversation. Both Bell and independent telephone companies tried at times to prevent eavesdropping, with limited success. They passed rules against it, editorialized against it in trade journals and rural newspapers, and occasionally levied fines against offenders. They experimented with lock-out devices meant to prevent other subscribers from listening in on a party line once a connection had been made. But rubbering remained widespread, and many rural telephone users defended it as a perfectly friendly and legitimate practice. Certainly, many farmers opted for multiparty lines long after private lines became available and reported missing the sociability of the old telephones when they were gone. "You got better programs on it than you ever did on the radio," one reminisced.[67]

The prank call was another innovation, even less welcome, that became an enduring application of flat-rate telephone service. In 1905, *Sound Waves* described an incident that was typical, it said dryly, of the "advantages and pleasures" of small-town telephone use. A woman in rural Maine was awakened at three in the morning by the "furious ring" of her telephone: "Feeling from the wildness of the ring that it must be something mortally important, she scampered downstairs and nervously seized the receiver, only to hear a shrill soprano voice shriek, 'Got your washing done yet? Had mine out half an hour ago!'" The flat rates and automated switchboards preferred by the independents were far more hospitable to prank callers than Bell company lines. On most Bell systems, connections went through a human operator who could trace calls back to their source, but flat-rate, automatic systems gave pranksters access and anonymity. In 1899, the small city of Janesville, Wisconsin, established a free public telephone booth; the independent telephone company hoped to encourage more local merchants to subscribe. But the telephone was soon disconnected and the booth dismantled: "youngsters and irresponsibles" had defaced the booth and used the telephone "recklessly and viciously, making calls for mischief and worse."[68]

Not all innovations are good ones. Not all uses of the telephone were practical or mature. But while measured service let the Bell network grow in populous urban centers, the flat rates of the independents enabled change and innovation, creating a distinct telephone culture in rural and small-town America that was more informal, communal, and undisciplined than its big city counterpart. Again and again, choices about the operation of the network proved more than technical or economic in their import. Measured service let tens of thousands of city dwellers use Bell's networks for the first time. Flat rates let hundreds of thousands of small town and rural Americans make the independent networks their own.

Everyone His Own Operator

The legend of Almon Strowger, the man most often credited with inventing a practical system for automatic telephone switching, seems almost too picturesque to be true. In the first decades of the telephone, all calls were connected manually by operators at a central switchboard. Strowger, an undertaker in Kansas City, became convinced that Bell operators were diverting calls intended for him at the switchboard, connecting bereaved clients and their business to his chief competitor instead. Strowger stewed over ways to shift control of telephone switching from the perfidious "hello girl" to callers themselves, and in 1891 he patented an electromechanical switching device, allegedly constructed from a collar box and hat pins, that did the job. In Strowger's system, a row of buttons on each subscriber's telephone allowed callers to tap out the digits of the number they desired—a forerunner of dial and push-button phones.[69] Strowger's switch was not the first electromechanical connection device. Bell engineers had experimented in the 1880s with an automatic mechanism for small exchanges which they called the "village system." Nor was Strowger's switch necessarily the best. The amateur inventor soon partnered with others, like the Erickson brothers of Lindsborg, Kansas, who greatly improved his design.[70] But few captured better than Strowger that mix of mechanical ingenuity and chip-on-the-shoulder self-reliance that characterized independent telephony from its start. Strowger famously promoted his system as the "cuss-less, wait-less, out-of-order-less, girl-less telephone, where everyone is his own operator."[71]

Everyone his own operator—here was a vision that independent telephony could embrace. In 1892, a fully automatic exchange connecting sixty telephones went into service at La Porte, Indiana, constructed by Strowger's Automatic Electric Company and operated by the Cushman Telephone Company. The location was fitting. La Porte had been without telephones since the rate regulation battle of the 1880s, when American Bell sued Cushman subscribers there for patent infringement and a judge reputedly ordered the burning of their telephones. Automatic switching appealed to independent firms in modest markets because it was inexpensive, especially for a small village or rural exchange. A human operator worked only eight or ten hours a day, five or six days a week, and might be paid three hundred dollars per year. Strowger's switch and similar devices made it possible and cost effective to operate tiny exchanges twenty-four hours a day.[72]

Automatic switching also appealed because it shifted power over the telephone's operation from the company toward the consumer. Advertising for automatic devices played up distrust and resentment of the Bell company and its operators. Strowger switches, the Automatic Electric Company boasted, "never gossiped, [were] not interested in subscribers' affairs, [and were] never impudent or saucy."[73] Bell advertising portrayed the company's young female operators as surrogate servants, a characterization that fit with the company's vision, however out of date, of its genteel upper-class subscribers. But middle- and working-class Americans were less comfortable with virtual servants and less enamored of the operator. Bell publicity maintained that customers liked talking to operators and preferred manual over automatic switching, but private studies within the Bell System revealed that the opposite was true. Whenever customers had a choice, surveys revealed, they favored automatic systems over operators, just as they preferred flat rates to measured service.[74]

While the independents experimented with and improved automatic exchange systems, the Bell companies staunchly resisted this change. Bell engineers said that Strowger's technology could not be trusted with the crucial and complicated task of making telephone interconnections. Nor, they said more privately, could the average telephone user. Bell engineers and executives were strongly inclined to retain as much control as possible over the operation of the telephone. It was a matter of faith at Bell that reliable service meant insulating customers from the business of connecting calls. At a conference on switching technology in 1892, AT&T vice president Edward Hall said that "any attempt to take the user into our service and make him do a part of the work is a movement which is not in the right direction."[75] Thomas Lockwood, the Bell electrician who had experimented with and then abandoned an automatic "village system" in the 1880s, agreed. "An operation as complex as that of uniting two telephone subscribers' lines . . . can never efficiently or satisfactorily be performed by automatic apparatus, dependent on the volition and intelligent action of the subscriber," he advised John Hudson in 1891. Five years later, as independent systems and automatic exchanges spread across the Midwest, Lockwood was more blunt. Few subscribers could be trusted to remember their own telephone number, he said, let alone somebody else's.[76]

In public, Bell spokesmen soft-pedaled this mistrust of consumers and argued only that the technology for automatic switching was unreliable or unready. Strowger's system might serve in a tiny village like La Porte, admitted AT&T's chief engineer John Carty, but it would surely break down in a large urban exchange.[77] These doubts about automatic switching were not insincere. Scaling up a device like Strowger's to meet the demands of a massive urban network like Chicago or New York would prove a formidable technological challenge. Chicago's independent, the Illinois Telephone and Telegraph Company, installed an automatic system connecting nearly eight thousand telephones by 1905; it performed poorly. Automatic switching didn't sink the company, which went into receivership in 1909, but it didn't help. This mediocre performance in the very city where Automatic Electric was based was a black eye for Strowger's company and for the technology in general.[78]

But independent manufacturers kept tinkering, and the technology improved. By 1904, independent telephone companies were operating automated exchanges in dozens of small and medium sized cities across the United States. The U.S. Army adopted the mechanism on military bases. Besides Chicago, larger cities with automated exchanges included Indianapolis, Buffalo, and San Francisco. In 1905, the Strowger system in Los Angeles—no rural hamlet—connected nearly twenty thousand lines. By 1912, it would connect sixty thousand. Privately, Thomas Lockwood admitted that the newest Strowger switchboard was "a remarkable mechanism." Many European telephone systems were also embracing automation at this time. By 1910, AT&T's own internal analysis showed that automating switchboards would save money and improve service.[79] Even then, the Bell companies took another decade to begin introducing automated switching and did so only after a sharp increase in the wages and labor militancy of telephone operators during the First World War.[80] As a result of AT&T's reluctance, North American telephony, so far ahead of the rest of the world in many respects, lagged well behind Europe in the move to automated switching. In 1910, John Carty gave a controversial lecture at a conference of European telephone and telegraph managers in Paris, warning against the adoption of automatic switching. His advice went unheeded. By 1929, 40 percent of the telephones in Germany, over 50 percent in the Netherlands, and more than 70 percent in Austria allowed customers to dial their own connections. Only 26 percent of American lines did the same.[81]

There is, of course, more than one way to acquire an innovative technology. Around this time, AT&T and Chicago Telephone quietly purchased the failed Illinois Telephone and Telegraph. The bankrupt operating company was of little value in itself, but it owned a large stake in Automatic Electric, which in turn owned the industry's most valuable set of patents on automatic switching equipment. Clearly, the Bell companies intended a covert takeover of Strowger's old company. What is not clear is whether Bell planned to finally embrace automatic switching or to squash it once and for all. Independent manufacturers like New York's Bert Hubbell lobbied the Department of Justice to stop the sale and "save the automatic telephone." The purchase was indeed blocked by a government lawsuit in

1913, keeping automatic switching alive and out of Bell hands for another decade.[82]

John Carty was right that it would be difficult to bring reliable automatic switching to a large city like New York or Chicago. But building long-distance lines across the continent was difficult too, and AT&T embraced that challenge as central to its plans. The point to be made here is that certain technologies either fit or did not fit with Bell and the independents' competing visions of telephony. The dueling systems made choices and set priorities based on their immediate commercial and political environments and their views of the industry's future. These choices became investments, and soon each set of companies was deeply committed to a certain way of doing things. Patent portfolios, capital investments, and market positions reinforced corporate culture and vice versa. Automatic switching made sense to the independents for cultural, commercial, and political reasons. Automatic switching ran against Bell philosophies, and so the Bell companies dragged their feet.

This does not mean that the Bell companies were not refining and improving their own switching technologies. Indeed, the switchboard problem was a source of furious innovation at Bell. But while the independent companies chose to automate the switching process from the outside in, putting responsibility into the hands of their users, the Bell companies automated from the inside out. Bell engineers designed and redesigned their switchboards. They employed probability theory to track and monitor calling patterns. Efficiency experts streamlined and standardized the language and motions of telephone operators, and supervisors increasingly policed their operators' every move. In the 1910s, AT&T explored the idea of semiautomated exchanges in which customers would contact operators who would then dial their calls for them, effectively adopting the idea of automatic switching while still keeping the telephone user out of the loop. Carty argued that by 1910, most of Bell's large exchanges were already "semi-automatic," in that they employed automated machinery guided by human intelligence. That automation, however, was contained and concealed in a central exchange office. The workings of the Bell network remained invisible and inaccessible to the ordinary user—a conscious choice on the part of AT&T engineers. "The two systems are not so antagonistic as would at first appear," Carty said.[83] The real difference between Bell's central operator system and the customer-operated exchanges of the independents was in how much trust each system placed in its users.

Other differences in telephone design sprang from AT&T's commitment, and the independents' hostility, to standardization, centralization, and control. The Bell companies quickly embraced the common battery system, which replaced the bulky, messy batteries in old hand-cranked telephones with current from a central power source. Yet they fought for decades to keep third-party attachments of any kind off their telephones. This included not only electrical devices like loudspeakers, which might affect telephone transmission, but even items as innocuous as writing pads for jotting down numbers and messages. "That is what the fine page in the front of the directory is for," grumbled Bancroft Gherardi, Carty's successor as AT&T's chief engineer.[84] This near obsession with maintaining complete control over every element of the telephone network would ultimately contribute to the breakup of the Bell System in the 1980s, but it was for decades an entrenched and unquestioned part of Bell's corporate and technical culture.[85]

The "French phone," which, like modern telephones, integrated mouthpiece and earpiece in one handset, was another case in point. Handsets of this type became popular in Europe by the 1890s but were rarely seen in North America before 1900. Around 1905, independent telephone manufacturers like Strowger's Automatic and the Kellogg Switchboard and Supply Company began making one-piece handsets for the American market. Kellogg called his version the "grab-a-phone." For decades, AT&T and Western Electric opposed the use of integrated handsets. According to AT&T engineers, the French phone suffered from feedback and loss of signal clarity. But as with automatic switching, the real problem, from AT&T's point of view, was controlling the telephone user. The traditional two-piece telephone forced users to maintain a more or less stationary position, speaking with their lips an optimum distance from the telephone receiver. One-piece sets allowed telephone users to move around, and Bell engineers did not believe they could be trusted to handle the device gently or to hold their hand sets a correct distance from their mouths.[86]

Demand for the French phone—unaccountably, the name "grab-a-phone" did not take hold—spread in spite of AT&T's stern disapproval. It came to be seen as more fashionable and stylish than the Bell companies' utilitarian candlestick model. Independent manufacturers promoted this angle—"Why should a telephone be ugly?" asked advertisements for Strowger Automatic's Monophone—and by the 1910s and 1920s Bell customers began violating their terms of service by buying French phones and connecting them to Bell lines. AT&T ran advertisements warning customers not to use "foreign" telephones and ordered its operating companies to disconnect subscribers who did. The Bell companies would not adopt integrated handsets until the 1930s; even then, they charged a premium for these telephones and did not advertise their availability.[87].

Bell officials were similarly loath, despite public demand, to manufacture telephones in any color other than black. Home decorating magazines promoted a fad for painting telephones in the 1920s. In 1928, AT&T's Walter Gifford called the idea of colored telephones "a little silly," and Bell Laboratories president Frank Jewett spoke scornfully of the "fickle" public and its "color craze." Western Electric did begin producing a limited number of colored candlestick telephones for the Bell System in 1929, but Bell managers were warned that it would be "clearly impractical to do anything which would stimulate the sales of these sets." In the hard times of the 1930s, escapist films about the idle rich became known as "white telephone movies," as they were the only place such luxuries appeared. White and colored telephones would not become widely available to Bell customers until the late 1950s.[88]

The independents' early embrace of automatic switching and other telephone refinements refutes the idea that the Bell companies were the only important source of innovation in early telephony. Neither Bell nor the independents can be declared more or less open to innovation than the other. Instead, each pursued innovations that fit with their own business strategies and philosophies. AT&T embraced centralizing and standardizing technologies like common batteries and long-distance lines. The independent companies turned to automatic switching, which worked best in rural and small-town exchanges, saved smaller companies money, and shifted power toward the people. It was a natural innovation for Bell to resist, and for the independent movement to adopt.

Arguing against automatic switching in 1895, Thomas Lockwood made a telling distinction between Bell and independent philosophies. Bell's competitors might be drawn to automatic switching, Lockwood said, because they were free to consider things from "the point of view of the subscriber." But Bell engineers, he continued, had a much greater responsibility. They had to consider at all times the requirements of the entire telephone system.[89] Lockwood aptly described the commitment to system stability and integration that took hold at AT&T in the 1890s and 1900s. But to the independent way of thinking, Lockwood's distinction must have seemed perverse. Who was "the system" if not the people who used it?

The Infernal Nuisance of Duplication

The aspect of telephone service in this era that is most foreign to us today was the lack of interconnection between telephones on competing networks. Today, government regulations and corporate policy both mandate the interconnection of competing telephone systems. A century ago, this was not the case. A customer with a Bell telephone could not call an independent telephone, nor could the independent telephone connect to the Bell, unless an interconnection agreement had been arranged. The industry called this separation "dual service," and it meant just that—two entirely separate telephone systems fighting for subscribers and supremacy in the same city or town.[90]

Dual telephone service seems strange and unworkable from our vantage point in an era of universal, legally mandated interconnection. It meant two networks of poles and wires in each city, two sets of operators and exchanges, two solitudes of nonconnecting telephones. Many reading this book will have lived through eras of competing and incompatible computer operating systems, video cassette formats, or automated banking networks. In each case, the era of incompatibility ended with the arrival of interconnection or the obsolescence of one system. But dual, nonconnecting telephone service was too widespread and too long lasting to be simply dismissed as an error or aberration. Between 1900 and 1915, half the cities in the United States with populations over five thousand had two or more separate and competing telephone exchanges.[91] The last major city with dual service was Philadelphia, where the Keystone Telephone Company remained isolated from the Bell network until 1945. In Clay City, Indiana, dual service continued until the late 1950s.[92]

The nuisance of dual service was the single best argument against competition in telephony, and the Bell companies harped on it constantly. "TWO SYSTEMS MAKE TROUBLE," insisted Bell publicity. Nonconnecting telephone systems were "a constant irritation," "an infernal nuisance," and "the height of absurdity." "What form will Satan appear in next?" asked Bell executive Walter Vincent in 1907. "One telephone system is sufficient and more than one a nuisance," AT&T president Theodore Vail wrote in the *Atlantic Monthly* in 1913. "Everyone desiring service must be connected with the same system." This was the meaning of Vail's famous slogan, "universal service."[93]

Dual service was not an intrinsic characteristic of independent telephony, simply the result of competition between any two nonconnecting systems. Yet while Bell publicity constantly attacked dual service, some independents felt obliged to defend it. Philadelphia's Edward Cooke said that choice between telephone systems was as natural and desirable as choice in any other part of life. "On the same desk where you object to having two telephones, perhaps you have two ink wells," he told a hypothetical critic of telephone competition. "You don't confine yourself to one door in your house. You don't object to half a dozen elevators in yonder store. . . . You undoubtedly find a plurality of rubber stamps a convenience." Independent spokesmen drew analogies between the telephone and other industries where duplication of competing services was taken as a matter of course. "From the railroad and telegraph companies, with their parallel lines and their duplicate machinery and organizations, to the grocery men, the ice men and the milk men, who . . . criss-cross each other's paths daily like a spider's web, we have duplication," said Indiana independent A. C. Lindemuth. "What forces the business man to take two telephones?" asked *Telephony* in 1906. "The same thing that forces him to advertise his goods in two newspapers in a town instead of one—to reach the people."[94] In any of these other industries, the independents argued, a single monopoly might seem to offer more efficiency, but only through free and open competition could the people be assured of good service and reasonable rates.

These analogies had obvious flaws. It did not matter to most people if their neighbors did not read the same newspaper or employ the same milk man as they did. Each of the elevators in a department store presumably opened onto every floor, and the existence of a second inkwell or rubber stamp did not reduce the utility of the first. If, however, a telephone user's friends and relatives used different telephone systems, the value of the telephone to the user decreased. Edward Cooke's only answer to this challenge was an odd, and oddly gendered, ad hominem attack. "That is the argument of the unthinking—the namby-pamby—the effete," he blustered. "It is hardly the opinion of the red-blooded doers of the world."[95]

Defenders of dual service had a more convincing argument when they compared the telephone situation before and after the arrival of competition. The "bugaboo of divided service" held "no terrors" for those who remembered the monopoly years, maintained Illinois independent E. J. Mock.[96] In most cities with dual service, subscribers to either the Bell or independent networks enjoyed connection to a larger number of telephones at a lower price than they had during the monopoly era. In some cities, prices had dropped so far since the coming of competition that subscribing to both telephone networks was still cheaper than subscribing only to Bell in the monopoly years had been. In Columbus, Ohio, for instance, Bell subscribers had paid $96 per year in 1894 to connect with a network of about two thousand telephones. In 1907, subscribers could pay $54 per year to connect with Bell's eleven thousand telephones in the city, pay $40 per year to connect with the independent's eleven thousand phones, or pay $94 per year to connect to both. "Competition has brought to the alleged burdened businessman who has to keep two telephones 20,000 more telephones to talk with and has handed him a $2 yearly rebate in the bargain," the Columbus independents concluded.[97]

What did ordinary consumers think of dual service? Was it the terrible nuisance Bell claimed? Attitudes to dual service changed over time but generally split along lines of class, geographic region, and occupation. A survey conducted by the Merchants Association of New York found "unanimous hostility" to dual service among "bankers, brokers, newspaper men, and public officials." Another survey in Los Angeles found that one hundred percent of businessmen but only two-thirds of housewives considered dual service an inconvenience.[98] Such a divide should not be surprising, because the cost of dual service was not borne evenly by different classes of telephone users. Many large businesses installed both companies' telephones and paid both companies' rates in order to connect with every potential customer. But few individual telephone users found it necessary to connect with every other telephone. On average, about one-fifth of the telephone users in cities with dual service found it necessary to install both telephones.[99] (The calculations of the Columbus independents were therefore somewhat exaggerated. A Columbus businessman in 1908 had twenty thousand more *telephones* to talk with than in 1894, but only about fifteen thousand more telephone *subscribers*.)

A detailed study of dual service in Louisville, Kentucky, in 1910 divided subscribers into occupational categories, offering a useful look at who bore the costs of dual service. Eighty-seven percent of Louisville's railroads had both telephones, as did 86 percent of the city's banks and trust companies, compared with 35 percent of the plumbers with telephones, 25 percent of the grocers, and only 9 percent of residential telephone subscribers.[100] It is clear that Louisville's business users were far more likely than residential users to bear the cost of dual service, and that among businesses, large-scale, capital-intensive enterprises were more likely than smaller, locally oriented firms to have both telephones.

Thus, the cost of duplication was unevenly borne. In effect, dual service was subsidized by larger and wealthier businesses—the clients whom the Bell companies were primarily organized to serve. Bell's leaders recognized the uneven class pattern of duplication. "If there are two companies, *the subscriber having considerable business interests* finds it almost indispensable that he should be connected with both companies," said AT&T president Frederick Fish in 1904. His successor Theodore Vail concurred: "If there are two systems, neither of them serving all, *important users* must be connected with both." Bell publicity insisted that the full value of the telephone depended on being able to reach anyone and everyone. "It must be a system that will afford communication with any one that may possibly be wanted, at any time," Vail wrote in 1910.[101] But not all telephone users shared this belief. Some were content to pay less and reach a smaller segment of the population.

In simple models of competition between two or more nonconnecting networks, one network will almost always reach a tipping point after which it is difficult for any weaker network to survive. Once most of the population joins network A, who will join network B? But real-world social dynamics, along with divisions of geography and class, complicated and delayed these effects. In choosing to join one telephone system or the other, turn-of-the-century telephone subscribers reconstructed and reinforced their existing social networks. In cities with dual service, new users naturally tended to join the network to which their friends and associates already subscribed. The choice between Bell and independent often split along lines of occupation or class. In Muncie, where General Kemper's son Arthur separated his friends into "Cream," "Buttermilk," and "Skimmed Milk" castes, the Bell or Central Union telephone was said to be the instrument of "the Cream set"—the city's wealthiest families and biggest businesses—while the local independent served the "Skimmed Milk crowds"—more middle-class families and the farmers of Muncie's hinterland. These dynamics reduced, though hardly removed, the nuisance of dual service competition.[102]

When such divisions also mapped on to ethnic or linguistic divides, the separation of networks could be dramatic and long-lived, as in the secret telephone system that allegedly flourished in San Francisco's Chinatown during the patent monopoly years.[103] One of the few cities in Canada to experience vigorous telephone competition was bilingual Montreal. Bell Canada was slow to recognize French Canadians as a promising market for the telephone and became so unpopular in French-speaking Quebec that independent companies owned and operated by French Canadians were able to capture much of the Francophone market. In Montreal, that business went to the cooperatively owned Compagnie de Téléphone des Marchands, or Merchants' Telephone Company, which had about fifteen hundred subscribers in 1905 and stayed in operation until 1913. That a small independent could survive so long in Bell Canada's home city was remarkable to some. But once a company became established in a given community as either the Francophone or Anglophone system, that identity quickly became self-reinforcing. So clear was the split between the French and English networks of Montreal that some said Bell Canada and the Compagnie des Marchands were not really in competition. "The Merchants' Telephone Exchange of Montreal cannot be classed as an active competitor insomuch as it caters only to the French speaking population and can never hope to be of universal benefit to the entire business community," argued one Canadian senator in 1901. "As it is, the Merchants' Company serves the Bell interests by furnishing Mr. Sise [Bell Canada's president] with an excuse for misleading the public into the belief that they are not a monopoly."[104]

Even when divisions between social networks were not this stark, predictable patterns of telephone adoption emerged. Telephone users whose contacts were primarily local, whose horizons and aspirations were generally contained in the counties or regions in which they lived, often found that their local independent system gave them all the telephone connections they desired. Those with contacts and interests farther afield, or those who hoped one day to make such contacts, were drawn to the more expensive but also more extensive Bell affiliate. And so these two orientations, with all the cultural and political implications each carried, were built into the physical networks that the Bell and independent companies constructed.

Connecting Town and Farm

After the price of telephone service, perhaps the most significant difference between Bell systems and their competitors was the actual physical shape of the networks each built. A resident of Muncie, Indiana, who wanted telephone service in 1905 had to choose whether to install a Central Union telephone or a Delaware and Madison County telephone—in other words, whether to connect to Bell or to the local independent. With a Bell or

Central Union telephone, that resident could speak to anyone else in Muncie who also used the Bell telephone. He or she could also make long-distance calls, for a fee, to Bell subscribers in major cities like Chicago, Philadelphia, and New York. With a telephone from the local independent, our Muncie resident could not talk to these distant financial centers. He or she could, however, call farmers in Roverton, ten miles outside of Muncie, or in Mill Grove Township, just over the county line. One could not make those calls with a Central Union telephone. The Bell affiliate had not built connections to those rural areas or those very minor towns and villages. AT&T's extensive long-distance network offered real advantages to certain kinds of telephone users, but so too did the "middle distance" connections of the local and regional independents.

While building networks in and between urban centers, the Bell companies had generally ignored rural areas and the suburban regions between cities and the countryside. Bell's early owners regarded these territories as less profitable than urban exchanges or long-distance service. And building rural lines was expensive, particularly when maintaining the level of technical quality to which the Bell companies aspired. "We cannot afford to cover that territory with toll lines of the character of construction which we have adopted as a standard," one Bell manager wrote in 1896.[105]

But by leaving the hinterland to the independents, Bell gave its opponents a powerful commercial and political weapon. The desire to connect with rural areas that Bell did not serve created an opening for the independents, not only in the countryside, but also in towns and cities. In particular, the desire of town and city merchants to have telephone links to farmers in their immediate hinterland led them to install or build their own independent phones. "The business men who are our patrons insist that farmers' lines are to them a necessity," wrote Iowa Bell executive Casper Yost in 1902, "and unless we give them connection with farmers' lines, then they must organize mutual companies in order to protect their trade which might go to some nearby town with which farmers' lines are connected."[106] Thus, there was competition between towns as well as between telephone companies to capture rural telephone connections. In building telephone networks between town and farm, merchants and farmers were building or protecting local networks of commerce and trade. Urban-rural interconnection also gave a political boost to independent telephony, as municipal governments closely tied to merchant groups granted franchises and concessions to independent companies willing to connect their rural customers and suppliers.

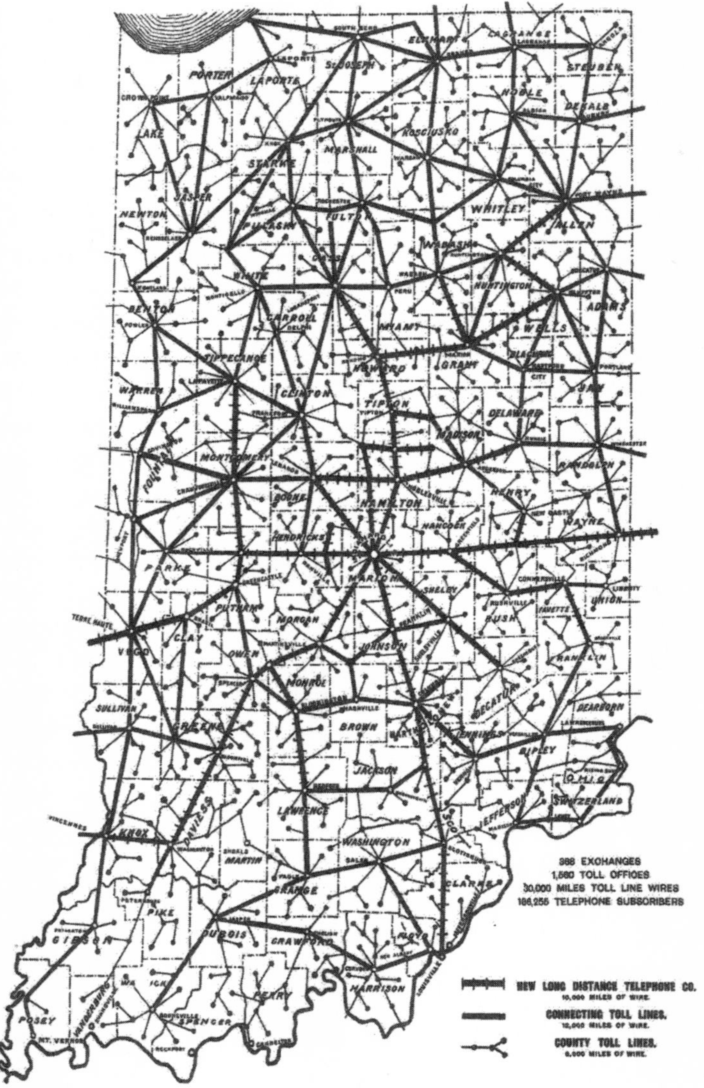

Figure 7. Independent Telephone Toll Lines of Indiana, 1905
Independent networks were distinguished by the density of their local and regional coverage rather than the distance of their reach. Compare to Figure 8, below. Reprinted in Canada, House of Commons, Select Committee Appointed to Inquire into the Various Telephone Systems in Canada and Elsewhere, *Report*, 2 vols. (Ottawa: King's Printer, 1905).

Contemporaries sometimes called this urban-rural interconnection "kitchen-to-farm" service.[107] In the jargon of a later age, the kitchen-to-farm call might have been dubbed one of the telephone's "killer applications"—a new use of the technology that opened up unforeseen markets and demand. Henry Barnhart declared the interconnection of town and farm the key to success in independent telephony. "Get into the field first and your case is won," he wrote.[108] When Robert and Helen Lynd studied Muncie in the 1920s, one question they asked their interview subjects was whether they had a telephone and what they used it for. Only a handful of replies to this question survive in the Lynds' papers. Nevertheless, five out of eight respondents mentioned calling between the city and the hinterland among their chief reasons for owning a telephone. None, by comparison, listed longer-distance calling as a reason for installing or keeping a telephone.[109]

In Central Canada, where Bell maintained a monopoly in most towns and cities, rural lines remained marginal. Although some Canadian farmers did establish their own telephone systems, there was little competition to induce Bell Canada's urban managers to connect with them. Bell Canada resisted interconnecting with rural systems or charged fees for interconnection that many small systems were unwilling to pay. Without links to urban exchanges, rural telephone systems in Central Canada remained "feeble efforts," in one observer's words. The director of a failed rural system near Waterloo, Ontario, put it succinctly: "There is no use in having a separate company in the rural districts without also being able to connect with the towns."[110]

By 1908, independent leaders in the United States declared it an "undisputed fact" that "the rural phone [had] been the potent weapon in the hands of the independents." But the real key to independent success in the Midwest was the development of regional networks that connected rural telephones to the town. A small-town Minnesota newspaper celebrated a new telephone line in 1901 by saying, "The merchants and farmers can hello back and forth as much as they wish to."[111] In the networks they built, the independents eschewed transcontinental connections and made physical the alliance of merchant and farm.

Long Lines and Short Lines

One strength of the Bell companies which the independents never duplicated was their national long-distance network. As the long-distance arm, and later the parent company, of the Bell System, AT&T invested tremendous money and effort into building a national long-distance network. Its executives regarded long-distance service as their major competitive weapon. In 1892, AT&T's long lines first connected New York and Chicago. In 1912, New York could speak to Denver. And by 1915, the Bell network crossed the continent, sending the human voice from New York to San Francisco, and interconnecting over nine million telephones.[112] This was a technological achievement that the independents never approached. Indeed, it was a feat unrivalled anywhere else in the world.

Theodore Vail and other AT&T executives argued that the independents would and should be defeated in the marketplace because of their inability to offer long-distance service on a truly national scale. "It is extremely important that we should control the whole toll line system of intercommunication throughout the country," AT&T executive George Leverett wrote in 1901. "We need not fear the opposition in a single place provided we control the means of communication with other places."[113] For over a century, histories of the telephone have taken AT&T's word that controlling long-distance service was essential to the company's ultimate victory over the independents.[114]

It is certainly true that the independent telephone movement in America failed to build a long-distance network on the scale of AT&T's. Independent companies did interconnect with one another and, in so doing, established profitable regional networks in the Midwest and upstate New York and on the West Coast. But these lines were never consolidated into a truly transcontinental network. It is far from evident, however, that this was the fatal weakness AT&T's publicity held it to be. Many independent executives disavowed any interest in offering long-distance service. Their customers, they said, were happy without it. "Ninety-eight percent of all telephoning is local, and of long distance telephoning, ninety-eight percent is to points within a radius of one hundred miles," said Frederick Dickson, the president of Cleveland's Cuyahoga Telephone Company, in 1905. "The Bell argument is that if we would connect with them, we could talk to Boston, New York, etc.," said William Crownover, the director of a small telephone system in rural Iowa. "True, we can if we have money enough to pay the bill," he continued, "but telephone service is not valued by the number of miles of naked wire we have at our disposal, but by the number of patrons in our immediate vicinity."[115]

Telephone traffic patterns seemed to bear out the independents' claims. As impressive a technological achievement as it was, AT&T's transcontinental network was no money maker. In its first few years of operation, the

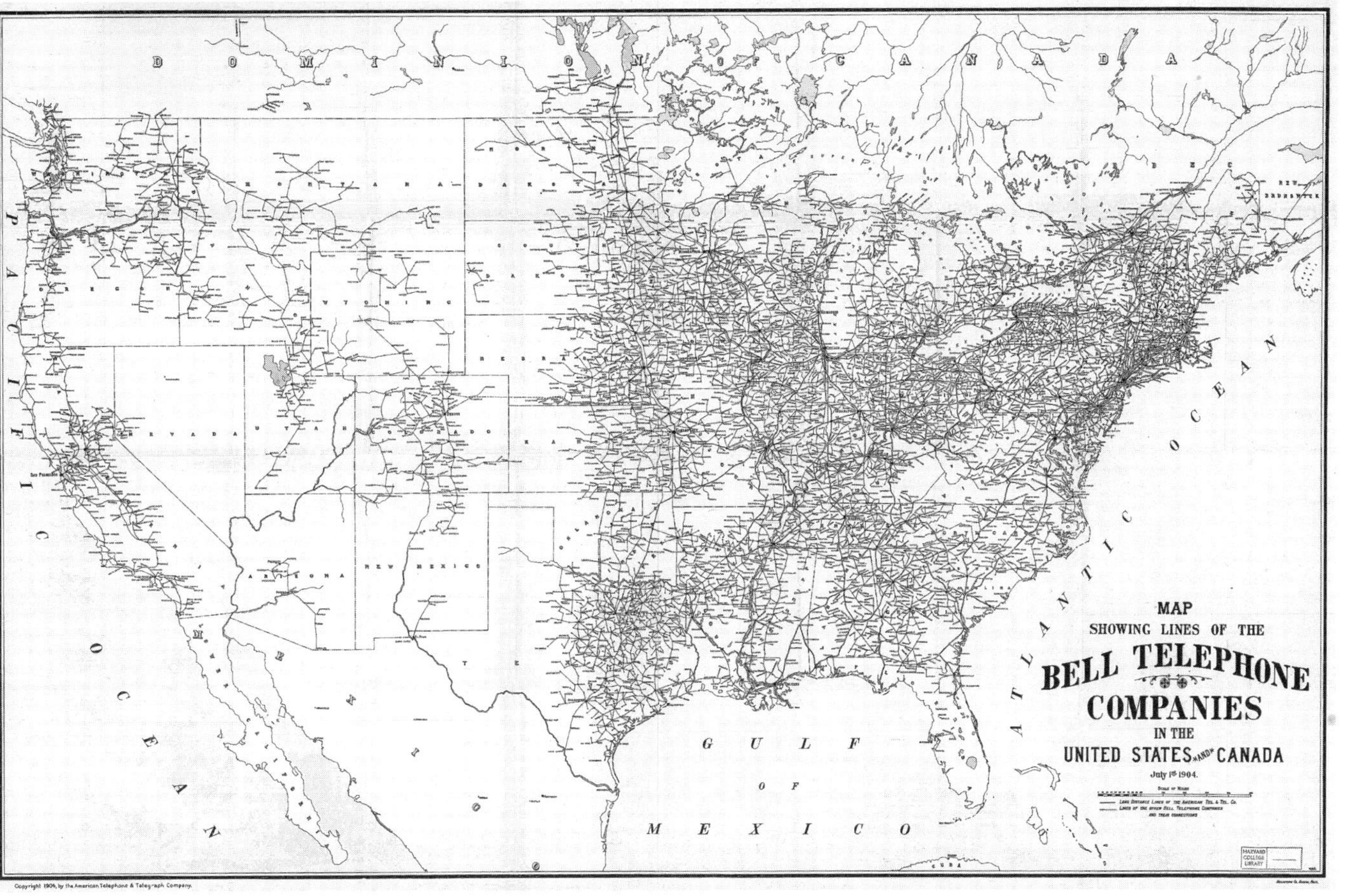

Figure 8. The Bell Long Distance Network, 1904
By 1904, AT&T's long distance lines connected half of the continent. Compare to Figure 7, above. Map Collection, Widener Library, Harvard University.

coast-to-coast network averaged only two calls per day. Dickson reported that the Bell exchange in Cleveland connected an average of forty calls per day between Cleveland and Chicago, and perhaps fifteen calls per day between Cleveland and New York. Dickson's company, by contrast, connected nearly ninety calls a day between Cleveland and the little village of Lorain, Ohio, and an equal number with dozens of other communities in the immediate vicinity.[116] Long-distance lines were expensive, both to build and to use. AT&T's decision to emphasize long-distance service imposed other technical choices on the system, including more powerful transmitters in each telephone, higher quality wires, and some sacrifice of local construction. Many subscribers "strenuously resist[ed]" the company's efforts to replace their early telephones with more expensive instruments suitable for long-distance transmission. The *American Telephone Journal* reported in 1907 that Bell customers in Wisconsin would "throw aside" their telephones rather than pay the extra fees for instruments "of the 'long distance' type."[117]

Middle- and working-class residents of Muncie, Cleveland, or rural Iowa had little reason to telephone New York or San Francisco, and no inclination to pay five or more dollars per call to do so. Wealthier Americans, particularly those involved in large region-spanning businesses, were more likely to have contacts and interests farther afield. Given the high costs, low revenues, and apparently limited demand for long-distance service, one could argue that the independents' failure to construct a transcontinental network gave them some competitive advantages over their Bell rivals in the 1900s and 1910s.[118] Successful independent systems found a market niche by offering less expensive service and a different sort of coverage than Bell. But the significance of this contest between locally and nationally oriented networks runs deeper than the commercial struggle between Bell and the independents. In the competitive heyday of independent telephony, these dueling networks embodied in poles and wire a debate between the defenders of a local or regional economy populated by small firms and the advocates of an increasingly integrated national or continental economy dominated by the new nation-spanning corporations.

It is clear from the language of independent propaganda that the principals in the telephone fight understood their struggle in this way. Independent leaders and promoters asked why a "foreign" company should be allowed to take money from midwestern consumers, or what business an Indiana farmer even had in calling San Francisco or New York. "Cleveland does not need the kind offices of a foreign corporation to supply its people with telephones," wrote Cuyahoga's Frederick Dickson in 1904. "Corporations should be owned by the people whose interests they attempt to serve, and the profits of the enterprise should be divided among those who make profits possible, and not go to swell the income of the residents of distant cities."[119]

Choosing between Bell and the independents thus became both personal and political. What kind of network did American telephone users want to be a part of? Where did their friends, livelihood, and future lie? The difference between AT&T's national network and the regional clusters of the independents ultimately represented alternate visions of American economic life. Bell's long-distance network was both symbol and agent of the new national economy. The kitchen-to-farm lines of the independents made concrete the older codependence of midwestern towns and farms. Independent networks recapitulated in physical form the independent movement's local orientation and dedication to the autonomy of regional commerce and life.

The Independent Idea

Henry Barnhart seemed to be a classic Main Street businessman and local booster, his interests and horizons closely centered on his own home town. "I like Rochester as no other place and I'll fight it out here," he often said. In 1902, Barnhart's friend Hugh Dougherty had to plead with him to travel to Indianapolis, a distance of less than one hundred miles, to mediate a conflict between two independent companies in another part of the state. "It might occur to you that it is asking too much to have you go to Indianapolis for this purpose, while the troubles are so far from you," Dougherty wrote, "but whatever affects the independent telephone business in the southern part of the state indirectly affects it in the northern part."[120]

Barnhart's political career would take him much farther than Indianapolis in the end. Still, he remained a small town Hoosier, or at least never forgot how to play the part. In 1912, when news reached Congressman Barnhart in Washington that his beloved fox terrier Bob had died, he read a long and sentimental eulogy for the dog into the *Congressional Record*. In eulogizing Bob, Barnhart might have been describing the independent movement, and the qualities he valued in it: "No boy ever soaked you . . .

and got away with it without being bitten; no man ever violently attacked you who didn't cry, 'Call off your dog'; and no one ever approached your home in an unseemly manner except to hear warning of your strenuous vigil. . . . Of course, you occasionally erred in judgment . . . and you were not sociable with other people. But your mistakes were due to your loyalty to me and mine."[121]

Was Barnhart's emotion sincere or a deliberate performance of rustic hokum? As is often the case with politicians, as it was with the rhetoric of independent telephony, it is difficult to tell and perhaps irrelevant. The independents as a whole shared Henry Barnhart's blend of small town parochialism and larger ambition. Defending their vision of a locally owned and oriented telephone industry ultimately required organizing, building, and lobbying on a national scale. These were tasks for which the independents often proved poorly suited or equipped. Like Bob, independent entrepreneurs could err in judgment and were not always sociable with others. But their loyalty to a more local, egalitarian model of telephony was real.

The rise and fall of the independent telephone movement was hardly, as partisans like Paul Latzke insisted, a second American Revolution. It was, however, an episode in which deep connections between physical infrastructure, corporate structure, and political culture were laid bare. The overheated rhetoric of the independent movement was of course a self-serving performance, but it shaped the development of the telephone just the same. The political economy and culture of the Midwest was particularly hospitable to certain kinds of localist and populist appeals. These appeals found expression in the vision of a people's telephone. Instead of matching AT&T's technical standards, the independents undercut its prices. Instead of linking the nation's leading financial centers, they connected modest towns to their own rural hinterlands. Instead of centralizing corporate and operational control, they radically decentralized. Competing ideas about the scale of social and economic life, about the value of different kinds of speech, and about the proper relationship of the periphery to the core, were thus mapped onto contests over the physical layout of poles and wires.

Our standards for evaluating historical schemes and visions often turn on whether or not they won out over their rivals, rather than on the intrinsic value of the ideas themselves. Yet by such a measure, each and every alternative to the present state of affairs must ultimately be judged a failure. The counterfactual question—could the independents have defeated

AT&T?—should not be posed too starkly. Total victory against such a resourceful opponent was imaginable but always unlikely. It was absolutely possible, however, to build a telephone system less centralized than AT&T's, one better oriented to regional economies, more responsive to local concerns, and friendlier to third-party innovation and experimentation. For this is exactly what the independents did.

When we try to look back toward the 1890s, 1900s, and 1910s, our line of vision is blocked by the Bell System's long decades of dominance in the mid-twentieth century. It is difficult to see AT&T's priorities and values as choices or accidents rather than nature or the market's laws. But there was indeed more than one path that the telephone could have followed. The independents offered a genuine alternative in their day, changing the industry and forcing the Bell companies to change themselves too. AT&T's victories in the decades to come were not the inevitable unfolding of some technological or economic destiny. They were politically constituted, just as the rise of independent competition had been. The independents themselves played an ironic role in that victory. The next chapter tells that story.

Chapter 5

The Politics of Scale

The "struggle for democracy," the crusading lawyer and future Supreme Court justice Louis Brandeis declared in 1910, was "the struggle of the small man against the overpowering influence of the big." The battle between the regional independents and the national Bell System was only one front in a larger war over the proper scale on which American social and economic life should be organized. Agrarian populism, urban progressivism, anti-monopoly sentiment, and municipal home rule—all these movements were, like independent telephony, reactions to the growth of giant corporations and assaults on what Brandeis famously called "the curse of bigness."[1] The hydras, spiders, and octopuses of the era's political iconography were testaments to the unease provoked by the size and geographic scale of the new business giants. It was not simply a matter, as Theodore Roosevelt would have had it, of distinguishing the good trusts from the bad. For many Americans, "bigness" itself was the crime.

As we have seen, the dueling telephone systems of this era embodied competing arguments about scale. Every wire strung was a prediction and a prescription about where information and commerce would travel, and about who should expect to talk to whom. Federal political systems can also be seen as arguments about scale—not "arguments" in the sense of being statements or lines of reasoning, but in the sense of requiring ongoing discussions or debates. In the United States and Canada, the U.S. Constitution and the British North America Act each laid out the relationship between different levels of government in terms of jurisdiction at different scales. Which powers and duties are reserved to the national government, which to the states and provinces, which to cities and towns? The founding documents are very clear on some subjects and not at all clear on others. Thus, a great deal of politicking in each country always concerns questions of jurisdiction, or arguments about scale.

Different political environments rewarded or encouraged different answers to these questions. Ideas about the telephone, and plans for its development, contained within them arguments about geographic scale. Such arguments found friends and adherents in a given region when they fit with or flattered the prevailing political structure. When they did not, such arguments struggled to find a home. Thus, the populism of the independent telephone movement grew not from some special quality of the midwestern soil, but from the political economy and history of the region, in particular from the interests and outlooks of municipal politicians and the history of their struggle against Bell. But the fight for the telephone was a travelling show. In both Canada and the United States, political struggles over the telephone moved from venue to venue, shifting from one level of government to another, and between different branches and departments of each government. When venues changed, the tilt of the playing field changed. Arguments and strategies that found favor with the Muncie city council might fail to impress a state commissioner, a federal judge, or a Canadian member of Parliament. The Department of Justice saw the telephone industry differently than the post office or the Interstate Commerce Commission. Political structures did not determine outcomes in any simple or automatic way, but they provided the environments in which individual actors had to fight for their interests and plans. In both Canada and the United States, the state channeled debates and constrained choices. To understand the outcome of both countries' battles over telephony and scale, we must appreciate the interplay of political structures and ideas.

George Monro Grant and Canadian Technological Nationalism

Since Confederation, and indeed well before, Canadians have been powerfully drawn to technological remedies for their cultural and geographic divisions. This tendency is hardly unique to Canadians, though its intensity and ubiquity may be. The continent is vast and the ties of Canadian nationalism weak, or so the theory goes. Only technology makes the nation possible and real. Each new development in long-distance travel or communication—railway, radio, satellites, the Internet—has thus been enlisted in the service of nation building and national unity. Of course, performances of technological nationalism play differently in different regions of the country, but there is one place they have almost always found an appreciative audience: the Canadian Parliament in Ottawa. Technological nationalism need not be seen as the expression of some essential Canadian character.[2] Like the technological populism of the American independents, technological nationalism in Canada is best understood as a symbolic strategy, the predictable result of a political economy that put control over transportation and telecommunication in an arena where such language would be welcomed and rewarded. As long as the telephone fell under Ottawa's jurisdiction, it made sense for Bell Canada to embrace a nationalist mission for the telephone. But when the venue changed, the efficacy of such a strategy changed too.

In the summer of 1872, Kingston clergyman and educator George Monro Grant accompanied his friend Sandford Fleming in a journey across the continent, surveying a route for the proposed Canadian Pacific Railway. Grant's account of that expedition, written to promote further railway and telegraph construction, was published in 1875 under the title *Ocean to Ocean*. The book, which simultaneously celebrated and lamented the fledgling confederation's vast size and rugged geography, became a best seller and a founding text of Canadian technological nationalism. Grant said the problem of distance was Canada's "Gordian knot," and long-distance communication its only solution. "Let there be a line of communication from the Pacific to the St. Lawrence, through a succession of loyal Provinces bound up with the Empire by ever-multiplying and tightening links," he wrote, "and the future of the Fatherland [Canada] and of the Great Empire of which she will then be only the chief part is secured." Steam-driven transportation and electrical communication would unite the far-flung nation and "open wide the door to the free play of sympathy and sentiment, and the broad Imperial patriotism of . . . kith and kin." Only then, Grant said, would Canada's unity and prosperity be assured.[3]

Grant and Fleming's railway to the Pacific, completed in 1885, remains the most mythologized example of Canadian technological nationalism, but the telephone was also cast in this nationalizing role. As we have seen, a national mission for the telephone was written into Bell Canada's founding charter in 1882. Ruling on James Carrel's fight with Bell Canada in Quebec City, the chief justice of Quebec had challenged Bell's federal charter on the grounds that it did not offer interprovincial service and therefore ought to be subject to provincial or municipal jurisdiction. But Bell Canada promised Parliament it would construct long-distance lines as soon as possible and so secured the crucial clause declaring Bell "a work for the general advantage of Canada."[4] That clause removed the company from provincial or municipal authority to the more tender mercies of the federal government. As earlier chapters have shown, this gave the company virtual immunity from both private competition and municipal reform. It also defined Bell Canada almost from the start as a national and nationalist undertaking, an agent of Canadian unity.

Even if actual construction was slow in coming, the idea of a national network seems to have taken hold at Bell Canada in the 1880s. While long-distance construction remained controversial among the Bell affiliates in the United States, Charles Sise and others spoke expansively of a Canada united by telephone wires. Sise often solicited American Bell for money to build long-distance lines in Canada, money the Bostonians were loath to provide.[5] When Bell Canada petitioned Parliament for permission to increase its capitalization in 1892, it again made efforts to unite the country with long-distance service the center of its appeal. "The company has already constructed nine thousand miles of long distance telephone [line] and are continuing that expenditure," said Senator Richard Scott. "Is that not a good service to the people of Canada?"[6] The apocryphal story about Theodore Vail commanding Sise in 1885 to "unify and save" his company with long-distance lines makes sense in this context.[7] Long lines and national unity became a central part of Bell Canada's corporate identity and mission well before the lines themselves were built. "Bell talks the long distance argument threadbare," grumbled one of the company's independent rivals in 1908.[8]

The Mulock Commission

In 1905, the creation of a parliamentary commission to investigate nationalizing the telephone triggered an important confrontation over the future of the telephone in Canada. Once again, questions of jurisdiction and the local, regional, or national character of networks would dominate the hearings and determine their outcome. In the first decade of the twentieth century, Prime Minister Wilfrid Laurier's Liberal government pursued a policy of free trade and close commercial relations with the United States. The Conservatives were then the party of nationalist protection. For several years, the Conservative opposition in Parliament, in particular the fiery

"Red Tory" William Findlay Maclean, had criticized the government for its cozy ties with Bell Canada. Laurier's minister of railways, Andrew George Blair, was also the president of the New Brunswick Telephone Company, a Bell affiliate. Two other Liberal senators were on the board of directors of both Bell Canada and New Brunswick Telephone. Under daily attack from Maclean in the House of Commons, Blair resigned his ministry in July 1903, though ostensibly for other reasons. But almost immediately after giving up his cabinet post, Blair was appointed to head the newly created Board of Railway Commissioners, Canada's first national regulatory agency and the body most likely to be tasked with regulating the telephone.

Maclean kept up his attacks and allied himself with the Union of Canadian Municipalities and others calling for tougher regulation of the telephone. By the spring of 1905, Laurier's government had received petitions from nearly two hundred counties and municipalities demanding that Bell Canada be prevented from erecting poles and wires without municipal consent. As pressure in Parliament mounted, Laurier announced the creation of a special committee of the House of Commons, the Select Committee on Telephone Systems, to report on the telephone industry and recommend regulatory action. The committee would be chaired by William Mulock, the postmaster general and a senior member of Laurier's cabinet. After the British post office took over long-distance telephony in the 1890s, Mulock made it no secret that he hoped to do the same in Canada. "I cannot see why it is not as much the duty of the state to take charge of the telephone as it is to conduct the postal service," he told Parliament in March 1905. Laurier did not share this conviction, but with his government perceived to be in Bell Canada's pocket and the opposition clamoring for reform, an investigatory commission seemed a prudent suggestion of action.[9]

Mulock's commission met for the first time in March 1905. Expectations among Bell's opponents were high, probably higher than warranted. Early remarks by William Maclean, who secured himself a seat on the committee, encouraged many to think that the government was on the verge of nationalizing the telephone network in its entirety. But a complete takeover of the industry was never Mulock's aim. The government's purpose, he told the press, should be to bring telephone service "within the reach of residents in a municipality through machinery to be established in the municipality itself," and also to furnish telephones "to the people in the sparsely-settled districts."[10] The plan that Mulock seemed most inclined to support was for the federal government to take over long-distance telephony, leaving local systems to be run either by municipal governments or private local enterprise. This plan was essentially the one that had been proposed by the Union of Canadian Municipalities in 1903. One of Mulock's first actions was to hire Francis Dagger, author of the Union's telephone plan, as a consulting expert and engineer. And the first witness Mulock called before the committee was Frederick Cook, mayor of Ottawa and president of the Union.[11]

It is interesting that a plan backed by municipal politicians to restore local control of the telephone placed such importance on a national long-distance network. Francis Dagger declared the long-distance telephone "so important a factor in the life of the people" that the industry's whole future depended on it. "The municipalities can never reach the summit of their ambition until the handicap of trunk [long-distance] lines worked by hostile agencies has been removed," he told Kingston's *British Whig* in the first days of the commission. Dagger went so far as to lecture the American independents on their neglect of long distance. "Even in your great republic, the time is not far distant when this problem of government ownership of the long distance service will have to be seriously considered," Dagger told a possibly bemused convention of independent telephone entrepreneurs in 1908. "If you are to continue to retain the local control of your independent systems . . . I am convinced that the long distance problem will have to be tackled."[12]

The plan of the Union of Canadian Municipalities to split ownership of local and long-distance lines appealed to municipal politicians by reconciling their desire for increased local control with the compelling vision of a national long-distance network. It may be significant in this regard that the union was dominated by central Canadian mayors. Nationalism in Canada has always been strongest in the power centers of prosperous Ontario and the English-speaking population of Quebec. Francophone Canadians, and Canadians in the eastern and western provinces, have been far more skeptical of Central Canada's "national" projects. Despite their municipal power base, union leaders like Frederick Cook of Ottawa; Thomas Urquhart of Toronto; and William Lighthall, mayor of Montreal's Anglophone suburb Westmount, were central Canadian nationalists. The "civic populism" of such men was not, like American populism, an expression of regional grievance or radical agrarian dissent.[13] And, of course, their battle with Bell Canada would be waged in Ottawa, where central Canadian nationalism went largely unchallenged and the ideal of a national long-distance network prevailed on both sides.

Mulock himself was the lone exception. He challenged the priority of long-distance service on the very first day of the select committee's deliberations:

> Take a farmer for instance. He is chiefly interested in having telephone communication with his immediate neighbours. Whilst trunk lines connecting his district with the whole telephonic world might be useful, I fancy that the farmer, from the standpoint of usefulness, would prefer a telephone system that will enable him to be in telephonic communication with his neighbours and with his market town. He would prefer that to what might appear to be a much more extensive service, but which would not be so useful to him, namely the long-distance.[14]

Here the postmaster general sounded very much like an American independent. But Mulock's views on long distance were in the minority in Ottawa. Witnesses on both sides of the telephone fight—Bell partisans like Charles Sise and Bell Canada's chief lawyer, Allan Aylesworth, but also municipal boosters like William Lighthall and Francis Dagger—all agreed on the importance and desirability of a coast-to-coast national network. Where they differed was on the question of who should own these long-distance lines, and whether the operation of long-distance networks could be separated from the operation of local exchanges.

Sise and Aylesworth quickly went on the offensive against what Aylesworth called "this new cult" of municipal ownership. But they attacked the idea of government-owned long-distance lines in a deliberate way. They did not, by and large, make ideological arguments about the virtues of private versus public ownership. Nor did they rely heavily on legal precedent or the shield of Bell Canada's original charter. Instead, they made technical arguments about the inherent nature of the telephone system, reading closely from the scripts of AT&T's master centralizers, John Carty, Edward Hall, and Theodore Vail. Allan Aylesworth told the select committee it would be "manifestly impossible" to "sever in the slightest degree" the control of local and long-distance systems. "It must manifestly be one system, one owned and connecting system." "You cannot very well separate local and long distance services," agreed Alexander Johnston. "They are so intimately associated that you cannot separate them."[15]

Bell's opponents disputed these claims. Local and long-distance service might be "intimately associated" from "the commercial standpoint," said one American independent appearing before the committee, but "from the electrical standpoint," he insisted, "they are entirely divorced." Hartley Dewart, a lawyer for the city of Toronto, argued that Parliament had failed to recognize "the dual character" of the telephone, and the technical distinctions between local and long-distance service. They operated on entirely different principles, he maintained, and it was a mistake to regulate them in the same way. Dewart urged Parliament to take control of Canada's long-distance lines and leave local networks to the municipalities. "But where is the line of demarcation?" challenged Joseph Bergeron, one of Bell's allies on the committee. Allan Aylesworth interrupted Dewart to offer his own reply. "It is all one system," he said.[16]

These exchanges were representative of the hearings in general. Aylesworth and Dewart were not engineers or scientists or even in the telephone industry; they were lawyers. Yet neither man and neither side based their arguments on matters of law. Instead, each made claims about the character of telephone technology, the inherent nature of the network, and the qualities they held to be manifestly obvious or true. Were telephone networks divisible or indivisible? Was the telephone local or national in character? As so often happened in the politics of telephony—as so often happens in the politics of any new technology—different interests fought for advantageous interpretations of the technology but insisted they were only hoping for its true nature to be revealed. The select committee of 1905 did not speak of choosing between alternative paths for the telephone. It behaved as if the character of the telephone had already been fixed and merely needed to be discovered. The Mulock commission did not see its job as deciding whether telephone networks should be locally or nationally oriented, but rather discovering what they "naturally" were and then devising regulatory instruments to conform to that inherent nature.

In a different arena, a different view of the telephone's inherent nature might have obtained. But Parliament was always going to hear arguments for nation-building networks more clearly than arguments for localism or municipal control. The committee's capitulation to technological determinism also worked to Bell Canada's advantage. Bell's near monopoly on the telephone business in Central Canada appeared to give them a similar monopoly on technical knowledge and expertise. From Sise on down, the Bell men spoke with authority and conviction as to the technical nature of the telephone. They presented reams of evidence and scoffed at their critics' expertise. "The people of any community would have a better telephone service under a system where there is some experience and some expert knowledge," said Allan Aylesworth. "A municipal service is an unmitigated nuisance to the citizens and an unmitigated loss." Most of the witnesses against the company were municipal politicians or rural entrepreneurs with limited technical expertise. The only witness on the other side with experience to match the Bell men was Francis Dagger, and Bell witnesses took pains to undercut and dispute his testimony.[17]

The Mulock commission began its work in March with a lion's roar but went out four months later as meekly as a lamb. At the end of May, William Mulock was called away to attend the Pacific Cable Conference in England. Adam Zimmerman, member of Parliament for Hamilton, Ontario, took over as acting committee chairman. The hearings were notably friendlier to Bell Canada from that point on. In July, with Parliament about to end its session for the year, Zimmerman declared that it would be impossible for the select committee to "come to any conclusions or to make any recommendations to the House."[18] In lieu of any recommendations, Zimmerman submitted the entire transcript of the commission's forty-three meetings and all documents submitted to the committee—more than two thousand pages of inconclusive testimony and often tedious detail. Laurier's government accepted the report without comment.

If Bell's opponents harbored any hopes that these three undigested volumes would spur the government to action, those died in October 1905, when William Mulock abruptly resigned from the government, because, he said, of his declining health. The next day, Wilfrid Laurier appointed none other than Allen Aylesworth, Bell's chief legal counsel, to take Mulock's seat in Parliament and his place as postmaster general of Canada.[19] When Parliament met again in 1906, the Conservative opposition—not just the irrepressible William Maclean but also Robert Borden, the leader of the opposition—called for a new select committee to continue the telephone inquiry. Instead, Laurier's government closed the issue by introducing legislation making all federally chartered telephone companies—in other words, Bell Canada—subject to regulation by the Board of Railway Commissioners. Thereafter, Bell would have to ask the board for permission to raise its rates, and independent or municipal systems could petition the board for permission to connect to Bell's long-distance lines. In practice, Bell Canada found regulation by the railway commission quite agreeable. In virtually every telephone case that came before the board between 1906 and 1921, the commissioners would rule in Bell's favor. The 1906 law also closed the door to any nationalization of the long-distance network or other radical action at the federal level. If regulation had to come, this must have been the form that Bell Canada most preferred.[20]

Bell's opponents were deeply dismayed by this turn of events. William Maclean was apoplectic. Bell Canada had many well-placed friends in Laurier's government, and it was widely and reasonably assumed that the company had used its influence to neuter the select committee and force Mulock out of Parliament. In a letter to AT&T president Frederick Fish, Charles Sise strongly intimated that Mulock's resignation was indeed the company's doing.[21] Mulock's claim of poor health seems dubious to say the least. He lived for four more decades, enjoying a long and distinguished career in the judiciary, becoming chief justice of the Province of Ontario, and celebrating his one-hundredth birthday in 1944.

It is tempting to speculate as to the backroom dealings that muzzled the Select Committee on Telephone Systems. But we should not attribute too much importance to this cabinet shuffle, hardly an unprecedented political maneuver, or feign great shock that wealthy corporations could shape government policy in their interest. Even before Mulock's departure, the select committee was hardly a powerful instrument for reform. And the range of options Laurier's government was willing to consider for the telephone had never been too broad. The shared assumptions of decision makers in Ottawa in 1905—in particular, the definition of the telephone as a national undertaking and the framing presence of technological nationalism—meant that many questions would never be raised and many options would not be considered. The goal of a single national long-distance network was not seriously questioned or debated in 1905, only the regulatory instruments necessary to achieve it. Nor did anyone challenge the naturalness of monopoly in telephone ownership, or the undesirability of direct competition. For all its drama, what may be most significant about the select committee of 1905 was how little was really at issue, and how many assumptions about the telephone had already come to be shared by Canadians on both sides of the telephone fight.

Public Ownership on the Prairies

In a federal system, no grievance need ever be truly abandoned. The legislation of 1906 settled the telephone question in Ottawa, at least for the duration of Laurier's long-lived Liberal government, but agitation against Bell Canada continued at the provincial and municipal levels—and moved west. The nationalist rhetoric that had served Bell Canada so well in Ottawa played rather differently in the Prairie Provinces. After 1905, the boldest steps against the company would be taken by the young provincial governments of Manitoba, Saskatchewan, and Alberta. The rapid growth of the Prairies and the creation of two new provinces at precisely this moment created a window of opportunity for Bell's opponents, in the form of an altered political economy where a very different sense of what was natural or inevitable would prevail.

Manitoba became a Canadian province in 1870. The neighboring provinces of Saskatchewan and Alberta were officially created in September 1905. While immense in area, the region that would become the three Prairie Provinces was thinly populated. Given Bell Canada's preference for serving commercial customers in urban centers, the Prairies did not seem an attractive territory for development. Labor and equipment were more expensive there than in Central Canada; the population was less affluent; wires had to be slung across far greater distances. Western settlers clamored for telephones, but Bell Canada was slow to respond. "We had better use of our money," Sise told the West. Bell's North West Department remained a minor adjunct of the company's business in Ontario and Quebec.[22] By 1896, the company had installed only two thousand telephones west of Ontario. Most of these were in Winnipeg, then the only prairie city of any size. Long-distance development was extremely limited. No lines linked the Prairie Provinces to British Columbia in the West, Ontario in the East, or even to each other. (One line south from Winnipeg to North Dakota did appear on company maps by 1904.)[23]

A great tide of immigration upset Bell's policy of indifference to the West. Between 1881 and 1911, Manitoba's population grew from 62,000 to 461,000; the population of the territory that became Saskatchewan rose from thirty thousand to 492,000; and the territory that became Alberta from barely one thousand to 374,000. In 1905, the year of the Mulock commission, the population of the Prairies broke one million. Bell's eight thousand telephones in the region were spread rather thin.[24] The northwest division made belated efforts to meet the growing demand, more than doubling its operations between April 1905 and December 1907. But ultimately Bell Canada had neither the capital nor the desire to keep up with such explosive growth. By 1904, the company had almost reached the upper limit of its authorized capitalization of $10 million, so the need to allocate resources carefully was acute. And the economics of serving the West were not changed completely by its population boom. Even a million residents could be scattered sparsely across the Prairies, and Bell still did not see rural farmers as a promising market. James Mavor, a Canadian political economist commissioned by AT&T to write a book critiquing government telephony on the Prairies, said the new immigrants were "primarily of the peasant class, with slender knowledge of the English language, self-contained habits, and small purchasing power." The West was not the sort of territory, and the new immigrants not the sort of customers, that Bell Canada preferred to serve. "It is obvious," Mavor concluded, that "the telephone business [in the West] could not grow otherwise than slowly."[25]

Bell's disdain for western consumers was more than reciprocated. The growth of the Prairie Provinces in the 1900s and 1910s was accompanied by growing alienation from Central Canada. Problems of economic development and uneven distribution of wealth fed a deepening distrust of eastern commerce in the West. The nationalist dreams of Ontario and English-speaking Quebec could be read on the Prairies as blueprints for the region's exploitation. Western farmers were particularly resentful of the Canadian Pacific Railway and their own dependence on it. And Bell Canada had infamously partnered with the railway, securing an exclusive arrangement to install telephones in CPR stations and build telephone lines along the railroad's rights of way. Bell also wrapped itself in the rhetoric of technological nationalism pioneered by the builders of the Canadian Pacific. This made it extremely easy for western Canadians to see and portray Bell Canada as one more agent of Central Canada's economic imperialism.[26]

Charles Sise dismissed agitation against Bell Canada in the West as "a purely political matter," cooked up by opportunistic politicians rather than stemming from genuine public unrest. Some historians have accepted this characterization; some have not.[27] But the move for public ownership of the telephone on the Prairies came from the same place as the Mulock commission, the Indiana rate law, and the whole independent telephone movement. It grew out of local battles with Bell in the 1880s and 1890s, and the realization that municipal governments could not tackle the telephone monopoly on their own. What was different is that, when action against Bell came to fruition in the Canadian West, it came not in the streets of municipalities but in the legislative assemblies of the new provincial governments. This would shape the form and impact of telephone populism on the Prairies. Like their countrymen in Ontario and Quebec, and unlike the American independents, telephone reformers in the Prairie Provinces generally rejected competition as a means of regulating the telephone industry. Most accepted the idea that the telephone was a natural monopoly and saw government ownership as the best course of action. And although these reformers were interested in municipal telephone systems, political structures ultimately pushed the Prairies toward provincial solutions—another example of political economies shaping and channeling ideas and reforms.

Telephony in the Northwest Territories, the vast region from which the provinces of Alberta and Saskatchewan would be carved in 1905, remained embryonic and disorganized before the turn of the twentieth century. Scattered lines and exchanges were installed and operated by Bell Canada, various telegraph companies and local entrepreneurs, the Canadian Pacific Railway, and even the Northwest Mounted Police. Bell made few friends in the region as it tried to control and rationalize the business. In western Canada, as one historian put it, Bell could "achieve unpopularity in two main ways: (a) by going into a town; (b) by staying out."[28] In 1892 and again in 1903, the Legislative Assembly of the Northwest Territories rejected bills that would have affirmed Bell Canada's federal charter and its ability to erect poles and wires in the territories without municipal consent. In Ontario and Quebec, where Bell had secured such legislation in the 1880s, municipal politicians were basically powerless against the company and always had to petition provincial or federal governments for assistance or relief. In the Northwest Territories, however, the municipal and territorial authorities were very often the same men. The five-member municipal law committee of the Legislative Assembly that denied Bell's request for an ordinance in 1903 contained four municipal politicians and one manager of an independent telephone cooperative. Their response to Bell's petition was perhaps preordained.[29]

Bell's failure to secure an act affirming its federal charter in the territories did not mean its charter was invalid there; it meant that nobody knew if it was valid. So the company continued to establish exchanges in markets it deemed promising, while municipalities and independent entrepreneurs established their own systems too. In 1899, the province of Manitoba also passed legislation permitting the creation of municipally owned telephone exchanges. Dozens of municipal and quasi-municipal independent systems were established in Manitoba and the Northwest Territories, but most remained tiny and remote, typically connecting between five and fifty telephones. Bell Canada refused as a matter of course to connect such systems to its long-distance lines.[30] The largest independent system in the territories was the Edmonton District Telephone Company, established in 1887. By 1904, it had 390 subscribers and 150 miles of wire, connecting telephones in Edmonton to the neighboring settlements of Strathcona, St. Albert, and Fort Saskatchewan. Bell Canada offered to buy the system in that year for $12,500 but was outbid by the city of Edmonton, after a referendum there found citizens overwhelmingly in favor of municipal ownership. The city then encouraged the smaller communities connected by its wires to create their own exchanges in a joint municipal network.[31]

This was the situation in 1905, when the Select Committee on Telephone Systems briefly raised and then deflated hopes of federal action on behalf of municipal telephony. In the summer of 1905, while the Mulock commission was compiling its indigestible report, the Union of Canadian Municipalities held its annual general meeting in Winnipeg, Manitoba, a symbolic shift in venue from Central Canada to the West. Rodmond Roblin, the Conservative premier of Manitoba, attended the meeting with interest. Roblin had launched his career in Manitoba politics fighting the monopoly privileges of the Canadian Pacific Railway. In 1901, he secured an agreement that broke the CPR's monopoly in Manitoba by leasing several hundred miles of track to the Canadian Northern Railroad, a quasi-public competitor that gave the province control over its freight rates in return for the lines. Like many on the Prairies, Roblin viewed Bell Canada as the CPR's junior partner in exploiting the West. In September 1905, when the new provinces of Alberta and Saskatchewan were created, many former municipal politicians with similar sensibilities filled their new legislative assemblies.[32]

In November 1905, Roblin's government announced its plan to create a jointly owned municipal-provincial telephone network in Manitoba. This was a variation on the scheme Francis Dagger and the Union of Canadian Municipalities had proposed for Canada as a whole in 1903, with municipalities running their own local systems and the province owning the long-distance lines between them. Confident of widespread hostility to Bell Canada, Roblin's Conservatives hoped to make the telephone a winning issue in the next provincial election, until their Liberal opposition also came out in favor of the plan. Trade unions, farm organizations, and town councils also embraced a provincial takeover of the telephone. A similar proposal was one of the very first acts of the new Liberal government in Alberta, which sat for the first time in March 1906. Calgary Mayor William Henry Cushing, who became Alberta's first minister of public works, denounced Bell's federal charter as "the most pernicious and iniquitous piece of legislation that has ever been perpetrated upon people claiming to be free." "The Alberta Government believes that if it has any function at all," Cushing declared on another occasion, "it is to protect the people from such monopolies."[33] Saskatchewan's first government, led by the pro-Ottawa Liberal Walter Scott, was slower to move on the telephone question; there it was taken up by the opposition, Frederick Haultain's Provincial Rights Party. But by the spring of 1907, under rising pressure from municipalities and farm and trade organizations, Scott's Liberals also endorsed the principle of public telephone ownership and hired Francis Dagger to advise them on the matter.[34]

In Manitoba, Roblin's government initially hoped to expropriate Bell's operations in the province, but Ottawa denied their authority to do so. Roblin then offered to purchase Bell's operations in Manitoba, but the company at first refused to sell. Finally, the province began constructing its own lines at Winnipeg, in direct competition with Bell Canada. Charles Sise wrote to American Telephone and Telegraph for aid, but that company was in turmoil too, in the midst of the takeover by New York financiers that pushed the Bostonians off its board and returned Theodore Vail to power. At this point, Sise wrote in his journal, he had a choice: "to lose the territory with the money or without it." Sise chose to take the money. Without conducting any kind of formal valuation, Sise told Roblin he wanted $4 million for his company's facilities in Manitoba. In January 1908, the province paid Bell Canada $3.4 million for its holdings—over loud objections from Francis Dagger that this was at least $1 million too generous. A few months later, Bell Canada sold its considerably smaller holdings in Alberta for $650,000, and in Saskatchewan for about half that amount.[35]

Bell Canada had lost control of the Prairies but was well compensated for its withdrawal and had reason to be satisfied with the results. Sise sacrificed some of his company's geographic scope in order to maintain its profit margins, a decision that William Forbes and the Bostonians who originally hired Sise would likely have endorsed. Despite its rhetorical commitment to building a single national network, Bell Canada was willing to trade away territory in order to protect its core investment in Central Canada's populous urban corridor. The nationalist rhetoric and the federal charter that had made Bell Canada invulnerable in Ontario and Quebec were far less effective in the West, where rapid growth and the creation of new provinces transformed the political environment and shifted the balance of power toward the company's foes.

The fortunes of the prairie telephone systems in the years that followed offer mixed evidence on the virtues of public ownership. The early years of government telephony in Manitoba were rocky. Each city, town, and village in the province held a referendum on whether to establish a municipally owned exchange. Although a slight majority of the total vote was in favor of the Roblin plan, 67 out of 122 municipalities elected not to establish their own systems. Already committed to government ownership, Roblin's government saw little choice but to go beyond its hybrid municipal-provincial plan and take full control of both long-distance and local telephone service across the province. Upon taking control of the industry, the province lowered the price of both urban and rural telephones and extended service rapidly, growing the network from seventeen thousand subscribers in 1908 to thirty-six thousand in 1910. But it also incurred and then concealed large financial losses. After deficits grew too big to hide, an investigation in 1912 exposed evidence of gross mismanagement. Rates were raised sharply and Roblin's Telephone Commission forced to resign. Opponents of public ownership in both Canada and the United States made hay of the mess in Manitoba. The province's telephone system was only put on a secure footing after 1915, when a separate scandal involving the construction of public buildings exposed corruption at every level of the Manitoba government. Roblin and his cabinet were forced to resign en masse, and criminal charges were brought against them all.[36] The Manitoba Telephone System was reorganized as a government-owned but independently operated crown corporation and escaped most of the opprobrium heaped on Roblin's administration. For the rest of the century, it was quite successful on the whole. Its rates were consistently among the lowest in Canada and its service regarded as excellent. Now known as Manitoba Telecom Services, the corporation was privatized in 1996.[37]

Alberta's early years in the telephone field were less dramatic but also had their ups and downs. As in Manitoba, the original plan to split long-distance and local service was revised when many municipalities proved unready or unwilling to operate their own systems. Alberta's Department of Public Works thus took over both local and long-distance lines in most communities. One important exception was Edmonton, already in the telephone business, which operated its own successful municipal system until 1995. Alberta's Department of Public Works avoided the scandals seen in Manitoba but remained underfinanced through the 1910s and 1920s. When the hard times of the 1930s hit, the cash-starved provincial government was forced to turn over its rural telephones to farmers' cooperatives, moving back toward the original hybrid plan. Born out of desperation, this move proved astute. A renaissance of rural telephone construction ensued, more than doubling the number of rural telephones in the province during the very worst years of the Depression. In 1958, Alberta shifted control of telephony to a crown corporation called Alberta Government Telephones. AGT and Edmonton's municipal system, EdTel, both returned to prosperity and growth in the postwar years. Like Manitoba Telecom, they were privatized in the 1990s, and the two corporations merged with British Columbia's BCTel to become Telus Communications in 1999.[38]

The most successful of the prairie telephone systems was Saskatchewan's. Only Saskatchewan followed the blueprint laid out by Francis Dagger and the Union of Canadian Municipalities from the start. Unlike Manitoba and Alberta, the Saskatchewan government took over only the long-distance lines between towns and cities and some of the largest urban exchanges. For most local and rural service, the province encouraged the development of municipal systems, private independents, or rural farmers' cooperatives, building a mixed public-private-cooperative network that soon became the envy of other Canadian provinces. By early 1913, the portions of the network directly under provincial control had quadrupled in size and connected with five new municipal systems, fifteen private independents, and 337 rural telephone companies. The provincial network had also turned a profit, something Manitoba and Alberta's systems would not do for decades. Although long-distance service remained more expensive in Saskatchewan than elsewhere, Saskatchewan's system as a whole cost the province far less than Manitoba's and Alberta's had cost them, and it charged its subscribers much less than those in Ontario and Quebec. By splitting ownership of long-distance and local lines—in other words, by doing precisely what AT&T and Bell Canada had maintained was impossible—Saskatchewan's hybrid telephone system outpaced both Bell and the more centralized government systems.[39] Through the Depression and into the postwar years, it consistently outperformed its neighbors, and SaskTel was at the start of the twenty-first century the only government-owned system remaining in the Canadian telephone industry. The province of Saskatchewan is still known as Canada's "cooperative province" for its long history of successful collectives, co-ops, and crown corporations. Most famously, Saskatchewan created Canada's first government-run health insurance program in the 1960s. It would go too far to attribute this achievement to the province's earlier success in telephony, but it is certainly true that the political economy of Saskatchewan has long been receptive to local innovation and experimentation in organizational forms.[40]

Patchwork Nation

Independent telephony was not wholly extinguished in Central Canada after the legislation of 1906. Small independent systems actually grew in Ontario and Quebec in the decade after the Mulock commission, reaching their relative peak between 1915 and 1920. In Ontario, this was largely the doing of Francis Dagger, whom the province hired as supervisor of telephone systems in 1910. There as in Saskatchewan, Dagger encouraged the formation of semicooperative municipal systems for small towns and rural areas. Over one hundred small and remote communities in Ontario established their first telephone service under the Dagger plan. These systems were independent of Bell Canada, but the rural independents in Ontario after 1910 should not be confused with the kind of independent competition Bell faced in the midwestern United States. Bell Canada retained its monopoly in Ontario's major cities and on the long-distance lines between them. The new Ontario independents were tiny systems in remote and rural areas. They never competed with Bell in its profitable urban markets, nor did they pose any real challenge to the company's social or political legitimacy. Indeed, they brought telephones to marginal areas Bell Canada had little interest in serving and reduced pressure on the company to expand beyond its profitable urban base.[41]

Bell Canada's unpopularity in French-speaking Quebec created a slightly larger niche for independent telephones there. As we have seen, Bell Canada under Charles Sise did not consider French Canadians a promising market for the telephone and did little to invite their business or even their goodwill. Independent entrepreneurs exploited this opening, reaching out to French-speaking customers in Quebec and emphasizing their own Francophone origins. Some were extremely successful. Jacques Demers's Compagnie de Téléphone de Métis began among the tiny villages of the lower St. Lawrence and grew into a substantial regional network that still exists today.[42] For many years, telephone networks in Quebec would recapitulate the province's linguistic and cultural divides, with Bell Canada serving most English speakers and independents serving many French. "Racial sentiment has contributed largely to Dr. Demers' phenomenal success," said the *Canadian Engineer* in 1907. "All his work has been achieved in that part of eastern Canada where the fleur de lis reigns supreme."[43] Such divides cast doubt on the allegedly unifying qualities of the telephone in Canada.

On Valentine's Day 1916, two hundred Canadian businessmen gathered in Montreal's Ritz-Carlton Hotel to hear a telephone conversation with an equal number of leading citizens at Vancouver's Globe Theatre. The event was touted as the first "trans-Canada" telephone call. "Science has placed at naught time and distance and the human voice is wafted from ocean to ocean across thousands of miles of hills and plains," opined the Vancouver *Province*. "The East and West have met, have joined, and are as one." It did not seem to mar the festivities, but neither was it stressed that the long-distance network the Canadians had gathered to inaugurate was largely the work of an American corporation. Nobody present was so gauche as to remark that their proclamations of Canadian unity and triumph were carried for almost the entirety of their journey along AT&T lines—from Montreal down to Buffalo and then west through Chicago, Omaha, Salt Lake City, Portland, and finally north to Vancouver. Nor was it mentioned that Montreal lies six hundred miles west of Canada's Atlantic coast. It would be five more years before true coast-to-coast telephone service in Canada, and sixteen more years before one could speak across the nation on entirely Canadian wires.[44]

A similar ceremony had been held thirteen months earlier to celebrate the United States' first coast-to-coast telephone call, kicking off a series of demonstrations in both countries. By this time, AT&T was well on its way toward reconsolidating the telephone industry in the United States under its control. The industry in Canada, by contrast, remained deeply divided by political boundaries, geography, and corporate structure. No telephone wires crossed the Canadian Rocky Mountains, a situation that forced British Columbia Telephone to route even relatively short-distance calls from the coast to the interior down through the United States via Washington and Montana. There were another thousand miles of wilderness between Winnipeg and Sudbury where no telephone poles stood, and a third long break in the wires between Quebec City and Saint John. Corporate divisions mirrored these geographic barriers. Bell Canada remained the country's largest telephone company and dominant in the urban centers of Ontario and Quebec, though Quebec's independents had captured a significant portion of the French-speaking market there. The eastern provinces were served by the New Brunswick Telephone Company and the Maritime Telephone and Telegraph Company. In the far west was British Columbia Telephone. Originally Canadian-owned, BC Tel was purchased by Theodore Gary and Company in 1926, becoming part of the Missouri-based independent's growing collection of telephone and utility companies around the world. Completing the map of telephony in Canada were the publicly owned systems of Manitoba, Alberta, and Saskatchewan.

The obstacles that hindered the construction of a single Canadian telephone network were the same obstacles that have always faced national unity in Canada—vast distances, rough terrain, quarreling regions, and linguistic and cultural divides. But jurisdictional regimes were the crucial element shaping outcomes in Canadian telephony. The language of technological nationalism that was so useful to Bell Canada when dealing with the federal government in Ottawa, or with Anglophone elites in Ontario and Quebec, did little to win the company favor with the new provincial governments of the Prairies. For all the talk of unification through technology, the telephone network that Canadians ultimately created was a patchwork quilt of separate telephone systems with a complicated mix of Canadian and American ownership and public and private firms.

One thing that is striking about the rhetoric of telephony in Canada is the way Bell Canada's spokesmen remained committed to the AT&T argument that coast-to-coast long distance demanded centralized control, even as events belied these determinist claims. "It is all one system. . . . It must manifestly be one system, one owned and connecting system," Bell counsel Allan Aylesworth told the Mulock commission in 1905. He warned of disaster if control of the telephone was decentralized or allowed to break along regional lines: "we should have the most unmitigated and unbearable nuisance that could be imagined, namely not one connected system of telephoning from town to town and from house to house in different parts of the country, but a series of disconnected cells, so to speak, not having any connection with another, not being under any one general management, but each part of it under a different and continually changing management."[45]

Aylesworth's "unbearable nuisance" is essentially what Canadians created: seven major regional systems, each enjoying a monopoly or near monopoly within their own territory, but also interconnecting with dozens of much smaller local systems. And Canada's patchwork network has served for over a century. Its alleged impossibility did not prevent Canada's public and private telephone companies from establishing uniform standards and practices for interconnection. Nor did it stop them from coming together in the 1920s to build a true coast-to-coast line on entirely Canadian soil.[46] Yet even after this system had been in operation for decades, many at Bell Canada insisted it should not function as well as it did. Bell engineers dubbed the country's decentralized long-distance network "the bumblebee of communications," referring to the myth that it ought to be impossible for bumblebees to fly.[47] In different regulatory environments, it would seem, the impossible becomes possible, the unnatural natural. Yet such was the strength of AT&T's rhetorical commitment toward end-to-end system integration that not even the Canadians' empirical success in constructing an alternate technical and corporate organization convinced them that it could actually be done.

Reconstructing the Bell Monopoly in the United States

In the United States, as in Canada, questions of scale and jurisdiction played a powerful role in shaping the fight over the telephone. Was the telephone a creature of municipal government and a tool for local service? Was it an instrument of interstate commerce, properly regulated by the federal government? Was it both, or something in between? As in Canada, venues mattered. Different arguments played differently in different regions, departments, and jurisdictions. Though the regulatory regime that emerged by the mid-1920s was perhaps more uniform in the United States than Canada, the road to that regime was winding and indirect.

The outcome of this story has to be seen as a victory for the American Telephone and Telegraph Company, but AT&T was hardly the only actor on the stage. Municipal, state, and federal regulators all played a role, even if they were often reacting more than acting. Telephone users, especially organized business groups, were also key players in the construction of Bell's regulated monopoly. They had helped launch the independent movement in the 1890s, and their defection by the 1910s and 1920s was an important contributor to its demise. And the independents themselves were highly active participants in the political struggles of the 1900s and 1910s. They did not win these battles in the end. They rarely agreed on the best course of action, and disputes over strategy split the independent movement at perhaps the most critical juncture. But it is remarkable how active individual independents remained in this political endgame. Often it was they who set the agenda, spurring action and reaction by both government and AT&T.

To an extent that few histories of the telephone have acknowledged, the Bell monopoly was broken by competition and then reconstructed, city by city, in the years after 1907. Business users played a crucial role in the monopoly's fall and rise. Local merchant associations, chambers of commerce, and boards of trade brokered negotiations between city governments, the Bell affiliates, and their independent rivals. Through both forced and voluntary buyouts and interconnections, dual service gradually came to an end in city after city, and a consensus among business users for some kind of regulated monopoly emerged.[48] When state governments began establishing telephone regulatory commissions in large numbers, they were reacting to this new consensus. The regulatory structure of the state commissions was ultimately embraced from above by Theodore Vail, but its details bubbled up from below in the interactions of local governments, telephone managers, and business users.

No group was more important in this shift than the business community—not the great titans of industry like Morgan and Rockefeller, but local and regional businessmen, those Main Street merchants around the country whose capital and support had been so crucial to the rise of independent telephony. Urban businessmen had, of course, been Bell Telephone's first and most important customers. Bell's old Boston owners built their whole strategy around such users, so it is hardly surprising that their views on the telephone had harmonized in certain ways. Yet as we have seen, many business users grew fiercely unhappy with the nineteenth-century telephone monopoly and backed independent telephone systems in the 1890s and early 1900s in a bid for cheaper service and more local control. The independents called themselves a movement for all the people, but they would never have gotten as far as they did without this particular group of people as customers, investors, and political allies. When local business leaders around the country began to return to the Bell fold, believing that they would be better served by one big telephone system than by competition, the independent movement lost a key constituency and much of its motive force.[49]

New York City's businessmen were important early movers in this shift. Bell's New York Telephone Company enjoyed a lucrative monopoly in the city; in 1904, AT&T vice president Edward Hall estimated that Manhattan alone accounted for one-fifth of all Bell operating company profits.[50] Independent entrepreneurs had lobbied for years to establish a competing system in New York. But business interests there were divided on the desirability of telephone competition, a split reflected in two of the city's leading commercial associations. The New York Board of Trade and Transportation supported the introduction of competition and in 1905 pressured the state government to launch a new investigation of the telephone situation in New York. The Bell company then reached out to a rival commercial group, the Merchants Association of New York, opening their books to that association and inviting them to perform their own private investigation of the company. In exchange for a reduction in telephone rates, the Merchants Association reported back to Albany that no public investigation of New York Telephone would be necessary and blocked an application by the independent Atlantic Telephone Company to compete in the city against Bell.[51]

The Merchants Association then published a report praising the Bell System and criticizing competition in telephone service. It conducted a nationwide survey of businessmen and other professional telephone users and reported growing dissatisfaction with the costs of dual service and duplication. The vast majority of those polled did believe that competition had been a good thing, forcing the Bell companies to offer better service and lower rates. Only fourteen respondents said it would be preferable to return to conditions prevailing before the coming of the independents; 1,245 respondents said it would not. But while almost all of those surveyed credited competition with making the telephone accessible and affordable, a growing number believed that its work was now done. A report the next year by Boston utility lawyer George Anderson reached the same conclusion. The lesson "taught by competition in the middle West has been taken to heart by telephone managers in other parts of the country," Anderson said. "It . . . does not at all follow that further demonstration . . . needs to be made."[52] Like the Merchants Association, Anderson made clear that business users, particularly larger firms with extensive geographic connections, bore the added cost of dual service. As more and more American businessmen came to work for such firms, or define their own interests in this way, support for independent competition dwindled and support for a single national system grew.

AT&T wasted little time in publicizing the Merchants Association report. Business groups around the country began to echo its findings, signaling a new willingness to accept monopoly in the telephone field in exchange for some kind of rate regulation. This transition began in the urban centers of the northeast, where the Bell monopoly was well entrenched and where businessmen were first and most inclined to see themselves as part of a national business community. Yet by the start of the 1910s dissatisfaction with telephone competition had spread well beyond New England and New York. It was not so surprising when the National Civic Federation, a nationally oriented organization of moderately progressive business elites, came out against competition in the telephone industry and in support of regulation by commission in 1909. But when local business groups in former independent hotbeds like Cincinnati, Milwaukee, or Indianapolis reached the same conclusions, a significant shift was clearly underway.[53] The choice between the intensive local networks of the independents and the extensive long lines of the Bell System had been, as we have seen, a kind of referendum on different models of the economy. By the 1910s, more and more telephone users, even in small to middle-sized midwestern cities, were willing to cast their lot with a national network. Still, they did not want to give up the local connections the independents had built. Taking their cues from local business, municipal governments in the Midwest stopped granting franchises to new independents and began pushing existing independents to interconnect with Bell.[54]

Internal histories of the Bell System and many outside histories written in their wake praise AT&T and Theodore Vail for embracing government regulation of the telephone industry in an act of farseeing corporate statesmanship. Vail himself was happy to take this credit, claiming in 1913 that "we believe in, and were the first to advocate, state or government control and regulation of public utilities."[55] In truth, the Bell companies had fought bitterly against regulation at the state or local level for decades. It is true that after 1907, Vail joined a growing consensus for utility regulation, provided such regulation was, in his words, "independent, intelligent, considerate, thorough and just, recognizing . . . that capital is entitled to its fair return."[56] But regulation of the telephone was not new in 1907. As we have seen, the telephone was politically constructed and contested from its very beginnings, actively and aggressively regulated by town and city governments around the country. What was new was a shift in the main arena of regulation, from the municipal level of government to state commissions and in some cases federal courts. Vail and AT&T endorsed this change of venue, understanding that the new state regulatory commissions would be far friendlier to the Bell System than most municipal governments had been.

By 1910, there was growing momentum for state regulation of the telephone industry. The eclipse of municipal power over the telephone by state commissions was part of a broad shift in this era that moved responsibility for many utilities from the cities to the states. The traditional narrative of reform-minded statehouse Progressives vanquishing corrupt urban machines has some truth, but has been overdrawn. Progressive reformers lined up on both sides of the debate between state commissions and municipal home rule. In most places, advocates of state-level utility control, backed by powerful business leaders like the National Civic Foundation, gained the upper hand in the 1910s. Before 1907, eight states had tried some form of telephone regulation, such as Indiana's experiment with rate control. Between 1907 and 1914, thirty states would pass legislation regulating the telephone, with many of them establishing permanent regulatory commissions. Within another decade such commissions could be found in nearly every state.[57]

After decades of wrangling with mayors and city councilors in hundreds of volatile municipal venues, the move to state regulation was a relief for the Bell companies, but often a blow for the independents, who owed their origins to these same municipal fights. Particularly in the Midwest, where independent telephony and local government had been so closely intertwined, state governments were far friendlier to Bell interests than the municipalities had been. In Indiana, for example, Republican Governor Frank Hanly was known as an ally of Bell's beleaguered Central Union Telephone Company, while the Republican Mayor of Indianapolis, Charles Bookwalter, was clearly a friend to the city's competing independent. One Central Union manager told his superiors at AT&T that state-level regulation was his company's "only hope" against hostile municipal governments and independent rivals.[58]

The Bell companies did not find every aspect of the state commissions to their liking. In particular, they balked at regulation of telephone prices, introduced in fifteen states by 1910. But in general, the Bell companies prospered under the new regulatory order. State utility commissioners were generally appointed, not elected. They saw themselves as rational and nonpartisan, standing above local political concerns, and had little to gain by grandstanding against "foreign" telephone companies—a description that fell into disuse after 1910. Efforts by regulators to improve and standardize telephone service often had the side effect of imposing the Bell System's own standards for proper quality and pricing on the rest of the industry. Many state commissioners shared Theodore Vail's enthusiasm for efficiency, quality, and systematic management, and in their deliberations and decisions, the language of system could often be heard. Vail's words echoed, for example, in a 1918 declaration by the California Utility Commission that "the telephone being a natural monopoly, there should be one universal service, as this will enable complete interchange of communications between all telephone users." The state regulatory commissions had little or no enthusiasm for the confusion of competition. In almost every case, they supported the elimination of dual service, whether by interconnection of competing systems or outright acquisition.[59]

Interconnection and the Independents

The independents could not ignore the growing consensus in favor of interconnection. While the number of independent telephones in the United States would continue to grow until about 1920, the number of independent phones with no physical connection to the Bell System peaked in 1907. After that year, a rising number of independent companies connected their lines to Bell wires and capitulated to increasing influence over their operations by AT&T executives and engineers. In 1911, several leaders of the independent telephone movement shocked their own followers by publicly embracing Theodore Vail's vision of one big telephone system. Other independents fought this shift and turned to the federal government to try to prevent consolidation of the industry. The independent telephone movement never really recovered from this split. Individual companies remained and prospered, but by the end of the 1910s, a new regulatory order would be established, and independent telephony as a movement of resistance to AT&T's domination of the industry was no more.

In 1906, about three hundred thousand independent telephones in the United States were connected to Bell wires under some kind of sublicensing agreement. By 1914, that number had increased tenfold. The percentage of independent telephones connected to Bell lines increased from 14 percent to 69 percent between those years.[60] AT&T histories credit Theodore Vail with liberalizing the Bell policy toward interconnection, and magnanimously allowing independent companies to connect their systems to Bell lines. In fact, the managers of Bell operating companies sought interconnection with independent systems well before Vail returned to AT&T. As early as 1898, Bell managers described sublicensing, or interconnection, as a useful way "to control [the opposition] and have [it] operated to our benefit."[61] In 1900, the Central Union Telephone Company reported that it had negotiated interconnection agreements with 151 independent telephone systems. That was only a fraction of the more than one thousand independent systems operating in Central Union's midwestern territory, but it demonstrates that the policy of interconnection predated Vail's and even Frederick Fish's leadership at AT&T.[62] Vail did not liberalize interconnection policy so much as standardize what local management was already trying to do. He set uniform technical standards for independents connecting to Bell lines and encouraged regional managers to pursue interconnection agreements in the rural areas that Bell companies chose not to serve.[63]

What changed after 1907 was less the Bell System's attitude toward interconnection than the independents'. Before around 1910, many independent entrepreneurs remained fiercely opposed to interconnection with AT&T or its affiliates. In 1905, Henry Barnhart wrote a stern letter of warning to a fellow Indiana independent that had entered negotiations with Central Union. "When you have been in the business as long as I, you will understand that the Bell Co. furnishes no equipment to any company it does not control," Barnhart wrote. "Experience has shown," Paul Latzke agreed, that whenever an independent connected with Bell wires, "the Independent company ultimately passes under the absolute control of the Bell and in the end is swallowed up."[64] Those independent entrepreneurs that did seek to connect their telephones with Bell lines, or even to sell their systems outright, risked the wrath of their comrades. Stories circulated of midnight meetings between Bell managers and independent owners where the independents arrived in false beards and dark glasses to hide their identities. When Barnhart's friend Hugh Dougherty, owner of an independent system in Bluffton, Indiana, connected his lines to Central Union's in 1905, he was ostracized by other independents and called "a traitor in the meanest form." "A rich man, [Dougherty] sacrificed all considerations of honor, of moral obligation, of manliness, for money that he does not need," spat Paul Latzke. One month later, when another Hoosier independent died of a stroke at an independent convention, Dougherty was even blamed for somehow killing his former comrade.[65] As time went on, however, angry editorials in *Telephony* and strident resolutions at independent conventions could not conceal the growing number of independents willing to make a separate peace with Bell.

The independents had always struggled to raise capital in large amounts, and AT&T and its financial allies did everything they could to exacerbate this weakness. "Every large bank in New York . . . has on its board a Bell Telephone director," complained Pennsylvania independent Robert Hall in 1912. "Slowly but surely," he said, the Bell interests were "strangling" all independent investment. Hall spoke from some experience; he claimed to be more heavily invested in independent telephone securities than "almost any man in the United States."[66] In 1905, Hall and several wealthy midwestern investors—among them Anheuser-Busch's Adolphus Busch, Eastman Kodak's George Eastman, and Hiram Sibley Jr., son of Western Union's first president—created the United States Independent Telephone Company, an ambitious attempt to compete with Bell in and around New York City. Based in Rochester, New York, and initially capitalized at $25 million, United States Independent acquired a franchise to build an independent system in New York City and promised to establish 225,000 telephones there within two years. It also took over Stromberg-Carlson, an important independent manufacturer, and made plans to buy and consolidate several independent operating companies in a wide territory around New York.[67]

But this upstate invasion of New York City did not get far. According to Hall, AT&T's influence with New York bankers and financiers—"a conspiracy as complete and thorough as well might be imagined"—froze United States Independent out of capital and resources. Others said the company had never been more than watered stock and hot air. Whatever the truth, the whole scheme hinged on establishing a competitive telephone system in Manhattan. When that effort crashed on the reefs of state and city politics, United States Independent was finished almost before it had begun. A state law passed during the pole and wire fights of the 1880s required all telephone lines in New York City to be buried underground. This meant that United States Independent needed permission either to use existing underground conduits or to open the streets and lay their own. But the existing conduits were owned by the Empire Subway Company, a subsidiary of AT&T. And Bell's allies in the New York City government launched a challenge to the new company's franchise, which, they argued, had originally been issued for the purpose of constructing a burglar alarm service, and did not authorize construction of a telephone exchange. The New York City Comptroller denied United States Independent the right to open the city's streets until the matter was resolved. By 1907, the company had made no inroads into New York City and investors were dumping their shares. AT&T then made a move to buy out the whole concern, but independents outside the company convinced the New York attorney general to block such a takeover on antitrust grounds. The state's action prevented AT&T from acquiring Stromberg-Carlson and several independent operating companies at fire sale prices, but it doomed United States Independent to bankruptcy. The messy, well-publicized collapse of the venture put a chill into independent investors from coast to coast.[68]

Another attempt to consolidate the independent movement was thwarted in 1909. Several independents operating regional long-distance lines signed agreements in that year to form the Independent Long Distance Telephone and Telegraph Syndicate, not a holding company but a looser federation that could offer long-distance service over a wide swath of territory from Kansas to New York. AT&T's response showed some of the advantages conferred by the Bell System's increasing unification and coordination. At first, the independent syndicate offered lower prices than the Bell System and immediately began cutting into its long-distance profits. Rather than compete with independent rates in all places, AT&T chose a few strategic points and drastically cut its prices there. In particular, it targeted the United States Telephone Company of Cleveland (not related to United States Independent), which operated the syndicate's lines across Ohio and Indiana. Central Union, already the weak sister of the Bell System, became something of a sacrificial lamb. It cut its toll rates in Indiana and Ohio by two thirds, a drastic move the independent could not match. AT&T could order Central Union to operate at a loss; the independent syndicate could not ask the same of United States Telephone. Bell lawyers also challenged the legality of the exclusive contracts United States Telephone had signed with hundreds of small Ohio independents. (Antitrust laws could work in Bell's favor too.) By the end of 1909, United States

Telephone had gone into receivership and was purchased through a dummy corporation by J. P. Morgan and Company, cutting a large hole in the heart of the independents' long-distance network.[69]

AT&T stepped up its acquisition and absorption of independent companies in 1909 and 1910. Though Theodore Vail's annual reports to AT&T shareholders had never been timid, his 1910 report displayed a new boldness in discussing such moves. "Wherever it could be legally done, and done with the acquiescence of the public, opposition companies have been acquired and merged into the Bell System," Vail wrote. "There is no question but that the public are tired of dual telephone exchange systems, and that . . . opposition against mergers will decrease." Boldest of all was AT&T's secret purchase, in 1909, of a controlling interest in its first great rival, the Western Union Telegraph Company. In 1910, Vail became president of Western Union and began merging the telephone and telegraph networks into what he called a "universal wire system," with connections all the way to Europe and South America. "There can be no boundaries to the telephone system as it is now understood and demanded," he proclaimed.[70]

In the wake of all these events, each independent operator faced a difficult choice. Interconnect with the Bell System? Sell out completely? Or keep fighting? And the decentralized nature of the movement meant that every independent had to make this decision on their own. In early 1911, several big independents came out in favor of negotiating collectively with the Bell System to interconnect en masse and end direct competition. Chief among them was Nebraska's Frank Woods. Woods was the president of the prosperous Lincoln Telephone and Telegraph Company and was elected president of the National Independent Telephone Association in 1909. In December 1910, Woods invited several of the leading independents to a secret meeting in Chicago with Henry Pomeroy Davison, a senior partner at J. P. Morgan and Company, and AT&T's Nathan Kingsbury and Theodore Vail. Kingsbury handled the nuts and bolts of negotiations for AT&T, but Vail laid out his vision: to consolidate the Bell System and all the major independents in the country. The House of Morgan would underwrite the mergers, creating a single $1.3 billion combine. According to one of the independents present, Milo Kellogg's son Leroy DeWolf Kellogg, Vail did admit that this was an enormous sum, but, Vail allegedly said, the public had clamored for the "waste" and inefficiency of competition, and so the public "ought to pay the damages."[71]

Frank Woods and his colleagues balked at the idea of a billion dollar telephone trust, but talks continued in Chicago and New York. A committee of seven independent executives—all, like Woods, directors of large, commercially successful systems—formed to negotiate with the bankers and AT&T. Vail told the independent men that he didn't care about the specific details of the mergers, only that competition be eliminated and one universal system remain. Essentially, Vail offered the major independents a place in his one big system. It would indeed be one system, and the system would be Vail's, but the independents at the table could continue to own and profit from their lines as long as they followed directions and all "strategic points"—presumably all large urban markets—were controlled by AT&T. Woods agreed with Vail that the days of direct competition were numbered. The public and their political representatives no longer desired it, he said. If interconnection was inevitable, Woods argued, it was better for the independents to negotiate collectively with Bell to secure the best deal possible, rather than make individual deals one by one. Another member of Woods's group of seven was the ambitious Missouri independent Theodore Gary, whose large holdings would eventually form a significant part of GTE and Verizon. "If we are wise," Gary wrote in March 1911, "we can perpetuate thousands of Independent companies on a much better basis than they are today."[72]

Word of these secret meetings soon got out, throwing the independent movement into an uproar. Woods defended his actions at the next meeting of the National Independent Telephone Association. Conditions were different than when the independent movement began, Woods told a shocked convention. "The public . . . demanded progress," Woods said, and progress meant—here his words must have warmed Vail's heart—"universal service." Woods proposed to lobby Congress and the states for laws compelling interchange of service between all companies and ensuring fair dealing through nonpartisan regulation. The controversy opened a bitter split in the independent movement. The rank and file of the NITA passed a resolution repudiating the actions of its own president and attempted to unseat him. The dispute soon split the organization. The largest, wealthiest independents—including six of the seven men named to negotiate with Davison and Vail—stood by Woods and supported continuing negotiations. But the smaller independents, less wealthy yet far more numerous, vigorously opposed such talks. They had learned through experience to hate and mistrust AT&T and doubted they would be well treated by any deals it made. If the big independents merged with Bell, what would become of the little ones?[73]

Woods regained control of the NITA and called for "intelligent co-operation of Bell and Independent under government supervision." Talks between AT&T, the big independents, and J. P. Morgan and Company continued in New York. Although no billion-dollar combine was created, many large mergers and consolidations were effected. Independent properties were sold to Bell and, less frequently, Bell properties to the big independents, all with an eye to eliminating direct competition across the country. In 1907, 60 percent of American cities with a population of five thousand or more had competing telephone systems. By 1913, that proportion was reduced to 37 percent. Woods's purchase of Bell operations in Nebraska was negotiated at this table, as were plans for AT&T to absorb the United States Telephone Company of Cleveland, the long-distance provider acquired by J. P. Morgan in 1909. Woods and Theodore Vail seem to have become friends in the course of these negotiations, or at least developed a strong mutual respect. According to James Geist, a later president of Woods's Lincoln Telephone and Telegraph, the most acrimonious negotiations were not between the independents and AT&T but between the independents and the Morgan group, in the form of banker Henry Davison. Woods felt Davison had concealed his true ties to the Bell System, and Vail apparently had to mediate between the two. At one point talks broke down completely until Vail invited Woods to his estate in Vermont and personally coaxed him back to the negotiations. On consummating the consolidation of Bell and independent properties in Nebraska, Vail, with characteristic modesty, gave Woods a portrait of himself. It bore the inscription: "To the Great Independent, from his friend Theo. N. Vail." The gift symbolized a great change in relations between Bell and the independents. Some independent telephone men might have hidden such a portrait, or burned it. Woods hung Vail's picture over his desk for the next thirty years.[74]

John Wright and the Antitrust Strategy

Those independents who remained opposed to interconnection with Bell broke away from the National Independent Telephone Association in 1911 and formed a new organization they called the United Independent Telephone Association, as if to advertise the one thing the independent movement was not. The new group attracted the support of smaller independent operators, those not invited to any secret meetings with AT&T and the Morgan banks. It also included several independent manufacturers, who saw they had little to gain from consolidation or the end of dual service. The association took a much harder line against any negotiation with their rivals and was open only to independents that remained wholly unconnected to Bell lines. "A strong, aggressive organization is needed to withstand the onslaughts of the enemy," declared the UITA's first president, West Virginia independent Walter Barnes.[75]

Only one of the seven big independents negotiating with Davison, and Vail broke with his colleagues to join the new association. Bert Hubbell, president of Buffalo, New York's, Federal Telephone and Telegraph Company, left the talks after AT&T secretly acquired the Kansas City Long Distance Telephone Company and accused Vail and Kingsbury of negotiating in bad faith. Hubbell advised his fellow independents to keep fighting. He said he did not believe that public service commissions could be counted on to control a telephone monopoly. "The American Telephone and Telegraph Company is beyond the physical, mental, and financial ability of any one set of men to encompass and control for the public good," Hubbell charged in 1913. It had resorted to "the most dastardly, malicious, unprincipled, and illegal practices," and could only be contained by healthy, uncompromising competition.[76]

But the most important spokesman for the new association and for the independents that still resisted interconnection was Jamestown, New York's, John Henry Wright. Wright had entered independent telephony by way of the newspaper business in the 1890s, when he was publishing a half dozen country weeklies for small towns and villages in Pennsylvania. The Bell Telephone Company of Pennsylvania refused to extend service to these little communities, so Wright built his own lines to connect them. By 1910, Wright was managing three separate telephone companies in Pennsylvania and New York and owned substantial shares in maybe a dozen more. (He was also one of the founders and first presidents of the American Automobile Association and has been credited with conceiving the idea of elementary school safety patrols.) Though he was a successful and ambitious businessman, Wright's interests and point of view remained those of the small independent. He was staunchly committed to local control of telephony and communication. "Localism is an inherent and controlling factor in ninety percent of the telephone business," he said. And he opposed "the Bell-Morgan alliance" as "one of the largest and most unscrupulous trusts on the face of the earth."[77] The independents had never been short on passionate spokesmen, but Wright targeted a new and important audience: the United States Department of Justice. He acquired the ear of two attorneys general, for a time, and gave the smaller independents a new strategy that opened the political endgame of their fight with AT&T.

Before 1910, American independents had rarely looked to the federal government for aid. The National Independent Telephone Association, from which Wright and the other small independents had just split, actually argued that the federal government had no authority to regulate local or intrastate telephony.[78] It is true that without Milo Kellogg's federal suit against the Berliner patent in 1892, the independent movement might never have gotten off the ground. But the independents were local in their origins and outlook and disinclined to see Washington, D.C., as an ally. AT&T certainly won more fights than it lost in federal courts and other venues. And Republican administrations in particular were thought to be friendly to the Bell System.

By 1910, however, Wright was convinced that local and state regulators offered no counter to AT&T's growing reach and power. Municipal governments could do little, he said, to prevent the "capture" and "wrecking" of independent systems, and the new state regulatory commissions were actively abetting this process. Wright was driven to action when word of the negotiations between AT&T and the big independents got out. If the large independents were absorbed by the Bell System, Wright predicted, both the small independents and the public would be left "to the tender mercies of the great telephone trust." Not only that, but "millions of dollars invested in Independent telephone securities"—including more than a few of Wright's own dollars—would "be rendered worthless." In defense of localism and his own investments, Wright turned to the federal government and urged his fellow independents to do the same. The nature of the telephone business, he argued, made every telephone "an instrument of state commerce one minute and an instrument of interstate commerce the next." In other words, all telephone business was interstate business and might rightly be subject to federal regulation.[79]

In November 1911, Wright sent his first of many long and detailed letters to Attorney General George Woodward Wickersham. Wright's letter told the history of the telephone in the United States from the small independents' point of view. His chronicle of events was less rabid than Paul Latzke's *Fight with an Octopus* but followed the same outline. (In 1908, when an independent telephone group sent a copy of Latzke's book to Wickersham's predecessor, he called it a "scurrilous pamphlet" and threw it out.)[80] Like Latzke, Wright stressed the local and political origins of independent telephony. He celebrated the municipal fights against Bell's monopoly in the patent era, calling the Rochester telephone strike of 1886 an "uprising of the people" that "smacked strongly of the days of '76." He assured the attorney general that independent telephony was no "mushroom growth"—that is, no creation of speculators and promoters—but a substantial industry playing an important role in the commercial welfare of the country. He credited the independent movement with lowering the price, extending the reach, and improving the quality of telephone service across the nation. Competition, Wright said, had made the telephone "less scarce, less poor, and less dear." Wright's letter then described Bell's tactics in fighting the independents. He accused the Bell companies of trying to restrain commerce, illegal under the Sherman Antitrust Act. He complained of the "conspiracy" between the Bell System and the House of Morgan, and its influence over banking interests, the press, telephone experts, and state regulatory commissions. He reported with alarm the acceleration of Bell mergers and acquisitions since 1910, and with dismay the capitulation of the large independents to Vail's plans. Even the National Independent Telephone Association and Harry MacMeal's magazine *Telephony*, Wright charged, had fallen under control of the Bell-Morgan alliance.[81]

Wright told Wickersham that he did not want or expect the Department of Justice to break up the Bell System. Nor, he said, did the independents seek to drive Bell from the field. All they sought, Wright claimed, was to preserve the existence of independent competition. He called for the Justice Department to put a stop to the takeover and consolidation of independent properties by AT&T, takeovers that Wright insisted were illegal attempts to monopolize commerce under the terms of the Sherman Act. The "Bell conspiracy should be stopped at its inception, not at its completion," Wright warned. Once the mergers were finalized, it would be too late to act. The Bell and independent systems would be too integrated to break apart, and AT&T would have become too powerful for even the federal government to control. "I am speaking to you as a practical telephone man and not as a lawyer," Wright wrote in a subsequent letter, "when I say it is not possible, even . . . under the mandate of the Supreme Court, to resolve a Bell monopoly once completed into its original competitive elements."

An effectively regulated monopoly, Wright insisted, was "at the most an ideal dream."[82]

Wright's letter and memorandum found a receptive reader not in George Wickersham, but in James Alexander Fowler, the assistant to the attorney general in charge of antitrust suits. Fowler responded to Wright's letter, which began a steady correspondence between the two, and dispatched attorney George R. Benham to meet with Wright and begin a preliminary investigation of the telephone industry.[83] For several weeks, Wright accompanied Benham on a tour of independent telephone systems in the Northeast and Midwest. He introduced Benham to Minnesota independent George W. Robinson and others who had taken part in negotiations with AT&T and the Morgan interests. And he zealously promoted the antitrust strategy to his fellow independents, encouraging them to lodge formal complaints with Fowler's office against any and all of the Bell companies' pending acquisitions.[84] The small independents roundly answered Wright's call. By March 1912, more than a thousand independent companies had petitioned the Justice Department for antitrust action against AT&T. By the following year, Wright could declare that "thousands of complaints" had been lodged as a direct result of his efforts.[85]

Benham submitted his report to Fowler and Wickersham at the end of April 1912. Wright and the other independents had convinced him that antitrust action against AT&T was appropriate and required. Benham's report pointed to a number of transactions and contemplated transactions that might be considered illegal under the Sherman Antitrust Act. At the top of this list was AT&T's planned acquisition of United States Telephone, the Cleveland company purchased by J. P. Morgan in 1909 with the intent of transferring it to Bell. James Fowler was also convinced. He said that if the pending transfer of United States Telephone to AT&T was permitted, it would "almost entirely destroy all competition" in Ohio and parts of Indiana and also destroy competition in long-distance service across an even larger section of the United States. Also on the list was AT&T's effective control of Western Union. The telephone situation, Fowler concluded, was the "most serious problem which the Department of Justice now has to deal with."[86]

In August 1912, Attorney General Wickersham met several times with AT&T vice president Nathan Kingsbury. Wickersham's memorandum of these meetings noted with perhaps a little pique that he had actually sent for Theodore Vail, but only Kingsbury came. Wickersham warned Kingsbury that the Department of Justice was conducting a general investigation of his company. He said they were not yet ready to take formal action, but he asked Kingsbury to put on hold any pending acquisitions or consolidations that might seem objectionable under the law. According to Wickersham's memo, Kingsbury agreed to do so. Also in August 1912, Wickersham met with John Wright, undoubtedly at Fowler's urging. Wright's energetic lobbying had made him the voice of the independent movement as far as the Justice Department was concerned. But from Wright's point of view, this meeting was not successful. The attorney general assured Wright that the Justice Department would prosecute any outright violations of the Sherman Act. But Wickersham also told Wright, frankly, that he personally was opposed to dual service in telephony and that he agreed with Vail and Kingsbury that the nation's telephones must ultimately be united in one system. The only long term solution to the telephone problem, Kingsbury concluded, was some kind of regulated monopoly.[87]

Wickersham told James Fowler much the same thing. He was not enthusiastic about taking formal action against AT&T. Kingsbury had been "very pleasant," he said, and Wickersham believed the Bell interests would "meet the Government frankly" by abandoning any transactions deemed to violate the Sherman Act. The larger question of how the telephone industry ought to be regulated was not, Wickersham said, within the Justice Department's jurisdiction.[88] A few months later, as he prepared to step down as attorney general, Wickersham turned over all the data gathered by Fowler and Bentham to the Interstate Commerce Commission, urging the ICC to conduct its own investigation of the telephone industry. Once again, a shift in regulatory venue had major implications for the future. The Department of Justice could really act only to preserve competition, by preventing consolidations or prosecuting illegal restraints of trade. The Interstate Commerce Commission, by contrast, could really only act to regulate commerce. It could not prevent mergers or break up monopolies once formed. Passing the baton from Justice to the ICC in this way effectively endorsed the end of government-enabled competition and the establishment of a government-regulated monopoly. Wickersham understood these implications and indeed embraced them. In a letter to ICC commissioner Charles Prouty, he echoed the AT&T argument that all telephones in America must ultimately be linked into one big system. Regulating that system, he argued, was the proper work of the ICC.[89]

But the Department of Justice did not entirely let go of the baton. For while George Wickersham left office with the rest of the Taft administration in March 1913, James Fowler did not. The incoming Wilson administration would prove inconsistent in its trustbusting efforts, but it contained many who were skeptical of corporate monopoly and at least rhetorically committed to small business and the preservation of competition. Woodrow Wilson replaced Wickersham as attorney general with James Clark McReynolds, a veteran of major antitrust lawsuits against coal railroads and the tobacco industry. The new attorney general kept Fowler in his position as assistant in charge of antitrust suits. And within days of Wilson's inauguration, John Wright was lobbying Fowler, McReynolds, and the new president to resume action against AT&T. Fowler, too, urged his new bosses to quickly reopen the Justice Department's investigation of the telephone industry. The ICC's powers, he argued, were not sufficient to control AT&T, and the Justice Department could not pass on its responsibility to protect competition in telephony. In particular, Fowler worried that AT&T might regard Nathan Kingsbury's promise to delay any major acquisitions as no longer binding once Wickersham left office. "Within a few weeks time," Fowler warned McReynolds in April 1913, independent telephone interests with properties worth millions of dollars might "suffer irreparable loss." McReynolds was persuaded. In July 1913, the Department of Justice formally initiated federal antitrust proceedings against AT&T.[90]

"Apparently, We Have Won"

For the next six months, the Justice Department held public hearings around the country and took depositions from independent telephone operators and others to build a case against AT&T and its affiliates. The government's lawsuit came to center on the Pacific Northwest, where Pacific Bell had recently acquired Northwestern Telephone, a regional long-distance provider connecting independent systems in Portland, Seattle, and Tacoma.[91] The United States Telephone Company of Cleveland could not be made the centerpiece of the government case because AT&T, reading the political weather, had abandoned its plans to acquire the company from J. P. Morgan.[92] But the Bell interests also faced dozens of state-level lawsuits regarding antitrust issues and rates in almost every section of the country.

Speculation grew that the courts might order the breakup of the Bell System, just as they had ordered the divestiture of Standard Oil and American Tobacco two years earlier. Or they might go further still. In November 1913, Postmaster General Albert Sidney Burleson issued a report advocating outright government ownership of the telephone and telegraph. In December, Democratic congressman David Lewis brought forward a bill to "postalize"—that is, take over and operate by the government—all long-distance telephone lines. An internal memo at AT&T reported that twenty senators and forty-four congressmen approved the postalization plan.[93]

Under political pressure on several fronts, AT&T offered to negotiate with Attorney General McReynolds, and a compromise was patched together. On the day that David Lewis introduced his postalization bill to Congress, the telephone company and the Department of Justice announced an agreement that would settle the federal antitrust case out of court and at least temporarily ward off any move to nationalize the telephone. The deal was made public in an open letter to McReynolds from AT&T's Nathan Kingsbury. In this letter, Kingsbury agreed to three stipulations the Justice Department had made: First, AT&T would give up its control of Western Union, selling all its shares in the telegraph company. Second, it agreed to stop taking over competing telephone systems. Third, it offered to allow independent systems that did not compete directly with Bell companies to connect, under certain conditions, to AT&T's long-distance lines. In exchange for these assurances, the Justice Department dropped its antitrust proceedings against the company.[94]

AT&T publicists christened this arrangement "the Kingsbury Commitment," and in most histories of the telephone, the name has stuck. AT&T's boosters presented the deal as a generous gift, an act of corporate statesmanship that would end the war between Bell and the independents and inaugurate a new era of intelligent cooperation.[95] The independents were not so sure. A headline in the trade journal *Transmitter* captured the mix of optimism and skepticism many must have felt upon learning of the deal: "Apparently, We Have Won." Some independents, certainly, were jubilant. "It is the greatest boon the Independents could desire," cheered an editorial in *Telephony*. "The fight for recognition of Independent telephony has been won."[96] But others quickly rejected the truce, calling it "insane" or "absurd." When the United Independent Telephone Association, by then calling itself the Independent Telephone Association of America, held its annual convention in January 1914, members condemned the agreement as "unfair to the public and independent operating companies" and vowed there would be "no withdrawal" in the fight against Bell. Some waffled between these positions. In the first days after the settlement was announced, J. C. Kelsey, a columnist for *Telephony*, assured his readers that AT&T's "voluntary surrender" was "not a miracle—not a trick—every Napoleon must meet his Waterloo." Yet in the same pages just two weeks later, Kelsey harshly criticized the specific terms of the deal.[97] Other independents took a wait-and-see attitude. The true implications of the settlement could not really be judged until it became clear how the specific terms of the interconnection offer and the ban on acquisitions would be interpreted or enforced.

One thing the independents could agree on was who deserved credit for AT&T's "surrender." It was not Nathan Kingsbury or James McReynolds. "We praise Wilson and McReynolds," began an editorial in *Transmitter*, "but the man behind the president and the attorney general . . . is John H. Wright of Jamestown, New York." It was Wright, *Transmitter* reminded its readers, who convinced and cajoled his fellow independents to take their fight to the federal government. It was Wright who brought the telephone question to the Justice Department's attention and who, when George Wickersham tried to shelve the matter, would not let it rest. Wright convinced George Benham and James Fowler to build an antitrust case against AT&T, and with the material Wright helped him gather, Fowler ultimately convinced the Wilson administration to launch a federal suit. Though Wright's name appeared nowhere in Kingsbury's letter and he did not get to set its terms, the deal reached in 1913 was as much the result of Wright's efforts as Kingsbury's or McReynolds's. Wright's work, *Transmitter* said, had brought about "the general surrender of the telephone trust to the government." The independent movement could never repay him for this service.[98]

Perhaps not. Yet Wright did well enough in the years to come—better, it must be said, than the independent movement as a whole. The so-called Kingsbury Commitment was not a magnanimous act of statesmanship on AT&T's part. It was a deal cut under duress by a company eager to evade more serious government action. But Vail and Kingsbury had hardly surrendered, and the independents had not won. The concessions imposed on AT&T in 1913 did not inaugurate peaceful cooperation between industry and government, or between the Bell System and its rivals. The deal was certainly not the beginning of telephone regulation—as we have seen, the telephone was always regulated by one level of government or another. And it did not, as is sometimes imagined, put in place the regulatory system that would govern the telephone industry for the next seventy years.

In the short term, AT&T's settlement with the Justice Department did help to shore up independent financing by reassuring potential investors that independent telephony was around to stay. It gave heart to independent manufacturers for the same reason. And it generated enough good feelings for the NITA and UITA to reunite, forming the United States Independent Telephone Association in 1915.[99] Giving up Western Union was a painful setback for Theodore Vail, though not as painful as a federal antitrust suit might have been. And the deal slowed the Bell System's march toward monopoly, for a time. But in the long run, the Kingsbury-McReynolds agreement was no great triumph for the independents. The terms of the agreement were not as generous as they may have initially seemed, and within a few years, most of AT&T's promises had been broken or made moot.

Kingsbury's provision regarding interconnection of independents with AT&T's long-distance lines was not a radical change in policy. It did little more than affirm an offer Vail had made almost two years earlier in his meetings with the big seven independents.[100] AT&T would allow noncompeting independents to pay for access to its long-distance lines, but it imposed a significant surcharge over and above the regular toll for each call and stipulated that the entire long-distance portion of any call so connected must be carried on Bell lines, effectively freezing out independent long-distance providers. Also, this agreement was nonreciprocal; it allowed independents to transfer calls and tolls to Bell systems but did not permit traffic or money to flow the other way. In effect, the interconnection provision proposed to turn independent exchanges into one-way feeders for AT&T's long-distance network, much as Bell's 1879 truce with Western Union had made Bell's local exchanges into feeders for the telegraph giant. An important difference was that in 1879, Theodore Vail had carefully protected Bell's right to develop long-distance telephony. The fine print of the Kingsbury-McReynolds agreement would spell the eventual demise of the independent's long-distance lines.[101]

It did not take long for the independents to realize this and begin protesting the terms of the interconnection provision. William Orthwein, president of the Kinloch Long Distance Company, said the contract should be "universally rejected" as "unfair to the public and discriminating against the Independent Companies." Bert Hubbell, struggling to reach better terms on which he could connect his subscribers to AT&T's long-distance lines, soon pleaded with Attorney General McReynolds to intervene again. "As the matter now stands," Hubbell wrote, "the Independents are unable to make any move . . . and except through action by your department I know of no way to get the relief we are so greatly in need of."[102] But in August 1914, McReynolds was appointed to the U.S. Supreme Court and left the Justice Department without answering Hubbell's plea. In 1916, the reunited USITA passed a resolution calling on AT&T to fulfill "the intent of the Kingsbury Commitment rather than its provisos" and petitioned President Wilson and the Justice Department for aid. USITA vice president F. B. MacKinnon insisted that "the independents as a group have *never* considered the contract [of 1913] a solution to the toll connection problem —and after three years but few companies have entered into it." Wilson asked McReynolds's successor, Attorney General Thomas Gregory, if there was any way the government could help, but Gregory said that as long as the law was not being broken, there was nothing the Justice Department could do to force AT&T to grant the independents more favorable terms.[103]

Kingsbury's promise to suspend acquisition of competing systems was more welcome to the independents than the interconnection provision, but this part of the agreement would be undone by changing circumstances and another shift in regulatory jurisdiction. In the years after 1913, pressure continued to develop for the consolidation of telephone systems and the end of dual service. More and more states placed telephony under the control of state utility commissions, which pressed for the consolidation of competing telephone exchanges. Municipal governments and business groups, once the motive force behind the creation of competing systems, no longer stood in the way of their absorption into regulated monopolies. And the number of independents who were themselves ready to sell out or be absorbed by the Bell System only grew.

So it was that in August 1916, Bert Hubbell and John Wright, the very men who had led the smaller independents in their last stand against consolidation, again approached the U.S. Department of Justice. This time, instead of seeking to block the Bell takeover of an independent system, they asked the Justice Department to allow it. Hubbell's Buffalo-based Federal Telephone Company was failing. Its network had shrunk from over fifty thousand subscribers to barely thirty thousand. The rival Bell exchange connected nearly three times as many subscribers in the city. Hubbell cut his rates, advertised aggressively, and went deep into debt to install a $1.5 million automatic switching system, but nothing staunched the flow of customers to the larger Bell exchange. By early 1916, Federal Telephone defaulted on its debts and was facing foreclosure. Hubbell was ready to sell, and Bell's New York Telephone Company was ready to buy, but of course the terms of the agreement between AT&T and the Justice Department prohibited the deal. This is where John Wright came in. Unlike Hubbell's company, Wright's Jamestown, New York, system was prospering, with nearly twice as many subscribers there as the rival Bell exchange. And in Rochester, New York, a third independent system in which both Wright and Hubbell had invested was competing neck and neck with the Bell exchange. So Hubbell, Wright, and representatives of Bell's New York Telephone sought permission for Hubbell to sell his Buffalo independent to Bell and offset the purchase by having Wright purchase Bell's operations in Jamestown and Rochester. The effect of the swap would be to end direct competition in all three cities—giving Bell a monopoly in Buffalo and the independents monopolies in Rochester and Jamestown—but roughly maintain the total number of Bell and independent telephones.[104]

The four companies involved moved carefully to secure government approval before going forward with their deal. They petitioned the municipal governments of Buffalo, Rochester, and Jamestown for support, then the New York State Public Utility Commission, and finally the U.S. Department of Justice, in effect retracing the regulatory history of the telephone. In Buffalo, Federal and New York Telephone obtained the signatures of fifty thousand telephone users (about half the subscribers in the city) on a petition supporting their merger. They also worked with the Buffalo Chamber of Commerce, which conducted an investigation of telephone rates and produced a report calling for the end of dual service in western New York. A last-minute counterproposal to start a municipally owned system in Buffalo was rejected as "a joke." If the people of Buffalo really wanted competition, they should have supported Federal Telephone, said the Chamber of Commerce's E. H. Hutchinson. The cities and the state gave their assent to the deal, as did George Carroll Todd, an assistant to the U.S. attorney general. Not wanting to thwart the will of all parties involved, the Justice Department accepted the fiction that creating three separate monopolies did not end competition and thus did not contravene antitrust laws or the agreement of 1913.[105]

This is, in microcosm, how competition in American telephony came to an end. Support for dual service dwindled among business users and municipal governments, the very groups that had given birth to independent telephony. State utility commissions pressed for interconnection, on the grounds that regulation could do the work competition had once done. City by city and market by market, swaps and consolidations like the one arranged in western New York eliminated direct competition, parceling out the country to Bell and independent firms. Failing independents, like Hubbell in Buffalo, were taken over by their Bell rivals. More successful independents, like Wright in Jamestown, could earn themselves pieces of out-of-the-way territory and were allowed to connect to the Bell System on AT&T's terms. Both groups of independents often had to eat some earlier words. In 1913, Bert Hubbell had insisted that the "dastardly, malicious" Bell monopoly could never be controlled by regulation. In 1916, he said that the telephone industry was "so well developed that with regulation there is no longer any need for competition." John Wright, so voluble in his fight to stop the consolidation of Bell and independent systems, was laconic when asking for permission to consolidate. "There are now new conditions," he allowed.[106]

Those negotiating these consolidations had to step lightly around antitrust laws and the terms of Nathan Kingsbury's agreement with the attorney general. But when telephone users, city councils, and the independents themselves were in favor of consolidation with AT&T, federal officials were not eager to stand in their way. By requiring that Bell's acquisition of independent properties be offset by sales of Bell property to independents in other areas, the Justice Department kept up the pretense that competition was being preserved. But the net effect of these consolidations was to increase the size of the Bell System and to chip away at the remaining independents. Between 1913 and 1917, Bell companies acquired independent networks totaling 241,000 subscribers; the independents acquired Bell networks totaling 58,000.[107] The replacement of dual service with interconnected monopolies was not really competition, but rather the cartelization of the telephone industry. In 1911, there had been competing telephone systems in 2,290 communities in the United States, including more than half of all cities with populations larger than five thousand. In 1913, the year of the Kingsbury-McReynolds agreement, more than eighteen hundred American cities and towns still had competing exchanges. By 1918, competition remained in fewer than one thousand communities. That was not a negligible number, but it did represent a significant decline, considering AT&T's promise that takeovers and consolidations had come to an end.[108]

Wartime Control of the Wires

The end of competition in telephony was hastened during the First World War, when the American government invoked its war powers to briefly take control of the nation's railroad, telegraph, and telephone lines. The immediate pretext for federal takeover of the wire systems was the threat of a telegraph operators' strike in the summer of 1918. Woodrow Wilson's government was anxious to avoid any disruption of national telecommunications or of the trans-Atlantic cables connecting Washington to the American Expeditionary Force. Wilson appealed directly to the leaders of the nation's two biggest telegraph companies, Western Union's Newcomb Carlton and Postal Telegraph's Clarence Mackay, to reach some agreement with the telegraphers' union. Mackay—a foe of Western Union who had also tried to launch an independent long-distance telephone network—complied with the president's request, but Carlton—a former AT&T vice president and protégé of Theodore Vail's—said he would rather see the government take over his company than ever recognize a union. In July 1918, Wilson instructed Postmaster General Albert Burleson to "assume control and supervision of each and every telegraph and telephone system" in the United States.[109]

Many believed that wartime control was only the prelude to permanent nationalization of the telephone and telegraph. The postmaster general was already on record favoring such a move, as was Wilson's unofficial chief of staff, Joseph Tumulty. Wilson himself had privately told Burleson he supported the postalization of the telegraph, without specifically mentioning the telephone one way or the other. When Congress debated the bill authorizing a temporary takeover of the wire systems, leading Republicans expressed doubts about the government's claims of wartime necessity. In the Senate, Warren Harding declared that "no one pretends to believe" Wilson's ultimate goal was not "to initiate Government ownership." But the Democrats controlled both houses, and Congress authorized the White House to take control of the nation's wires on 1 August 1918.[110]

This had been AT&T's chief nightmare for many years. Yet government control would prove only fleeting, and the experience was, in the end, not only painless but beneficial to the Bell System. From the start, Postmaster General Burleson imposed no significant changes on either AT&T or Western Union in terms of strategy or personnel. Burleson directed the nation's telephone and telegraph companies to continue all operations as usual. AT&T's chief engineer became the government's chief engineer; Theodore Vail's head counsel became Burleson's head counsel. Burleson and Vail struck up a close friendship, and Burleson made Vail his own "personal advisor" on creating a "universal wire service and a unified cable system." In many ways, the postmaster general already shared Vail's vision for the telephone and telegraph—both men believed the nation's telecommunications should be one united system, centrally controlled. "Our interests are exactly the same," Vail told Burleson at their first meeting, and Burleson agreed. Vail called the federal takeover "a golden opportunity" to centralize control of both industries. "Much can be accomplished" under government control, Vail said, "that could not be accomplished under private ownership, because of antagonism and competition." He would take full advantage of the chance.[111]

Unthreatened by antitrust legislation, Burleson and Vail called for "the coordination and consolidation of competing systems whenever possible." The postmaster general created a committee to consider merging all the telephone systems in the country at one fell swoop. While that never actually came to pass, Burleson did authorize dozens of mergers and the sale to Bell of many independent systems that the Justice Department had previously put on hold. In this way, for example, competition finally ended in both Muncie and Indianapolis, when the independent systems in both cities were sold, with Burleson's blessing, to their old foe Central Union, soon to be reorganized as Indiana Bell. The postmaster general put Bell and Western Union executives in charge of a Wire Operating Board empowered to reintegrate control of the telephone, telegraph, and undersea cables. In effect, wartime control undid whatever was left of the so-called Kingsbury Commitment, reuniting Western Union with the Bell System while accelerating the takeover and absorption of independent telephone companies and competing telegraph firms.[112]

The independents did not find wartime control nearly as agreeable as AT&T. On technical and operational questions, Burleson deferred to Vail and Newcomb Carlton, ignoring the views of their smaller competitors. He let AT&T and Western Union set the terms and procedures for interconnecting diverse systems. And, the independents charged, the government was unfair in awarding compensation for deficits incurred under federal control. AT&T and Western Union seem to have secured considerably more lucrative compensation agreements than the independent telephone and telegraph companies. The Bell System ultimately received $9.2 million in compensation from the government, on top of its regular income for the period. All other telephone and telegraph companies combined received a total of $5.2 million. Clarence Mackay and others called this blatant discrimination. Indiana independent Henry Barnhart, now a Democratic congressman in Washington, threatened to break with his party over such favoritism. By December 1918, Mackay declared that the postmaster general was out to destroy his company, a charge echoed by Republican politicians and the press. Burleson barely denied it, calling Mackay's Postal Telegraph, and by extension other rivals to AT&T and Western Union, "a parasite" that formed "no essential part of a broad, comprehensive national system." In March 1919, Burleson used his authority to remove Mackay from control of his own company and put Postal Telegraph under the supervision of Vail and AT&T.[113]

Federal control of the telephone and telegraph did not last. Despite predictions of permanent nationalization in the summer of 1918, a number of factors ensured that the wartime experiment would be short-lived. First, Republicans gained control of both the House and Senate in the midterm elections of November 1918. Less than a week later, the armistice with Germany was signed. Peace came sooner than Burleson and other government officials had expected; this threw a wrench into their plans for long-term control of the wires. Claims of wartime necessity suddenly rang hollow, and the new Republican Congress felt much freer to block and criticize the government than it had during the war. But perhaps the most significant factor preventing more permanent nationalization was the ham-fisted administration of Postmaster General Burleson and the post office. One year of Burleson's management discredited government control more widely and thoroughly than decades of lobbying by AT&T.

Advocates of government ownership, who had long insisted the government would lower the cost of telephone and telegraph service, were sorely disappointed. Instead, Burleson raised long-distance telephone and telegraph rates by about 20 percent and authorized local rate hikes in hundreds of markets. Getting forty-odd state regulatory commissions plus the ICC to approve such increases would have been a formidable task for private industry, but Burleson's office forced the new rates through over the objection of consumers and state commissioners. Burleson also instituted a fee for new telephone connections that the Bell companies had sought, but that state commissions had blocked, for some time. Finally, he abolished flat rates for telephone service, ending by fiat the battle over billing structures that Bell and the independents had waged since competition began.[114]

Those who believed that the government would treat its workers more kindly than private industry were also disappointed. In fact, the postmaster general was harsh and stingy to telephone and telegraph employees. He refused to honor War Labor Board policies allowing collective bargaining and let Western Union and many Bell companies continue their practice of firing anyone who joined a union. Indeed, Burleson did not allow company managers to negotiate with workers, even when management wanted to do so. Far from preventing unrest, government control provoked a series of strikes and walkouts, alienating labor and angering the public. The most publicized strike came in April 1919 when, after four months without a contract, operators at Bell's New England Telephone and Telegraph walked off the job. Telephone service was paralyzed in Maine, Massachusetts, New Hampshire, Rhode Island, and Vermont. The press and public poured sympathy on the plucky "hello girls" and scorn on the post office, while the Bell corporation itself escaped serious criticism. Labor groups, which had agitated for government control of the wire systems since the 1880s, quietly slunk away from this position. Samuel Gompers called Burleson a dictator and demanded his resignation.[115]

The New England operators' strike brought criticism of government control, and of Burleson in particular, to a crescendo. On the fifth day of the walkout, the staunchly pro-Democratic *New York World* published and attempted to syndicate an article calling for the postmaster general to resign. But Western Union and Postal Telegraph, both under control of Burleson's Wire Board, refused to transmit the article to other cities around the country. When news of this refusal got out, the howls of protest could not be silenced. The *Washington Star* reported that Democratic leaders were imploring Woodrow Wilson "to decapitate Postmaster General Burleson" on his return from the peace talks at Versailles. The *New York Times* declared wartime control of the telephone and telegraph an "abject and exemplary failure." The din reached Wilson's ears in France; on April 28, Wilson cabled Joseph Tumulty, telling him to instruct the post office to relinquish control of the wires. The undersea cables were returned to their owners days later, but the telegraph and telephone remained in government hands for three more months. Burleson used this lame duck period to push through more than sixty additional increases to telephone rates, even over Tumulty and Wilson's objections.[116]

"The newspapers never liked me," Burleson later reflected, "but they always liked Mr. Vail." In May 1919, as the American experiment with postalization collapsed in disgrace, the *New Republic* joked that "one bond and one alone" held the country together, uniting socialist and capitalist, trade unionist and banker: everyone had come to detest Albert Burleson. Everyone, that is, except Theodore Vail. When control of the telephone and telegraph returned to private hands in August 1919, Vail's company was considerably better off than it had been twelve months earlier. The government had raised its prices, broken some of its workers' unions, eliminated many of its remaining competitors, and absorbed almost all the criticism resulting from this process, discrediting public ownership of the telephone so thoroughly that it would rarely be contemplated in the United States again. Government control was so kind to the Bell System that Nathan Kingsbury felt obliged to assure the Senate's interstate commerce committee that it had not been Vail's idea from the start. While the government took the unusual step of decorating AT&T and Western Union as corporations for their distinguished wartime service, Vail praised Burleson's management and thanked him for his friendship. "I was never better treated in my life," Vail said.[117]

The End of the Independent Movement

The remains of the Kingsbury-McReynolds agreement were laid to rest soon after the end of wartime control. The Harding administration's "return to normalcy" brought the rolling back of many earlier efforts to regulate corporations and the economy. In 1921, Congress passed the Willis-Graham Act, which transferred authority over telephone mergers and consolidations from the Justice Department to the Interstate Commerce Commission and explicitly exempted telephone and telegraph companies from antitrust regulation once the ICC had determined that a proposed consolidation was in the public interest. Deliberations over the act make clear that most lawmakers by then agreed that the telephone was a natural monopoly, and that the industry should be regulated but free from competition. "There is nothing to be gained by local competition in the telephone business," declared the House committee that drafted the bill.[118] The Willis-Graham Act mooted any of AT&T's remaining commitments to the Justice

Department and cleared the way for a final wave of mergers and acquisitions that effectively ended independent competition in telephony.

In September 1921, for example, the Bell System finally absorbed the Ohio State Telephone Company, formerly the United States Telephone Company of Cleveland, the long-distance independent whose pending acquisition had triggered government action against AT&T eight years earlier. In 1922, Southwestern Bell purchased the once-mighty Kinloch Telephone Company of St. Louis, and in 1925, Theodore Gary sold his Kansas City Telephone and the Tri-State Telephone Company of St. Paul to their respective Bell rivals. Only a few diehard independents kept up the fight. In 1907, there had been 2.2 million independent telephones in the United States not connected to the Bell System. By 1920, there were less than nine hundred thousand, and by 1930, there were only one hundred thousand, most in remote areas.[119] The last major city to have two competing telephone systems (before competition returned to American telephony with the breakup of the Bell System in 1984) was Philadelphia, where the Keystone Telephone Company remained in operation, remarkably, until 1945.[120]

Those independents that connected with Bell wires rather than selling out entirely were not swallowed up but tamed. Their numbers and their market share would remain relatively constant for the next several decades. From the 1920s through the 1980s, ostensibly independent telephone companies operated about 15 percent of the telephones in the United States and earned about 10 percent of the revenues. But they could hardly be called a movement, and they did not represent an alternative to AT&T's domination of the industry. Connecting independents had to accept AT&T's authority on technical and financial issues, and there was never a possibility of their posing a competitive or political threat to Bell. From AT&T's point of view, the old foes of the system eventually became a political asset. One student of public relations in the 1930s observed that the Bell System had built a "protective fringe" out of the "numerous though economically unimportant swarm of independents" that largely shared its interests. It was often politic to send these tame independents before state utility commissions to complain about some issue or to petition for higher rates.[121]

As the years went on, local and long-distance charges were rebalanced so that long distance came to be the more lucrative part of the industry. In the first decades of telephony, long lines had been money losers, loss leaders bordering on folly. The real money was in local service for concentrated urban markets. In the second half of the twentieth century, however, this pattern would be reversed. Long-distance rates went up and up and eventually came to subsidize local service. Regulators liked this, as did consumers, because it helped keep the price of local service low. Eventually, cross-subsidies from long-distance revenues allowed the Bell System to return to flat rates for local service. But this rebalancing worked against smaller systems with no long-distance lines. The Bell companies and state regulatory commissions set a standard for low local rates, which the independents were obliged to match, even when they served rural territories where costs per telephone were greater. And because AT&T completely controlled the nation's long-distance network, the remaining independents had no long-distance profits with which to offset this squeeze.[122]

Individual independents could still make a living as junior partners to the Bell System, but it was not a growth industry, and the independent movement as any kind of opposition to AT&T or national incorporation was no more. John Wright stayed in the business until his death in 1951 but devoted more and more of his time to aviation and other pursuits. Frank Woods prospered, teaming up with Theodore Gary to buy the independent manufacturing company Automatic Electric. After the New England operators' strike of 1919, Woods and Gary negotiated a long term contract with AT&T to make automatic switching equipment for the Bell System. Gary was perhaps the most successful individual independent, using Automatic Electric's valuable patents to build an empire that forms part of today's Verizon. Woods was content to remain in Nebraska, where he ran the Lincoln Telephone and Telegraph Company until 1946. In 1925, Woods marked a symbolic end to the independent movement by leading a drive among the state independent telephone associations to open their membership to Bell employees and officially drop the word "independent" from their names. His sons and grandsons managed Lincoln Telephone until the 1980s; it was acquired by Alltel, now another subsidiary of Verizon, in 1999.[123]

Ironic Outcomes

The politics of telephony and scale produced ironic outcomes. In Canada, nationalist elites embraced the telephone in its earliest years as an instrument of Canadian unity. This effectively removed the telephone from the control of Canadian municipalities and other local interests. Yet Canada never built a unified national system. Bell Canada gave up the western provinces to an uprising of prairie populism and was punished for its failure to adequately serve French Canadians in Quebec. A functional but balkanized telephone system emerged. In the United States, by contrast, municipalities and local entrepreneurs were active and important in the telephone industry from the start. Indeed, the telephone was enlisted by the independents and others in the defense of local and regional autonomy. Yet in the crucible of the telephone fight, AT&T built a single, tightly unified telephone system, both revered and notorious for its commitment to standardization and centralized control.

These outcomes mirror the development of federalism in each country. The United States was deeply imbued at its founding with the doctrine of states' rights, and suspicion of centralized power remains an important thread in American political culture. Yet in comparative terms, modern American federalism is highly centralized. The individual states are weak compared to Canadian provinces, and the federal government is strong, while the American economy is remarkably integrated and robust. Canada's nineteenth-century founders had much less fear of centralization, and many sought a strong national government. Yet today the provinces enjoy a degree of autonomy seen in few federal systems, and Canada's economy remains distinctly divided along regional lines.[124] Explaining these reversals is beyond the scope of this book, but they support the conclusion that differences in political economy trumped any inherent features of telephone technology in shaping the map of telephony in the United States and Canada.

That is not to say that outcomes were inevitable or that individuals and events did not play determining roles. AT&T's ultimate victory in the United States not only allowed it to dominate the telephone industry for most of the twentieth century; the victory also let AT&T write the history of the telephone, and in a way that concealed the political battles of its first forty years. That version of the telephone's history remembers few individuals beside Alexander Graham Bell and Theodore Vail. Many others left their mark on the development of the industry and indeed on our ideas about communication, nation, and scale: John Wright and Frank Woods, Francis Dagger and William Maclean, James Fowler and, alas, Albert Burleson. These names have largely been forgotten.

Telephone networks were shaped by individuals and ideas, but ideas and individuals were also shaped by their environments. Federal systems and the political economy of telecommunications influenced both business strategies and cultural values. Political structures and venues channeled the debate over the telephone, especially when it turned, as it so often did, on questions of jurisdiction or geographic scale. Rather than shaping the nation in its image, telephony in Canada took on the shape and image of its nation. Hanging together in spite of itself, combining public and private enterprise, divided by language and distance yet linked by slender wires, Canada's telephone infrastructure may be a more telling model of Canadian federalism than its builders ever intended. In the United States, the Bell System both assisted in and served as a model for the incorporation of America. As the next chapter argues, AT&T's leaders and publicists used their coast-to-coast telephone network as a model for the incorporation of the nation as a whole, crafting a defense of big business and national integration that would be employed by many industries beside the telephone.

Chapter 6

The System Gospel

In October 1927, a new president of the American Telephone and Telegraph Company spoke in Dallas, Texas, at a national conference of state and federal utilities commissioners. Walter Gifford was born in 1885, the same year as AT&T. By the time he came to head the company in 1925, independent competition had been all but eradicated, and a regulated monopoly paradigm was in place that would stand for sixty years. Before this audience of the civil servants responsible for overseeing his industry, Gifford pledged AT&T's commitment to public service over profit and praised the commissioners for their work. "You as Public Utility Commissioners and we in the telephone business are engaged in a common enterprise," he said. "Our policy and purpose are the same as yours—the most telephone service and the best, at the least cost to the public."[1]

At a private meeting of Bell advertising and publicity agents just six months later, Gifford presented a different attitude toward the public and its political representatives. "Every minute . . . we are faced with the fact that we are hindered from doing what we would like to do because of a public reaction," he complained. He called it "perfectly criminal" that Bell executives had to beg state commissions for telephone rate increases, and his subordinates accused commissioners of invariably ruling against the Bell companies in order to curry public favor. "I should like to see the day," Gifford said, "when if we want to raise rates . . . we can raise rates without mean, dirty, vicious attack." But that day was "a long way off," he concluded, calling it "a millennium that may never come."[2]

When the minutes of this conference were collected and published, Gifford's remarks had been edited and revised. His talk of "mean, dirty, vicious" attack was expunged and that passage rewritten to read, "I should like to see the day . . . when we have so accurately gauged the public desires and met them, and so well acquired public confidence . . . that we could even raise rates if that was necessary without attack."[3] We should hardly be shocked that the president of AT&T might express one view of utility regulation in public and another in private, or that a conference of public relations experts would edit their words before publication. But the revision of Gifford's remarks is symbolic of AT&T's considerable success in rewriting its own history and effacing political conflict from its own past.

Back in 1907, when Theodore Vail became president of AT&T for the second time, the company's fortunes had seemed dire. The Bell octopus was widely mistrusted by the public and in many quarters actively despised.[4] Bell's subsidiaries in the Midwest were hemorrhaging business to their independent competitors, and a government takeover of the industry seemed very possible. Yet by the time Vail retired in 1919, and certainly by the time Walter Gifford became president in 1925, the Bell System was stronger, more prosperous, and more united than ever. In little more than a decade, AT&T had locked up control of the regional Bell operating companies, divided and conquered its independent rivals, completed construction of a transcontinental telephone network, and navigated grave political dangers largely unscathed. The company's victory was so complete that in the years to come, it would begin to seem there had been no victory. By the 1920s, virtually every significant actor in the American telephone industry came to share in, or at least surrender to, the vision of telephony long espoused at AT&T. In retrospect, its success began to seem inevitable. Once it did, the history of the telephone could be revised so that the political and commercial battles of its early days were obscured and ultimately forgotten.

And not only this. In promoting the Bell System, Vail and AT&T articulated a new, more positive vision of monopoly capital and big business in general. Rejecting the narrow horizons of Bell's old Boston owners, and outflanking the independents by borrowing the style if not the substance of their rhetoric, AT&T's leaders and promoters constructed a positive defense of consolidation, centralization, and integration through commerce. Ultimately, AT&T succeeded both in constructing a national telephone system and in selling that system as a worthy model for the nation itself. The Bell System was not only a useful tool for the new nation-spanning corporations; it was an argument for the rightness and inevitability of the dawning corporate age.

The Gospel of Herbert Casson

History may be written by the winners, but it relies heavily on the quotable. Besides Theodore Vail and Alexander Graham Bell, both of whom could turn a phrase, there is perhaps no individual whose words appear more often in the historiography of the telephone than Herbert Newton Casson. Casson, a Canadian Methodist minister turned American labor activist turned British efficiency expert, is little known today. But his unusual career path and powers of persuasion put him near the center of ideas about systems and human organizations one century ago. In particular, Casson wrote a book called *The History of the Telephone* in 1910. Commissioned by AT&T, Casson's book was a reverential history of the company that never strayed from Theodore Vail's point of view. A review at the time by public utility expert Delos Franklin Wilcox saw through Casson's puffery. "Mr. Casson's book might tend to give youthful readers an unwholesome notion of the unimportance of ordinary civic institutions as compared with the Bell Telephone Company," Wilcox wrote. "Every man connected in any important way with this company . . . is seen in Mr. Casson's book as a divinely appointed agent" and a "heroic benefactor of the human race." But the book was so lively, so full of clever anecdotes and vivid descriptions of early telephony, that it has proven irresistible to subsequent historians. Casson's words and stories have been endlessly quoted over the years—sometimes with attribution, though often not—especially in internal histories of AT&T but also in popular and academic works.[5]

The History of the Telephone was only one of more than one hundred books penned by Casson between the 1890s and the 1940s. Taken as a whole, his career illustrates the power and appeal of systems in this era. System was a word to conjure with in the late nineteenth and early twentieth centuries, an idea and organizing concept that seemed to cross traditional political boundaries and hold out the promise of resolving the technical, commercial, and economic challenges of the day. Yet system was neither a neutral nor a static concept. It had political and technical implications, and those implications changed over time, shaping the development of technologies like the telephone even as those technologies altered the public understanding of system.[6]

Herbert Casson's life is difficult to summarize in brief. Born near Kingston, Ontario, in 1869, he entered the ministry as a young man but soon alarmed his rural congregations by preaching the gospel of Christian socialism. In 1893, Casson was convicted of heresy by the Methodist Church of Canada. He left Canada for Boston, where he founded a radical labor church. After four years of activism in Massachusetts, Casson joined the Ruskin Colonies, utopian communes in Georgia and Tennessee, and became one of their most prolific promoters. But commune life did not suit him, and in 1899 he went to work for the progressive mayor of Toledo, Samuel "Golden Rule" Jones. Then in 1901, Casson interviewed John Henry Patterson, the president of the National Cash Register Company, and was, in his own words, "converted to capitalism." He began a new career writing magazine profiles of entrepreneurs and inventors, and worshipful books about the romance of big business. *The History of the Telephone* was commissioned and written at this time.[7]

Casson became friendly with many towering figures in American industry, including John D. Rockefeller and Theodore Vail. He advised Rockefeller on how to handle negative publicity during the government antitrust suit against Standard Oil. After that company's breakup in 1911, Casson helped his friend Harry McCann, a former advertising manager at Bell's New York Telephone Company, found a firm that would one day become McCann Erickson, the world's largest advertising agency. Standard Oil of New Jersey was their first client. By 1914, Casson was able to sell out and retire a wealthy man. But he did not retire. After moving to Britain on the eve of the First World War, Casson discovered that American-style scientific management was little known there. He threw himself into wartime mobilization efforts and became one of Britain's best-known efficiency experts. (Among other things, he agitated strenuously for the expansion of the telephone.) In the next three decades, he published over one hundred books on topics ranging from the psychology of management to the social organization of insects to Europe after Hitler (confidently published in 1939).[8]

Described in this way, Casson's career sounds eccentric if not schizophrenic. Yet in his writing, the common thread is apparent. Casson was always fascinated by systems or organizational structures. His politics changed radically over the years, yet whether he was promoting Ruskin's cooperative commonwealth or Vail's long-distance network—or even championing the "highly developed civilization" and "elaborate social organization" of the ant—Casson remained an apostle of system. He believed and argued that human organizations were perfectible, and that, so perfected, they could solve all political and economic challenges. For

Casson, the Ruskin commune was not a utopian retreat but a socialist workshop for perfecting a new form of Christian industrial organization. Cyrus McCormick's genius, as extolled in Casson's *The Romance of the Reaper*, lay not in the invention of the mechanical harvester but in "the McCormick System" by which he organized his business. The lesson of the ants was the efficiency and adaptability of the collective. And AT&T's "grand telephonic system" was a working model, in both human beings and wires, of the corporate order that would save democracy by replacing it.[9]

That Casson's ideas could remain so consistent in his journey from labor activism to monopoly capitalism to management technocracy demonstrates the power and adaptability of the system gospel. The allure of system crossed and confounded traditional political categories. Indeed, much of system's appeal came from the promise that new forms of organization might transcend the bitter political conflicts of the time. System, to its champions, meant human organization elevated to a rational, objective science. This was the star by which Herbert Casson charted his peripatetic career path. It was also the idea with which AT&T would vanquish its opponents and redeem the image of the nation-spanning corporation.

"The System Must Be First"

"The Bell System! Here we have the *motif* of American telephone development," Casson enthused in his *History of the Telephone*. "Explanations of it are futile," he continued, though his entire book was an attempt to provide one that wasn't. The telephone system, Casson argued, could not be reduced to "the simple telephone itself, nor the maze and mileage of its cables." The true Bell System consisted of all the telephones, all the switchboards, all the operators—"as many girls as would fill Vassar College a hundred times and more"—and all the corporations acting in unison under AT&T's control. Unsurprisingly, AT&T's leaders echoed this holistic vision. "It is not the telephone apparatus, central office equipment, or wires" that provide service, Theodore Vail wrote in 1917. "It is the machine as a whole; all the telephones, all the equipment, all the central offices are vital and necessary parts of that machine. That machine is the Bell System."[10] For Vail and his followers, this was the heart of the system idea—the inseparability of mechanical and human parts, and the essential unity of the physical plant and the corporate institutions that operated it.

In particular, system at AT&T meant centralized control. "A nationwide intercommunicating system," Vail insisted, "can be obtained only through one system, one policy, one centralized administration."[11] Here Vail echoed the famous slogan he had introduced in 1908—"One System, One Policy, Universal Service"—but spelled out the demand for centralization that the shorter slogan only implied. Considerable ink has been spilled on the precise meaning of "universal service": what Vail meant by it, whether he was the first to think of it, and when and how the concept emerged.[12] Less has been said about the slogan as a whole. But Vail's vision of "universal service" must be understood as part of that triptych. System, not service, came first in the slogan and in Vail's heart.

"There was no policy of universal service until the independent companies forced its adoption," the New York independent John Wright insisted in 1911.[13] Wright was right, to a point. The independents—along with the managers of some of the regional Bell operating companies—were calling for more universal access to telephones at least a decade before Vail and AT&T. But what Vail meant by "universal service" was not the same as the independents. Vail rarely argued, as many independents did, that every American could or should afford a telephone in their home. As a sales pitch and a political slogan, it did not hurt that "universal service" could be interpreted to mean telephones for all. But Vail was on record saying that he did not believe this was truly feasible or desirable. "Instantaneous and immediate transmission of communication is as yet a convenience or luxury," Vail told AT&T stockholders in 1911, three years after embracing "universal service" as a slogan. "It is not a necessity and is still confined to the comparatively few, and for that reason should be at the cost of the few that find benefit and profit in that use."[14] "Universal service," for Vail, meant that every telephone in the country—and every telegraph line, if he could manage it—should be part of one single system, under centralized control. It was the system, not access to it, that Vail aimed to make universal.

Herbert Casson did not invent the gospel of system. Nor did Theodore Vail or anyone at AT&T. When Casson or Vail sang the praises of system, they borrowed from a discourse that had grown up around the nineteenth-century railroads and the new forms of business management they pioneered. Daniel McCallum, superintendent of Pennsylvania's Erie Railroad in the 1850s, blamed the failures of earlier roads on their "want of system" and predicted future profits "in proportion to the perfection of the system adopted." Charles Perkins, president of the Chicago, Burlington, and

Quincy Railroad, wrote a famous memorandum in the 1880s calling the railroad a "great machine" that could be operated with "systematic principles."[15]

The influence of system as a metaphor peaked in the half century after the telephone's birth. The prestige of engineers and other system builders was never higher. "The system must be first," said the famed efficiency expert Frederick Winslow Taylor, delivering a maxim for the age. Factories, of course, were systematized. "System, system, system" was the mantra behind Henry Ford's automobile assembly lines and the disassembly lines of the great Chicago slaughterhouses. Beyond the factory floor, all sorts of activities and organizations could be imagined as systems and analyzed as engineering problems, or machines with moving parts. The post office, where Vail had made his name, was routinely described as a system and praised for its machine-like efficiency. In Britain, it became common in the nineteenth century to describe the entire civil service as an enormous, all-purpose machine.[16] While Thorstein Veblen and others made the intellectual case for a systematic industrial society, publishers offered self-help courses in "systematizing the office and the man." Business theorist Arch Wilkinson Shaw launched a magazine called *System* to spread the system gospel and to publicize the ideas of system heroes like Taylor, Ford, and Vail. (When Herbert Casson arrived in Britain, he founded his own journal, *Efficiency*, modeled on *System*.) "Systematic agriculturalists" exhorted farmers to farm with system, replacing old-fashioned trial-and-error methods with new efficiency regimes. Advocates of domestic science applied Taylor's methods in the home, systematizing cooking and household chores.[17]

What did all this talk of system mean? A tidy office, a factory assembly line, a nation-spanning network of telephone wires—any idea that could be applied in all these places had to be generously defined. Indeed, much of the power of the system gospel came from a sense that it could be used anywhere. Frederick Taylor insisted that his principles of scientific management could and should be "applied with equal force to all social activities."[18] But all this would mean little if system was merely a figure of speech, a trope for describing the interconnection of various things. It was not. Like the idea of the people's telephone, the language of system was prescriptive as well as descriptive. It had implications that were technical, commercial, and political. Like all such models and metaphors, the system idea served certain interests and worked against others by guiding and constraining thought. Somewhere between a technology and an ideology, system was at once a way of doing things and an argument about the way things ought to be done.

In the late nineteenth century, those who embraced the system idea generally did so because it seemed to promise efficiency, standardization, and control. One of Vail's signature achievements at the U.S. Postal Service was to eliminate the practice of hiring private contractors, thus maintaining central control over the entire postal circuit from mailbox to mailbox. Daniel McCallum's major innovation at the Erie Railroad was a similar system of comprehensive control. Charles Perkins's memo on railroad organization and Theodore Vail's pronouncements on the telephone industry all carried the same message of centralized authority.[19]

Though framed with talk of disinterested efficiency, the rise of system was hardly apolitical. A major thrust of the system idea was to shift power away from workers and indeed lower-ranking managers in favor of imposing fixed operating procedures and following predefined rules. Harvard economist Frederick Taussig celebrated this aspect of system in 1900. "Nothing is more wonderful in the industrial history of the past generation than the new vista opened as to the possibilities of organization," Taussig wrote. "The increasing application of machinery has made it possible to reduce operations more and more to routine and system, and to lessen the need of independent judgment for every step."[20] Why was this "wonderful"? What was wrong with independent judgment? For true believers like Taylor and Taussig, centralization of control meant greater efficiency, and efficiency could be its own reward. But systematic management also shifted the balance of power in the American workplace. Consider the factory: before the late nineteenth century, most industrial labor in America was performed by skilled workers. Through their monopoly over craft knowledge and skills, these workers maintained considerable control over factory production. In the 1890s and after, factory owners increasingly aimed to adopt systems that replaced the knowledge and initiative of skilled workers with more mechanized routine. This freed employers from dependence on their workers and bolstered their power in labor disputes. The literature of scientific and systematic management was forthright in asserting this goal. Even if no earthly factory ever lived up to the clockwork perfection of Taylor's dreams, systematic management was one of the weapons by which the autonomy and authority of skilled labor in America was broken.[21]

Centralizing the Bell System

AT&T used ideas of system and efficiency to justify ever tighter control of its labor force after 1907. Engineers plotted the precise movements of the female operators who served as the system's "human switches," and supervisors scripted the exact words and pronunciation they were to use in connecting every call.[22] Yet the operator was less of an obstacle to AT&T's program of systematization and standardization than were the entrepreneurs who owned America's local and regional telephone networks. Vail's insistence that universal service demanded "one system, one policy, one centralized administration" was obviously an attack on the legitimacy of independent telephone systems. But it was also directed at the managers of Bell's own regional operating companies. Vail's call for "that complete harmony and cooperation . . . that can only come through centralized or common control" was meant for their ears too. For the universal telephone system to reach perfection, Vail argued, local managers had to give up their autonomy and authority. The regional Bell companies had to accept AT&T's authority in setting standard practices, while independent systems had to be taken over or purged.[23]

In the 1880s and 1890s, the Bell operating companies had considerable autonomy in their operations. Owners and managers like Cumberland Telephone's James Caldwell and Southern New England Telephone's Morris Tyler fiercely guarded their independence from American Bell in Boston and later AT&T in New York. As we have seen, this recalcitrance played a role in Theodore Vail's frustrated departure from the telephone industry in 1889. But even then, a drive toward centralization and standardization was beginning at AT&T, a process Theodore Vail would complete and consecrate after his return in 1907.

In 1889, the year Vail left the telephone business to build hydroelectric plants in Argentina, AT&T engineer John Carty presented a paper entitled "The New Era in Telephony" at the annual meeting of the National Telephone Exchange Association, the trade organization for Bell operating companies and the main counterweight to Boston's control of the Bell interests. Carty's paper, coauthored by Angus Hibbard and Frank Pickernell, began by asserting the importance of long-distance telephone service and praising the work of the American Telephone and Telegraph Company in bringing such service about. Rising demand for a "perfected" long-distance system "may be said to have created a new era in telephony," Carty and his coauthors declared. This new era, they argued, would be marked by three major and inseparable elements: long-distance service, interconnection between operating companies, and uniform technical standards across the system. "During the past, very much has been lost by a lack of uniformity," Carty said. "The methods of the east and the west have differed widely. . . . In this 'new era' in which a perfected service is to be given, such engineering cannot possibly be successful." Local management must begin "adhering to uniform practices," he insisted, and "remedy . . . the loose methods of past years."[24]

Carty's "New Era" paper, dubbed seminal in later years by AT&T's centralizers and systematizers, proved controversial at the time. It was an attack on the autonomy of local operating companies and their ability to define their own standards and procedures. Appreciating the negative reaction he would receive from an audience of local managers, Carty did not read his paper to the entire membership of the NTEA, only to a special closed-door executive session. The few local managers who were present demanded to know whether Carty's paper was officially "backed" by AT&T or "simply the opinion of three of their experts." No answer to this question was forthcoming. A vote had to be held on whether or not to publish Carty's paper in the minutes of the conference. The motion to publish was carried by a close vote of 11 to 9 but was immediately followed by passage of a resolution that the NTEA did not officially endorse the views of any papers presented at its meetings.[25]

At the NTEA's next annual conference, AT&T's Edward Hall extrapolated from the "New Era" paper, arguing that the human organization of the telephone industry should be standardized along with its technical operations. Hall began by calling the Bell corporate system an "artificial person," but the metaphor at the heart of his paper was that of the corporation as a mechanism or machine. "I do not see why we should not go at this [organizing the corporation] just as we would at the construction of any piece of mechanism," Hall said. "Surely [our corporation] is more complicated and more delicate than any of our electrical apparatus, and at the same time, its motions are attended with such consequences that we cannot afford to make any mistake." Hall criticized the "tangled . . . old-fashioned 'rule of thumb' method" in practice at most local operating companies, and displayed organizational charts—a novelty in 1890, the first some present had ever seen—that made explicit his analogy between telephone circuits and lines of managerial communication and control. Hall's view of the new era was a simple extrapolation of Carty and Vail's. The connection of wires across the country required the connection of telephone companies across the country, and that, Hall argued, required centralization of authority and power. "As all the parts [of the Bell corporate system] are interrelated," Hall said, "it is evident that there must be somewhere a single central authority, or division means chaos."[26]

Hall's thinking was in step with the business culture of his time. The innovations in business organization pioneered by the railroads—hierarchical management, new methods of accounting and information gathering, and the like—inspired executives in other industries to imagine their corporations as engineering problems, embracing the language of system while eliding distinctions between humans and machines. But the managers of Bell's regional operating companies were much less enamored by talk of centralization, and few of them rushed to adopt Hall or Carty's schemes. "Will it not always be true that the parent Company must vitally depend on men who are in charge locally?" asked E. B. Field, president of the Colorado Bell Telephone Company. Field challenged Hall's machine metaphor directly, saying, "I would rather be building an organization that makes *man* supreme and not the Company, that is, all round intelligence, which administers the Company's affairs, and not a machine."[27]

Money, not metaphor, would drag Bell's reluctant managers into this new era of centralized control. After AT&T replaced American Bell as parent company of the Bell organization, it began to increase its ownership of the various regional operating companies. At the turn of the century, AT&T controlled just 45 percent of the total voting stock of all the local and regional licensees. By 1910, that figure was more than 80 percent. Eventually, distinctions between the parent company and its subsidiaries would be almost meaningless; by 1934, AT&T owned at least 99 percent of the stock in sixteen of the twenty-one operating companies. Centralization hastened after 1907, when the syndicate of George F. Baker, J. P. Morgan, and others completed their takeover of AT&T, forcing out the Bostonians who had owned the Bell companies since 1880 and returning Theodore Vail to the post he had resigned twenty years before.[28]

J. P. Morgan's personal influence over Bell has been exaggerated by histories of the company in the robber baron mold, but the affinity between Morgan and Vail was real. Like Vail, Morgan was a builder of systems. Both men believed in stability and profit through corporate consolidation. It was Morgan's investment firm, more than any other, that imposed order and oligopoly on the American railroad industry in the 1880s and 1890s, combining dozens of regional railroads into a few giant systems. In the 1890s and early 1900s, it was often rumored that Morgan was planning to take over the independent telephone movement in the same way, merging thousands of local systems into one giant rival to Bell. Yet in the end, it was the Bell companies that the House of Morgan would consolidate and control.[29]

Vail and his lieutenants used AT&T's growing financial leverage to consolidate the once autonomous operating companies into a single, centrally controlled Bell System. "When we acquire the ownership of all the stock of any company, we are in a position for the first time to say just how it should be handled," Edward Hall wrote in 1909. Vail made John Carty AT&T's chief engineer and expanded the power of Carty's department over the engineering practices of the operating companies. Carty shut down Bell laboratories in Boston and Chicago, centralizing all research and development in New York, and ordered Western Electric, the manufacturing arm of the system, to stop taking orders for equipment from the regional companies. In order to eliminate what Carty called "excessive and uneconomic diversity," all decisions regarding equipment and operations would be made thereafter by the central engineering department at AT&T.[30]

The system builders agreed that technological and human standardization were inseparable. "It is a grave mistake to regard our problem as being one for the mechanician only," said Carty in 1910. "It is much broader and deeper than this, involving important questions of political economy." As Carty centralized control of Bell's technical systems, Vail and Edward Hall worked to centralize its human organization. All problems "must be dealt with on broad lines," Hall wrote, "and by methods which are applicable to the whole territory." In the spring of 1908, Vail and Hall restructured AT&T's management completely, beginning with long-distance operations, in order to centralize decision making and standardize procedures. Reorganization of the regional operating companies followed. In the words of one internal company history, these changes faced "pockets of resistance" from local management, but such resistance was ultimately broken by Vail's unshakeable commitment to system integration, a constant drumbeat of publicity and propaganda from New York, and the steady extension of AT&T's financial control.[31]

The national long-distance network was a crucial weapon in this fight. In 1909, Vail and Carty vowed that AT&T would inaugurate transcontinental telephone service before the completion of the Panama Canal. Company histories praise Vail's boldness in making such a promise, for in 1909, the technology to transmit an intelligible conversation three thousand miles did not exist.[32] Yet such histories do not mention how long distance and the transcontinental project in particular served AT&T in curtailing the autonomy of local operating companies and justifying this change. AT&T's growing holdings of operating company stock made it possible for Vail to centralize control of Bell's affiliates, forging a single Bell System. What the transcontinental network gave him was a compelling reason to do so.

The national network required "uniformity in operating methods and instrumentalities," Vail wrote in 1914. "For interconnecting service and distant communication, uniformity in methods of operation and apparatus is necessary, in fact, imperative." In local telephone service, he conceded, a variety of methods might be adequate, but in operating a national long-distance network there could be only one best way. "When the supreme test comes," Vail said, "the best and only the best can be used." No aggregation or loose affiliation of smaller systems, he argued, could have achieved a coast-to-coast telephone call. The transcontinental telephone link was the "supreme test" of the Bell System, perhaps the only application that truly demanded the kind of integration and centralized control Vail worked so hard to attain. Whether or not anyone would actually pay to use it was almost beside the point.[33]

AT&T publicity returned repeatedly to this theme, not only in material directed to the general public, but also in internal publications. Bell employees were fed a steady diet of speeches and memoranda explaining and justifying the system's corporate reorganization. They were led in songs at company gatherings that extolled the virtues of centralization and standard operating procedures. The "Blue Bell Song," just one example out of many, described the three branches of the reorganized company to the tune of "My Country 'Tis of Thee": "Contract, quote proper rate / Plant, keep the wires straight / Traffic, all woes abate / Ring clear the Bell." Everything within the Bell System was standardized: not only equipment and technical practices, but business and accounting methods, office furniture, janitorial supplies, even cutlery and china.[34] For the telephone to reach its full potential, Bell employees were told again and again, local management had to surrender its old autonomy and authority. Embedded in the project of the transcontinental telephone system was a technological justification for this otherwise unpopular organizational change.

The success of this program can be read in the archives of James Caldwell's Cumberland Telephone and Telegraph Company. Caldwell and his employees prided themselves on their independence and autonomy from the parent company and resisted all attempts by American Bell or AT&T to take control of their operations. Caldwell's father had been a slave-owning Mississippi planter, and Caldwell's own memoirs smarted with indignation at "Yankee carpetbaggers" who descended on the South after the Civil War. When AT&T "wise men" came down to Nashville and criticized Cumberland's local people and methods, Caldwell saw them as carpetbaggers too. He was barely on speaking terms with Edward Hall, whom he considered the most meddlesome of "our New York friends," and he chose whenever possible to "rely upon native valor." The southerners argued frequently with New York over issues of upkeep and obsolescence, arguing, much like the independents, that AT&T's technical standards were far more exacting than necessary. And they fought increases in the licensing fees owed to AT&T by the regional operating companies, fees that cut into Cumberland's profits but also, they argued, kept telephone prices out of reach for middle- and working-class homes.[35]

In 1906, Caldwell engaged in a war of words with the independent partisan Paul Latzke, which led to each man suing the other for libel. Caldwell called the independent movement a "disreputable swindle," and, noting Latzke's "foreign" name, declared him a member of "that cracked brain class . . . represented by Czolgosz and Guiteau"—the assassins of presidents William McKinley and James Garfield. But what was the slander that provoked such outrage in Caldwell? It was that Latzke had said, of the Bell companies, "no matter how far a man is removed from Boston, he must abide by the rules and regulations laid down in Boston." Of all the charges in Latzke's long and lurid campaign of anti-Bell propaganda, what set Caldwell off was the "contemptible and unwarranted falsehood" that he was not wholly his own man.[36]

Caldwell managed to be more civil with Theodore Vail than with Latzke or Hall but held "no high opinion" of Vail's plans for the Bell System. "Mr. Vail . . . conceived a great notion about systematizing the working rules and plans for the telephone companies," Caldwell wrote in his memoirs, published in 1923. "It seemed to organize the business until it would be stiff and frigid, and the individual dwarfed into a mere cog in a wheel," he scoffed. "It reminded me too much of the Massachusetts regiment, which was all officers but one, and they ordered him to form a hollow square, and he killed himself trying to execute it." Caldwell also resented the way Vail took credit for the success and growth of the telephone industry, when in fact he had been out of the business for nearly twenty years. He made jokes about Vail's weight, accused him of "petty vanity and jealousy," and believed Vail was determined to be rid of him because he did not genuflect to Vail's organizing genius and expertise. "It was impossible for me to look to Mr. Vail for advice and direction, which clearly irritated him," Caldwell wrote. "Step by step, he moved toward bringing me under the yoke, or putting me out."[37]

Yet in 1911, when AT&T finally did acquire a controlling interest in Cumberland Telephone and Telegraph, buying out its stockholders and accepting Caldwell's resignation, the southerner conceded to the takeover in language that seemed to come directly from Theodore Vail. In a letter explaining the purchase to his shareholders, Caldwell specifically cited the technological and organizational imperatives of a national long-distance network. "The absorption of your Company into the national system was both logical and inevitable," Caldwell wrote: "the very nature of the art and the public convenience compelled it, for the telephone on the desk must be in contact with, and in speaking reach of every other telephone throughout the continent, and this can only be done through one unbroken homogenous system where every hand that touches has an incentive to push in the same direction. . . . Practically and psychologically, that one universal system can only be the American Telephone and Telegraph Company."[38]

It is remarkable how thoroughly Caldwell capitulated in this letter to the determinist arguments of Carty, Hall, and Vail. There must be a single, national, long-distance network, Caldwell said, a "universal system." And the technology seemed to demand that that network be organized in a certain way. Therefore, the argument went, the corporate system that operated that network must also be organized in that fashion. This was the power of the system gospel at Bell. Technological objectives shaped corporate organization and vice versa. In building and celebrating a national network, AT&T executives blurred distinctions between the actual physical system of telephones and wires, and the corporate structure of companies and people around it. Ideas about how the technology worked or was thought to work were extrapolated to the organization of human systems too.

AT&T's use of the system idea was thus in keeping with the era's movement toward corporate integration and consolidation, a transformation of the economy that reduced the power of small businesses and local entrepreneurs in nearly every industry and region. Complaints of overproduction and cutthroat competition served the same legitimizing purpose in this process as those of inefficiency in the factory did for the deskilling and mechanization of industrial labor. Thousands of American companies were absorbed in these years in a great wave of mergers, takeovers, and combinations.[39] System and systematic management were the ideological handmaidens of this transformation. As an economy populated almost exclusively by local firms gave way to one dominated by nation-spanning corporations, the gospel of system offered an explanation and a justification for the change.

Selling the Bell System

"It is a dangerous thing to be a monopoly at the present time," AT&T vice president Nathan Kingsbury told an audience of telephone executives in February 1914. "Business is uncertain, harassed, worried. Many predict panic and disaster." Only weeks before, Kingsbury had negotiated his agreement with Attorney General James McReynolds to settle the federal antitrust suit against AT&T. But the company was not out of political danger, and Kingsbury remained anxious. The legitimacy of the nation-spanning corporation remained an open question. The muckraking, trust-busting spirit seemed to be on the march. "The results of this new movement," Kingsbury said, had already been "economically and socially greater than the results of the French Revolution"—a preposterous claim, but testament to the anxiety in the boardrooms of America's biggest companies.[40]

Two years earlier, in July 1912, the leaders of some of the largest industrial and financial concerns in the country had met to discuss the crisis of corporate legitimacy Kingsbury was describing. Present were J. P. Morgan, his partner Henry Davison, Standard Oil heir John D. Rockefeller Jr., banker and senator Nelson Aldrich, and AT&T's Theodore Vail. These men discussed plans to develop a bureau of investigation and publicity that would promote the legitimacy of big business and counter public hostility to the consolidation of corporate power. Nothing came of this meeting directly, but several present praised one of their number for doing the kind of publicity work they believed was required. "Mr. Vail, as president of the Telephone Company, has done this kind of work . . . for many years with great success," Rockefeller wrote after the meeting. Just a few months before, the Supreme Court had ordered the breakup of Rockefeller's own

Standard Oil, while AT&T survived its federal antitrust suit relatively unscathed. Rockefeller was openly envious of Vail's achievement. "The fact that his Company, one of the greatest, if not the greatest single monopoly in the country, is allowed to continue unmolested . . . is indication enough of his success," Rockefeller said.[41]

When Vail met with Morgan and Rockefeller, he was among his own kind—the great system builders and consolidators of the age. What made Vail stand out in this group was what Rockefeller called his "persistent . . . campaign of education." More than any contemporaneous captain of industry, Vail embraced the challenge of corporate public relations. Under his direction, AT&T after 1907 embarked on an innovative and important publicity campaign, one designed not to sell telephone service but to sell the telephone system as a whole, and indeed to promote the gospel of the system itself. This three-decade effort has been called "the first, the most persistent, and the most celebrated of the large-scale institutional advertising campaigns of the early twentieth century." Business leaders like Rockefeller and others would celebrate, study, and imitate the AT&T campaign for decades to come.[42] Not only did it transform the hated Bell octopus of the nineteenth century into the trusted and even beloved Ma Bell of the twentieth, it created a template for modern public relations and did more to pacify fears of America's new corporate order than any other advertising campaign.

"In all times, in all lands, public opinion has had . . . the last word," Vail wrote in 1911. Winning over the public was a crucial step in Vail's ambitions for the Bell System. "Before we can accomplish our plans for a universal wire system," he said on a different occasion, "the public mind must be thoroughly imbued with its economies and advantages."[43] One of Vail's first acts after returning to AT&T was to take control of its public relations activities, firing Bell's old external press agency but hiring its best man, James Ellsworth, to head a new in-house Information Department and oversee publicity for the entire Bell System. With a budget for advertising and publicity unprecedented in American business history, Ellsworth pioneered many of the modern practices of corporate public relations. Indeed, Ellsworth and Vail together did much to popularize the term "public relations" and to introduce American business to the concept. Just as John Carty centralized control of Bell engineering practices, Ellsworth centralized publicity for the system, standardizing the look and message of Bell advertisements and aiming to control nearly every aspect of the telephone's public image. His Information Department courted reporters, editors, authors, politicians, librarians, and schools. It prepared "magic-lantern lectures"—slide shows—for Bell employees to give before local audiences around the country. It planted press releases in friendly newspapers and magazines and published a flood of "educational" pamphlets, booklets, and films. By subsidizing books like Herbert Casson's worshipful *History of the Telephone*, AT&T was even able to write its own history. The historiography of the telephone would genuflect to AT&T's—and particularly Theodore Vail's—version of events for decades to come.[44]

Vail and Ellsworth also secured the advertising agency of N. W. Ayer and Son for what became a thirty-year campaign of advertising in newspapers, trade journals, and even children's magazines. These advertisements would adapt and evolve their message over the years, but their primary goal never changed. They were political, not commercial, advertisements, intended not simply to sell telephone service but to remake the image of the Bell companies and indeed of American big business in general.[45]

Given public anxiety about the curse of corporate bigness, one might have expected Vail and Ellsworth to deemphasize the size, unity, and power of the Bell System. Given the regional basis of so much anti-Bell populism, one might have expected a retreat from arguments about the way the telephone was shrinking and unifying the nation. But AT&T's grand publicity campaign did neither. Instead, the company offered a positive defense—indeed, an enthusiastic celebration—of its own size, and of economic integration and corporate consolidation more broadly.

It was at this time that the term "Bell System" came into frequent use in AT&T advertisements and the press. Before about 1907, Bell executives rarely used the term. It was their independent competitors and political foes who insisted on the unity of the system, calling Bell an octopus and a monolithic trust. Bell's friends and allies spoke instead about "American Bell Telephone and its associated companies," carefully emphasizing the independence of the regional operating firms. After 1907, however, Bell publicity was increasingly forthright about describing the Bell System as a single entity. Vail even used and embraced the dreaded word "monopoly" in arguing against the wastefulness of independent competition. He also introduced the slogan "One System, One Policy, Universal Service" at this time and made it a part of nearly every Bell advertisement. N. W. Ayer and Son actually balked at introducing this motto in 1908. It was an election year, and the ad men feared that such open advocacy of monopoly would provoke a political backlash. Yet Vail insisted. "Let's say it ourselves first, and beat anybody else to it!" he is alleged to have said.[46] In the words of one AT&T executive, Vail's slogan was "sent forth to do battle with the slogans of the 'curse of Bigness.'"[47]

The People's Bell

How did Vail and Ellsworth advocate monopoly in telephony without provoking the backlash earlier executives had feared? How did AT&T celebrate the size and complexity of its nation-spanning network without arousing fear and envy of the huge corporation that owned it? Part of its success came from simply sanding down the rough edges of Bell's public image. In the patent monopoly years, Bell's Boston owners seemed haughty and aloof, if not openly contemptuous of their customers and the public. Even friends of the system admitted as much. As AT&T's Walter Gifford put it, the attitude of early Bell employees to their customers was "For heaven's sake, don't come in here and bother us!" But by the 1910s, the Bell System began to change its public face. Complaints about incompetent telephone users gave way, at least in public, to friendly solicitude. "Don't bristle at the man who makes a complaint," Edward Hall told his managers, "but make him feel that he is doing you a favor." Telephone experts who once fretted about "training" the public in proper telephone behavior were instructed, in Casson's words, to "fit telephony like a garment around the habits of the people." The incorrigible Charles Fay, who had railed against the impertinence of his own customers in the 1880s, was scornful of the change in attitude. "I . . . longed to get into some open competitive field," Fay recalled after leaving the industry: "a *man's* competition, where I could call my soul my own, and tell people to go to my competitors or to the devil if my ways did not suit."[48]

Yet the shift in Bell publicity was more fundamental than simply declaring, "the customer is always right." One of AT&T's more audacious maneuvers was to adopt their enemies' own populist rhetoric. In the years before 1907, nobody could have confused AT&T and independent advertising. (The ads of the regional Bell operating companies could be closer to the independents in content and tone.) Over time, however, Ellsworth's Information Department as well as Ayer and Son's ad agency borrowed from the Bell operating companies and from their independent foes certain ideas and images and a more rustic, "populist" style. They worked to portray the Bell System as a kind of industrial democracy, its local operating companies as good neighbors and folksy friends, and the telephone itself as an instrument of local communities and ties. AT&T adopted, to a point, the language and postures of the people's telephone, even as it waged commercial warfare on the independent telephone movement. "What's the matter with Kansas? Nothing to speak of that the telephone won't solve," declared *Bell Telephone News* in 1915.[49]

AT&T's Information Department targeted particular audiences for attention. James Ellsworth made a point of reaching out to the groups that had been most crucial to the rise of independent telephony. This meant midwestern farmers and small to middling entrepreneurs. Early in his work for AT&T, Ellsworth traveled in person to hot spots of anti-Bell sentiment like Milwaukee, Kansas City, and Rochester, New York, where he lobbied newspaper editors and other opinion makers directly. He earmarked a substantial portion of AT&T's advertising budget for newspapers and agricultural journals in the Midwest, to carry the Bell System's message directly to farmers and also to influence editorial positions toward Bell. As late as 1927, AT&T still spent approximately one-third of its institutional advertising budget on the agricultural press.[50] By the 1920s, Ellsworth had repudiated the practice of using advertising money to directly influence editorial content, but he was forthright about doing so in earlier years. With proper cultivation, Ellsworth's colleague Walter Allen advised company management in 1904, "each new story presented [in the press] can be made more and more frankly a Bell advertisement."[51]

As AT&T publicists targeted the key constituencies of the independent movement, they also appropriated some of independent propaganda's defining images and themes. One central element of the people's telephone philosophy, going back to Gardiner Hubbard and his battles with Western Union, was the idea of the telephone as an "instrument of democracy," innately or at least potentially liberating and empowering. Independent publicists routinely used this notion to attack the Bell monopoly and its alleged tyranny, going on at length about the democratic mission of the people's telephone. But around 1911, AT&T advertisements also began speaking expansively of the telephone's contributions to democracy. Bell publicity would elaborate several implications of this theme. For example, Bell advertisements after 1910 started to describe the telephone as essentially democratic because it could be used by almost anyone. "[The telephone] carries the voice of the child and the grown-up with equal speed and directness," read an AT&T magazine ad from 1915. It serves "all the people all the time."[52] The independents had made this argument at least a decade before, at a time when Bell management still instructed operators not to connect calls made by children or servants.[53]

Other advertisements described the Bell System as an "investment democracy," because of the wide public ownership of AT&T stock. "The Bell System . . . is the most democratic of all our so-called 'monopolies,'" Elbert Hubbard wrote in 1913. "It has 75,000 stockholders and 25,000,000 users." By the 1920s, more people owned shares in AT&T than in any other American corporation. This, the company argued, made AT&T "a democracy in business, owned by the people it serves." That phrase—"owned by the people it serves"—had been a refrain in independent publicity for years. Company publicists boasted that "no one person owns as much as one percent of the total stock of AT&T." That was true but overlooked the fact that 1 percent of AT&T stock would have represented an investment of more than $20 million. The statistic hardly proved an absence of business titans behind the Bell System. Also, business analysts know that small shareholders have little power in the day-to-day operations of very large companies. The wider the distribution of stock holdings, the more power passes from individual shareholders to professional management. Yet the idea of AT&T as an industrial democracy, owned by an army of average Americans, was a powerful counter to older images of Gilded Age robber barons or octopus trusts.[54]

The visual and literary style of AT&T advertising also moved toward examples set by the independents and the more progressive Bell affiliates. AT&T's earliest magazine advertisements were famously wordy and didactic, but they adopted an increasingly folksy tone in the 1910s and 1920s, as the independent movement itself declined.[55] Images of friendly telephone operators and linemen replaced long sermons from on high. Farmers and housewives appeared in ads alongside the well-heeled businessmen ubiquitous in earlier years. In the 1920s and 1930s, AT&T advertisements became increasingly nostalgic. Often they compared the social space created by the telephone to the old village post office or general store—by then, vanishing symbols of the local sociability that the independent and farmers' telephone systems had first embraced. The telephone, these ads said, made "a single community out of our vast busy continent" or "a neighborhood of a nation"—metaphors of shrinking scale that promised the preservation of local community in an era of national commerce and communication.[56]

In the 1920s, AT&T began publishing a series of telephone almanacs for "farmers, businessmen, housewives, students, and other telephone users." These almanacs combined testimonials on the virtues of the Bell System with weather forecasts, farming data, homilies, jokes, and household hints. Their rustic style, while hardly invented by the independents, was strongly reminiscent of old independent journals like *Sound Waves* and *Telephony*. Ellsworth was explicit about the almanacs' target audience and didactic purpose: "No doubt there will be considerable demand for it from rural subscribers," he wrote. "It should be useful also in the cities where the intelligent interest of the subscriber needs to be accelerated." The Bell System "belongs to Main Street and the farm," declared AT&T's almanac for 1928, claiming what had once been the twin pillars of independent telephony. As if to underline the absorption and appropriation of their old enemies' rhetoric, the 1934 almanac described the Bell System as "The People's Telephone."[57]

In adopting these rhetorical elements of the people's telephone idea, Bell executives did not convert to the actual policies or philosophies of the independents. Nor did they move away from Vail's vision of "One System, One Policy, Universal Service." These years were marked by the centralization of power at AT&T and the standardization of all its operations—a determined effort to quash local initiative and autonomy in the telephone industry. Yet the promoters of the Bell System increasingly described it in words that echoed the independent defense of local business and regional economies. Blending the populist language of the people's telephone with a commitment to standardization and system integration, AT&T's promoters found a new way to talk about the telephone. Ultimately they constructed a new, friendlier portrayal of the original system idea, and a kinder, gentler vision of the emerging corporate economy.

The Octopus Redeemed

In August 1908, *Harper's Weekly* published a flattering portrait of the new Bell System that was typical of the press Ellsworth and his Information Department engineered for AT&T. It also foreshadowed some of the ways the company would revise and reframe the system gospel in the years to come. Entitled "The Nerve-Centre of Modern Business," and written by John Kimberly Mumford, the article began with a breathless recitation of statistics describing the size and complexity of the Bell System. Four million telephones. Eight million miles of wire. Six billion connections made every year. Then Mumford described the fragility of the system. "The company . . . is wholly at the mercy of the employee," he said. "A single incompetent can put the whole system out of business." The article then turned to the restructuring of the Bell companies since Morgan's takeover in 1907 and Vail's return to the presidency of AT&T. "Within the past six months this whole extraordinary machine—more extraordinary the more you study its workings, and involving a minute and everlasting detail such as no other business in the world knows—has been wholly reorganized, from top to bottom," Mumford reported. And he made a surprising claim. "The change was wrought for one purpose, and one only—to give to the gifted or industrious man or boy, or even the girl, hitherto kept down in the ranks of the employment, a straight, uninterrupted way by which they may travel most quickly to the top." This was a remarkable take on a reorganization that had actually served to centralize power at AT&T and quash the autonomy of the regional Bell companies. Described in this way, AT&T's digestion of the regional Bells and its continued battle against independent competition seemed far less threatening. "They call this the age of machinery," Mumford concluded, "but rather it is the age of men."[58]

In Bell publicity after 1907, calls for order, hierarchy, and centralized control were increasingly replaced by praise for flexibility and decentralization. Another new slogan appeared in Bell advertisements: "Every Bell Telephone Is the Center of the System." Once, executives like Charles Fay had fumed about the incompetence and ingratitude of ordinary telephone users. In private, Vail and his followers remained committed to centralizing power away from the user, the operating company, or the local manager. But as they worked to restructure the Bell System along these lines, their publicity took a far more solicitous pose. AT&T advertisements now declared that the telephone network had as many masters as it had users.

This revision of the system idea grew bolder as years went on. Organic metaphors joined and superseded the merely mechanical. In 1910, Herbert Casson described the Bell System as "a living conscious being." In 1914, Vail described AT&T as "an ever-living organism." Such metaphors enjoyed a vogue in the era's political culture. They seemed to capture the holistic complexity of modern systems, and the need for careful stewardship and intimate cooperation. "Government is not a machine, but a living thing," Woodrow Wilson said in his 1912 "New Freedom" speech. "It is accountable to Darwin, not to Newton."[59] An AT&T advertisement from that year compared the Bell System to a tree:

> A noble tree thrives because the leaves, twigs, branches, trunk and roots are all working together, each doing its part so that all may live. . . . The existence of the tree depends not only on the activity of all the parts, but upon their being always connected together in the "tree system." This is true also of that wonderful combination of wires, switchboards, telephones, employees, and subscribers which helps make up what is called the Bell Telephone System. It is more than the vast machinery of communication, covering the country from ocean to ocean. Every part is alive, and each gives additional usefulness to every other part.[60]

The "tree system" was interconnected and united, yet also alive and "interdependent"—by then a favorite word of Theodore Vail's. More than a machine, it was a living being. Each of its parts depended on the others. This was the subtle revision of the system idea in which AT&T publicity was engaged.

Vail liked to tell reporters an anecdote about a time he saw "something new" in a telephone exchange. "I asked Mr. Carty to explain it . . . but he did not understand it," Vail would say. "We called the manager. He didn't know, and called his assistant. He didn't know, and called the local engineer, who was able to tell us what it was. . . . No man knows all the details of the System," Vail concluded.[61] Would Frederick Taylor have boasted of such an incident? Would Frederick Taussig? This was reverence for system, but a different sort of reverence than that which dubbed employees "human switches" and found nothing more "wonderful" than the removal of independent judgment. Vail's story was not an admission of failure but a rather disingenuous denial of centralized, hierarchical control.

What Vail might have liked best about this story was the role the telephone itself played in resolving his quandary. Vail called John Carty on the telephone. Carty called his assistant. Carty's assistant called a local engineer. The telephone, in other words, was the very instrument that allowed information and ideas to flow through the giant corporation, from chief executives to middle managers to lowly workers and back again. The telephone made this vision of a large but flexible, decentralized yet united, corporation possible. The technological system that AT&T operated might reform and redeem the corporate system that AT&T was.

For adherents to the system gospel, this reformation had profound implications: Large corporations need not be feared or vilified if the telephone could transform them, replacing rigid hierarchy with agile democracy. "The telephone arrived in time to prevent big corporations from being unwieldy and aristocratic," Herbert Casson wrote. "The foreman of a Pittsburg coal company may now stand in his subterranean office and talk to the president of the Steel Trust."[62] Thus, the telephone was enlisted to defuse the very fears of corporate bigness that AT&T's size had raised. Because anyone could call anyone else, it was argued, the telephone would break down organizational hierarchies and make rigid chains-of-command obsolete. Large companies would not only become more nimble and efficient as they adopted the telephone, they would become more egalitarian and democratic—not octopuses but trees, not plutocratic trusts but interdependent organisms.

AT&T publicity after 1907 never sought to deny or downplay the scope and power of the telephone network. Instead, it aimed to redeem that power by offering it to telephone users. "Your line is connected with the great Bell highways, reaching every state in the union," promised one of AT&T's monthly magazine ads. "Wherever you may be, a multitude is within reach of your voice," said another. Advertisements like these courted business customers like the Main Street merchants and entrepreneurs who had fuelled the rise of independent telephony, beguiling them with the reach and power that, they argued, only the Bell System could provide. "The multiplication of power in a businessman . . . depends upon the increased number of people whom he can, by personal contact, interest in his purposes," said another advertisement in the series. "He does this by the telephone."[63] AT&T publicity emphasized not the power of the telephone company, but the power it might afford its users.

As an answer to the monstrous spiders and octopuses so popular in independent caricatures of the Bell System, AT&T advertisements offered striking images of giant operators and businessmen looming over a nation the telephone had made manageable and small.[64] America's local businessmen need not imagine themselves as the helpless prey of the octopus, these images argued. They could see themselves instead as masters of the national network, empowered rather than threatened by its size. Awestruck descriptions of nation-spanning machinery were juxtaposed with seemingly contradictory celebrations of individual empowerment. The national telephone network was indeed immense—but AT&T's customers were, or could be, bigger still.

AT&T's publicists also worked to counter fears of ethnic and sectional difference with a rhetoric of national union through communication and commerce. "In a country like ours, where there are eighty nationalities in the public schools, the telephone has a peculiar value as a part of the national digestive apparatus," argued Casson. "When the telephone was invented," one of Ellsworth's pamphlets claimed, "the United States consisted of 37 commonwealths loosely held together . . . lacking in organization and efficiency of action." The arrival of the telephone changed all that. "Loose ends were gathered up. . . . Social and business methods were put on a broader and more efficient basis, and the passing of sectionalism and race feud began." The telephone had conquered not only "sectionalism" but "race feud"—a bold assertion in 1915. AT&T's long-distance network "blots out North, South, East and West, leaving in their stead one national family," declared another piece of publicity from that year.[65]

To be sure, there were limits to the company's boldness, and lines that AT&T's promoters were loathe to cross. A half century after the Civil War, AT&T's representations of sectional interconnection almost invariably ran from east to west rather than north to south. The first telephone calls from New York to Atlanta or New Orleans did not receive anything like the publicity around the first calls to Denver or San Francisco. Though AT&T constructed long-distance circuits in every direction, they did not trumpet their north-south connections as they did their east-west lines. It was safer for AT&T to illustrate national unity as a matter of east-west communication. This could be done without raising the ghosts of sectional conflict or pressing modern questions around politics and race. Those wires were still too live to touch.

A magazine advertisement from 1913 illustrated the delicacy of the company's position. Under the headline "The Merger of East and West," the ad depicted two smiling men speaking on the telephone from either side of the United States. The text of the advertisement paraphrased Rudyard Kipling's "Ballad of East and West," a story about an Indian bandit who befriends an English colonel's son. "These men were of different races and represented widely different ideas of life," the copy read. Yet "each found in the other elements of character which made them friends." If this text stood alone, it might seem remarkably progressive, offering a call for friendship

Figure 9. AT&T publicity answered images of the octopus with visions of giant businessmen empowered by the long-distance phone. "Annihilator of Space," AT&T Advertisement, August 1910; "Your Telephone Horizon," AT&T Advertisement, December 1913.

and interconnection across sectional and racial lines. But the illustration told another story. The two men speaking on the telephone were not of different races. Nor did they seem to come from different walks of life. Both appear to be white, business-class Americans. The easterner had a moustache and the westerner wore a hat, but otherwise they could be twins.[66]

The telephone, this ad went on to say, had "broken down the barriers of distance" and made Americans "a homogenous people." AT&T's offer of homogeneity must have had a powerful appeal in 1913. Technology and commerce were altering space, connecting Americans to continent-spanning networks of information and exchange. Still, AT&T promised its customers, the telephone need not threaten regional identities or lines of race and class and outlook. The people on the other end of the line would be people who looked just like them. AT&T's publicity for the national telephone network combined the rhetoric of national integration with subtle assurances that everyone to be so connected was essentially the same.

Clearly, AT&T's long and influential publicity campaign did more than simply promote telephone service. Ultimately, the company was selling nothing less than national commercial integration. It was promoting the legitimacy of big business and the whole transformation the American economy had recently undergone. "To shrivel up the miles and to stretch out the minutes—this has been one of the master passions of the human race," wrote Herbert Casson. "The larger truth about the telephone is that it is vastly more than a mere convenience. . . . It is nothing less than the high-speed tool of civilization, gearing up the whole mechanism to more effective social service. It is the symbol of national efficiency and cooperation."[67]

This was an audacious and successful campaign that helped to change Americans' understanding of the economy and their place in it. It celebrated a new corporate order and cast the telephone as a solution to the very problems that new order seemed to raise. The telephone would not erase local communities; it would turn the entire nation into one close-knit neighborhood. The telephone did not threaten the autonomy of middling entrepreneurs; it would magnify their power. The telephone was not a tool of monstrous corporate trusts; it would transform those trusts into more dynamic, democratic institutions. One AT&T advertisement from the 1920s seemed to directly address the entire transformation of society in this era when it said, "[the telephone] helps the individual man and woman to triumph over the complexities of a vast world."[68] Slowly, skillfully, and patiently, AT&T was teaching Americans to stop worrying and love the octopus.

A remarkable book called *Romance of the Machine*, published in 1929 by the physicist Michael Pupin, took AT&T's ideas to their millennial extreme. Pupin was one of the fathers of the long-distance telephone network. In 1899, he invented the loading coils that made truly long-distance telephony possible. Selling his patents to AT&T in 1900 made Pupin a wealthy man and something of a public figure. His patriotic autobiography *From Immigrant to Inventor* received a Pulitzer Prize in 1924. And in *Romance of the Machine*, Pupin turned the telephone into an instrument not only of democracy, but of technocratic utopia. "I wish to describe the romance of the telephone," Pupin began. But it was not the telephone so much as the telephone company that Pupin found romantic. He praised the Bell System as "the largest and most perfectly co-ordinated industrial organization in the world." AT&T offered a model of a flexible, cooperating system, Pupin argued, not only for other industries, but also for government and every human endeavor. The United States was pioneering a new kind of economic democracy, he said, and the telephone lay at the heart of that transformation. It consolidated the nation without controlling it, it "harmonized interests" without ever reducing freedom. "Who can contemplate . . . the industrial democracy inaugurated by our telephone industry," Pupin asked, "without being assured that it is a joyful message of an approaching civilization which will be more just and generous to the worker than any which the world has ever seen?"[69] From Pupin's vantage point in the heady summer of 1929, the future looked bright indeed.

Portraits of Vail

On 25 January 1915, AT&T held the first of many lavish ceremonies to commemorate the United States' first coast-to-coast telephone call. Alexander Graham Bell, in New York, spoke by telephone to his old assistant Thomas Watson, in San Francisco. "Mr. Watson, come here, I want to see you," Bell said, repeating the words he had spoken in the very first telephone call, nearly forty years before. "Why, Mr. Bell," replied Watson, "it would take me a week to do that now!" This premeditated witticism traveled thirty-five hundred miles from San Francisco to New York, across thirteen states

Figure 10. Alexander Graham Bell (center) with Mayor John Purroy Mitchell of New York (at Bell's right) and other dignitaries at the official opening of transcontinental telephone service, New York, 25 January 1915. Plate 4.644, *The Pageant of America* Photograph Archive, vol. 4: "The March of Commerce," New York Public Library.

and over nearly three thousand tons of copper wire supported by 130,000 telephone poles. Another circuit connected Bell and Watson with President Wilson in Washington and with Theodore Vail, vacationing in Georgia. And the real achievement, AT&T executives were quick to point out, was not this one call but the system in its entirety, a now truly national long-distance network connecting more than nine million telephones from sea to sea.[70]

Two photographs of this ceremony appear in numerous histories of the telephone. The first and more famous photo shows Alexander Graham Bell sitting with New York mayor John Purroy Mitchell and other dignitaries at the New York end of the transcontinental call. A second photograph shows Thomas Watson at the Panama-Pacific Exhibition in San Francisco with a similar collection of West Coast notables. Conspicuously absent from either picture is Theodore Vail. (In the New York photograph, Vail's portrait appears on the wall behind Bell.) There is another photograph, however, that never appeared in AT&T publicity or any official histories of the company. It shows Vail listening in on the inaugural call from the Jekyll Island Club, an exclusive resort on the Georgia coast owned and frequented by America's wealthiest business leaders. At Vail's side are four men. Two of them are architects, there to consult with Vail on the AT&T Building then under construction in New York. The other two men are William Rockefeller and J. P. Morgan Jr.

One can guess why AT&T would choose not to publicize this particular photograph in the days of muckrakers and trustbusters. It made perfect sense, however, for Theodore Vail to be joined by a Rockefeller and a Morgan at this moment of triumph. Vail and his company had not only built a coast-to-coast telephone system. They were well on their way to owning the entire industry, locking up control of the Bell operating companies and bringing even the independents to heel. Another portrait of Vail, after all, was hanging on Frank Woods's wall. When Vail retired from the presidency of AT&T in 1919, the structure of the telephone industry for the next sixty years was essentially in place. AT&T had redeemed its public image, beaten back the challenge of independent competition, escaped major antitrust action, and cemented its near monopoly over the telephone in America with congenial government regulation.

And that is not all. In the crucible of telephone competition and the larger crisis of corporate legitimacy in the United States, AT&T forged a powerful defense of integration, consolidation, and big business, all wrapped in the gospel of system. AT&T pioneered the tactics of corporate public relations, constructing the template for a positive image of big business that virtually every large American company would imitate in years to come. And it offered Americans around the country a reassuring way to imagine themselves within the new national economy, and vivid metaphors with which to do so. In embracing the Bell System, Americans came to embrace their nation's new political economy. Finally, AT&T wrote the history of the telephone—just as Walter Gifford would edit his words—so that the many battles of its first fifty years were downplayed and eventually

Figure 11. AT&T president Theodore Vail (seated far right, on the telephone), with William Rockefeller (seated), J. P. Morgan Jr. (behind Rockefeller) and two other men, participating in the opening of transcontinental telephone service from Vail's summer home on Jekyll Island, Georgia. Courtesy of AT&T Archives and Historical Center, Warren, New Jersey.

forgotten. Herbert Casson's *History of the Telephone* and all its later imitations were also portraits of Theodore Vail. They praised his vision in predicting the future of the industry but effaced from history the battles his company had fought and won to fulfill its own prophecies. AT&T's vision of the telephone and the economic order it sustained came to seem natural and inevitable. If it is difficult for us to imagine alternatives—if, in retrospect, the heyday of independent telephony seems an aberration and the idea of a people's telephone sounds naïve—that too is a measure of Vail's triumph and its cost.

Conclusion

Return to Middletown

When Robert and Helen Lynd returned to Muncie in the 1930s to write a sequel to *Middletown*, the Depression had radicalized the scholars but not the town. *Middletown in Transition*, published in 1937, was more political than the Lynds' original study and more critical of Muncie and its values. The sense of loss that had been a subtheme in the earlier book became the sequel's dominant chord. In particular, *Middletown in Transition* mourned Muncie's absorption into America's national economy, the loss of its local autonomy, and the deference of its middle and upper classes to the new corporate order. "Local giants . . . have shrunk in stature," the Lynds wrote. Big business had invaded Muncie, displacing its old middle class of "independent manufacturers, independent merchants, and . . . independent professional people" with a new class of salaried dependents.[1]

Middletown in Transition devoted an entire chapter to a group the first *Middletown* had not even mentioned—the "X" family, the Lynds' pseudonym for Muncie's wealthiest clan, the Balls. The Ball brothers—Lucius, William, Edmund, Frank, and George—had once been independents of a sort. They were glass makers who had invaded the market in glass canning jars after John Mason's patent expired in 1883. The Balls were not involved in Muncie's telephone fights, although in the days of competition, Ball Brothers Glass and its subsidiaries always subscribed to both telephones. By the 1920s, Ball jars were sold nationwide, and the three living brothers were millionaires. The Depression did little to hurt sales of canning jars and only widened the economic gap between the Balls and their neighbors. In 1935, George Ball became a player on the national economic scene when he bought several railroads at auction from J. P. Morgan and Company. At least one group of Muncie's "local giants" was thriving in the new national economy.[2]

A profile of George Ball published by the *Saturday Evening Post* in 1937 held him up as a model for America's local businessmen to follow. The *Post*, a magazine that played its own role in training Americans to embrace the national grid, lauded the scope of Ball's ambitions, calling him "a small-town man with big-town interests." It also highlighted the technology George Ball used to operate on a national scale. "With one telephone he manages to keep in pretty constant communication with New York, Chicago, Cleveland and the West," the *Post* reported, sounding not unlike an advertisement for AT&T. "He has developed telephoning into a fine art, and there are people all over the country who know George Ball well and have never met him except at the other end of a wire."[3] The message was clear. America's small-town businessmen could prosper in the new national economy without giving up their hometown identities. The telephone and other new technologies could make them national players, rather than the victims of big business and its rise.

Middletown in Transition was not critical of the Balls themselves. The Lynds took pains to praise the "X" family for public spirit and philanthropy. What the Lynds lamented was the way the rest of the town deferred to its "reigning royal family," and the way one success story concealed the larger truth of Muncie's capitulation to outside economic forces. The Ball Corporation was no longer a local enterprise, the Lynds argued. It belonged with "outside big units" in "Middletown's big-business bloc." *Middletown in Transition* eulogized the independence of local manufacturers, merchants, and professionals—the same Main Street businessmen who once organized and patronized the independent telephone movement. Muncie had been "built around the theory of local autonomy," the Lynds wrote; now the slogans of local boosterism rang hollow and false. "The town's old backbone . . . holds its own as best it can, insisting that *it* still is Middletown," they said. But in all important matters, the native middle class now genuflected to outside corporate interests.[4]

Other observers shared the Lynds' assessment but not their dismay. "Mr. and Mrs. John Citizen of Middletown, U.S.A. do not believe that there is anything inherently wrong with business corporations because they are big," concluded *Sales Management* magazine after a survey of Muncie residents in 1938. "They mention nearly twelve times as many good points as bad points about ninety leading corporations." One of those leading corporations, of course, was AT&T. Fifty-seven percent of the Muncie residents queried said that AT&T gave its customers good value for their money; only 4 percent considered it an unfair monopoly.[5] In the years around the turn of the century, little had stirred more passionate protest in Muncie and its neighbors than the rapid rise of giant corporations and the threat they seemed to pose to the autonomy and integrity of small-town life. Yet by the 1940s, one Bell executive would testify, "the bigness so recently deplored" was widely seen as "fundamental to the nation's strength."[6]

In 1908, Muncie's General Kemper had called electrical communication "the greatest vital issue . . . both economically and politically, before the American people."[7] The communication networks constructed in Kemper's day were at the center of protest and debate over America's political economy and economic geography. The telephone wired homes and offices and individuals into the national economy and into this debate. The questions facing Americans and Canadians in the late nineteenth and early twentieth centuries played out in the arenas of politics and commerce and also in networks of switchboards and telephone wires. By the time the Lynds returned to Muncie in 1935, its business leaders and even its broader middle class had come to see themselves as participants in a national economy created and symbolized by the grid of telephones, telegraphs, and trains.

"Railroads reach cities, towns, and villages. The telephone reaches the individual." So boasted an AT&T advertisement from 1920.[8] The railroads may have catalyzed the centralization of wealth and power in the United States, but the telephone and the battle for its future domesticated and legitimized that corporate order. As AT&T built a national telephone network, it pioneered new tactics of corporate public relations, constructing the template for a positive image of big business that virtually every large American company would imitate in years to come. And it did more than that. It gave Americans a new way of imagining the national network and their place in it. As the commercial threat of independent competition declined, AT&T appropriated the rhetoric of its former foes, promoting the telephone itself as an innately democratic and democratizing technology, a cure for the curse of bigness. This brand of technological populism has become our default way of talking about new communication technologies in the twentieth century and beyond. Wireless telephony in the 1910s; broadcast radio in the 1920s; television in the 1940s and 1950s; personal computers in the 1970s and 1980s; the Internet in the 1990s; and at the start of the twenty-first century, wireless telephones again: each would be described in their day as empowering the individual and rejuvenating democracy, even when those technologies were owned and controlled by monopoly-seeking corporations still larger and more powerful than AT&T.[9]

The Political Construction of the Telephone

Born in the United States and tempered in the crucible of the midwestern telephone fight, AT&T's defense of corporate integration and consolidation was also exported to Canada. Themes and ideas developed by Theodore Vail and his subordinates can be seen in Bell Canada's publicity, particularly after the retirement of president Charles Sise in 1915. But a vigorous defense of corporate consolidation proved less necessary in Canada. Though Canadians have been less hostile than Americans to public enterprise, and arguably less friendly to private business, they have placed less emphasis than Americans on bigness as a particular evil. (Of course, in Canada, corporations were simply never so big.) And AT&T's new rhetoric of technological populism fit awkwardly with the Canadian tradition of technological nationalism, which continued through the twentieth century unabated. Canadians, and particularly federal politicians, would turn again and again to new communication technologies in hopes of securing cultural and economic unity—with limited success.

In the development of telephony, the politics of localism and nationalism had ironic outcomes. In Central Canada, a nationalist mission for the telephone was articulated strongly from the start. By the 1880s, Bell Canada and the federal government had both embraced the vision of a single telephone system reaching from sea to sea. But the nationalist idea was not as strong in other parts of the country, and close association with central Canadian nationalism undermined attempts to construct a single coast-to-coast system. As the provinces demanded authority over the telephone, Bell Canada retreated, only somewhat reluctantly, from its stated nationalist aims. The telephone system that emerged in Canada was less a national network than a quilt of distinct regional monopolies, representing a mixture of public and private ownership, federal and provincial regulation, and Canadian and American control.

Some students of Canadian federalism have called this a "great mystery." Why did modern technologies and institutions not lead to centralization in Canada, but rather to heightened regionalism, both in the telephone industry and in broad aspects of Canadian cultural, political, and economic life?[10] The implicit comparison in this characterization is, of course, to the American experience, where modernization meant the centralization of political and economic power. But one could easily reverse the terms of this mystery. In the midwestern United States, the Bell System faced criticism and competition on a scale seen nowhere else in the world. The independent challenge to Bell's national network was fuelled by a fierce defense of localism and by an antitrust tradition unique to the United States in its longevity and force. Yet what emerged from this fight was a highly centralized telephone system and an argument in favor of consolidation that many Americans found compelling for decades to come. Both of these outcomes—in Canada and the United States—were unique. Most European countries created government monopolies to operate their telephones. No other nation created a patchwork telephone system like Canada's. No other nation created a private telephone conglomerate that rivaled the size and scope of the Bell System in the United States.[11]

The answer to the mystery is that neither the development of the telephone nor its effects were predetermined by any innate logic of modernity or technological change. Nor was the destiny of the telephone chosen by the natural selection of the market or the agency of individual consumers. The telephone networks of the United States and Canada were politically constructed, in a complex struggle of overlapping interests and ideas. Paul Latzke was only half right: there was not one fight for the telephone but many. And these fights were rarely fought on level political ground. Different political structures encouraged different kinds of appeals. They made different visions of telephony seem reasonable and different outcomes seem natural. The political economies of Ontario and Quebec—though not the Prairie Provinces to the west—rewarded Bell Canada for its pose of Canadian nationalism. The political economy of the American Midwest was extremely hospitable to the localism and populism of the independents. And the United States federal courts and Interstate Commerce Commission were friendly to centralization and the dominance of AT&T.

In many ways, neither Canadians nor Americans got the telephone system they said they wanted. Individual consumers had a hand in the development of telephony, but they were hardly sovereign in this process. The telephone systems Americans and Canadians constructed did not emerge from free market competition or individual consumer choice. But Americans and Canadians were not only private consumers. They were also citizens and voters, who debated and disputed the legitimacy of the telephone monopoly, along with all the other corporate systems and networks that emerged in their time. Telephone users organized in groups to assert their interests. They voted for politicians willing and able to do the same. Some even built their own telephone systems in both commercial and collective forms.

Telephone networks were political entities from their very creation, the products and the subjects of collective action and debate. The actors in these contests constantly, even perversely, denied the political nature of telephony themselves. They reached for assertions that what they were doing was "natural"—natural monopolies, natural selection, the nature of the telephone—as if to evade responsibility for the decisions they were making or to deny that they were making decisions at all. But the telephone was never a product of nature. It was constructed, by people, in the untidy world of politics and power.

After the People's Telephone

The independent telephone movement had barely begun by the turn of the century, yet as a meaningful challenge to AT&T's dominance of the industry, the movement was over by the end of the First World War. Was anything lost when it ended? We do not need to romanticize the independents, or ignore the challenges facing them, to feel that there was. Americans and Canadians born in the middle of the twentieth century may remember when the telephone was a rather forbidding device.[12] One used it for serious business, then relinquished the wires. To many, a long-distance call or even a local call after dark once signaled terrible news. Yet for the first generation that grew up with the telephone, this wasn't necessarily so. Rural Americans, especially those in the heartland of the independent movement, created and enjoyed a telephone culture that was lively, social, and easily characterized as frivolous. This telephone culture was predicated on flat rates and local networks. A Muncie farm girl in the early 1900s might have giggled for hours on the telephone, then got off the line to let the neighbors hear her father play his banjo for a spell. And if Pa had strung the wire from town himself, he might not have appreciated being asked to get off the line.

By the 1920s, those unmeasured days had come to a close. As AT&T achieved full control of its industry, the vibrant, generative culture of flat-rate local telephone use went into decline. Thousands of little telephone systems sold out to Bell or went bankrupt. Bell's own operating companies, once another source of variation and innovation, surrendered their autonomy to serve the demands of long-distance service and efficiency. State and federal regulation trumped municipal engagement with the telephone and entrenched the near-monopoly of the Bell System. Both billing structures and the protocols of "polite behavior" served to define and suppress casual and informal use of the wires. Small-town and rural telephone use would not be as affordable, innovative, or fun for decades to come. It is true that as the twentieth century wore on, improved technology, lower rates, and the eventual return of competition would restore inexpensive access and revive some of what had been lost in the decline of the people's telephone. But by then the world had turned. The economic structures on which the people's telephone was based—small towns and their hinterlands linked in healthy, locally oriented economies—have never really been restored.[13]

This story runs counter to many expectations about technology and communication technology in particular. We are so used to technological progress that we take it for granted. We are trained to assume that new technologies can only get cheaper and better. Historians may have replaced chronicles of technological determinism with narratives of consumer agency and triumph, but the trajectory of these stories is still almost always toward better access, cheaper service, and more freedom. The history of technology is generally written "for boys of all ages," one historian has complained, and the endings are almost always happy.[14] The sputtering out of the people's telephone in the early twentieth century confounds our expectations and offers a more cautionary tale.

The People's Internet?

This book is a work of history, and I have made every effort to approach that history on its own terms. I have tried to avoid drawing direct parallels between the early history of the telephone and our own era of rapid change and innovation in communication technology. Such parallels are never exact. And given the pace of technological change, I know that any references I make to contemporary events will only date this work. But I will not be unhappy if readers make their own connections.

In many ways, the American and Canadian telephone industries at the start of the twenty-first century look more like their counterparts of a century ago than like the industries of the intervening years. Competition returned to the American industry with the court-ordered breakup of the Bell System in 1984. The alliance that toppled Bell—among the Justice Department, new long-distance providers like MCI, and users lobbying for lower rates—would have been quite familiar to John Wright. A second era of competition followed in the 1980s and 1990s, although, just as in the late nineteenth century, there was no such thing as unfettered free-market competition, but rather a complex political environment where rival corporations contended with each other, with consumers, and with public officials from multiple levels of government. By the early 2000s, the North American telephone industry had reconsolidated into the hands of just a few big corporate players. Most were descendants of the Bell operating companies split off from AT&T in 1984. A few, such as Sprint Nextel, had historical ties to the old independent movement. In 2005, a much-diminished AT&T was acquired, and its name adopted, by SBC Communications, a firm that was once the Southwestern Bell Corporation and originally Bell's Missouri and Kansas affiliate.

In the years before and after the turn of the millennium, the Internet entered the lives of millions and new wireless technologies radically altered the grids laid down a century ago. Those years saw dreams of technological convergence and fears of monopoly. They saw a boom and then a crash among entrepreneurs whose enthusiasm for the Internet's democratizing power would have been entirely familiar to the apostles of independent telephony. They saw a surge of interest by local governments in deploying municipal wireless networks and fierce opposition to this move by the Bell System's corporate descendants. And they saw the largest corporations in the computer and telecommunications industries appropriate the language of consumer empowerment to beat back competition and ward off political attack. At the start of the twenty-first century, Theodore Vail's strategies and ideas were alive and well.

Are there lessons in the history of the telephone for us to learn or use today? I hesitate to suggest that twenty-first-century technologies will or should develop like the telephone in any detailed or determining way. We have seen how earlier systems like the railroad, the post, and the telegraph shaped ideas about the telephone; such precedents obscured original thinking and narrowed possibilities at least as often as they provided useful strategies or ideas. Still, the general shape of the story may offer some insights.

First and foremost, the history of the telephone demonstrates the inescapably political nature of communication technology. It challenges notions of our own political impotence, and indeed the impotence of politics generally, in the face of rapid technological change. Perhaps the most common refrain of the early Internet era was of the irrelevance of politics. A new world was dawning, it was said, because the technology itself demanded it. Not only were governments and citizens powerless to control this process, they would have been foolish to try.[15] But claims that politics cannot shape technology are themselves political maneuvers and ought to be met with skepticism. The history of the telephone—and, already, the history of the Internet—demonstrates that communication networks are always political, and that collective action, even on a small scale or local level, can shape their construction in meaningful ways.

The history of the telephone also makes an interesting case against centralization and standardization, even against efficiency per se. Early telephone networks grew fastest and furthest—they were at their most generative, to borrow an anachronistic but useful concept—precisely when they were least organized and efficient.[16] The competitive era in telephony from the 1890s to the 1910s produced furious innovation from both the independents and the regional Bell operating companies, and a pace of growth and change never matched in the decades that followed. The telephone industry in its first competitive era was wasteful and chaotic but also responsive to the public and surprisingly egalitarian. Barriers to entry were low, and barriers to influencing the industry were lower still. The sticky fingers and clumsy bylaws of a hundred municipal governments often proved a better spur to innovation and a better defense of the public interest than expert federal regulation. The digital revolution of our own time has been suffused with democratic rhetoric, but that rhetoric is often qualified by impatience with the messiness that true democracy entails. Technically minded people admire centralization, uniform standards, and the efficiency these bring. But these are not the signal virtues of democracy. And they are not the only criteria by which technological systems should be judged.

Today we have the opportunity and responsibility to make decisions about the future of our communication networks, just as Americans and Canadians did one century ago. The ways we communicate with one another are, or should be, at the very center of political debate. Will we trade away genuine choices for the simplicity and efficiency of one big system? Will we give up what power we have as citizens and stakeholders while parroting slogans of consumer empowerment? Will we accept that space and distance, and therefore local autonomy, have been annihilated because we are told technology makes it so? I hope we will not be quick to surrender the authority of the political process over such matters, or to take the words of interested parties as to what new devices "naturally" mean or require.

A sense has already set in, I think, that the Internet and related media will not be all we once hoped. In particular, the widely heard predictions that the Internet would be a fundamentally democratizing force in economic as well as political life—a people's Internet?—already seem naïve. A frontier gold rush of perhaps a hundred thousand little start-ups has given way to an oligopoly of corporate giants, old and new. Great fortunes have been made, but the barriers to making new ones have largely been rebuilt. Data throttling and usage-based billing by large service providers (reminiscent of Bell's measured service, though as always the parallels are not exact) threaten the neutrality and some say the underpinning philosophy of the Internet. The open, generative web is being replaced, many fear, by tethered appliances and walled social media gardens. Whatever ingenious toys are still in store for us, fewer and fewer people will admit to believing that the communication revolution we are living through will fulfill the more utopian hopes of the 1990s or early 2000s.

Of course those hopes were always mostly hype. Like visions of the people's telephone, they were overblown and ahistorical, and generally peddled by people out to make a buck. Yet they resonated and found a receptive audience, perhaps because buried in them were old and compelling ideas about communication and democracy, and a hope that some historical missteps might be put right. But people hate to be fooled, and they desperately hate to be disappointed. As hopes for a people's Internet sour, early enthusiasm for the democratic potential of the technology may well become embarrassing, like the fashions of a prior decade. It would be easy to comfort ourselves by dismissing the idea of a people's Internet as naïve and obsolete. We could conspire to forget the history of the Internet and the roles of human choice, politics, and power in its development. We could chide ourselves for thinking that things could have been different. We could reassure ourselves that it was the free market or the inherent logic of the technology that decreed that things must be just as they are. It has happened before.

But there are elements of the people's telephone worth remembering. There is the idea that ordinary people should imagine and work toward the best possible use of a new technology in light of their democratically determined needs. There is the view that community-scaled networks might be more egalitarian or humane than a single national or global grid. And there is the notion that governments and markets can work profitably together to build and operate such networks. These ideas have gone in and out of fashion, but they are not necessarily obsolete. Nor are they so very radical or naïve. What would be naïve, however, would be to think that these things could happen automatically, or that public policy and political economy would play no role, or that the octopuses of the world will give up their power without a fight.

Notes

Introduction

1. Paul A. Latzke, *A Fight with an Octopus* (Chicago: Telephony Press, 1906).

2. Latzke, *A Fight with an Octopus*, 11.

3. Latzke, *A Fight with an Octopus*, 5, 9; U.S. Census Bureau, *Telephones and Telegraphs: 1912* (Washington, D.C.: Government Printing Office, 1915), 35; U.S. Census Bureau, *Historical Statistics of the United States* (Washington, D.C.: Government Printing Office, 1975), 2: 783–784.

4. James E. Caldwell, *Recollections of a Life Time* (Nashville: Baird-Ward Press, 1923), 178.

5. See, e.g., Herbert N. Casson, *The History of the Telephone* (Chicago: A. C. McClurg, 1910); Horace Coon, *American Tel & Tel: The Story of a Great Monopoly* (New York: Longmans, Green, 1939); Alvin Von Auw, *Heritage and Destiny: Reflections on the Bell System in Transition* (New York: Praeger, 1983).

6. The independents have their own partisan histories, but most are privately printed books that never reached the audience of the AT&T versions: Latzke, *A Fight with an Octopus*; Harry B. MacMeal, *The Story of Independent Telephony* (Chicago: Independent Pioneer Telephone Association, 1934); Charles A. Pleasance, *The Spirit of Independent Telephony* (Johnson City, Tenn.: Independent Telephone Books, 1989).

7. See, e.g., Ithiel de Sola Pool, ed., *The Social Impact of the Telephone* (Cambridge, Mass.: MIT Press, 1977); and the Johns Hopkins/AT&T series in telephone history, published between 1985 and 1989: Robert W. Garnet, *The Telephone Enterprise: The Evolution of the Bell System's Horizontal Structure, 1876–1909* (Baltimore: Johns Hopkins University Press, 1985); George David Smith, *The Anatomy of a Business Strategy: Bell, Western Electric, and the Origins of the American Telephone Industry* (Baltimore: Johns Hopkins University Press, 1985); Neil H. Wasserman, *From Invention to Innovation: Long-Distance Telephone Transmission at the Turn of the Century* (Baltimore: Johns Hopkins University Press, 1985); Kenneth Lipartito, *The Bell System and Regional Business: The Telephone in the South, 1877–1920* (Baltimore: Johns Hopkins University Press, 1989). The first three volumes of the Johns Hopkins/AT&T series are detailed, useful works, but strongly shaped by their origins in the AT&T Archives. The last and best volume in the series, Ken Lipartito's *The Bell System and Regional Business*, incorporates a wider range of sources, actors, and views.

8. In the 1980s and 1990s, historians and sociologists interested in the social construction of technology challenged the determinism of the old AT&T narrative and highlighted ways ordinary men and women shaped the use and meaning of telephony. But their sources led them to see AT&T as representative of the telephone industry as a whole, and they typically overlooked the variety and dynamism of the independents and indeed the other Bell companies. And while this literature celebrated the agency of individual consumers, it had less to say about their collective actions as citizens and the political struggles that profoundly shaped the telephone industry and its development. See, e.g., Carolyn Marvin, *When Old Technologies Were New: Thinking About Electric Communication in the Late Nineteenth Century* (New York: Oxford University Press, 1988); Michèle Martin, *Hello, Central? Gender, Technology, and Culture in the Formation of Telephone Systems* (Montreal: McGill-Queen's University Press, 1991); Claude S. Fischer, *America Calling: A Social History of the Telephone to 1940* (Berkeley: University of California Press, 1992).

9. Scholarship employing this broader source base to tell a story that goes beyond AT&T includes Roy Alden Atwood, "Telephony and Its Cultural Meanings in Southeastern Iowa, 1900–1917" (Ph.D. diss., University of Iowa, 1984); Milton L. Mueller, *Universal Service: Competition, Interconnection, and Monopoly in the Making of the American Telephone System* (Cambridge, Mass.: MIT Press, 1997); Ronald R. Kline, *Consumers in the Country: Technology and Social Change in Rural America* (Baltimore: Johns Hopkins University Press, 2000); Richard R. John, *Network Nation: Inventing American Telecommunication* (Cambridge, Mass.: Harvard University Press, 2010).

10. Richard R. John, "Recasting the Information Infrastructure for the Industrial Age," in *A Nation Transformed by Information: How Information Has Shaped the United States from Colonial Times to the Present*, ed. Alfred D. Chandler and James W. Cortada (New York: Oxford University Press, 2000), 55–105.

11. Latzke, *A Fight with an Octopus*, 9.

12. Robert MacDougall, "The Wire Devils: Pulp Thrillers, the Telephone, and Action at a Distance in the Wiring of a Nation," *American Quarterly* 58, no. 3 (September 2006), 715–741.

13. The literature on these topics is enormous. On the railroads and their impact, begin with Alfred D. Chandler, *The Visible Hand: The Managerial Revolution in American Business* (Cambridge, Mass.: Harvard University Press, 1977); but see also Gerald Berk, *Alternative Tracks: The Constitution of American Industrial Order, 1865–1917* (Baltimore: Johns Hopkins University Press, 1994); and Richard White, *Railroaded: The Transcontinentals and the Making of Modern America* (New York: W. W. Norton, 2011). On the telegraph, standard works include Robert L. Thompson, *Wiring a Continent: The History of the Telegraph Industry in the United States, 1832–1866* (Princeton, N.J.: Princeton University Press, 1947); and James W. Carey, "Technology and Ideology: The Case of the Telegraph," in his *Communications as Culture* (Boston: Unwin Hyman, 1989), 201–230; but see the important revisions in John, *Network Nation*, and

David Paul Hochfelder, *The Telegraph in America, 1832–1920* (Baltimore: Johns Hopkins University Press, 2012). On the telephone, begin with John Brooks, *Telephone: The First Hundred Years* (New York: Harper and Row, 1976); but again see John, *Network Nation*, and the other histories of telephony cited above.

14. Richard B. DuBoff, "The Telegraph and the Structure of Markets in the United States, 1845–1890," *Research in Economic History* 8 (1983): 253–277; Naomi R. Lamoreaux, *The Great Merger Movement in American Business, 1895–1904* (Cambridge: Cambridge University Press, 1985); William G. Roy, *Socializing Capital: The Rise of the Large Industrial Corporation in America* (Princeton, N.J.: Princeton University Press, 1997); plus the works cited in previous note.

15. Some historians question the fairness and utility of the term "Gilded Age." Rebecca Edwards and Richard R. John both believe the label is pejorative, emphasizing the role of greed and corruption in this era. I do not disagree but am inclined to find this a point in the label's favor. To be consistent, we ought to come up with equally pejorative labels for all the other eras in American and Canadian history, including our own! In this book, I use the term "Gilded Age" advisedly: not as a neutral label for the late nineteenth century, but to specifically connote the crimes and crises of these years. As political corruption and the concentration of wealth were hardly vanquished after 1901, I think it is fair to speak of a "Long Gilded Age" from the 1870s through the 1920s (the years covered in this book), one coexistent and contemporaneous with the "Long Progressive Era" Edwards has described. See Rebecca Edwards, Richard R. John, and Richard Bensel, "Forum: Should We Abolish the 'Gilded Age'?" *Journal of the Gilded Age and Progressive Era* 8, no. 4 (2009): 461–485; Rebecca Edwards, *New Spirits: Americans in the Gilded Age, 1865–1905* (New York: Oxford University Press, 2006), 4–7.

16. Jackson Lears, *Rebirth of a Nation: The Making of Modern America, 1877–1920* (New York: Harper Collins, 2009), 42.

17. Menahem Blondheim, *News over the Wires: The Telegraph and the Flow of Public Information in America, 1844–1897* (Cambridge, Mass.: Harvard University Press, 1994), 182.

18. Robert Bruce, *1877: Year of Violence* (Indianapolis: Bobbs-Merrill, 1959); Philip S. Foner, *The Great Labor Uprising of 1877* (New York: Monad Press, 1977).

19. Ida M. Tarbell, *All in the Day's Work* (New York: Macmillan, 1939), 82.

20. Ian McKay, *Rebels, Reds, Radicals: Rethinking Canada's Left History* (Toronto: Between the Lines Press, 2005), 103–104.

21. For discussion of the phrase see Leo Marx, *The Machine in the Garden: Technology and the Pastoral Idea in America* (New York: Oxford University Press, 1964), 194–196.

22. Thomas L. Haskell, *The Emergence of Professional Social Science: The American Social Science Association and the Nineteenth-Century Crisis of Authority* (Chicago: University of Illinois Press, 1977), 15, 40.

23. The phrase "island community" is Robert Wiebe's, in Robert H. Wiebe, *The Search for Order, 1877–1920* (New York: Hill and Wang, 1967), 4, 44, 111. Thomas Bender observes that American historians have located the "breakdown" of America's isolated communities in, variously, "the 1650s, 1690s, 1740s, 1780s, 1820s, 1850s, 1880s, and 1920s." Thomas Bender, *Community and Social Change in America* (New Brunswick, N.J.: Rutgers University Press, 1978), 50–51.

24. On the social construction of space or scale, see Henri Lefebvre, *The Production of Space*, trans. Donald Nicholson-Smith (Cambridge, Mass.: Blackwell, 1991), esp. 28–31; Sallie A. Marston, "The Social Construction of Scale," *Progress in Human Geography* 24, no. 2 (2000): 219–243; Richard White, "What Is Spatial History?" (working paper, Spatial History Project, Stanford University, 2010).

25. White, *Railroaded*, xxix, 140–178; Roland Marchand, *Creating the Corporate Soul: The Rise of Public Relations and Corporate Imagery in American Big Business* (Berkeley: University of California Press, 1998), 3.

26. Berk, *Alternative Tracks*; Gretchen Ritter, *Goldbugs and Greenbacks: The Antimonopoly Tradition and the Politics of Finance in America* (Cambridge: Cambridge University Press, 1997); Roy, *Socializing Capital*; Richard R. John, "Robber Barons Redux: Antimonopoly Reconsidered," *Enterprise and Society* 13, no. 1 (2012): 1–38.

27. Most famously, in Richard Hofstadter, *The Age of Reform: From Bryan to FDR* (New York: Random House, 1955).

28. On the modernity of antimonopolism, see Charles Postel, *The Populist Vision* (New York: Oxford University Press, 2007).

29. Robert S. Lynd and Helen Merrell Lynd, *Middletown: A Study in Modern American Culture* (New York: Harcourt, Brace, 1929), 10–12. Henry Adams, born one year before Kemper, used the same trope as the Lynds to describe the changes in his own lifetime, declaring his boyhood in the 1850s to have been "nearer the year 1 than to the year 1900." Henry Adams, *The Education of Henry Adams: An Autobiography* (Boston: Houghton Mifflin, 1918), 53.

30. General William H. Kemper, *A Twentieth Century History of Delaware County, Indiana* (Chicago: Lewis, 1908), 210.

31. Among iconic titles from a literature far too large to list here are Samuel P. Hays, *The Response to Industrialism, 1885–1914* (Chicago: University of Chicago Press, 1957); Wiebe, *The Search for Order*; and Alan Trachtenberg, *The Incorporation of America: Culture and Society in the Gilded Age* (New York: Hill and Wang, 1982).

32. Kemper, *History of Delaware County*, 77.

33. George Monro Grant, *Ocean to Ocean* (Toronto: Rose Belford, 1879), 344; William Lawson Grant and Frederick Hamilton, *George Monro Grant* (Edinburgh: T. C. and E. C. Jack, 1905), 243. It is hard to overstate the significance of communications in Canadian historiography and culture. The classic work is Harold A. Innis, *Empire and Communications* (Oxford: Clarendon Press, 1950); a more recent version is Gerald Friesen, *Citizens and Nation: An Essay on History, Communication, and Canada* (Toronto: University of Toronto Press, 2000). On the history of Canadian ideas about

communication, see Robert E. Babe, *Canadian Communication Thought: Ten Foundational Writers* (Toronto: University of Toronto Press, 2000).

34. For Bell's biography, see Robert V. Bruce, *Alexander Graham Bell and the Conquest of Solitude* (Boston: Little, Brown, 1973).

35. Graham D. Taylor, "Charles F. Sise, Bell Canada, and the Americans: A Study of Managerial Autonomy, 1880–1905," *Historical Papers* (Ottawa) 17, no. 1 (1982): 11–30.

36. Useful exceptions include Lipartito, *The Bell System and Regional Business*; Meighan Jeanne Maguire, "The Local Dynamics of Telephone System Development: The San Francisco Exchange, 1893–1919" (Ph.D. diss., University of California at San Diego, 2000); Claire Poitras, *La cité au bout du fil: Le téléphone à Montréal de 1879 à 1930* (Montreal: Presses de l'Université de Montréal, 2000).

37. A comparative history sets two or more narratives side by side and seeks to explain their similarities and differences; a transnational history tells one single story that crosses national boundaries. The stellar example of the transnational approach to the history of this period is Daniel T. Rodgers, *Atlantic Crossings: Social Politics in a Progressive Age* (Cambridge, Mass.: Harvard University Press, 1998). Comparative history may actually be more common in the histories of technology and business than in other fields. See, e.g., Thomas P. Hughes, *Networks of Power: Electrification in Western Society, 1880–1930* (Baltimore: Johns Hopkins University Press, 1983); Tony Freyer, *Regulating Big Business: Antitrust in Great Britain and America, 1880–1990* (Cambridge: Cambridge University Press, 1992); Colleen A. Dunlavy, *Politics and Industrialization: Early Railroads in the United States and Prussia* (Princeton, N.J.: Princeton University Press, 1994).

38. A standard comparison of the United States and Canada is Seymour Martin Lipset, *Continental Divide: The Values and Institutions of the United States and Canada* (New York: Routledge, 1990), but see also Jason Kaufman, *The Origins of Canadian and American Political Differences* (Cambridge, Mass.: Harvard University Press, 2009). A rare work comparing U.S. and Canadian telecommunications, focused primarily on the 1980s and 1990s, is Kevin G. Wilson, *Deregulating Telecommunications: U.S. and Canadian Telecommunications, 1840–1997* (New York: Rowman and Littlefield, 2000). For comparison of telephony in the United States and the United Kingdom, see Christopher Beauchamp, "The Telephone Patents: Intellectual Property, Business and the Law in the United States and Britain, 1876–1900" (Ph.D. diss., University of Cambridge, 2006).

39. "Although it was its characteristic rather than its exceptional features which led to the selection of Middletown, no claim is made that it is a 'typical' city," the Lynds wrote. It was really the absence of exceptional features that made Muncie suitable for their purposes. Lynd and Lynd, *Middletown*, 9. On the representativeness of Muncie or lack thereof, see Richard Jensen, "The Lynds Revisited," *Indiana Magazine of History* 75 (December 1979): 303–319; Sarah Elizabeth Igo, *The Averaged American: Surveys, Citizens, and the Making of a Mass Public* (Cambridge, Mass.: Harvard University Press, 2007), 23–102.

40. My use of Muncie in this way was inspired, of course, by *Middletown*, but also by David E. Nye, *Electrifying America: Social Meanings of a New Technology, 1880–1940* (Cambridge, Mass.: MIT Press, 1990).

41. Thomas Hughes has argued that patterns of technological development are most often regional in nature. Thomas Hughes, "Shaped Technology: An Afterword," *Science in Context* 8, no. 2 (1995): 451–455.

42. Kaufman, *The Origins of Canadian and American Political Differences*, 20–22.

43. On the "structuring presence of the state," see Dunlavy, *Politics and Industrialization*, 4.

Chapter 1. All Telephones Are Local

1. John Updike, "Telephone Poles," in *Telephone Poles and Other Poems* (New York: Alfred A. Knopf, 1963), 43.

2. *Quebec Daily Telegraph*, 5 January, 9 February, 26 April, 2 May, 20 June 1881.

3. "The Tyranny of Monopolies," *Harper's Weekly*, 14 May 1881, 312–315.

4. See, e.g., "Telephone Poles Cut Down," *New York Times*, 3 July 1883; "Telegraph Poles Cut Down," *New York Times*, 4 November 1883; "An Inside View of the Telephone Business," *Indianapolis Daily Sentinel*, 8 April 1886; Bell Telephone Company of Canada, *Telephone History of London, Ontario* (Montreal: Bell Telephone Company of Canada, 1972), 2; "Wiggins's Great Discovery," *New York Times*, 21 June 1891.

5. William Patten, *Pioneering the Telephone in Canada* (Montreal: privately printed, 1926), 74; Robert J. Collins, *A Voice from Afar: The History of Telecommunications in Canada* (Toronto: McGraw-Hill Ryerson, 1977), 120–124.

6. George L. Priest, "The Origins of Utility Regulation and the 'Theories of Regulation' Debate," *Journal of Law and Economics* 36, no. 1 (1993): 289–329. On the importance of municipal politics in parallel industries, see Mark H. Rose, *Cities of Light and Heat: Domesticating Gas and Electricity in Urban America* (University Park: Pennsylvania State University Press, 1995). On the "invisibility" of the state in nineteenth-century America, see Brian Balogh, *A Government Out of Sight: The Mystery of National Authority in Nineteenth-Century America* (Cambridge: Cambridge University Press, 2009).

7. Helen Merrell Lynd, *Possibilities* (Bronxville, N.Y.: Sarah Lawrence College, 1983).

8. See, e.g., Gerald Tulchinsky, ed., *To Preserve and Defend: Essays on Kingston in the Nineteenth Century* (Montreal: McGill-Queen's University Press, 1976).

9. In this respect, Muncie and Kingston were not truly representative of many other cities: In Kingston in 1901, 99 percent of the population was white, and 72 percent Protestant. In Muncie in 1920, the first census year for which these data are available, 94 percent of the population was white, 98 percent native born, and according to the Lynds, approximately 88 percent Protestant. Canada, Dominion Bureau of Statistics, *Census of Canada, 1901* (Ottawa: Dominion Bureau of Statistics, 1901), vol. 1;

U.S. Census Bureau, *United States Census, 1920* (Washington, D.C.: U.S. Census Bureau, 1920), vol. 3. Years later, Helen Lynd recalled that "Bob visited various cities, and decided that he didn't want a city with a large foreign population or a racially-mixed city." Helen Merrell Lynd, "Middletown" (paper presented to American Sociological Association, August 1980), Center for Middletown Studies, Ball State University, Muncie, Indiana (hereafter cited as CMS); Igo, *The Averaged American*, 55–60, 75–85.

10. On Muncie in this period, see also Lynn I. Perrigo, "Muncie and Middletown, 1923 to 1934" (Ph.D. diss., University of Colorado, 1935); Dwight W. Hoover, *Magic Middletown* (Bloomington: Indiana University Press, 1986). On Muncie's early history, see Kemper, *History of Delaware County*; Frank D. Haimbaugh, *History of Delaware County, Indiana* (Indianapolis: Historical Publishing Company, 1924). Eric Morser's history of La Crosse, Wisconsin, a city not unlike Muncie, offers a detailed portrait of the municipal political economy of a midwestern city at this time. Eric J. Morser, *Hinterland Dreams: The Political Economy of a Midwestern City* (Philadelphia: University of Pennsylvania Press, 2011).

On Kingston in this period, see Anne MacDermaid, "Kingston in the 1890s: A Study of Urban-Rural Interaction and Change," *Historic Kingston* 20, no. 1 (1972): 35–45; Tulchinsky, *To Preserve and Defend*; Brian S. Osborne and Donald Swainson, *Kingston: Building on the Past* (Westport, Ont.: Butternut Press, 1988). On the telephone in Kingston, see Robert M. Pike, "Kingston Adopts the Telephone: The Social Diffusion and Use of the Telephone in Urban Central Canada, 1876 to 1914," *Urban History Review* 18, no. 1 (1989): 32–47; Robert M. Pike, "Using the 'Talking Machine': Telephone Diffusion in Kingston, 1876–1911," *Historic Kingston* 42, no. 1 (1994): 60–70.

11. *Indianapolis News*, 21 September, 16 October 1877; Stephen R. Shearer, *Hoosier Connections: The History of the Indiana Telephone Industry* (Indianapolis: Indiana Telephone Association, 1992), 12–16.

12. *Kingston Daily British Whig*, 11 September 1877; Bell Telephone Company of Canada, "Out of the Past, into the Future: The History of the Telephone, Kingston 1877–1981," n.d., Bell Canada Historical Collection, Montreal (hereafter cited as BCHC).

13. National Telephone Exchange Association (hereafter cited as NTEA), *Proceedings of the Fourth Annual Meeting of the National Telephone Exchange Association*, September 1882, 18–21, Historical Collections, Baker Library, Harvard Business School (hereafter cited as HBS).

14. Indianapolis Common Council, *Proceedings of the Common Council, Board of Aldermen, and the Joint Conventions of Said Bodies*, 1878–1879, 646–649, 674, 692, 774–775, Indiana State Library, Indianapolis (hereafter cited as ISL).

15. City of Muncie, *Records*, 16 February 1880, CMS; "The Telephone Company Granted the Right of Way Through the City," *Muncie Daily News*, 17 February 1880.

16. Rosario Joseph Tosiello, "The Birth and Early Years of the Bell Telephone System, 1876–1880" (Ph.D. diss., Boston University, 1971), 81–91.

17. "Muncie's First Operator," *Indiana Telephone News*, July 1928, 29–30.

18. The original thirty-seven subscribers are listed in *Muncie Daily News*, 25 January 1880, and Kemper, *History of Delaware County*, 129–130.

19. *Muncie Daily News*, 4 March, 6 March, 8 March, 22 March 1880. See also Indiana Bell Exchange Files: Muncie, AT&T Archives and History Center, San Antonio, Texas (hereafter cited as AT&T-TX).

20. *Kingston Daily British Whig*, 22 April 1881.

21. Osborne and Swainson, *Kingston: Building on the Past*, 213.

22. Kaufman, *The Origins of Canadian and American Political Differences*, 232, 245, 301.

23. Bell Canada, *Out of the Past, into the Future*; Lawrence Surtees, *Pa Bell: A. Jean de Grandpre and the Meteoric Rise of Bell Canada Enterprises* (Toronto: Random House, 1992), 73–74.

24. City of Kingston, *Bylaws*, No. 29, 27 November 1883, City of Kingston Collection, Queen's University Archives, Kingston, Ontario (hereafter cited as KQUA).

25. "They Talked," *Muncie Morning News*, 14 November 1894; Bell Canada, *Out of the Past, into the Future*; Pike, "Kingston Adopts the Telephone."

26. Haimbaugh, *History of Delaware County*, 398; Central Union Telephone Company, *Annual Report of the Directors of the Central Union Telephone Company*, various years, HBS. Chicago remained separate from the Central Union territory, as did the southern part of Indiana, served by Nashville-based Cumberland Telephone and Telegraph.

27. Garnet, *The Telephone Enterprise*, 55–73.

28. American Bell Telephone Company, *Annual Report of the Directors of the American Bell Telephone Company to the Stockholders*, 1882, 3, HBS.

29. "Telephone Rents," *Indianapolis Daily Sentinel*, 4 April 1885; "Telephone Rentals," *Indianapolis Daily Sentinel*, 13 April 1885; Cuyahoga Telephone Company, *Annual Report to Stockholders of the Cuyahoga Telephone Company*, 1903, HBS.

30. Caldwell, *Recollections of a Life Time*, 140.

31. Thomas Sherwin, *Exchange Statistics* (Boston: American Bell Telephone Company, 1886), 8–15, HBS.

32. U.S. Census Bureau, *Telephones and Telegraphs: 1902* (Washington, D.C.: Government Printing Office, 1906), 9; Beauchamp, "The Telephone Patents," 288–289; MacMeal, *The Story of Independent Telephony*, 28.

33. "With Axes and Nippers," *New York Times*, 15 December 1889.

34. NTEA, *Proceedings*, 1882, 22; 1885, 93; 1887, 24; Indianapolis Common Council, *Proceedings*, 1881, 603, 693, 824, 856, 866.

35. "The Wires Underground," *New York Times*, 19 April 1884; "Met Death in the Wires," *New York Times*, 12 October 1889.

36. Muncie, *Records*, 8 August 1890.

37. Caldwell, *Recollections of a Life Time*, 186.

38. NTEA, *Proceedings*, 1882, 20.

39. David Paul Nord, *Newspapers and New Politics: Midwestern Municipal Reform, 1890–1900* (Ann Arbor, Mich.: UMI Research Press, 1981), 23–24; Morton Keller, *Affairs of State: Public Life in Nineteenth Century America* (Cambridge, Mass.: Harvard University Press, 1977), 324–326.

40. *Statutes of Canada*, 1880, 43 Vic., c. 67; 1882, 44 Vic., c. 95. In this way, the regulatory structure of Canada differs from that of the United States. In the United States, the federal government regulates interstate commerce, while the individual states have jurisdiction over almost all economic activity within their borders. Thus, different activities of the same corporation—or different circuits of the same telephone network—are routinely subject to regulation by different levels of the American federal system. In Canada, by contrast, each company is in theory the creation and jurisdiction of only one government. Thus, all of Bell Canada's activities were subject to federal jurisdiction, whether or not they crossed provincial lines, while all the activities of a smaller telephone company chartered in Ontario would be regulated by the Ontario provincial government alone. In practice, this division of powers is often contested, but the principle is there.

41. *R. v. Mohr* (1881), 7 QLR,183–192; *Quebec Daily Telegraph* 3 June, 6 June, 8 June 1881.

42. *R v. Mohr*, 184.

43. Canada, Senate, *Debates*, 27 April 1882, 438; 5 May 1882, 612; see also Canada, House of Commons, *Debates*, 13 March 1880, 624–625; Christopher Armstrong and H. V. Nelles, *Monopoly's Moment: The Organization and Regulation of Canadian Utilities, 1830–1930* (Philadelphia: Temple University Press, 1986), 72.

44. Patten, *Pioneering the Telephone*, 99–100; Armstrong and Nelles, *Monopoly's Moment*, 164–165.

45. Armstrong and Nelles, *Monopoly's Moment*, 314–315.

46. "The Telephone in New England and Illinois," *Electrical World*, 23 May 1885, 208; "Legislation in Massachusetts," *Electrical World*, 6 June 1885, 229; "A Bluff Game," *New York Times*, 4 March 1886; "Telephones in the West," *New York Times*, 15 March 1886.

47. Indiana House of Representatives, *Journal*, 14 January 1885, 117; 3 April 1885, 1435–1436; 11 April 1885, 1565.

48. *National Cyclopaedia of American Biography* (New York: James T. White, 1928), 20: 468–469.

49. Indianapolis Common Council, *Proceedings*, 1881–1882, 693, 856, 866, 1091, 1128–1129, 1220–1221, 1475, 1545, 1549.

50. Indianapolis Common Council, *Proceedings*, 1884, 101, 210, 230, 342–343, 356, 411–412. Indianapolis had a bicameral city government, with a mayor, a board of aldermen representing city districts, and a separate common council elected at large.

51. Charles N. Fay, "Telephone Subscribers as Knights of Labor," in NTEA, *Proceedings*, 1887, 28, Crerar Library, University of Chicago.

52. Indianapolis Common Council, *Proceedings*, 1882–1883, 759.

53. Indianapolis Common Council, *Proceedings*, 1884, 81.

54. The companies named were the Indiana Overland Telephone and Telegraph Company, the Pan-Electric Telephone Company, and the American Co-operative Electric Company. The city also granted telegraph franchises to the Bankers and Merchants Telegraph Company and the Baltimore and Ohio Telegraph Company. Indianapolis Common Council, *Proceedings*, 1884, 211, 212, 600, 671, 761.

55. Equivalent to about $75 per month and $125 per month in 2014 dollars.

56. Indianapolis Common Council, *Proceedings*, 1884, 206, 769; 1885, 18, 68; Indiana House of Representatives, *Journal*, 14 January 1885, 117.

57. Indiana House of Representatives, *Journal*, 3 April 1885, 1435–1436; 11 April 1885, 1565. House and Senate debates on the bill are reprinted in "Telephone Rents," *Indianapolis Daily Sentinel*, 4 April 1885; "Telephone Rentals," *Indianapolis Daily Sentinel*, 13 April 1885.

58. "The Bell Conspiracy," *Indianapolis Daily Sentinel*, 19 April 1886; American Bell, *Annual Report*, 1886, 19–22.

59. *Hockett v. State*, 5 N.E. 178, 182 (Ind., 1886). Justice W. E. Niblack's decision is reprinted in "The Record of the Courts," *Indianapolis Journal*, 22 February 1886.

60. "Telephone Tinkering," *Indianapolis Daily Sentinel*, 4 March 1886. See also "Going Out of Business," *New York Times*, 3 March 1886; "Telephone Tinkering," *Indianapolis Daily Sentinel*, 4 March 1886; "The Telephone in Indiana," *New York Times*, 5 March 1886; "The Telephone Situation," *Indianapolis Journal*, 1 April 1886; "Taking Out the Telephone," *Indianapolis Journal*, 7 April 1886.

61. "The Telephone in Indiana," *Electrical World*, 26 September 1885, 132; American Bell, *Annual Report*, 1886, 19–21.

62. *New York Times*, 3 March, 5 March, 1 April, 4 April, 17 April 1886; *Indianapolis Journal* 1 April, 7 April, 9 April 1886; *Indianapolis Daily Sentinel* 7 April, 10 April, 17 April 1886.

63. *Indianapolis Journal* 16 April, 23 April, 24 April 1886; *Indianapolis Daily Sentinel* 19 April, 24 April 1886. The quoted phrase is from John Caven, president of the Citizens' Cooperative Telephone Company, in Indianapolis Common Council, *Proceedings*, 1886, 514.

64. "A Violation of the Orders," *Indianapolis Journal*, 16 April 1886; "The Telephone Question," *Indianapolis Journal*, 23 April 1886.

65. "Thirty-Seven Telephone Suits," *New York Times*, 17 October 1887; "The Bell Company's Victory over Cushman," *Electrical Review*, 10 November 1888, 1; Stanley Swihart, "Early Automatic Telephone Systems," *Telecom History* 2 (1995): 8.

66. Indianapolis Common Council, *Proceedings*, 1886, 867; "Indiana's Telephone Muddle," *New York Times*, 24 April 1886; "An Undesirable Franchise," *Indianapolis Journal*, 1 July 1886.

67. Indiana Senate, *Journal*, 26 February 1889, 941; *Indianapolis Journal*, 27 February 1889; American Bell, *Annual Report*, 1889, 8.

68. Beauchamp, "The Telephone Patents," 133.

69. Central Union Telephone Company, *Central Union Telephone Directory: Muncie, Indiana* (Central Union Telephone Company, 1909), CMS; "The Talking Machine: 10 Years of the Telephone," *Kingston Daily British Whig*, 21 January 1891.

70. For all statistics on telephone diffusion in Muncie and Kingston, and discussion of my method in analyzing them, see Robert MacDougall, "The People's Telephone: The Politics of Telephony in the United States and Canada, 1876–1926" (Ph.D. diss., Harvard University, 2004).

71. *Muncie Daily News*, 3 March 1880; *Muncie Daily News*, 27 March 1880.

72. *Kingston Daily British Whig*, 11 November 1902.

73. American Bell, *Annual Report*, 1886, 14.

74. Armstrong and Nelles, *Monopoly's Moment*, 72–73; Surtees, *Pa Bell*, 75.

75. *New York Times*, 9 April 1887. See also *New York Times*, 27 January 1885; 11 June, 11 October 1887.

76. Charles F. Sise to H. P. Dwight, 1 April 1882, Sise Letterbooks, BCHC; S. C. Wood to Charles F. Sise, 19, 20, 26 January 1885, Correspondence, BCHC.

77. "Report of Meeting of C. F. Sise with Local Managers," 16–17 May 1887, Document File 26606, 43, BCHC.

78. Armstrong and Nelles, *Monopoly's Moment*, 108–112.

79. "The Telephone War," *Peterborough Review*, 11 December 1890; Canada, House of Commons, Select Committee Appointed to Inquire into the Various Telephone Systems in Canada and Elsewhere, *Report*, 2 vols. (Ottawa: King's Printer, 1905), 1: 676; 2: 205.

80. After the charade had been revealed, Sise wrote to his Winnipeg manager: "I did not wish to tell you this before, as I wished your opposition to be in earnest, and in good faith." Charles F. Sise to F. G. Walsh, 20 April 1886, BCHC; Armstrong and Nelles, *Monopoly's Moment*, 107–114; Surtees, *Pa Bell*, 75–76.

81. Select Committee on Telephone Systems, *Report*, 1: 79–87, 130, 622, 630–631; Robert E. Babe, *Telecommunications in Canada: Technology, Industry, and Government* (Toronto: University of Toronto Press, 1990), 85.

82. Charles F. Sise to John E. Hudson, 5 January 1895, BCHC; F. Page Wilson, "Telephone Requirements in Canada," *Telephony*, March 1908, 190–192. See also A. F. Wilson, "The Relation of Rural Telephones to Towns and Cities," *Telephony*, January 1907, 42–44, and Francis Dagger, "The Common Cause," *Telephony*, April 1908, 262–264.

83. Select Committee on Telephone Systems, *Report*, 1: 660; Collins, *A Voice from Afar*, 172. For railroad and municipal contracts, see, e.g., Select Committee on Telephone Systems, *Report*, 1: 179–209, 660–666; Canada, Board of Railway Commissioners, *Papers*, vol. 530, Exhibit 65, 7 January 1907, Record Group 46, National Archives of Canada, Ottawa, Ontario (hereafter NAC).

84. Kingston, *Bylaws*, No. 441, 28 September 1892. On Toronto, see Armstrong and Nelles, *Monopoly's Moment*, 110.

85. W. G. Raymond to Edward Ryan, 20 January 1899, KQUA; Donald M. McIntyre to Edward Ryan, 30 January 1899, KQUA.

86. A. T. Smith to W. M. Drennan, 11 February 1899, KQUA; A. T. Smith to Chairman of Finance Committee, 17 February 1899, KQUA; Edward Ryan to A. T. Smith, 20 March 1899, KQUA; William T. White to Edward Ryan, 22 March 1899, KQUA; A. T. Smith to Edward Ryan, 24 March 1899, KQUA; A. T. Smith to Chairman of Finance Committee, 22 April 1899, KQUA.

87. H. W. Snelling to City Clerk, 22 June 1903, KQUA; H. W. Snelling to Mayor and Council, 29 June 1903, KQUA; Kingston, *Bylaws*, No. 58, 4 August 1903. The new contract was also to increase the company's yearly payment to $500.

88. Ontario Municipal Association, *Proceedings of the Ontario Municipal Association* (Guelph, Ont.: 1903), KQUA.

89. Charles F. Sise to L. W. Shannon, 20 August 1903, KQUA.

90. Kingston Board of Works, Correspondence Files, KQUA; City of Kingston, *Proceedings*, 12 October 1903, 11 April, 27 May, 6 June, and 24 October 1904, KQUA; City of Kingston, Finance and Accounts Committee, *Report*, No. 93, 5 December 1904, KQUA.

91. Babe, *Telecommunications in Canada*, 73–90.

92. Some of Bell's opponents in Ontario tried to argue that if municipalities had no jurisdiction over Bell Canada, they should not have the power to grant it an exclusive franchise. In 1894, however, Bell induced the government to pass a bill specifically authorizing this one municipal right.

93. The Berliner patent decision is discussed in Chapter 3.

94. U.S. Census, *Telephones and Telegraphs: 1902*, 8–9; U.S. Census, *Telephones and Telegraphs: 1912*, 35; MacMeal, *The Story of Independent Telephony*, 39–41; Mueller, *Universal Service*, 61. The 1902 census counted commercial systems only (not farmers' cooperatives) and included only systems that were still operating in 1902.

95. U.S. Census, *Telephones and Telegraphs: 1902*, 8–9; U.S. Census, *Telephones and Telegraphs: 1912*, 35.

96. Other sources estimated only about twelve thousand independent telephones in Canada at this time. H. D. Fargo, "The Canadian Convention," *Telephony*, October 1907, 216–218; W. R. Rutherford, "Canada's Second Independent Telephone Convention," *American Telephone Journal*, 14 September 1907, 168–169; M. C. Urquhart, ed., *Historical Statistics of Canada* (Cambridge: Cambridge University Press, 1965), S323–331.

97. Charles F. Sise to John E. Hudson, 5 January 1895, BCHC; Charles F. Sise to F. G. Beach, 5 January 1895, BCHC.

98. George W. Anderson, *Telephone Competition in the Middle West and Its Lesson for New England* (Boston: New England Telephone and Telegraph Company, 1906); MacMeal, *The Story of Independent Telephony*; Dan Schiller, "Social Movement in Telecommunications: Rethinking the Public Service History of U.S. Telecommunications, 1894–1919," *Telecommunications Policy* 22, no. 4/5 (1998): 397–408.

99. "Competition Coming," *Muncie Morning News*, 9 June 1895.

100. The Muncie City Council Records for 1892–1897 were destroyed by fire, but these deliberations are described in "Franchise Wanted for a New Telephone System," *Muncie Morning News*, 19 May 1896; and "Franchise Granted," *Muncie Morning News*, 29 September 1896.

101. *Muncie Morning News*, 19 January, 12 May 1897.

102. *Muncie Morning News*, 29 September 1896, 9 March 1897. Muncie also embraced competition in the electrical industry. In 1897, Muncie Electric—the firm's full name was the Muncie Electric Light, Heat, Power and Telephone Company—was one of three systems generating electrical power for the city. On electricity in Muncie, see Nye, *Electrifying America*, 1–28.

103. *Muncie Morning News*, 12 May, 20 May 1897.

104. "The Financial Side of Independent Telephony," *Telephony*, January 1906; Mueller, *Universal Service*, 66.

105. *Muncie Morning News*, 30 December 1899.

106. *Muncie Daily Herald*, 26 November 1901.

107. "Telephones and Gas," *Muncie Daily Herald*, 27 November 1901.

108. Muncie, *Records*, 16 December 1901; "The Franchise Was Granted," *Muncie Daily Herald*, 17 December 1901.

109. *Muncie Daily Herald*, 10 November 1907.

110. Central Union, *Annual Report*, 1903, 1 and 1907, 5.

111. "The Telephone Industry," *Electrical World*, 30 March 1907, 619; "Telephony in Ohio," *Electrical World*, 25 May 1907, 1021; "Bell Proposal Rejected," *Telephony*, June 1907, 368–369; Charles S. Norton, "The Indiana Situation," *American Telephone Journal*, July 13 1907, 20–21; "Where Consistency Paid," *Telephony*, August 1907, 101.

112. Select Committee on Telephone Systems, *Report*, 1: 7, 827. The committee was presented with figures showing one telephone for every sixty-three residents in British Columbia, one phone for every eighty-nine residents in Ontario, every 102 residents in Quebec, every 122 residents in Nova Scotia, and every 129 residents in New Brunswick. Bell spokesmen challenged these figures, and they are lower than the national aggregates provided by Bell Canada and the Census Bureau would suggest. Still, there was no question that by 1905 the diffusion of telephones in the United States and the Midwest in particular had far outpaced development in any part of Canada.

113. MacDougall, "The People's Telephone," 76–83. I developed a detailed picture of early telephone subscribers by cross-referencing telephone directories with census data and other sources, especially the annual street directories published in these years. I am indebted to Robert Pike for suggesting this method and for the substantial data on Kingston telephony in Pike, "Kingston Adopts the Telephone."

114. Maguire, "The Local Dynamics of Telephone System Development," 81–98; John, *Network Nation*, 295–299.

115. Muncie, *Records*, 17 June, 1 July 1887; Edward Springer to City of Muncie, 23 June 1887, CMS; "Five Cents a Talk," *Muncie Daily News*, 1 July 1887.

116. Claude S. Fischer, "'Touch Someone': The Telephone Industry Discovers Sociability," *Technology and Culture* 29, no. 1 (1988): 32–61.

117. See, e.g., "Telephone Competition," *Telephony*, March 1907, 179–180; "Low Rates and Local Service," *American Telephone Journal*, 17 August 1907, 108; "Telephone Rates," *Telephony*, 11 April 1914, 41; Joan Nix and David Gabel, "AT&T's Strategic Response to Competition: Why Not Preempt Entry?" *Journal of Economic History* 53, no. 2 (1993): 377–381; Kenneth Lipartito, "Culture and the Practice of Business History," *Business and Economic History* 24, no. 2 (1995): 31. The fight over rate structures is discussed further in Chapter 4.

118. MacMeal, *The Story of Independent Telephony*, 224.

119. J. J. Hanselman and H. S. Osborne, "More and Better Telephone Service for Farmers," *Bell Telephone Magazine*, Winter 1944–1945, 213–226; see also Harriet Prescott Spofford, "A Rural Telephone," *Harper's Monthly*, May 1909, 830–837; Frank G. Moorhead, "End 'Phone Eavesdropping,'" *Technical World*, October 1914, 224–225.

120. On the operator as surrogate servant, see Martin, *Hello, Central*, 92–95.

121. Wilson, "Telephone Requirements in Canada."

122. "The Telephone Problem in Canada," *Canadian Engineer*, November 1901, 438; "Independent Telephony in Canada," *Canadian Engineer*, January 1903, 1–2.

123. Select Committee on Telephone Systems, *Report*, 1: 934.

124. Zimmerman was skeptical of Pickernell's explanation too. Asked Zimmerman: "Even at that, he [the midwestern farmer] would not buy a telephone if he had no use for it?" Pickernell answered, "I do not know about that. Men buy gold bricks when they do not need them." Select Committee on Telephone Systems, *Report*, 1: 934, 1030.

125. Kenneth Lipartito, "Component Innovation: The Case of Automatic Telephone Switching, 1891–1920," *Industrial and Corporate Change* 3, no. 2 (1994): 325–357; John, *Network Nation*, 269–339.

126. Fay, "Telephone Subscribers as Knights of Labor," 25.

127. John, *Network Nation*, 279. The threat of competition or hostile regulation can influence a monopolist's business strategy and so produce what David Hochfelder has called "a quasi-regulatory environment." David Hochfelder, "A Comparison of the Postal Telegraph Movements in Great Britain and the United States, 1866–1900," *Enterprise and Society* 1 (December 2000), 739–761.

128. U.S. Census, *Telephones and Telegraphs: 1912*, 27, 34–41.

129. Theodore Caplow et al., *Middletown Families: Fifty Years of Change and Continuity, Middletown III Project* (Minneapolis: University of Minnesota Press, 1982), 5.

Chapter 2. Visions of Telephony

1. Alexander Melville Bell, *Visible Speech: A New Fact Demonstrated* (Edinburgh: W. P. Kennedy, 1865).

2. Alexander Graham Bell to Alexander Melville Bell, 6 May 1874, Alexander Graham Bell Family Papers, Library of Congress, Washington, D.C. (hereafter BFP-LOC);

Deaf-Mute Voice, 2 February 1889, BFP-LOC; Jill Lepore, *A Is for American: Letters and Other Characters in the Newly United States* (New York: Alfred A. Knopf, 2002), 171–179.

3. Carey, "Technology and Ideology," 203–204. See also John Durham Peters, "Technology and Ideology: The Case of the Telegraph Revisited," in *Thinking with James Carey: Essays on Communications, Transportation, History*, ed. Jeremy Packer and Craig Robertson (New York: Peter Lang, 2006), 147.

4. Richard R. John, *Spreading the News: The American Postal System from Franklin to Morse* (Cambridge, Mass.: Harvard University Press, 1995); Paul Starr, *The Creation of the Media: Political Origins of Modern Communications* (New York: Basic, 2004); David Henkin, *The Postal Age: The Emergence of Modern Communications in Nineteenth-Century America* (Chicago: University of Chicago Press, 2006); John, *Network Nation.*

5. On populism as a rhetorical style, see Michael Kazin, *The Populist Persuasion: An American History* (New York: Harper Collins, 1995).

6. See Richard R. John, "Theodore N. Vail and the Civic Origins of Universal Service," *Business and Economic History* 28, no. 2 (1999): 71–81; W. Bernard Carlson, "The Telephone as Political Instrument: Gardiner Hubbard and the Formation of the Middle Class in America, 1875–1880," in *Technologies of Power: Essays in Honor of Thomas Parke Hughes and Agatha Chipley Hughes*, ed. Michael Thad Allen and Gabrielle Hecht (Cambridge, Mass.: MIT Press, 2001), 25–55.

7. Thomas Sanders to Gardiner Hubbard, 28 January 1878, Box 1193, AT&T Archives and History Center, Warren, New Jersey (hereafter AT&T-NJ).

8. Biographical Sketch of Gardiner Hubbard, n.d., Box 16, Hubbard Family Papers, Library of Congress, Washington, D.C. (hereafter HFP-LOC); Tosiello, "Birth and Early Years," 157–159; Carlson, "The Telephone as Political Instrument," 34–35.

9. Thompson, *Wiring a Continent*, 391–396, 406–426.

10. Gardiner G. Hubbard, "Government Control of the Telegraph," *North American Review*, December 1883, 529.

11. Carlson, "The Telephone as Political Instrument," 34–38; Hochfelder, *The Telegraph in America*, 34, 59–64.

12. Thomas A. Sanders to Charles Cheever, 23 April 1878, General Manager's Letter Books, 13: 420, AT&T-NJ; "Congress and the Telegraph," *Telegrapher*, 6 June 1875, 135. David Hochfelder argues that, contrary to many versions of this history, Hubbard and Orton remained on friendly terms despite their professional differences. David Hochfelder, "Constructing an Industrial Divide: Western Union, AT&T, and the Federal Government, 1876–1971," *Business History Review* 76, no. 4 (2002): 710.

13. Hubbard, "Government Control of the Telegraph," 522. See also Gardiner G. Hubbard, "The Postal Telegraph," 1869, HFP-LOC; Gardiner G. Hubbard, "Memoir of Gardiner G. Hubbard in Relation to the Postal Telegraph," 1873, HFP-LOC; Gardiner G. Hubbard, "The Proposed Changes in the Telegraphic System," *North American Review*, July 1873, 80–107.

14. Richard B. DuBoff, "Business Demand and the Development of the Telegraph in the United States," *Business History Review* 54, no. 4 (1980): 466–467; Dan Schiller, *Theorizing Communication: A History* (New York: Oxford University Press, 1996), 8.

15. Blondheim, *News Over the Wires*, 177–187.

16. Hubbard, "Proposed Changes in the Telegraphic System," 99–100.

17. See, e.g., "The Tyranny of Monopolies," *Harper's Weekly*, 14 May 1881, 312–315; William A. Phillips, "Should the Government Own the Telegraph," *North American Review*, July 1886, 35–44; Richard T. Ely, "The Telegraph Monopoly," *North American Review*, July 1889, 44–53; Katherine B. Judson, ed., *Selected Articles on Government Ownership of Telegraph and Telephone* (New York: H. W. Wilson, 1914).

18. Donald Bruce Johnson, ed., *National Party Platforms* (Urbana: University of Illinois Press, 1978), 1: 117; Schiller, *Theorizing Communication*, 8–17. See also Dan Schiller, *How to Think About Information* (Urbana: University of Illinois Press, 2007).

19. John, *Network Nation*, 156–199.

20. Thompson, *Wiring a Continent*, 426; Starr, *The Creation of the Media*, 175.

21. Hubbard, "Proposed Changes in the Telegraphic System," 81–82.

22. Hubbard, "Government Control of the Telegraph," 532.

23. Wayne E. Fuller, "The Populists and the Post Office," *Agricultural History* 65, no. 1 (1991); John, *Spreading the News*; Henkin, *The Postal Age*; John, *Network Nation*.

24. Alexander Graham Bell to Parents, 20 October 1874, BFP-LOC.

25. Tosiello, "Birth and Early Years," 11–12; Brooks, *Telephone*, 46–50.

26. *The Bell Telephone: The Deposition of Alexander Graham Bell in the Suit Brought by the United States to Annul the Bell Patents* (Boston: American Bell Telephone Company, 1908), 82. The famous patent is Alexander Graham Bell, "Improvement in Telegraphy," U.S. Patent No. 174,465, 7 March 1876.

27. Bruce, *Alexander Graham Bell*, 178–181, 231–235.

28. Gardiner G. Hubbard, "Trustee's Report to the Board of Managers," 1 August 1877, Box 1001, AT&T-NJ; Gardiner G. Hubbard, "Report to Stockholders and Directors of the Bell Telephone Company," 1879, BFP-LOC; J. Warren Stehman, *The Financial History of the American Telephone and Telegraph Company* (Boston: Houghton Mifflin, 1925), 9–10; Garnet, *The Telephone Enterprise*, 14–17.

29. See, e.g., Casson, *The History of the Telephone*; William Chauncy Langdon, "The Early Corporate Development of the Telephone," *Bell Telephone Quarterly* 2, no. 3 (1923): 133–152; Coon, *American Tel & Tel*.

30. Hubbard, "Proposed Changes in the Telegraphic System," 99.

31. Hubbard also pushed the company representing Bell's patents in Britain to organize the British telephone industry in this way. Beauchamp, "The Telephone Patents," 39–40.

32. Gardiner Hubbard to William H. Forbes, 20 January 1884, Box 1264, AT&T-NJ, emphasis mine.

33. "The Telephone and Its Uses," *New York Times*, 1 August 1877; "The Telephone," May 1877, Box 1097, AT&T-NJ.

34. "The Speaking Telephone," *New York Times*, 20 May 1877.

35. Tosiello, "Birth and Early Years," 58.

36. Tosiello, "Birth and Early Years," 156–160.

37. Thomas Sanders to Gardiner G. Hubbard, 5 December 1877, Box 1006, AT&T-NJ; Sanders to Hubbard, 30 January 1878, General Manager's Letterbook, AT&T-NJ; Sanders to Hubbard, 22 February 1878, Box 1193, AT&T-NJ.

38. National Bell Telephone Company, Director's Meeting, Minutes, 11 March 1879, AT&T-NJ; Stehman, *Financial History of AT&T*, 4–12.

39. Hubbard, "Proposed Changes in the Telegraphic System," 82.

40. Langdon, "Early Corporate Development," 18. On John Murray Forbes, see John Lauritz Larson, *Bonds of Enterprise: John Murray Forbes and Western Development in America's Railway Age* (Iowa City: University of Iowa Press, 2001). The only biography of William Forbes is the hagiographic Arthur S. Pier, *Forbes: Telephone Pioneer* (New York: Dodd, Mead, 1953).

41. A. P. Rockwell to William H. Forbes, 17 February 1877, William Hathaway Forbes Collection, Massachusetts Historical Society, Boston (hereafter WHF); William H. Forbes to John Murray Forbes, 17 September 1884, WHF.

42. Quoted in Pier, *Forbes*, 105; on Butler, see Margaret S. Thompson, "Ben Butler Versus the Brahmins: Patronage and Politics in Early Gilded Age Massachusetts," *New England Quarterly* 55, no. 2 (1982): 163–186; John, *Network Nation*, 164–166.

43. Johnson, *National Party Platforms*, 1: 65.

44. Gardiner Hubbard to William H. Forbes, 29 October 1885, Box 1115, AT&T-NJ; William H. Forbes to Alexander Graham Bell, 5 March 1879, Box 1003, AT&T-NJ.

45. Fay, "Telephone Subscribers as Knights of Labor," 24.

46. George S. Ladd to Theodore N. Vail, Response to Circular of December 28 1883, Box 1080, AT&T-NJ.

47. Larson, *Bonds of Enterprise*, 111–169.

48. American Bell, *Annual Report*, 1880, 8; American Bell, *Annual Report*, 1884, 7.

49. Anderson, *Telephone Competition in the Middle West*, 8.

50. Milton Mueller, "The Switchboard Problem: Scale, Signaling, and Organization in Manual Telephone Switching, 1877–1897," *Technology and Culture* 30, no. 3 (1989): 534–560. See also Babe, *Telecommunications in Canada*, 137–149; Mueller, *Universal Service*, 11–20.

51. Quoted in NTEA, *Proceedings*, 1887, 32.

52. Anderson, *Telephone Competition in the Middle West*, 10; Marion May Dilts, *The Telephone in a Changing World* (New York: Longmans and Green, 1941), 28; Edward J. Hall in NTEA, *Proceedings*, 1881, 46.

53. Norvin Green to Henry Bingham, 11 December 1890, quoted in John, "Recasting the Information Infrastructure for the Industrial Age," 79.

54. Prices varied widely by region and over time. John Kingsbury quoted prices of $100 per year for residential service in Chicago, Philadelphia, and Boston and $150 per year in New York, in John E. Kingsbury, *The Telephone and Telephone Exchanges: Their*

Invention and Development (New York: Longmans, Green, 1915), 469. Twenty years earlier, American Bell auditor Thomas Sherwin reported slightly lower rates in Sherwin, *Exchange Statistics*. Wage data appears in U.S. Census, *Historical Statistics of the United States*, 165.

55. Charles N. Fay, "Address of the President," in NTEA, *Proceedings*, 1886, 8.

56. American Bell, *Annual Report*, various years, and U.S. Census, *Historical Statistics of the United States*, 783–784.

57. Alexander Graham Bell to Mabel Bell, 21 February 1879, BFP-LOC.

58. National Bell Telephone Company, Director's Meeting, Minutes, 11 November 1879, BFP-LOC; Western Union Contract, 10 November 1979, Box 1006, AT&T-NJ. For detailed discussion of the agreement, see Garnet, *The Telephone Enterprise*, 44–54; George David Smith, "The Bell-Western Union Patent Agreement of 1879: A Study in Corporate Imagination," in *Readings in the Management of Innovation*, ed. Michael Tushman and William L. Moore (Cambridge, Mass.: Ballinger, 1988); Hochfelder, "Constructing an Industrial Divide," 707–717; John, *Network Nation*, 167–170.

59. Between 1879 and 1894, Bell Telephone paid about $7 million in royalties to Western Union. Stehman, *Financial History of AT&T*, 17.

60. "The Telephone: What Has Been Done in the First Ten Years of Its Existence," *New York Times*, 1 January 1886.

61. Tosiello, "Birth and Early Years," 486; American Bell, *Annual Report*, 1881, 1882.

62. Technically, the telephone made Mabel Hubbard Bell's fortune rather than Alexander Graham Bell's. On his wedding day, two days after founding the Bell Telephone Company, Alexander gave all but ten of his shares in the company to his bride.

63. Federal Communications Commission, *Proposed Report, Telephone Investigation* (Washington, D.C.: Government Printing Office, 1938), 96.

64. Pier, *Forbes*. See also Thomas K. McCraw, *Prophets of Regulation: Charles Francis Adams, Louis D. Brandeis, James M. Landis, Alfred E. Kahn* (Cambridge, Mass.: Harvard University Press, 1984), 1–79; Larson, *Bonds of Enterprise*.

65. See, e.g., American Telephone and Telegraph Company, *Annual Report of the Directors of the American Telephone and Telegraph Company to the Stockholders*, 1909, 18–19, HBS; and in general, Theodore N. Vail, *Views on Public Questions: A Collection of Papers and Addresses* (privately printed, 1917).

66. For a detailed history of one Bell operating company, and the complex relations between American Bell's agents, subagents, and local licensees, see J. Leigh Walsh, *Connecticut Pioneers in Telephony* (New Haven, Conn.: Telephone Pioneers of America, 1950).

67. One source that credits Alfred Vail with inventing Morse code is Franklin Leonard Pope, "The American Inventors of the Telegraph, with Special References to the Services of Alfred Vail," *Century Illustrated Magazine*, April 1888, 924–945.

68. The only book-length biography of Vail is Albert Bigelow Paine, *In One Man's Life: Being Chapters from the Personal and Business Career of Theodore N. Vail* (New

York: Harper and Brothers, 1921). On Vail's work at the post office, see John, "Civic Origins of Universal Service," 71–81.

69. Paine, *In One Man's Life*, 59.

70. Dionysius Lardner, *Railway Economy: A Treatise on the New Art of Transport* (London: Taylor, Walton, and Maberly, 1850), 503.

71. Paine, *In One Man's Life*, 113.

72. Hubbard quoted in Thomas A. Watson, *The Birth and Babyhood of the Telephone: An Address Delivered to the 3rd Annual Convention of the Telephone Pioneers of America at Chicago, October 17, 1913* (New York: American Telephone and Telegraph Company, 1934), AT&T-TX; "The Retirement of Messrs. Vail and Madden," *Electrical World*, 18 July 1885, 27.

73. Paine, *In One Man's Life*, 137–138; Walsh, *Connecticut Pioneers*, 110.

74. It is not clear when this vision was first born in Vail's mind. Sometimes he said it was "co-existent with the business." At other times, he said he could not say with any certainty when the idea of "one great big general system" first came to him. New York State, Joint Committee of the Senate and Assembly Appointed to Investigate Telephone and Telegraph Companies, *Report* (Albany: J. B. Lyon, 1910); AT&T, *Annual Report*, 1909, 18–19.

75. "The Telephone in Indiana," *Electrical World*, 26 September 1885, 132; *Cumberland Telephone Journal*, 15 May 1903, 12, AT&T-TX.

76. American Bell, *Annual Report*, 1883, 4.

77. Caldwell, *Recollections of a Life Time*, 196–197.

78. Southern New England Telephone Company, *Annual Report of the Directors of the Southern New England Telephone Company to the Stockholders*, 1885, HBS; NTEA, *Proceedings*, 1885, 61–62. (AT&T did not actually offer telephone service between the United States and Japan until 1934.)

79. Paine, *In One Man's Life*, 69.

80. "Telephone Interests," *Electrical Review*, 20 September 1884, 4; American Bell, *Annual Report*, 1885, 4.

81. American Bell, *Annual Report*, 1885, 4–7; "The New England Telephone Company," *Electrical World*, 16 May 1885, 195; Sherwin, *Exchange Statistics*; N. R. Danielian, *AT&T: The Story of Industrial Conquest* (New York: Vanguard, 1939), 336. Company statistics are not entirely consistent, but all show a contraction at this time. Forbes's report says that seventy-eight exchanges were shut down between 1884 and 1885, a net decline of just seventeen exchanges, but a comparison of annual reports from previous and subsequent years shows a net decline of 118 exchanges, and Thomas Sherwin's 1886 auditors' report shows a net decline of 134.

82. Casson, *The History of the Telephone*, 172; Walsh, *Connecticut Pioneers*, 143; SNET, *Annual Report*, 1885.

83. "The American Bell Company's Capital," *Electrical World*, 14 March 1885, 107–108; "The American Bell Petition," *Electrical World*, 30 May 1885, 214.

84. Paine, *In One Man's Life*, 173.

85. See, e.g., Casson, *The History of the Telephone*, 176–177; Danielian, *AT&T*, 58, 71; Angus Smith Hibbard, *Hello, Goodbye: My Story of Telephone Pioneering* (Chicago: A. C. McClurg, 1941), 139–142. James Caldwell is just about the only Bell memoirist to side with Hudson over Vail; see Caldwell, *Recollections of a Life Time*, 136–138, 194.

86. William H. Forbes to Theodore N. Vail, 1 July 1885, AT&T-NJ; American Bell, *Annual Report*, 1886, 7.

87. Theodore N. Vail to Edward J. Hall, 16 February 1885, Box 1010, AT&T-NJ.

88. Quoted in Frederick L. Rhodes, *Beginnings of Telephony* (New York: Harper and Brothers, 1929), 196–197.

89. Theodore N. Vail to Frederick P. Fish, 14 April 1906, quoted in Hochfelder, "Constructing an Industrial Divide," 719.

90. *New York Times*, 29 April 1886, 4.

91. Edward J. Hall to John E. Hudson, 21 January 1888, Box 1011, AT&T-NJ; Garnet, *The Telephone Enterprise*, 79–81.

92. Brooks, *Telephone*, 85.

93. Alexander Graham Bell to Parents, 5 May 1877, BFP-LOC; Alexander Graham Bell to Executive Committee of the Bell Telephone Company, 29 November 1878, Box 1104, AT&T-NJ. Bell Sr. and Jr. were not above encouraging a bidding war for their patents. "The great thing, I think, is to get some interest shown in the matter [the Canadian patents] by Jay Gould and the Dominion [Telegraph Company]," the younger Bell counseled his father. "In that case I am sure you will get all you want and more out of the Bell Telephone Company [of Boston]." Alexander Graham Bell to Alexander Melville Bell, 9 September 1879, BFP-LOC.

94. Taylor, "Charles F. Sise, Bell Canada, and the Americans."

95. R. C. Fetherstonhaugh, *Charles Fleetford Sise, 1834–1918* (Montreal: Gazette Printing, 1944); Jean-Guy Rens, *The Invisible Empire: A History of the Telecommunications Industry in Canada, 1846–1956*, trans. Käthe Roth (Montreal: McGill-Queen's University Press, 2001).

96. Fetherstonhaugh, *Charles Fleetford Sise*, 119.

97. Robert Steven Fortner, "Messiahs and Monopolists: A Cultural History of Canadian Communication Systems, 1896–1914" (Ph.D. diss., University of Illinois at Urbana-Champaign, 1978), 92–94; Poitras, *La cité au bout du fil*, 87–101.

98. Quoted in Poitras, *La cité au bout du fil*, 91.

99. "French at the Telephone," *Le Nationaliste*, 14 April 1907.

100. Charles F. Sise to W. A. Haskell, 28 January 1885, BCHC.

101. The earliest version of this story I have found is from forty years after the fact, in Patten, *Pioneering the Telephone in Canada*, 90. See also Fetherstonhaugh, *Charles Fleetford Sise*, 173.

102. Theodore N. Vail to Charles F. Sise, 17, 18 February 1885, Sise Correspondence, BCHC.

103. Armstrong and Nelles, *Monopoly's Moment*, 107–114; Babe, *Telecommunications in Canada*, 74–90.

104. Bell Canada retained a sizable, though not controlling, interest in the New Brunswick Telephone Company, and its relations remained close with both the New Brunswick and Nova Scotia firms. Bell Telephone Company of Canada, *Annual Report of the Directors to the Shareholders of the Bell Telephone Company of Canada*, various years, BCHC. See also Armstrong and Nelles, *Monopoly's Moment*, 109; Babe, *Telecommunications in Canada*, 74–75; Rens, *Invisible Empire*, 81–84.

105. Plus, theoretically, the territories that would become the provinces of Saskatchewan and Alberta in 1905, though Bell had little activity there before they began their rapid growth around the turn of the century.

106. Rhodes, *Beginnings of Telephony*, 196–197.

107. FCC, *Proposed Report*, 96; Gerald W. Brock, *The Telecommunications Industry: The Dynamics of Market Structure* (Cambridge, Mass.: Harvard University Press, 1981), 107–108.

108. Stehman, *Financial History of AT&T*, 44–45; U.S. Census, *Historical Statistics of the United States*, 165.

109. U.S. Census, *Historical Statistics of the United States*, 783–784; Mueller, "The Telephone War." A survey of diffusion rates for common household appliances in the United States found the telephone to be the slowest spreading of twenty twentieth-century appliances. Sue Bowden and Avner Offer, "Household Appliances and the Use of Time: The United States and Britain Since the 1920s," *Economic History Review* 47, no. 4 (1994): 725–748.

110. Office and workplace telephones made up 79 percent of the telephones in Muncie in 1891, and 84 percent of the telephones in Buffalo, New York in 1892. MacDougall, "The People's Telephone," 76–83; Mueller, *Universal Service*, 40.

Chapter 3. Unnatural Monopoly

1. Henry Carter Adams, *Relation of the State to Industrial Action* (Baltimore: American Economic Association, 1887). On the history of natural monopoly theory see William W. Sharkey, *The Theory of Natural Monopoly* (Cambridge: Cambridge University Press, 1982), 12–28.

2. On the difficulty of applying natural monopoly theory to the telephone, see Babe, *Telecommunications in Canada*, 137–149; Mueller, *Universal Service*, 11–20.

3. See, e.g., Fischer, "Touch Someone"; Fischer, *America Calling*; Martin, *Hello, Central*.

4. James J. Storrow to John E. Hudson, 17 November 1891, quoted in Leonard S. Reich, *The Making of American Industrial Research: Science and Business at GE and Bell, 1876–1926* (Cambridge: Cambridge University Press, 1985), 137.

5. "The Telephone Monopoly," *New York Times*, 8 April 1881; Sherwin, *Exchange Statistics*.

6. Fay, "Telephone Subscribers as Knights of Labor," 22, 34.

7. See, e.g., "The New England Telephone Company," *Electrical World*, 16 May 1885, 195; "Not Too Rosy," *Electrical World*, 10 October 1885, 155; "Discordance in

Concord," *Electrical World*, 31 October 1885, 185; "Telephone Troubles at Burlington, Vermont," *Electrical World*, 7 November 1885, 192.

8. Harry W. Laidler, *Boycotts and the Labor Struggle* (New York: John Lane, 1913), 82–85; Haggai Hurvitz, "American Labor Law and the Doctrine of Entrepreneurial Property Rights: Boycotts, Courts, and the Juridical Reorientation of 1886–1895," *Industrial Relations Law Journal* 8, no. 3 (1986): 310–312, 321–323.

9. Gardiner G. Hubbard to William H. Forbes, 29 October 1885, 12 November 1885, Box 1115, AT&T-NJ.

10. Fay, "Telephone Subscribers as Knights of Labor," 33.

11. Kazin, *The Populist Persuasion*; Shelton Stromquist, *Reinventing "the People": The Progressive Movement, the Class Problem, and the Origins of Modern Liberalism* (Chicago: University of Illinois Press, 2006).

12. For all material on the Rochester telephone strike, I am indebted to Derek Hoff, "The Rochester Telephone Strike of 1886 and the Problem of Monopoly in the Gilded Age" (paper presented to the Historical Society, Boothbay Harbor, Maine, June 2004).

13. *Rochester (N.Y.) Democrat and Chronicle*, 11 December 1886.

14. *Rochester (N.Y.) Democrat and Chronicle*, 5 November, 11 November 1886; *Rochester (N.Y.) Union and Advertiser*, 2 November 1886.

15. *Rochester (N.Y.) Democrat and Chronicle*, 2 November, 12 November, 17 December 1886; Edward J. Hall to John Hudson, 15 December 1886, Rochester File, AT&T-NJ.

16. Fay, "Telephone Subscribers as Knights of Labor," 30–33.

17. Hoff, "The Rochester Telephone Strike."

18. *Rochester (N.Y.) Democrat and Chronicle*, 19 October 1887; Lipartito, "Culture and the Practice of Business History," 30–32; Maguire, "The Local Dynamics of Telephone System Development," 83–85; John, *Network Nation*, 241, 290–305.

19. Charles Norman Fay, *Big Business and Government* (New York: Moffat, Yard, 1912), 14–15.

20. Edward J. Hall to William Mallett, 10 October 1886, Rochester File, AT&T-NJ.

21. "War on a Telephone Company," *New York Times*, 5 February 1894; "Vandalism in Tennessee," *American Telephone Journal*, 3 August 1907, 75. See also "Druggists' Commissions Reduced," *New York Times*, 28 November 1898; "Minneapolis Druggists Still Aggressive," *Western Electrician*, 17 February 1900, 105; "The Druggists and the Pay Station," *American Telephone Journal*, 2 November 1907, 288; David L. Cowen, *The New Jersey Pharmaceutical Association, 1870–1970* (Trenton: New Jersey Pharmaceutical Association, 1970), 131–132.

22. "The Telephone Dead Head Evil," *Electrical Review*, 28 February 1885, 5.

23. *Indianapolis News*, 16 May 1902.

24. "War on a Telephone Company," *New York Times*, 5 February 1894.

25. Schiller, *How to Think About Information*, 61–79. Frank Trentmann and Vanessa Taylor argue that the "consumer" as a self-conscious identity emerged around

nineteenth-century political debates over municipal utilities like water, rather than individual consumption of discretionary goods. Frank Trentmann and Vanessa Taylor, "From Users to Consumers: Water Politics in Nineteenth-Century London," in *The Making of the Consumer: Knowledge, Power, and Identity in the Modern World*, ed. Frank Trentmann (Oxford: Berg, 2006), 53–80.

26. American Bell, *Annual Report*, 1886, 14.

27. Bell's most important personal patents were "Transmitters and Receivers for Electric Telegraphs," U.S. Patent No. 161,739, 6 April 1875; "Improvement in Telegraphy," U.S. Patent No. 174,465, 7 March 1876; and "Telephone Receiver," U.S. Patent No. 186,787, 30 January 1877.

28. "Another 'Great and Only' Telephone Inventor," *Electrical World*, 9 February 1884, 45. Charlie Ross was the four-year-old son of a wealthy Philadelphia couple, who was kidnapped in 1874. For years afterward, children came or were brought forward purporting to be the lost heir. See, e.g., "The Charlie Ross Mystery," *New York Times*, 23 October 1883; "Not Charlie Ross," *New York Times*, 3 July 1884.

29. The best descriptions of Bell's many patent battles are in Christopher Beauchamp, "Who Invented the Telephone? Lawyers, Patents, and the Judgment of History," *Technology and Culture* 51, no. 4 (2010): 854–878; and Beauchamp, "The Telephone Patents."

30. Beauchamp, "Who Invented the Telephone," 857–858. See also Steven W. Usselman, *Regulating Railroad Innovation: Business, Technology, and Public Policy in America, 1840–1920* (Cambridge: Cambridge University Press, 2002), 146–153.

31. Usselman, *Regulating Railroad Innovation*, 143–176; Beauchamp, "The Telephone Patents," 118–122, 143, 251–262; Steven W. Usselman and Richard R. John, "Patent Politics: Intellectual Property, the Railroad Industry, and the Problem of Monopoly," *Journal of Policy History* 18, no. 1 (2006): 96–125.

32. A caveat is a prelude to a patent application. It states that an invention is being worked on but is not ready for a patent.

33. See, e.g., William Aitken, *Who Invented the Telephone?* (London: Blackie and Son, 1939); A. Edward Evenson, *The Telephone Patent Conspiracy of 1876: The Elisha Gray—Alexander Bell Controversy and Its Many Players* (Jefferson, N.C.: McFarland, 2000); Seth Shulman, *The Telephone Gambit: Chasing Alexander Graham Bell's Secret* (New York: W. W. Norton, 2008). Bernard S. Finn, "Bell and Gray: Just a Coincidence?" *Technology and Culture* 50, no. 1 (2009): 193–201, offers a skeptical review.

34. Stehman, *Financial History of AT&T*, 17; Rhodes, *Beginnings of Telephony*, 49–75, 207–208; Beauchamp, "Who Invented the Telephone?"

35. Jesse W. Weik, "The Telephone Movement: Another Point of View," *Atlantic Monthly*, February 1906, 263.

36. H. C. Merwin, "Daniel Drawbaugh," *Atlantic Monthly*, September 1888, 347.

37. Beauchamp, "The Telephone Patents," 125–126.

38. Chauncey Smith and James J. Storrow to William H. Forbes, 23 March 1881, in American Bell, *Annual Report*, 1881, 5.

39. "The Great Telephone Suit," *Scientific American*, 4 October 1884, 208–209; "The Bell Telephone Inquiry," *Electrical World*, 25 April 1885, 167–168.

40. William H. Forbes to James J. Storrow, 13 September 1884, quoted in Pier, *Forbes*, 150.

41. "The Bell-Drawbaugh Suit," *Electrical World*, 19 January 1884, 22; "The Great Telephone Suit," *Scientific American*, 4 October 1884, 208–209. The Pan-Electric case, briefly described below, may have received more publicity by virtue of government involvement. But if so, it was Drawbaugh's only competition in this regard, and it did not cost as much or last nearly as long.

42. *American Bell Telephone Company v. People's Telephone Company*, 22 F. 309, 321 (1884); Lysander Hill, *Argument of Hon. Lysander Hill in Support of the Drawbaugh Defense Before the United States Circuit Court* (New York: New York Evening Post, 1884).

43. *New York Times*, 2 December 1884; "The Drawbaugh Interests," *Electrical World*, 5 January 1884, 7.

44. A second battle raged outside the courtroom as to which side, if any, was unfairly favored by the press. Forbes loudly denied any intent on Bell's part "to carry the contest into the newspapers." "This seems to us unwarrantable and wholly unusual among business men of repute," he wrote, "a weapon only likely to be used by those who have no confidence in legitimate business methods for their ends." But the *New York Times* maintained that several New York papers were "subsidized" by friends of Bell, and that as much as $5,000 had been paid for a single favorable article. American Bell, *Annual Report*, 1884, 8; "The Case Against Bell," *New York Times*, 8 February, 30 April 1886.

45. William H. Forbes to James J. Storrow, 13 September 1884, quoted in Pier, *Forbes*, 149.

46. *New York Times*, 30 April 1886.

47. *Western Electrician*, 27 October 1888, and *United States of America v. American Bell Telephone Company and Emile Berliner*, 65 F. 86 (1894), both quoted in Beauchamp, "The Telephone Patents," 208.

48. Quoted in "Are Telephone Rates Exorbitant?" *Electrical Review*, 24 January 1885, 4.

49. *New York Times*, 18 December 1887.

50. *People's Telephone v. American Bell Telephone*, 126 U.S. (1888); quoted in Rhodes, *Beginnings of Telephony*, 64–68, 209, 273–274.

51. "The Parent Telephone," *New York Times*, 4 April 1886; "Another Telephone Suit," *New York Times*, 17 September 1886.

52. Rhodes, *Beginnings of Telephony*, 56–60, gives the standard account of this case. Meucci's advocates, still extant, have their say in Basilio Catania, *Antonio Meucci: The Inventor and His Times* (Turin, Italy: SEAT Publications, 1994), among others.

53. American Bell, *Annual Report*, 1886, 8–12. The clearest summaries of this convoluted case are in Beauchamp, "The Telephone Patents," 134–139, 191–203; and John, *Network Nation*, 205–208.

54. Beauchamp, "The Telephone Patents," 203–206.

55. "Well-Known Heads of Well-Known Houses," *Telephony*, July 1901, reprinted as "Milo Gifford Kellogg," *Telecom History* 1 (1994): 93–94. In 1883, Kellogg alarmed American Bell by lobbying the city of Chicago to enforce its underground wire ordinance, a move that would generate business for Western Electric, in the form of cable and wire-laying equipment, but would be very expensive for Chicago Telephone and American Bell. John, *Network Nation*, 224.

56. Beauchamp, "The Telephone Patents," 206–207.

57. *United States v. Emile Berliner*, quoted in Beauchamp, "The Telephone Patents," 208–209.

58. "The Effect of the Berliner Decision," *Electrical World*, 15 May 1897, 611–613; Beauchamp, "The Telephone Patents," 207–212.

59. MacMeal, *The Story of Independent Telephony*, 26.

60. U.S. Census, *Telephones and Telegraphs: 1902*, 8–9; MacMeal, *The Story of Independent Telephony*, 40–41.

61. U.S. Census, *Telephones and Telegraphs: 1902*, 8–9; U.S. Census, *Telephones and Telegraphs: 1912*; 14, 29.

62. Walsh, *Connecticut Pioneers*, 340; David Gabel, "Competition in a Network Industry: The Telephone Industry, 1894–1910," *Journal of Economic History* 54, no. 3 (1994): 563–564.

63. U.S. Census, *Telephones and Telegraphs: 1912*, 35–36.

64. Examples are legion. See, e.g., Frederick S. Dickson, *Telephone Investments—And Others* (Cleveland: Cuyahoga Telephone Company, 1905), HBS; W. H. Denlinger, "The Independence of Independents," *Telephony*, March 1908, 175–176; A. C. Lindemuth, *A Larger View* (Chicago: International Independent Telephone Association, 1908), Telephone Pamphlets, Widener Library, Harvard University (hereafter TPH).

65. E. J. Mock, "Story of the States—Illinois," *Telephony*, January 1907, 1–3; unnamed speaker quoted in Atwood, "Telephony and Its Cultural Meanings," 106.

66. "Competition Is Necessary," *Sound Waves*, December 1907, 274; Wilson, "The Relation of Rural Telephones to Towns and Cities."

67. Charles Norton quoted in H. D. Fargo, "The International Convention: A Complete Report of the Proceedings," *Telephony*, February 1908, 81–110; Lindemuth, *A Larger View*, 2; Latzke, *A Fight with an Octopus*, 17; William Crownover, "Should Independent and Mutual Companies Co-Operate," *Telephony*, May 1907, 309.

68. The literature on populism is extensive; useful recent works include Kazin, *The Populist Persuasion*; Ritter, *Goldbugs and Greenbacks*; and Postel, *The Populist Vision*.

69. John, "Recasting the Information Infrastructure"; Starr, *The Creation of the Media*, 47–111.

70. Richard R. John similarly reminds us that the epithet "robber baron" (and the critique of monopoly capitalism it implied) was not coined by Kansas populists in the 1880s but by Boston elites in the 1860s. John, "Robber Barons Redux," 3–4.

71. Jeffrey Ostler, *Prairie Populism: The Fate of Agrarian Radicalism in Kansas, Nebraska, and Iowa, 1880–1892* (Lawrence: University Press of Kansas, 1993).

72. *Western Electrician* quoted in MacMeal, *The Story of Independent Telephony*, 35–36; "The Telephone Question: The Effect of the Berliner Decision on the Industry," *Electrical Review*, 26 December 1894, 320; Garnet, *The Telephone Enterprise*, 90–92; Nix and Gabel, "AT&T's Strategic Response to Competition," 381–385.

73. Central Union, *Annual Report*, 1896, 2.

74. Quoted in Atwood, "Telephony and Its Cultural Meanings," 95–96. "The man who pulls that company out of the mire is sure to find life a burden and grief galore," Yost wrote in 1897. The following year he became president of the company.

75. "The ideal system would put every person in a community into telephonic communication with every other person," said a pamphlet published by Bell's New England subsidiary in 1906. "Of course, such a condition as this is impossible." New England Telephone and Telegraph Company (NET&T), *The Telephone: A Description of the Bell System with Some Facts Concerning the So-Called "Independent" Movement* (Boston: New England Telephone and Telegraph Company, 1906), 22, TPH. For predictions of ruin to the independents, see "The Leading Independent Telephone Company," 1903, HBS; Anderson, *Telephone Competition in the Middle West*; New England Telephone and Telegraph Company, *Competition in Telephony* (Boston: New England Telephone and Telegraph Company, 1909), TPH; Chester I. Barnard, "An Analysis of a Speech of the Hon. D. J. Lewis Comparing Governmental and Private Telegraph and Telephone Utilities," 2 March 1914, TPH.

76. See, e.g., Dickson, *Telephone Investments*, 14; A. H. McMillan, "Telephone a Household Necessity," *American Telephone Journal*, 3 February 1906, 61; Charles H. Schweizer, "Relation of the Rural Telephone to the Farmer," *Sound Waves*, November 1907, 259–260. For rate comparison, see Select Committee on Telephone Systems, *Report*, 2: 766–810; for a rural cooperative, see Valley Exchange Telephone Company, *Ledger*, 1918–1924, Bernice Gaskins Collection, ISL.

77. Cumberland Telephone and Telegraph Company, *Annual Report of the Directors of the Cumberland Telephone and Telegraph Company*, HBS, 1902; Caldwell, *Recollections of a Life Time*, 141; Crownover, "Should Independent and Mutual Companies Co-Operate," 309.

78. John, *Network Nation*, 269–310.

79. Maguire, "The Local Dynamics of Telephone System Development," 39–46.

80. R. S. Master, R. C. Smith, and W. E. Winter, "Historical Review of the San Francisco Exchange," 1926, Pacific Bell Subject Files, AT&T-TX, 58–59; Maguire, "The Local Dynamics of Telephone System Development," 57–98. Richard R. John points out that a nickel at this time was a small, but not trivial, expense—the price of a package of cigarettes, a Coca-Cola, or a streetcar ride. John, *Network Nation*, 297.

81. Home Telephone Company of San Francisco, *Automatic Telephone System Progress Report* (San Francisco: Home Telephone Company, [1909?]), AT&T-TX; Maguire, "The Local Dynamics of Telephone System Development," 108–153.

82. Central Union, *Annual Report*, 1898, 2; 1900, 2; White, Weld, and Company, "Memorandum on the Central Union Telephone Company," 1914, HBS; "The Central Union Telephone Company / Chicago Telephone Company," Case Histories on the Development of AT&T's Horizontal Structure, [1980?], AT&T-NJ.

83. Hibbard, *Hello, Goodbye*, 179–223; John, *Network Nation*, 279–301.

84. "The Central Union Telephone Company / Chicago Telephone Company," 5–6; Gabel, "Competition in a Network Industry," 541–555; John, *Network Nation*, 301–305. Some of Sabin's correspondence with American Telephone and Telegraph is in Box 1313, AT&T-NJ.

85. Central Union, *Annual Report*, 1903, 1; 1907, 5; "Bell Proposal Rejected," *Telephony*, June 1907, 368–369; Norton, "The Indiana Situation," *American Telephone Journal*, 13 July 1907, 20–21; David Gabel, "Divestiture, Spin-Offs, and Technological Change in the Telecommunications Industry: A Property Rights Analysis," *Harvard Journal of Law and Technology* 3 (1990): 75–102.

86. Stehman, *Financial History of AT&T*, 60, 73; Garnet, *The Telephone Enterprise*, 105–109.

87. AT&T, *Annual Report*, 1906, 8; Frederick P. Fish to Joseph B. Davis, 25 September 1901, Presidential Letter Books, vol. 16, AT&T-NJ; Frederick P. Fish to F. E. Pettingill, 21 April 1902, Presidential Letter Books, vol. 23–1, AT&T-NJ.

88. Garnet, *The Telephone Enterprise*, 117–118.

89. Stehman, *Financial History of AT&T*; Danielian, *AT&T*, 57–66.

90. Latzke, *A Fight with an Octopus*, 9; "Wide-Open Competition," *Sound Waves*, October 1907, 1. See also "Exit President Fish," *Sound Waves*, June 1907, 3–4; E. J. Mock, "Story of the States—Illinois," *Telephony*, January 1907, 1–3.

91. U.S. Census, *Telephones and Telegraphs: 1912*, 27; Claude S. Fischer, "The Revolution in Rural Telephony, 1900–1920," *Journal of Social History* 21, no. 1 (1987): 5–26; Mueller, *Universal Service*, 56–57.

92. Rens, *Invisible Empire*, 112.

93. Patten, *Pioneering the Telephone*, 114; Fetherstonhaugh, *Charles Fleetford Sise*, 197; Dunstan quoted in Thomas W. Eadie, *Too Startling for Belief! A Story of Telephone Development in Canada* (New York: Newcomen Society, 1955), 12.

94. Bell Canada, *Annual Report*, 1905; Frederick DeBerard, *Supplemental Telephone Report: Further Inquiry into Effect of Competition* (New York: Merchants Association of New York, 1905), 3, TPH.

95. Select Committee on Telephone Systems, *Report*, 1: 622.

96. Select Committee on Telephone Systems, *Report*, 1:19, 811.

97. Bell Telephone Company of Canada, Circular, 4 January 1902, BCHC. American telephone executives could also be blunt about their biases. An AT&T manual from 1915 estimated that "an average American city, in which practically everyone is white," could support one telephone for every eight inhabitants. "Where a large portion of the population belongs to the Negro race, or a considerable portion of the population is made up of very poor workers in factories, the requirements will be

less," the report continued. Arthur B. Smith and William L. Campbell, *Automatic Telephony* (New York: McGraw-Hill, 1915), 379.

98. "The Taxpayer and the Telephone," 2 January 1902, Document No. 12016, BCHC.

99. Kenneth J. Dunstan to Charles F. Sise, 19 April 1900, and Kenneth J. Dunstan to Local Manager, 2 January 1902, Box 80141b, File 3146–3, BCHC; "Telephone Rates in Canada," *Telephone Magazine*, July 1902, 66–67; *Toronto Globe*, 31 March 1905; Martin, *Hello Central*, 31.

100. Armstrong and Nelles, *Monopoly's Moment*, 164–165.

101. *Richmond v. Southern Bell Telephone and Telegraph Company*, 174 U.S. 761 (1899).

102. William D. Lighthall to Oliver Howland, 10 June 1901, and Oliver Howland to William D. Lighthall, 12 June 1901, William D. Lighthall Papers, vol. 16, NAC.

103. Armstrong and Nelles, *Monopoly's Moment*, 141–162. Richard R. John suggests calling civic populism "municipal capitalism" instead, finding it "less an alternative to capitalism than its complement." But populism and capitalism were never incompatible alternatives, as historians from Richard Hofstadter to Charles Postel have shown. John, *Network Nation*, 265.

104. William D. Lighthall to Mayor, 2 January 1906, Finance and Accounts, KQUA.

105. Quoted in Armstrong and Nelles, *Monopoly's Moment*, 145. See also William D. Lighthall, *Canada: A Modern Nation* (Montreal: Witness Printing House, 1904).

106. G. E. Britnell, "Public Ownership of Telephones in the Prairies" (M.A. thesis, University of Toronto, 1934), 11; "Grange Endorses Competition," *Sound Waves*, December 1907, 1; "The Farmers' Proclamation," *Telephony*, January 1908, 3–4. Testimonials of support for the union plan and others are collected in Select Committee on Telephone Systems, *Report*, vol. 2.

107. Dagger, "The Common Cause." See also Francis Dagger, "Is Telephone Competition in Canada Desirable?" *Telephony*, July 1903, 48–50; "Mr. Dagger Compliments Us," *Sound Waves*, December 1905, 3; Francis Dagger, "Telephone Competition and Monopoly," *Sound Waves*, August 1906, 297–300.

108. Select Committee on Telephone Systems, *Report*, 1: 709, 746–752, 831–839, 2: 54–55, 60–61, 80, 112–113, 120–125; NET&T, *Competition in Telephony*, 3.

109. James Bryce, *Modern Democracies* (New York: Macmillan, 1921), 467; *Canadian Methodist Magazine* quoted in Carl Berger, *The Sense of Power: Studies in the Idea of Canadian Imperialism, 1867–1914* (Toronto: University of Toronto Press, 1970), 155.

110. Michael Bliss, "Another Anti-Trust Tradition: Canadian Anti-Combines Policy, 1889–1910," *Business History Review* 47, no. 2 (1973): 177–188; Michael J. Trebilcock et al., *The Law and Economics of Canadian Competition Policy* (Toronto: University of Toronto Press, 2002), 3–36. Ashley is quoted in Bliss, "Another Anti-Trust Tradition," 181.

111. Edward M. Cooke, *The Case of the Keystone Telephone* (Philadelphia: Keystone Telephone Company, 1915), 3, TPH. See also John H. Ainsworth, Gansey R. Johnston, and Frank L. Beam, *A Discussion of Telephone Competition* (Columbus: Ohio Independent Telephone Association, 1908), TPH; Lindemuth, *A Larger View*.

112. See, e.g., a 1902 report of the Hamilton, Ontario, city council, reprinted in *The Independent Telephone Movement: Its Inception and Progress* (1906), 59, HBS.

113. Charles Fitzpatrick, "Memorandum in Reference to the Telegraph and Telephone Bill," Sir Wilfrid Laurier Papers, MG 26, G-2, vol. 247, p. 68747, NAC.

114. Dagger, "Telephone Competition and Monopoly"; Dagger, "Is Telephone Competition in Canada Desirable?"

115. Quoted in Babe, *Telecommunications in Canada*, 76–77.

116. Canada, Senate, *Debates*, 4 May 1882, 187–188.

117. Select Committee on Telephone Systems, *Report*, 2: 29.

118. Canada, Senate, *Debates*, 7 March 1907, 381.

119. In 1909, there were approximately 239,000 telephones in all of Canada (data for 1907 is not available). In 1907, there were approximately 280,000 independent telephones in Iowa, 285,000 in Illinois, and 312,000 in Ohio. Urquhart, *Historical Statistics of Canada*, 559; U.S. Census, *Telephones and Telegraphs: 1912*, 35.

120. Fay, *Big Business and Government*, 3.

121. Fay, *Big Business and Government*, 15, 18.

Chapter 4. The Independent Alternative

1. Henry A. Barnhart, "Address to the Interstate Independent Telephone Association," 10 December 1903, Henry Barnhart Papers, Indiana State Library (hereafter HAB).

2. U.S. Census, *Telephones and Telegraphs: 1912*, 35; U.S. Census, *Historical Statistics of the United States*, 2: 783–784.

3. Mueller, *Universal Service*, and John, *Network Nation*, are two important exceptions.

4. On the "decentralized alternative" in another industry and in other countries, see Berk, *Alternative Tracks;* Andrew Davies, *Telecommunications and Politics: The Decentralised Alternative* (London: Pinter, 1994).

5. "Interstate Independent Telephone Association," 1902, Box 1337, AT&T-NJ, quoted in Kenneth Lipartito, "Component Innovation," 344.

6. L. G. Richardson to Theodore N. Vail, 9 July 1909, Box 1375, AT&T-NJ.

7. Henry A. Barnhart to N. O. Fanning, 9 May 1905, HAB; "Some Things Henry Barnhart Stands For," [1908?], 18–21, HAB. See also William Jennings Bryan to Henry A. Barnhart, 29 March 1902, HAB. Biographical information on Barnhart appears in Barnhart Papers, ISL, and also in Wendell C. Tombaugh and John B. Tombaugh, "Fulton County Handbook," Fulton County Library, Rochester, Indiana.

8. Tombaugh and Tombaugh, "Fulton County Handbook."

9. Barnhart, "Address to the Interstate Independent Telephone Association."

10. Charles E. Tarte, "Long Distance Service—Its Development and Possibilities," *Sound Waves*, July 1907, 96–97.

11. MacMeal, *The Story of Independent Telephony*, 140. William T. Sennett's diary is in the Thomas J. McGan Record Books, ISL.

12. *Rochester (Ind.) Sentinel*, 3 March 1915, in Tombaugh and Tombaugh, "Fulton County Handbook."

13. Atwood, "Telephony and Its Cultural Meanings," 198–269.

14. Citizens Telephone Company, *Annual Report of the Secretary of the Citizens Telephone Company of Grand Rapids, Michigan*, HBS; William J. Etten, *A Citizens' History of Grand Rapids, Michigan* (Grand Rapids: A. P. Johnson, 1926). For a description of some small cooperative and quasi-cooperative telephone systems, see Stephen J. Keillor, *Cooperative Commonwealth: Co-ops in Rural Minnesota, 1859–1939* (St. Paul: Minnesota Historical Society Press, 2000), 236–255. For the records of one such system, see Valley Exchange Telephone Company, Ledgers, 1918–1924, Bernice Gaskins Collection, ISL.

15. See, e.g., "Consolidation Talk," *New York Times*, 30 December 1899.

16. See, e.g., M. J. Dillman to B. C. Carroll, 2 September 1907, Home Telephone and Telegraph Company of Portland Files, and other Predecessor and Subsidiary Company Files generally, AT&T-TX.

17. See, e.g., "Secrets of Telephone Promotion: How the Wily Stock and Apparatus Peddler Pulls Wool Over the Eyes of Unsophisticated and Credulous Investors," *Central Union News*, May 1905, 6–7.

18. James E. Geist, *The Lincoln Telephone and Telegraph Company: The Great Independent* (New York: Newcomen Society of North America, 1979), 12–13; Al Farmer, "Lincoln: The First Dial System in a Capital City," *Telecom History* 2 (1995): 36–39.

19. MacMeal, *The Story of Independent Telephony*, 75–76; Thomas McCarthy, *The History of GTE* (Stamford, Conn.: GTE Corporation, 1990).

20. Henry A. Barnhart to E. M. Coleman, 9 November 1904 and 9 December 1904, HAB; John H. Wright to J. P. Tumulty, 18 March 1913, Box 38, Record Group 60, Department of Justice, National Archives, Washington, D.C. (hereafter DOJ-NA).

21. Kempster B. Miller, *American Telephone Practice* (Chicago: American Electrician, 1899); J. A. Williams, *Manual of Rural Telephony* (Cleveland: Manual Publishing, 1902), Hagley Museum and Library, Wilmington, Delaware (hereafter HML); MacMeal, *The Story of Independent Telephony*, 66–68, 81–84.

22. Henry A. Barnhart to E. M. Coleman, 9 December 1904, HAB; see more generally Barnhart's correspondence with Coleman, Automatic Electric Company, Stromberg-Carlson Manufacturing Company, and others. See also Select Committee on Telephone Systems, *Report*, 1: 934.

23. Scholarship on the independents has been too ready to adopt this division. Sociologists and social historians have been drawn to the story of rural telephony and the tiny farmers' cooperatives, while economists and economic historians have studied

the larger commercial independents, apprehending them and the Bell companies as essentially like-minded organizations driven by the profit motive.

24. U.S. Census, *Telephones and Telegraphs: 1912*, 27. On Bigfoot Township, see Tombaugh and Tombaugh, "Fulton County Handbook."

25. Sample stock certificates, bylaws, and articles of incorporation can be found in Williams, *Manual of Rural Telephony*. For a detailed description of the spectrum of independent organizations in one midwestern state, see Atwood, "Telephony and Its Cultural Meanings," 134–145.

26. A list of examples appears in Kline, *Consumers in the Country*, 31.

27. Lindemuth, *A Larger View*, 4–5; Manford Savage to James C. McReynolds, 17 December 1913, Box 38, Record Group 60, DOJ-NA.

28. Williams, *Manual of Rural Telephony*, 24.

29. See, e.g., Henry A. Barnhart to Stromberg-Carlson Manufacturing Company, 15 December 1902, HAB.

30. William P. Barnett and Glenn R. Carroll, "Competition and Mutualism Among Early Telephone Companies," *Administrative Science Quarterly* 32, no. 3 (1987): 400–421.

31. On potential strengths and advantages of small-firm networks over large corporate organizations, see Charles Perrow, *Organizing America: Wealth, Power, and the Origins of Corporate Capitalism* (Princeton, N.J.: Princeton University Press, 2002).

32. Casson, *The History of the Telephone*, 194.

33. A. F. Wilson, "The Relation of Rural Telephones to Towns and Cities," *Telephony*, January 1907, 42–44.

34. NET&T, *Competition in Telephony*, 28.

35. "Bell and Independent Exchange Rates, 1912–1913," Box 29, AT&T-NJ. See also the data on telephone prices in dozens of Canadian and American cities collected by the Parliament of Canada in Select Committee on Telephone Systems, *Report*, 2: 766–810.

36. Williams, *Manual of Rural Telephony*, 25.

37. E. B. Fisher, quoted in Select Committee on Telephone Systems, *Report*, 2: 102–103.

38. Gabel, "Competition in a Network Industry," 545–555, 565–566.

39. Weik, "The Telephone Movement," 269; Gabel, "Competition in a Network Industry," 564–565.

40. NET&T, *The Telephone: A Description of the Bell System*, 11–12.

41. "The Leading Independent Telephone Company," 1903, pamphlet filed with Cuyahoga Telephone Company Reports, 6, 19, HBS.

42. Dickson, *Telephone Investments*, 19, 49.

43. Bert G. Hubbell to James C. McReynolds, 19 September 1913, Box 38, Record Group 60, DOJ-NA; George S. Shanklin, "Depreciation of Telephone Properties," *Telephony*, February 1908, 138. See also Vinton A. Sears, *Telephone Development* (Boston: Barta Press, 1903), HML; Gansey R. Johnston, W. Roy McCanne, and Charles E.

Tarte, *Some Considerations on Telephone Depreciation* (Chicago: National Independent Telephone Association, 1910), TPH.

44. "Measured Service Rates," Boxes 1127, 1213, 1287, 1309, AT&T-NJ. For discussion of measured service outside the AT&T archives, see Anderson, *Telephone Competition in the Middle West*; John B. Geijsbeek and Page Lawrence, "Report on the Denver Plant of the Mountain States Telephone and Telegraph Co.," January 1914, TPH.

45. *Western Electrician*, 6 July 1901, 8; John, *Network Nation*, 303–306.

46. Richard Gabel, *Development of Separations Principles in the Telephone Industry* (East Lansing: Michigan State University, 1967); Peter Temin and Geoffrey Peters, "Is History Stranger Than Theory? The Origin of Telephone Separations," *American Economic Review* 75, no. 2 (1985): 324–327.

47. Geijsbeek and Lawrence, "Report on the Denver Plant," 20.

48. Kenneth Train, *Optimal Regulation: The Economic Theory of Natural Monopoly* (Cambridge, Mass.: MIT Press, 1991), 211–213; Anja Lambrecht and Bernd Skiera, "Paying Too Much and Being Happy About It: Existence, Causes, and Consequences of Tariff-Choice Biases," *Journal of Marketing Research* 43, no. 2 (2006): 212–223.

49. See, e.g., Harry B. Thayer to George F. Durant, 24 February 1909, and Frank A. Pickernell to Harry B. Thayer, 2 June 1909, "Missouri," Box 4, AT&T-NJ; Nix and Gabel, "AT&T's Strategic Response to Competition," 378–380.

50. Quoted in Nix and Gabel, "AT&T's Strategic Response to Competition," 380.

51. "Notice to Public," July 1880, Box 12, AT&T-NJ.

52. Theodore N. Vail to Edward J. Hall, 28 January 1880, Box 1127, AT&T-NJ.

53. Marvin, *When Old Technologies Were New*, 22–32.

54. Mark Twain, "A Telephonic Conversation," in *The Complete Humorous Sketches and Tales of Mark Twain*, ed. Charles Neider (Garden City, N.Y.: Hanover House, 1961), 478–481.

55. This argument is made in Martin, *Hello Central*; Fischer, *America Calling*; Lana F. Rakow, *Gender on the Line: Women, the Telephone, and Community Life* (Urbana: University of Illinois Press, 1991). Carroll Purcell and Lisa Gitelman have both critiqued the ways "even the most affirmative, feminist-friendly accounts" of this history accept that "inventing the telephone is manly; talking on it is womanly." Carroll Purcell, "Seeing the Invisible: New Perceptions in the History of Technology," *Icon* 1 (1995): 9–15; Gitelman, *Always Already New: Media, History, and the Data of Culture* (Cambridge, Mass.: MIT Press, 2006), 61.

56. On fears of female speech, see Ned Schantz, *Gossip, Letters, Phones: The Scandal of Female Networks in Film and Literature* (New York: Oxford University Press, 2008).

57. Edward J. Hall to E. M. Burgess, 30 March 1905, Box 1309, AT&T-NJ.

58. Charles F. Sise, quoted in Collins, *A Voice from Afar*, 124.

59. Anderson, *Telephone Competition in the Middle West*, 8.

60. Anderson, *Telephone Competition in the Middle West*, 9.

61. Conference of Publicity and Personnel Representatives of the American Telephone and Telegraph Company (hereafter cited as AT&T Publicity Conference), *Proceedings*, April 1928, 33, HBS.

62. *Telephony*, 8 May 1909, 542.

63. "The Spectator," *Outlook*, 15 November 1902, 631; William Maver Jr., "Widening Applications of the Telephone," *Cassier's Magazine*, February 1907, 275–282; U.S. Census, *Telephones and Telegraphs: 1912*, 15–17.

64. E. M. Rothelle, "New Uses of the Telephone," *Telephony*, May 1907, 332–334; Kline, *Consumers in the Country*, 41–45.

65. *Iowa City Citizen*, quoted in Atwood, "Telephony and Its Cultural Meanings," 317–318.

66. Quoted in Kline, *Consumers in the Country*, 44.

67. Quoted in George Shepherd, *West of Yesterday* (Toronto: McClelland and Stewart, 1965), 93. See "The Rural Babel," *Telephony*, December 1907, 385; "Spread of the Rural Telephone Movement," *Scientific American*, 18 February 1911, 162; Eleanor Arnold, ed., *Party Lines, Pumps, and Privies: Memories of Hoosier Homemakers* (Indianapolis: Indiana Extension Homemakers Association, 1984), 150–152; Kline, *Consumers in the Country*, 45–48.

68. "Experience on a Rural Line," *Sound Waves*, February 1905, 87; "Free Telephone Service," *Outlook*, 25 August 1900, 946–947; "Free Telephone Service Abandoned," *Western Electrician*, 13 October 1900, 234.

69. "Almon Strowger Biography," Box 92 10 187 01, AT&T-NJ; Robert J. Chapuis, *100 Years of Telephone Switching* (New York: North-Holland, 1982), 1: 207.

70. Emory Lindquist, "The Invention and Development of the Dial Telephone: The Contribution of Three Lindsborg Inventors," *Kansas Historical Quarterly* 23, no. 1 (1957): 1–8.

71. Arthur Bessey Smith, "History of the Automatic Telephone," *Sound Waves*, January 1908, 5; "Independent Telephony, 1891–1935," Box 177 09 01 03, AT&T-NJ; Lipartito, "Component Innovation."

72. See advertisements for Strowger Automatic Telephone Exchange and other systems, Boxes 1109, 1152, 1291, 2026, AT&T-NJ; Lipartito, "Component Innovation," 337; Venus Green, *Race on the Line: Gender, Labor, and Technology in the Bell System, 1880–1980* (Durham, N.C.: Duke University Press, 2001), 118–120.

73. "The Automatic Electric Company," 1902, Box 11 06 03 04, AT&T-NJ.

74. "Tests of the Strowger Automatic System in Chicago, Illinois," 18 October 1904, 11–07–01–02, AT&T-NJ; Martin, *Hello Central*, 50–81; Kenneth Lipartito, "When Women Were Switches: Technology, Work, and Gender in the Telephone Industry, 1890–1920," *American Historical Review* 99, no. 4 (1994): 1101.

75. Committee on Switchboards and Telephonic Apparatus (hereafter cited as AT&T Switchboard Committee), *Proceedings*, March 1892, 123, AT&T-NJ.

76. Thomas Lockwood to John E. Hudson, 4 November 1891, Box 1286, AT&T-NJ; Thomas Lockwood to John E. Hudson, 3 March 1896, Box 1274, AT&T-NJ.

77. John J. Carty, "The Automatic Telephone: Its Merits and Its Faults," *Scientific American Supplement* 61, no. 1581 (1906): 25331.

78. Kempster B. Miller, *Report on the Automatic Telephone Situation in the City of Chicago* (Chicago, 1915), 5–17.

79. Thomas Lockwood to W. W. Hutchinson, 26 March 1900, Box 1253, AT&T-NJ; Mueller, "The Switchboard Problem," 544–545; Stanley Swihart, "Early Automatic Telephone Systems," *Telecom History* 2 (1995), 2–21; Lipartito, "Component Innovation," 328.

80. Venus Green, "Goodbye Central: Automation and the Decline of 'Personal Service' in the Bell System, 1878–1921," *Technology and Culture* 36, no. 4 (1995): 942–943; Green, *Race on the Line*, 116–117, 125–127.

81. John J. Carty, *Telephone Service in America* (New York: Smith, Jones, and Leigh, 1910), HML; Lipartito, "Component Innovation," 327.

82. Bert G. Hubbell to James C. McReynolds, 29 June 1913, Box 38, Record Group 60, DOJ-NA; John, *Network Nation*, 354–355.

83. Carty, *Telephone Service in America*, 17.

84. AT&T Publicity Conference, *Proceedings*, 1928, 32, 572, 585–588.

85. Wilson, *Deregulating Telecommunications*, 110–115.

86. Janin Hadlaw, "Communicating Modernity: Design, Representation, and the Making of the Telephone" (Ph.D. diss., Simon Fraser University, 2004), 62–77; Fagen, *Engineering and Science in the Bell System*, 140–141.

87. "Why Should a Telephone Be Ugly?" *Telephony* 5 May 1928, 28–29; Bancroft Gherardi to Frank B. Jewett, 4 May 1926, Box 73, Series 7, F. B. Jewett Collection, AT&T-NJ.

88. AT&T Publicity Conference, *Proceedings*, 1928, 32; Frank B. Jewett to Bancroft Gherardi, 10 April 1928, Frank B. Jewett to W. S. Gifford and Arthur W. Page, 25 September 1928, Bancroft Gherardi to Frank B. Jewett, 14 Feburary 1929, Box 73, Series 7, F. B. Jewett Collection, AT&T-NJ; Hadlaw, "Communicating Modernity," 95–103.

89. Thomas Lockwood to John E. Hudson, 23 May 1895, Box 1253, AT&T-NJ.

90. On the dynamics of dual service, or "access competition," see Mueller, *Universal Service*, 54–91.

91. In 1897, at least 220 cities in America with populations of five thousand or more, or 23 percent of such communities, had dual service. In 1904, 60 percent of American cities had dual service; in 1907, 57 percent. Mueller, *Universal Service*, 7, 61.

92. Keystone Telephone Company, *Annual Report of the Telephone Securities Inc. and Keystone Telephone Company of Philadelphia*, various years, HML; Peter Schauble, "Dual Telephone Service Ends in Philadelphia," *Bell Telephone Magazine*, Winter 1946, 311–316; Shearer, *Hoosier Connections*, 57.

93. "Universal service": Or at least part of the meaning. Vail also had in mind the interconnection of telephone and telegraph, discussed in Chapter 5. Central Union, *Annual Report*, 1900, 2; NET&T, *The Telephone: A Description of the Bell System*; Walter B. Vincent, "Argument in Behalf of the Providence Telephone Company Before the

Joint Special Committee of the City Council Against Establishment of a Duplicate Telephone System in the City of Providence," 7 January 1907, 22, TPH; Vail, *Views on Public Questions*, 128.

94. Cooke, *The Case of the Keystone Telephone*, 5; Lindemuth, *A Larger View*, 4; *Telephony*, June 1906.

95. Cooke, *The Case of the Keystone Telephone*, 5.

96. Mock, "Story of the States—Illinois."

97. Ainsworth, Johnston, and Beam, *A Discussion of Telephone Competition*.

98. DeBerard, *Supplemental Telephone Report*; "Double Telephone Service," *Electrical World*, 29 June 1907, 1298; Lloyd Heck Marvin, "The Telephone Situation in Los Angeles," (M.A. thesis, University of Southern California, 1916), plate II.

99. DeBerard, *Supplemental Telephone Report*, 3–6. DeBerard examined the telephone business in fifty cities, finding average duplication rates ranging from 5 to 40 percent.

100. Thomas Tracy to U. N. Bethell, 11 February 1911, Box 39, AT&T-NJ. The data are reproduced and discussed in Mueller, *Universal Service*, 81–85.

101. Emphasis mine, AT&T, *Annual Report*, 1904, 16; 1907, 18; 1909, 23.

102. Arthur Kemper, Scrapbook, 1889–1897, General William H. Kemper Collection, Indiana Historical Society, Indianapolis (hereafter IHS); Markus Möbius, "Death Through Success: The Rise and Fall of Local Service Competition at the Turn of the Century," Working Paper, Department of Economics, Harvard University, 15 January 2001.

103. MacMeal, *The Story of Independent Telephony*, 28.

104. Canada, Senate, *Debates*, 9 May 1901, 354; "The Merchant's Telephone Company of Montreal," October 1985, BCHC; Babe, *Telecommunications in Canada*, 77–78.

105. Quoted in Mueller, *Universal Service*, 57.

106. Casper E. Yost to Frederick P. Fish, 14 April 1902, Box 1214, AT&T-NJ.

107. See, for instance, David J. Lewis, "The Postalization of the Telephone," 5 January 1915, TPH.

108. Henry A Barnhart to L. C. Miller, 27 April 1902, HAB.

109. Containers 7–10, Robert and Helen Lynd Papers, Library of Congress, Washington, D.C. (hereafter RHL-LOC).

110. Select Committee on Telephone Systems, *Report*, 1: 19, 50, 265.

111. G. F. Wonbacher, "Proper Development of the Rural Telephone," *Western Telephone Journal*, July 1908, 242; *Republican Press* (Atwater, Minn.), quoted in Keillor, *Cooperative Commonwealth*, 244.

112. American Telephone and Telegraph Company, *The Story of a Great Achievement: Telephone Communication from Coast to Coast* (New York: American Telephone and Telegraph Company, 1915), 2, 16.

113. George Leverett to Frederick P. Fish, 17 October 1901, Box 1375, AT&T-NJ.

114. See, most recently, Wu, *The Master Switch*, 53–54.

115. Crownover, "Should Independent and Mutual Companies Co-Operate," 309; Dickson, *Telephone Investments*, 40.

116. H. H. Nance and R. M. Oram, "The Circuits Go Up," *Bell Telephone Quarterly* 19, no. 1 (1940): 35; Dickson, *Telephone Investments*, 40.

117. "Low Rates and Local Service," *American Telephone Journal*, 17 August 1907, 108.

118. Lipartito, *The Bell System and Regional Business*, 116.

119. Cuyahoga Telephone Company, *Annual Report to Stockholders*, 1904, HBS.

120. Henry A. Barnhart to James A. Terry, 25 May 1901, HAB; Hugh Dougherty to Henry A. Barnhart, 15 February 1902, HAB.

121. Quoted in Tombaugh and Tombaugh, "Fulton County Handbook."

Chapter 5. The Politics of Scale

1. Louis D. Brandeis, *Business—A Profession* (Boston: Small, Maynard, 1914), xlv; Louis D. Brandeis, *Other People's Money: And How the Bankers Use It* (New York: Frederick A. Stokes, 1914), 162.

2. On technological nationalism in Canada, see Maurice Charland, "Technological Nationalism," *Canadian Journal of Political and Social Theory* 10, nos. 1–2 (1986): 196–220; A. A. Den Otter, *The Philosophy of Railways: The Transcontinental Railway Idea in British North America* (Toronto: University of Toronto Press, 1997).

3. Grant, *Ocean to Ocean*, 344; Grant and Hamilton, *George Monro Grant*, 243. See also George Monro Grant, "The Canada Pacific Railway," *Century Illustrated*, October 1885, 882; and Grant's articles in *Scribner's Monthly* from May through August 1880. On Grant's contributions to Canadian nationalism, see Berger, *The Sense of Power*.

4. See Chapter 1.

5. See, e.g., Charles F. Sise to John E. Hudson, 9 March 1893, 2 May 1894, BCHC.

6. Canada, Senate, *Debates*, 29 April 1892, 177; 4 May 1892, 187–188; 5 May 1892, 190–197.

7. See Chapter 3.

8. Wilson, "Telephone Requirements in Canada."

9. Canada, House of Commons, *Debates*, 17 March 1905, 2600; Babe, *Telecommunications in Canada*, 95–99; Armstrong and Nelles, *Monopoly's Moment*, 169–170.

10. "The Government Telephone Enquiry," *Canadian Engineer*, June 1905, 170; *Canadian Annual Review*, 1905, 130–131.

11. Select Committee on Telephone Systems, *Report*, 1: ix–x, 1–8; See also "National-Owned Telephone System," *Toronto Globe*, 18 March 1905; "A Public Telephone," *Toronto Globe*, 20 March 1905; "Sir William Mulock's Case," *Kingston Weekly British Whig*, 16 October 1905; "Mulock Says," *Kingston Weekly British Whig*, 19 October 1905.

12. "Buying Up the Plants," *Kingston Weekly British Whig*, 27 March 1905; Dagger, "The Common Cause."

13. For civic populism, see Armstrong and Nelles, *Monopoly's Moment*, 141–162.

14. Select Committee on Telephone Systems, *Report*, 1: 1.

15. Select Committee on Telephone Systems, *Report*, 1: 766–767, 771–773, 987.

16. Select Committee on Telephone Systems, *Report*, 1: 754–763, 987.

17. Select Committee on Telephone Systems, *Report*, 1: 455, 776–780, 830, 842.

18. Select Committee on Telephone Systems, *Report*, 1: viii.

19. "A Splendid Administrator Lost to the Public Service," *Toronto Globe*, 11 October 1905; "Sir Wm. Mulock to the Bench," *Toronto Globe*, 12 October 1905; "Sir William Mulock's Retirement," *Toronto Globe*, 14 October 1905.

20. Armstrong and Nelles, *Monopoly's Moment*, 173, 270–280; Babe, *Telecommunications in Canada*, 114–125.

21. Canada, House of Commons, *Debates*, 28 March 1906, 751–761; Charles F. Sise to Frederick P. Fish, 11 October 1905, AT&T Letterbooks, BCHC.

22. Sise quoted in Fetherstonhaugh, *Charles Fleetford Sise*, 208; Ronald S. Love, *SaskTel: The Biography of a Crown Corporation and the Development of Telecommunications in Saskatchewan* (Regina, Sask.: SaskTel, 2003), 15–21.

23. American Telephone and Telegraph Company, *Map Showing Lines of the Bell Telephone Companies in the United States and Canada* (Boston: Heliotype Company, 1904), Map Collection, Widener Library, Harvard University, Cambridge, Massachusetts.

24. Urquhart, *Historical Statistics of Canada*, 14.

25. James Mavor, *Government Telephones: The Experience of Manitoba, Canada* (New York: Moffett, Yard, 1916), 14. But see also James Mavor, "Confidential Report on the Telephone Systems of Manitoba, Saskatchewan, and Alberta," 1914, HBS. Mavor's original manuscript included chapters judging Alberta and Saskatchewan's public systems much less harshly than Manitoba's and was less polemical than the published version overall.

26. Ronald S. Love, "For the General Good: The Debate over Private vs. Public Ownership of Telephones and the Canadian West, 1900–1912," *American Review of Canadian Studies* 35, no. 1 (2005): 67–97.

27. Christopher Armstrong and H. V. Nelles accept this characterization of agitation; Ronald Love and Tony Cashman do not.

28. Tony Cashman, *Singing Wires: The Telephone in Alberta* (Edmonton: Alberta Government Telephones , 1972), 23.

29. Cashman, *Singing Wires*, 89, 100–103.

30. Michael Denny, *Government Enterprise in Western Canada's Telecommunications*, Discussion Paper No. 301 (Ottawa: Economic Council of Canada, 1986), 33–35; Babe, *Telecommunications in Canada*, 102.

31. Cashman, *Singing Wires*, 119–121; Denny, *Government Enterprise*, 33–38.

32. Hugh R. Ross, *Thirty-Five Years in the Limelight: Sir Rodmond P. Roblin and His Times* (Winnipeg, Man.: Farmer's Advocate, 1936), 28–33; Denny, *Government Enterprise*, 41; Barry Ferguson and Robert Wardhaugh, *Manitoba Premiers of the 19th*

and 20th Centuries (Regina, Sask.: Canadian Plains Research Center Press, 2010), 118–128.

33. Cashman, *Singing Wires*, 137; *Canadian Annual Review*, 1907, 597–598.

34. Love, *SaskTel*, 56–68.

35. Mavor, *Government Telephones*, 16–17; Britnell, "Public Ownership of Telephones in the Prairies," 37; Rens, *Invisible Empire*, 107–109.

36. Ferguson and Wardhaugh, *Manitoba Premiers*, 134–137.

37. Babe, *Telecommunications in Canada*, 101–107.

38. Cashman, *Singing Wires*, 359–365; Denny, *Government Enterprise*, 39–48.

39. Armstrong and Nelles, *Monopoly's Moment*, 282–292; Babe, *Telecommunications in Canada*, 107–111; Love, *SaskTel*, 69–178.

40. David H. Laycock, *Populism and Democratic Thought in the Canadian Prairies, 1910–1945* (Toronto: University of Toronto Press, 1990); Brett Fairbairn, "Canada's 'Co-operative Province': Individualism and Mutualism in a Settler Society, 1905 to 2005," in *Perspectives of Saskatchewan*, ed. Jene M. Porter (Winnipeg: University of Manitoba Press, 2009), 149–173.

41. Thomas Grindlay, *The Independent Telephone Industry in Ontario: A History* (Toronto: Ontario Telephone Service Commission, 1975); Babe, *Telecommunications in Canada*, 116–117; Armstrong and Nelles, *Monopoly's Moment*, 289–290.

42. It is now Telus Quebec, a subsidiary of Telus Communications, the corporation created by the merging of Alberta Government Telephones, Edmonton Telephone, and British Columbia Telephone.

43. Quoted in Fargo, "The Canadian Convention."

44. "Hello Montreal! Vancouver Is Speaking," *Vancouver Province*, 15 February 1916; E. B. Ogle, *Long Distance Please: The Story of the Trans Canada Telephone System* (Toronto: Collins, 1979), 44–46; Robert MacDougall, "The All-Red Dream: Technological Nationalism and the Trans-Canada Telephone System," in *Canadas of the Mind: The Making and Unmaking of Canadian Nationalisms in the Twentieth Century*, ed. Adam Chapnick and Norman Hillmer (Montreal: McGill-Queen's University Press, 2007), 46–62.

45. Select Committee on Telephone Systems, *Report*, 1: 771–772, 776.

46. MacDougall, "The All-Red Dream," 53–56.

47. Ogle, *Long Distance Please*, 9.

48. See Walter S. Allen, "Facts and Comments on Consolidations and Mergers of Telephone Companies," 27 April 1913, and in general, the various Predecessor and Subsidiary Company Files in AT&T-TX.

49. Schiller, *How to Think About Information*, 63.

50. Edward J. Hall to Frederick P. Fish, 24 July 1904, Box 1348, AT&T-NJ.

51. "Split May Shelve Telephone Inquiry," *New York Times*, 23 February 1905; "Impugns the Motives of Telephone Probers," *New York Times*, 8 March 1905; "Lower Telephone Rates Promised by Company," *New York Times*, 14 March 1905.

52. The first Merchants Association report was reprinted by Bell's New York affiliate and widely circulated as *Telephone Competition from the Standpoint of the Public* (New York: New York Telephone Company, 1906); the second Merchants Association report is DeBerard, *Supplemental Telephone Report.*

53. "The National Civic Federation and Trust Legislation," *Telephony*, 6 November 1909, 458; Alan Stone, *Public Service Liberalism: Telecommunications and Transitions in Public Policy* (Princeton, N.J.: Princeton University Press, 1991), 160–164.

54. David F. Weiman and Richard C. Levin, "Preying for Monopoly? The Case of Southern Bell Telephone Company, 1894–1912," *Journal of Political Economy* 102, no. 1 (1994): 103–126.

55. Theodore N. Vail, "Mutual Relations and Interests of the Bell System and the Public," August 1913, TPH.

56. AT&T, *Annual Report*, 1907, 18.

57. David Nord, "The Experts Versus the Experts: Conflicting Philosophies of Municipal Utility Regulation in the Progressive Era," *Wisconsin Magazine of History* 58, no. 3 (1975): 219–236; Priest, "The Origins of Utility Regulation." For the National Civic Federation's support of state-level utility commissions, see National Civic Federation, Commission on Public Ownership and Operation, *Municipal and Private Operation of Public Utilities* (New York: National Civic Federation, 1907). A detailed compilation of telephone regulation in force by 1913 appears in American Telephone and Telegraph Company, *Comparative Summary of Laws Relating to the Regulation of Telephone and Telegraph Companies by Commission*, 3rd ed. (Boston: American Telephone and Telegraph Company, 1914).

58. "Ring Off, Mr. Hanly," *Telephony*, April 1908, 233–234; Central Union manager quoted in Lipartito, *The Bell System and Regional Business*, 194.

59. H. Erickson, "The Advantage of State Regulation," *Annals of the American Academy* 57 (1915): 123–162; Mueller, *Universal Service*, 119–128. California Utility Commission quoted in Stone, *Public Service Liberalism*, 126.

60. U.S. Census, *Historical Statistics of the United States*, 2: 783–784.

61. Quoted in Lipartito, *The Bell System and Regional Business*, 137.

62. Central Union, *Annual Report*, 1900, 1–2. The 151 companies connecting with Central Union in 1900 were only a fraction of the hundreds of independent companies in the territory it served. The Census Bureau counted 1,027 commercial and mutual companies, probably an underestimate, in the states of Illinois, Indiana, and Ohio (the area served by Central Union) in 1902. Thus, only about one in seven independent systems in the region were willing to connect with Central Union at this early date. U.S. Census, *Telephones and Telegraphs: 1902*, 9–10.

63. Theodore N. Vail to Local Managers, 10 February 1908, Box 1364, AT&T-NJ.

64. Henry A. Barnhart to Dr. E. B. Swift, 22 August 1905, HAB; Latzke, *A Fight with an Octopus*, 53.

65. Paine, *In One Man's Life*, 226; Latzke, *A Fight with an Octopus*, 71; MacMeal, *The Story of Independent Telephony*, 159.

66. Robert C. Hall to James A. Fowler, 11 June 1912, Box 37, Record Group 60, DOJ-NA.

67. "Independent 'Phone Companies Merged," *New York Times*, 9 October 1905; John, *Network Nation*, 320–321.

68. "Will Hold Up Telephone," *New York Times*, 16 November 1905; "May Get Independent Telephone Concerns," *New York Times*, 3 February 1907; "Jackson Fights Telephone Merger," *New York Times*, 28 February 1907; "Capital $50,000,000, with No Assets," *New York Times*, 13 February 1908; John, *Network Nation*, 320–321.

69. Harry B. Thayer to Theodore N. Vail, 18 November 1909, Box 1376, AT&T-NJ; MacMeal, *The Story of Independent Telephony*, 177–178; Gabel, "Competition in a Network Industry," 555–558.

70. AT&T, *Annual Report*, 1910, 21, 49–52; AT&T, *Annual Report*, 1909, 8–12.

71. Leroy D. Kellogg to William Howard Taft, 9 December 1911, Box 37, Record Group 60, DOJ-NA. MacMeal does not list Kellogg among "the famous 'Committee of Seven'" but says that "other Independent leaders also attended these conferences," so it is not clear exactly what significance the group of seven had. MacMeal, *The Story of Independent Telephony*, 184–185.

72. Geist, *The Lincoln Telephone and Telegraph Company*, 9–13; Gary quoted in MacMeal, *The Story of Independent Telephony*, 188.

73. MacMeal, *The Story of Independent Telephony*, 184–188.

74. James A. Fowler, "Memorandum for the Attorney General with Reference to the Telephone Situation," 28 April 1913, Box 38, Record Group 60, DOJ-NA; Geist, *The Lincoln Telephone and Telegraph Company*, 11–13; Mueller, *Universal Service*, 110–114.

75. MacMeal, *The Story of Independent Telephony*, 195–196.

76. "Says Vail Planned a Telephone Trust," *New York Times*, 21 November 1913; Bert G. Hubbell to James C. McReynolds, 19 September 1913, Box 38, and Bert G. Hubbell to James A. Fowler, 5 April 1912, Box 39, Record Group 60, DOJ-NA.

77. John H. Wright to George W. Wickersham, 4 November 1911, John H. Wright to George W. Wickersham, 12 September 1912, and John H. Wright to Joseph P. Tumulty, 11 March 1913, Boxes 37 and 38, Record Group 60, DOJ-NA; *National Cyclopaedia of American Biography* (New York: James T. White, 1954), 39: 470–471.

78. Manford Savage to James C. McReynolds, 17 December 1913, Box 38, Record Group 60, DOJ-NA.

79. John H. Wright to George W. Wickersham, 19 March 1912 and 12 September 1912, Box 37, Record Group 60, DOJ-NA.

80. Manford Savage to James C. McReynolds, 17 December 1913, Box 38, Record Group 60, DOJ-NA; Edwin P. Grosvenor, "Memorandum for the Attorney General," 2 December 1908, Box 37, Record Group 60, DOJ-NA.

81. John H. Wright to George W. Wickersham, 4 November 1911, Box 37, Record Group 60, DOJ-NA. See also John H. Wright to George W. Wickersham, 19 March 1912 and 12 September 1912, Box 37, DOJ-NA; John H. Wright, "Memorandum Submitted to the Honorable George W. Wickersham, Attorney General of the United

States, by John H. Wright, Jamestown, New York, in Behalf of the Independent Telephone Companies of the United States, Alleging Violation of the Sherman Law by the Bell Telephone Company," n.d., Box 38, Record Group 60, DOJ-NA.

82. John W. Wright to George W. Wickersham, 4 November 1911 and 19 March 1912, Box 37, Record Group 60, DOJ-NA.

83. Fowler, "Memorandum for the Attorney General," 1–2.

84. John H. Wright to George W. Wickersham, 26 December 1911, Box 37, and John H. Wright to Woodrow Wilson, 11 March 1913, Box 38, DOJ-NA.

85. John H. Wright to George W. Wickersham, 19 March 1912, Box 37, and John H. Wright to J. P. Tumulty, 11 March 1913, Box 38, DOJ-NA.

86. Fowler, "Memorandum for the Attorney General," 2, 7–13.

87. George W. Wickersham, "Memorandum for Mr. Fowler," 29 August 1912, Box 37, Record Group 60, DOJ-NA; John H. Wright to James A. Fowler, [date unclear but probably March 1913], Box 38, Record Group 60, DOJ-NA.

88. Wickersham, "Memorandum for Mr. Fowler."

89. George W. Wickersham to Charles A. Prouty, 7 January 1913, Box 37, Record Group 60, DOJ-NA.

90. Fowler, "Memorandum for the Attorney General," 13; James A. Fowler to John H. Wright, 18 March 1913, Box 38, Record Group 60, DOJ-NA.

91. C. J. Smyth to James C. McReynolds, 14 October 1913, Box 39, Record Group 60, DOJ-NA.

92. Stuck with the Ohio company, the Morgan interests found themselves in awkward competition with AT&T, their supposed ally. Within a few months, they sold United States Telephone to a new set of investors, who reorganized the concern as the quasi-independent Ohio State Telephone Company. "Ohio Men to Take 16 Telephone Lines," *New York Times*, 22 May 1914; Pleasance, *The Spirit of Independent Telephony*, 102.

93. Albert S. Burleson, *Government Ownership of Electrical Means of Communication* (Washington, D.C.: Government Printing Office, 1914); David J. Lewis, *The Postalization of the Telephone and the Telegraph* (Washington, D.C., 1914); Chester I. Barnard, "Review of the Government Ownership Situation," 6 March 1917, Box 1364, AT&T-NJ.

94. Nathan C. Kingsbury to James C. McReynolds, 19 December 1913. The letter is reprinted in several places, including AT&T, *Annual Report*, 1913, 24–26.

95. Richard R. John holds that the compromise of 1913 should be called "the McReynolds settlement," and that it was a major defeat for AT&T because it entrenched the existing segmentation of the market and thwarted Theodore Vail's dreams of controlling both the telephone and telegraph systems. Milton Mueller, by contrast, argues that the settlement only seemed like a defeat for Bell. Its terms, he says, were far from generous to the independents and merely provided political cover for AT&T's continued consolidation of the industry. John, *Network Nation*, 359–363; Mueller, *Universal Service*, 129–135.

96. "Apparently, We Have Won," *Transmitter*, January 1914, 17–18; "A Gift from Santa Claus Bell," *Telephony*, 27 December 1913, 21.

97. "Independent Ass'n of America Disapproves Bell Contract," *Telephony*, 18 April 1914, 23; *Telephony*, 17 January 1914, 1; J. C. Kelsey, "The Voluntary Surrender," *Telephony*, 27 December 1913, 23; J. C. Kelsey, "Some New Year Thoughts," *Telephony*, 10 January 1914, 23; MacMeal, *The Story of Independent Telephony*, 209.

98. "The Man Behind the Government," *Transmitter*, January 1914, 19–20. Richard R. John remarks that "the McReynolds settlement might just as plausibly be called . . . 'Wright's Vindication.'" John, *Network Nation*, 361.

99. MacMeal, *The Story of Independent Telephony*, 216–219; Richard John, *Network Nation*, 361–362.

100. MacMeal, *The Story of Independent Telephony*, 208–209.

101. Pleasance, *The Spirit of Independent Telephony*, 81–87; Mueller, *Universal Service*, 130–133.

102. Kinloch Long Distance Telephone Company, *Annual Report of the Kinloch Long Distance Telephone Company*, 1914, HBS; Bert G. Hubbell to James C. McReynolds, 21 August 1914, Box 38, Record Group 60, DOJ-NA.

103. United States Independent Telephone Association to Thomas W. Gregory, 8 December 1916; Thomas W. Gregory to Woodrow Wilson, 27 January 1917; F. B. MacKinnon to Woodrow Wilson, 16 February 1917, all Box 38, Record Group 60, DOJ-NA; Mueller, *Universal Service*, 130–133.

104. Bert G. Hubbell to Thomas W. Gregory, 30 August 1916, Box 29, Record Group 60, DOJ-NA; MacMeal, *The Story of Independent Telephony*, 224–225.

105. "Town Is Talked Out on 'Phones," *Buffalo (N.Y.) Morning Express*, 1 June 1916; Federal Telephone and Telegraph Company et al., "An Analysis of the Present Unsatisfactory Telephone Conditions Now Existing in Western New York and a Plan for Remedying Them," 5 October 1917, Box 25, AT&T-NJ; John H. Wright to G. Carroll Todd, 8 October 1917, Box 38, Record Group 60, DOJ-NA; Mueller, *Universal Service*, 136–140.

106. Bert G. Hubbell to James C. McReynolds, 19 September 1913, Box 38, Record Group 60, DOJ-NA; "Town Is Talked Out on 'Phones," *Buffalo (N.Y.) Morning Express*, 1 June 1916; John H. Wright to G. Carroll Todd, 8 October 1917, Box 38, Record Group 60, DOJ-NA.

107. Richard Gabel, "The Early Competitive Era in Telephone Communication, 1893–1920," *Law and Contemporary Problems* 34, no. 2 (1969): 340–359, at 353. When Bell companies acquired noncompeting independents, they were not obligated to offset their purchases in this way.

108. U.S. Census, *Historical Statistics of the United States*, 2: 783–784; Mueller, *Universal Service*, 81, 145.

109. Woodrow Wilson, Presidential Proclamation of 22 July 1918, reprinted in U.S. Post Office, *Government Control and Operation of Telegraph, Telephone, and Marine Cable Systems, August 1, 1918, to July 31, 1919* (Washington, D.C.: Government Printing

Office, 1921), 45–47; Christopher N. May, *In the Name of War: Judicial Review and the War Powers Since 1918* (Cambridge, Mass.: Harvard University Press, 1989), 28–34.

110. 56 *Cong. Rec.* 9064 (13 July 1918); May, *In the Name of War*, 34–37.

111. Public Statement of Postmaster General, 23 July 1918, reprinted in U.S. Post Office, *Government Control*, 47; Vail quoted in Paine, *In One Man's Life*, 322.

112. May, *In the Name of War*, 37–45.

113. U.S. Post Office, *Government Control*, 33–34, 84–85; Henry A. Barnhart to Claude R. Stoops, 15 February 1919, HAB; Burleson quoted in May, *In the Name of War*, 47.

114. "Basis for Metering Service," *Telephony*, 15 November 1919, 11; John, *Network Nation*, 396–397.

115. May, *In the Name of War*, 45–50.

116. *New York World*, 19 April 1919, 21 April 1919; "Mr. Burleson's Adventure," *New York Times*, 30 April 1919; May, *In the Name of War*, 50–54.

117. Burleson and Vail quoted in Paine, *In One Man's Life*, 323–324; "The Tie That Binds," *New Republic*, 3 May 1919, 8; Nathan C. Kingsbury, Statement Before Senate Interstate Commerce Committee, 1919, Box 37, AT&T-NJ; A. Lincoln Levine, *Circuits of Victory* (Garden City, N.Y.: Doubleday, 1921), 215; "Government Control—Confidential Report to Directors," 1919, Box 1, AT&T-NJ; Schiller, "Social Movement in Telecommunications," 406–408.

118. Quoted in G. Hamilton Loeb, "The Communications Act Policy Toward Competition: A Failure to Communicate," *Duke Law Journal* 1978, no. 1 (1978): 1–56.

119. U.S. Census, *Historical Statistics of the United States*, 2: 783–784.

120. Peter Schauble, "Dual Telephone Service Ends in Philadelphia," *Bell Telephone Magazine*, Winter 1946, 311–316.

121. Norton E. Long, "The Public Relations Policies of the Bell System: A Case Study in the Politics of Modern Industry" (Ph.D. diss., Harvard University, 1937), 17.

122. Mueller, *Universal Service*, 159–162. See also Babe, *Telecommunications in Canada*, 121–126.

123. ITPA, "John H. Wright," 2; McCarthy, *The History of GTE*; Geist, *The Lincoln Telephone and Telegraph Company*, 14–21; MacMeal, *The Story of Independent Telephony*, 231.

124. Iain Wallace, *A Geography of the Canadian Economy* (Oxford: Oxford University Press, 2002); 19–40; Kaufman, *The Origins of Canadian and American Political Differences*, 189–196, 302–303.

Chapter 6. The System Gospel

1. Walter S. Gifford, Address Before National Association of Railroad and Utilities Commissioners, Dallas, Texas, 20 October 1927. Much of Gifford's speech is reprinted in Arthur W. Page, *The Bell Telephone System* (New York: Harper and Brothers, 1941), 11–13.

2. AT&T Publicity Conference, *Proceedings*, 1928, 20, 75, 104.

3. AT&T Publicity Conference, *Proceedings*, 1928, 20. Gifford's original words (typed) and the later revisions (in pencil) appear in the copy of the proceedings at the Harvard Business School's Baker Library.

4. AT&T's first survey of its own press coverage in the early 1900s found that 90 percent of the newspaper clippings sampled were hostile to Bell. James D. Ellsworth, "Autobiographical Notes by J. D. Ellsworth," 1928, Box 1066, AT&T-NJ.

5. Delos F. Wilcox, review of *The History of the Telephone*, by Herbert N. Casson, *Political Science Quarterly* 26, no. 1 (1911): 163–164.

6. Historians of technology embraced *system* as a concept some time ago, and a generation of scholars has made the large technological system their basic unit of historical analysis. But fewer have interrogated the intellectual history of system as an idea, or acknowledged the role this notion played in constructing the very technological systems we chronicle. The classic works are Hughes, *Networks of Power*; Wiebe E. Bijker, Thomas P. Hughes, and Trevor J. Pinch, eds., *The Social Construction of Technological Systems: New Directions in the Sociology and History of Technology* (Cambridge, Mass.: MIT Press, 1987).

7. Herbert N. Casson, *The Story of My Life* (London: Efficiency Magazine, 1931), 57–61, 107–108; W. Fitzhugh Brundage, *A Socialist Utopia in the New South: The Ruskin Colonies in Tennessee and Georgia* (Chicago: University of Illinois Press, 1996), 55–59, 177–179.

8. Casson, *The Story of My Life*, 152–189; Mathew Thompson, *Psychological Subjects: Identity, Culture, and Health in Twentieth-Century Britain* (Oxford: Oxford University Press, 2006), 158–160.

9. See, e.g., Herbert N. Casson, *What We Believe* (Lynn, Mass.: Lynn Labor Church, 1896); Herbert N. Casson, *Organized Self-Help: A History and Defence of the American Labor Movement* (New York: Peter Eckler, 1901); Herbert N. Casson, "New Wonders of Ant Life," *Munsey's Magazine*, May 1905, 235–241; Herbert N. Casson, *The Romance of the Reaper* (New York: Doubleday, Page, 1908); Herbert N. Casson, *Factory Efficiency: How to Increase Output, Wages, Dividends, and Goodwill* (London: Efficiency Magazine, 1917).

10. Casson, *The History of the Telephone*, 141–142, 195; Vail, *Views on Public Questions*, 344.

11. AT&T, *Annual Report*, 1914, 42–43.

12. See, e.g., Mueller, *Universal Service*; John, *Network Nation*, 340–369.

13. Quoted in John, *Network Nation*, 348.

14. AT&T, *Annual Report*, 1911, 36–37.

15. Daniel C. McCallum quoted in Alfred D. Chandler, ed., *The Railroads, the Nation's First Big Businesses: Sources and Readings* (New York: Harcourt, Brace, 1965), 101; Charles E. Perkins, "Memorandum on Organization," [1885?], Chicago, Burlington, and Quincy Railroad Papers, Newberry Library, Chicago.

16. Frederick Winslow Taylor, *The Principles of Scientific Management* (New York: Harper, 1911), 2; David A. Hounshell, *From the American System to Mass Production,*

1800–1932: The Development of Manufacturing Technology in the United States (Baltimore: Johns Hopkins University Press, 1984), 229; William Cronon, *Nature's Metropolis: Chicago and the Great West* (New York: W. W. Norton, 1991), 207–212; Jon Agar, *The Government Machine: A Revolutionary History of the Computer* (Cambridge, Mass.: MIT Press, 2003), 45–74. On the prestige of engineering, see Cecelia Tichi, *Shifting Gears: Technology, Literature, Culture in Modernist America* (Chapel Hill: University of North Carolina Press, 1987); John M. Jordan, *Machine-Age Ideology: Social Engineering and American Liberalism, 1911–1939* (Chapel Hill: University of North Carolina Press, 1994).

17. See, e.g., Thorstein Veblen, *The Theory of Business Enterprise* (New York: Charles Scribner's Sons, 1904); "Com. N. Sense," ed., *Desk System: A Complete Laboratory Course in Systematizing the Desk and in Systematizing the Man* (Chicago: R. A. Daniels, 1907); Theodore N. Vail, "Business Training," *System*, November 1909; Siegfried Giedion, *Mechanization Takes Command: A Contribution to Anonymous History* (New York: Oxford University Press, 1948), 512–522.

18. Taylor, *Principles of Scientific Management*, 3.

19. John, "Civic Origins of Universal Service," 77. On the implications of system, see also James R. Beniger, *The Control Revolution: Technological and Economic Origins of the Information Society* (Cambridge, Mass.: Harvard University Press, 1986); JoAnne Yates, *Control Through Communication: The Rise of System in American Management* (Baltimore: Johns Hopkins University Press, 1989).

20. Frederick W. Taussig, "The Iron Industry of the United States," *Quarterly Journal of Economics* 14, no. 2 (1900): 158.

21. See, e.g., Taylor, *The Principles of Scientific Management*; Robert F. Hoxie, *Scientific Management and Labor* (New York: Appleton, 1915); James Livingston, "The Social Analysis of Economic History and Theory: Conjectures on Late Nineteenth-Century American Development," *American Historical Review* 92, no. 1 (1987): 69–95; David Montgomery, *The Fall of the House of Labor: The Workplace, the State, and American Labor Activism, 1865–1925* (Cambridge: Cambridge University Press, 1987), 216–256.

22. Martin, *Hello, Central*, 50–90; Green, "Goodbye Central" 930–934.

23. AT&T, *Annual Report*, 1909, 23.

24. John J. Carty, Angus Smith Hibbard, and Frank A. Pickernell, "The New Era in Telephony," in NTEA, *Proceedings*, 1889, 34–43.

25. NTEA, *Proceedings*, 1889, 43–45.

26. Edward J. Hall, "Corporate Organization," in NTEA, *Proceedings*, 1890, 43–56. Angus Hibbard remarked on the novelty of Hall's charts in Hibbard, *Hello, Goodbye*.

27. E. B. Field to John J. Carty, 8 September 1909, Box 2029, AT&T-NJ, emphasis in original.

28. FCC, *Proposed Report*, 26–28; Danielian, *AT&T*, 57–66.

29. See, e.g., "Consolidation Talk," *New York Times*, 30 December 1899; Stehman, *Financial History of AT&T*, 56–59; MacMeal, *The Story of Independent Telephony*, 112. On exaggeration of Morgan's role, see John, *Network Nation*, 312–313.

30. Edward J. Hall to Theodore N. Vail, 27 September 1909, Box 1010, AT&T-NJ; John J. Carty to Edward J. Hall, 17 July 1907, Box 6, AT&T-NJ. See also Hugh G. J. Aitken, *The Continuous Wave: Technology and American Radio, 1900–1932* (Princeton, N.J.: Princeton University Press, 1985), 78–79; Wasserman, *From Invention to Innovation*, 110; Louis Galambos, "Theodore N. Vail and the Role of Innovation in the Modern Bell System," *Business History Review* 66, no. 1 (Spring 1992): 95–126.

31. Carty, *Telephone Service in America*, 17; Edward J. Hall to Frederick P. Fish, 30 October 1902, AT&T-NJ; "Application of Some General Principles of Organization," October 1909, Box 2029, AT&T-NJ; Garnet, *The Telephone Enterprise*, 135–138; "The Central Union Telephone Company / Chicago Telephone Company," 1.

32. Nance and Oram, "The Circuits Go Up," 23. On the technical history of the transcontinental line see Frank B. Jewett, "Transcontinental Panorama," *Bell Telephone Quarterly* 19, no. 1 (1940): 38–58; Fagen, *Engineering and Science in the Bell System*, 195–348; Aitken, *Continuous Wave*, 233–245.

33. AT&T, *Annual Report*, 1914, 42–43.

34. American Telephone and Telegraph Company, *Everybody Join In: The Blue Bell Songbook* (New York: American Telephone and Telegraph Company, [1920?]), Donald McNicol Collection, Queen's University Special Collections, Kingston, Ontario (hereafter QUSC); Andrew L. Russell, "Standardization Across the Boundaries of the Bell System, 1920–1938," in *By Whose Standards? Standardization, Stability, and Uniformity in the History of Information and Electrical Technologies*, ed. James Sumner and Graeme J. N. Gooday (London: Continuum, 2008), 37–52.

35. Cumberland Telephone, *Annual Report*, various years; Caldwell, *Recollections of a Life Time*, 142–148.

36. Caldwell, *Recollections of a Life Time*, 174–179.

37. Caldwell, *Recollections of a Life Time*, 190–198, 209.

38. James E. Caldwell to Cumberland Telephone and Telegraph Company Stockholders, 27 December 1911, HBS. Caldwell retired after writing this letter, and AT&T moved the headquarters of Cumberland Telephone and Telegraph from Nashville to Atlanta.

39. Lamoreaux, *The Great Merger Movement*; Livingston, "The Social Analysis of Economic History," 82–85.

40. Nathan C. Kingsbury, "Address Before the Telephone Society of New York," 17 February 1914, TPH, 3–6.

41. John D. Rockefeller Jr. to Frederick T. Gates, 27 July 1912, reprinted in John M. Jordan, "'To Educate Public Opinion': John D. Rockefeller, Jr. and the Origins of Social Scientific Fact-Finding," *New England Quarterly* 64, no. 2 (1991): 292–297. Vail's proposals are described in Theodore N. Vail, "Memorandum Concerning a Proposed Economic Bureau," Rockefeller Foundation Draft Report, April 1914, quoted in David M. Grossman, "American Foundations and the Support of Economic Research," *Minerva* 20, nos. 1–2 (1982): 59–82. Discussions apparently trailed off because Rockefeller sought to create a comprehensive research institute, while Vail and Morgan envisioned

only a public relations bureau. See also John Ensor Harr and Peter J. Johnson, *The Rockefeller Century* (New York: Charles Scribner, 1988), 127.

42. Rockefeller quoted in Jordan, "To Educate Public Opinion," 295; Marchand, *Creating the Corporate Soul*, 48–87; Stuart Ewen, *PR! A Social History of Spin* (New York: Basic, 1996), 85–101.

43. Vail quoted in Prescott C. Mabon, *A Personal Perspective on Bell System Public Relations* (New York: American Telephone and Telegraph Company, 1972), 2; Theodore N. Vail, "Address at Annual Conference of the Bell Telephone System in New York," October 1913, reprinted in Vail, *Views on Public Questions*, 143–157.

44. Ellsworth, "Autobiographical Notes"; James D. Ellsworth, "Introduction to Historical Memoranda on Bell System Publicity," 1929, 4, Box 1066, AT&T-NJ; James D. Ellsworth, "The Start of General Magazine Advertising," 1931, Box 1066, AT&T-NJ; Noel L. Griese, "James D. Ellsworth, 1863–1940: PR Pioneer," *Public Relations Review* 4, no. 2 (1978): 22–31.

45. Extensive collections of AT&T advertisements can be found in both AT&T Archives locations (at Warren, New Jersey, and San Antonio, Texas), as well as in the Bell Canada Historical Collection, Montreal, Quebec, and the N. W. Ayer Advertising Agency Records, National Museum of American History, Smithsonian Institution, Washington, D.C. They can also be found in many of the period's major magazines, including *Life*, *Scribner's*, and the *Saturday Evening Post*.

46. Theodore N. Vail, "Report on the Operations of the Telephone Business," 19 March 1880, Box 1080, AT&T-NJ; Robertson T. Barrett, "The Beginnings of Institutional Advertising in the Bell System," 1931, Box 1198, AT&T-NJ; Robertson T. Barrett, "Bell System Advertising and Publicity," 1931, Box 1066, AT&T-NJ.

47. Quoted in Marchand, *Creating the Corporate Soul*, 86.

48. Gifford quoted in AT&T Publicity Conference, *Proceedings*, 1928, 33–34; Edward J. Hall, "General Policy," 2, File on Public Relations-Securities-Competition to 1920, Box 56, AT&T-NJ; Herbert N. Casson, "The Future of the Telephone," *World's Work*, May 1910, 12903–12918; Fay, *Big Business and Government*, 30.

49. *Bell Telephone News*, August 1915, 1.

50. Ellsworth, "Autobiographical Notes"; Ellsworth, "Introduction to Historical Memoranda on Bell System Publicity"; Barrett, "Institutional Advertising in the Bell System"; James D. Ellsworth to Edward J. Hall, 18 February 1908, Box 1317, AT&T-NJ; AT&T Publicity Conference, *Proceedings*, 1916, 36, Box 1310, AT&T-NJ.

51. Walter S. Allen to Frederick P. Fish, 22 July 1904, Box 1398. AT&T-NJ.

52. Quoted in Marchand, *Creating the Corporate Soul*, 75.

53. See, e.g., "Ultimate Telephony," *Telephony*, September 1908, 125–126; Edward J. Hall to E. M. Burgess, 30 March 1905, Box 1309, AT&T-NJ.

54. Elbert Hubbard, *Our Telephone Service* (East Aurora, N.Y.: Roycrofters, 1913), 28; Marchand, *Creating the Corporate Soul*, 76–80.

55. See remarks of William Banning in AT&T Publicity Conference, *Proceedings*, 1921, 3–13, Box 1310, AT&T-NJ.

56. Marchand, *Creating the Corporate Soul*, 74–80.

57. James D. Ellsworth to G. E: McFarland, 10 March 1922, President's Files, Pacific Telephone and Telegraph Company, AT&T-TX; American Telephone and Telegraph Company, *Telephone Almanac*, various years.

58. John Kimberly Mumford, "This Land of Opportunity: The Nerve-Centre of Modern Business," *Harper's Weekly*, 1 August 1908, 22.

59. Woodrow Wilson, *The New Freedom: A Call for the Emancipation of the Generous Energies of a People* (New York: Doubleday, Page, 1913), 47.

60. "The Tree System—The Bell System," AT&T Advertisement, June 1912.

61. Quoted in Casson, *The History of the Telephone*, 167.

62. Casson, *The History of the Telephone*, 206.

63. "The Cost of a Telephone Call," AT&T Advertisement, December 1914; "The Telephone Doors of the Nation," AT&T Advertisement, December 1913; "The Multiplication of Power," AT&T Advertisement, September 1909.

64. See, e.g., "Annihilator of Space," AT&T Advertisement, August 1910; "Where Woman's Service Looms Large," AT&T Advertisement, February 1919.

65. Casson, *The History of the Telephone*, 80; "Coordinating the Nation," 24; "The Master Builder's Triumph," *Bell Telephone News*, February 1915, 1.

66. "The Merger of East and West," AT&T Advertisement, August 1913.

67. Casson, *The History of the Telephone*, 80.

68. Quoted in Marchand, *Creating the Corporate Soul*, 73.

69. Michael Pupin, *Romance of the Machine* (New York: Charles Scribner's Sons, 1930), 77–81. On Pupin, see also Louis Galambos, *The Creative Society, and the Price America Paid for It* (Cambridge: Cambridge University Press, 2012), 22–28. The engineer and quasi-socialist Charles Proteus Steinmetz made similar arguments in this era about his employer, General Electric. "The industrial corporation is far from the inflexible, rigid machine which it appears to the outsider," Steinmetz wrote in 1916. "It is this flexibility which gives it economic power and strength." Charles P. Steinmetz, *America and the New Epoch* (New York: Harper, 1916), 175.

70. The inauguration of the transcontinental line was described in numerous company publications. See, e.g., AT&T, *The Story of a Great Achievement*; "Coordinating the Nation," *Telephone Review*, January 1915, 24; Arthur Pound, *The Telephone Idea: Fifty Years After* (New York: Greenberg, 1926); and John Mills et al., "A Quarter-Century of Transcontinental Telephone Service."

Conclusion

1. Lynd and Lynd, *Middletown in Transition: A Study in Cultural Conflicts* (New York: Harcourt, Brace, 1937), 76, 457–459. On differences between the first and second *Middletown* studies, see Dwight W. Hoover, *Middletown Revisited* (Muncie, Ind.: Ball State University, 1990), 11–17; Igo, *The Averaged American*, 60–64.

2. Lynd and Lynd, *Middletown in Transition*, 74–101. For the Balls, see Frank C. Ball, *Memoirs of Frank Clayton Ball* (privately printed, Muncie, Ind., 1937), CMS;

Edmund S. Ball, *From Fruit Jars to Satellites: The Story of Ball Brothers Incorporated* (New York: Newcomen Society, 1960).

3. Charles Wertenbaker, "Mr. Ball Takes the Trains," *Saturday Evening Post*, 6 February 1937, 5–6; on the *Saturday Evening Post* and the national grid, see Louise Appleton, "Distillations of Something Larger: The Local Scale and American National Identity," *Cultural Geographies* 9, no. 4 (2002): 421–447.

4. Lynd and Lynd, *Middletown in Transition*, 77, 458–459.

5. "Sales Management's Public Relations Index to 90 Large Corporations," *Sales Management*, 1 May 1938, 18–20, 64–65.

6. Von Auw, *Heritage and Destiny*, 23.

7. Kemper, *History of Delaware County*, 77, 210.

8. "A Bee-Line to Everyone," AT&T Advertisement, February 1917.

9. See, e.g., Susan J. Douglas, *Inventing American Broadcasting: 1899–1922* (Baltimore: Johns Hopkins University Press, 1987); Robert W. McChesney, *Telecommunications, Mass Media, and Democracy: The Battle for the Control of U.S. Broadcasting, 1928–1935* (New York: Oxford University Press, 1993); Fred Turner, *From Counterculture to Cyberculture: Stewart Brand, the Whole Earth Network, and the Rise of Digital Utopianism* (Chicago: University of Chicago Press, 2006).

10. Richard Simeon, "Considerations on Centralization and Decentralization," *Canadian Public Administration* 29 (1986): 445–461; Alan C. Cairns, *Constitution, Government, and Society in Canada* (Toronto: McClelland and Stewart, 1988).

11. On the development of telephony in Europe, see Eli Noam, *Telecommunications in Europe* (Oxford: Oxford University Press, 1992); Davies, *Telecommunications and Politics*; Beauchamp, "The Telephone Patents."

12. Fischer, *America Calling*, 222–254.

13. Richard O. Davies, *Main Street Blues: The Decline of Small-Town America* (Columbus: Ohio State University Press, 1998).

14. David Edgerton, *The Shock of the Old: Technology and Global History Since 1900* (Oxford: Oxford University Press, 2007), ix.

15. See, famously, John Perry Barlow, "A Declaration of the Independence of Cyberspace," e-mail to Electronic Frontier Foundation, 8 February 1996. For critiques of these ideas, see Lawrence Lessig, *Code, and Other Laws of Cyberspace* (New York: Basic, 1999); Jack Goldsmith and Tim Wu, *Who Controls the Internet? Illusions of a Borderless World* (Oxford: Oxford University Press, 2006); Robert W. McChesney, *Communication Revolution: Critical Junctures and the Future of Media* (New York: New Press, 2007).

16. On generative platforms, see Jonathan Zittrain, *The Future of the Internet—And How to Stop It* (New Haven, Conn.: Yale University Press, 2008), 67–100.

Index

Adams, Henry Carter, 93
Alberta, 184, 186–190
Alberta Government Telephones (AGT), 190
Aldrich, Charles Henry, 107
Aldrich, Nelson, 242
Allen, D. E., 151
Allen, David, 50
Allen, Walter, 246
American Automobile Association, 206
American Bell Telephone Company, 77–85, 89–90, 120; and Bell Canada, 13, 86–88, 177; and Bell operating companies, 26–29, 38, 69, 79–82, 107, 235; and independents, 37, 47, 112, 115–116; and Indiana rate regulation, 37–38; patent rights, 29–30, 37, 40–41, 43, 47, 101–109; and telephone users, 94–95, 148. *See also* American Telephone and Telegraph Company; Bell System; National Bell Telephone Company
American Telegraph Company, 66
American Telephone and Telegraph Company (AT&T), 2, 85–86, 120–121, 257–258, 266; advertising and public relations, 17, 197, 227–228, 231–232, 242–255, 260–261; antitrust investigation, 208–214, 243; and Bell operating companies, 119–120, 235–242; financing, 121, 145; and historiography, 3–4, 225, 229; and independents, 2, 17, 141, 144, 172–173, 199–207, 212–214, 245–248; and long distance, 85–86, 119, 165, 168–171, 192–193, 238–239, 255–257; and regulation, 194–195, 197–199, 227–228; and telephone design, 155–159; and telephone users, 148, 155; wartime control, 218–222. *See also* American Bell; Bell System
American Telephone Journal, 170
American Tobacco Company, 212
Anderson, George, 74–75, 150, 196
antimonopolism, 5, 10–11, 113–114
Anti-Monopoly Party, 72
ants, 230–231
Ashley, W. J., 127
Atlantic Monthly, 160
Atlantic Telephone Company, 196
AT&T. *See* American Telephone and Telegraph Company
Automatic Electric Company, 138, 154, 156, 158, 224
automatic switching, 55, 136, 153–159, 224
Aylesworth, Allan, 180–182, 193–194

Baker, George F., 237
Ball Brothers, 259
Ball, George Alexander, 259–260
Barnes, Walter, 206
Barnhart, Henry A., 132–138, 140–141, 167, 171–172, 200, 220
Battle of Little Big Horn, 8
Beers, George, 50
Bell, Alexander Graham, 13, 61, 67–68, 255–256; American patents, 24, 29, 37, 47, 71, 106–108; and Bell companies, 8, 70, 73, 76, 288 n.62; Canadian patents, 43, 86–87; controversy over telephone's invention, 1, 40, 77, 101–104
Bell, Alexander Melville, 61, 86–87
Bell, Eliza Symonds, 61
Bell, Mabel Hubbard. *See* Hubbard, Mabel
Bell Atlantic, 137
Bell Canada, 86–89, 122–129; advertising and public relations, 16–17, 94, 177, 193–194, 262–263; and American Bell, 13, 86–87; federal charter, 33–35, 58–59, 93–94, 125, 176–177, 186, 188; and historiography, 14; and independents, 43–44, 88–89, 124–125, 190; in Kingston, 27, 42, 45–46, 56; and

Bell Canada (*continued*)
long distance, 34, 88–89, 176–177, 192–194; and Select Committee on Telephone Systems, 176–178, 180–183; in the Prairie Provinces, 184–188; in Quebec, 19–20, 33–34, 87–88, 163–164, 191–192
Bell Laboratories, 159, 238
Bell octopus, 1–2, 7, 64, 112, 243
Bell operating companies, 28–29, 81–82, 115–121, 264–265; and American Bell, 79, 107; and AT&T, 119–120, 235–242. *See also specific companies*
Bell System, 2, 3, 26, 90, 228, 231, 244, 249; breakup of, 158, 223, 266
Bell Telephone Company of Boston, 63, 68–71
Bell Telephone Company of Buffalo, 97–99
Bell Telephone Company of Canada. *See* Bell Canada
Bell Telephone Company of Pennsylvania, 206
Benham, George R., 209, 213
Bergeron, Joseph, 181
Berliner, Emile, 107
Bethell, Union, 117
Beveridge, Albert, 151
Big Business and Government (Fay), 129–130
Blackford, E. G., 95
Blair, Andrew George, 178
Board of Railway Commissioners (Canada), 178, 182
Bookwalter, Charles, 198
Borden, Robert, 182
Boston, 84, 86; Bell investors, 71–78, 82–89, 94, 120–122, 188
boycotts, 94–95, 100–101; Rochester boycott, 96–99, 208
Brandeis, Louis, 174
British Columbia Telephone (BCTel), 190, 192–193
British North America Act, 33, 174
Bryan, William Jennings, 135
Buffalo, New York, 98–99, 156, 216–217
Burleson, Albert Sidney, 212, 218–222
Busch, Adolphus, 135, 201
Butler, Benjamin Franklin, 72

Caldwell, James, 29, 32, 81–82, 116–117, 235, 239–241
Canadian Engineer, 57, 192
Canadian Independent Telephone Association, 44
Canadian Methodist Magazine, 127
Canadian Northern Railroad, 187
Canadian Pacific Railway, 13, 43, 176, 185, 187
Carey, James, 61
Carlton, Newcomb, 218–219
Carrel, James, 20, 33
Carty, John Joseph, 119, 155, 157, 235–238, 243, 250
Cassier's Magazine, 151–152
Casson, Herbert Newton, 229–233, 244, 249, 251–252, 254, 258
Central Canada, 45–46, 122–125, 131, 179; compared to Midwest, 5, 14–16, 24–25, 42, 51–60, 93–94, 167, 262–263. *See also* Ontario; Quebec
Central Union Telephone Company, 28, 100, 107, 219; and independents, 51, 115, 118–120, 144, 200, 202; and Indiana rate regulation, 36–41; in Muncie, 12, 28, 32, 49–51, 55, 164–165
Chicago, 31, 54, 57–58, 119, 123, 155–156
Chicago, Burlington, and Quincy Railroad, 232–233
Chicago Telephone Company, 31, 58, 81, 119, 146, 156
cities. *See* federalism; municipal governments.
Citizens Cooperative Telephone Company (Indianapolis), 40
Citizens Mutual Telephone Company (Rochester, N.Y.), 98
Citizens Telephone Company, 112
Citizens Telephone Company (Grand Rapids, Mich.), 57, 136
civic populism, 125, 127, 179
Civil War, 7–8, 64, 87, 252
Cleveland, Grover, 106
Colorado Bell Telephone Company, 237
Compagnie de Téléphone de Métis, 191–192
Compagnie de Téléphone des Marchands, 164
comparative history, 14–15, 275 n.37
competition, 47–48, 92–93, 115–122, 160–165, 195–197, 265–266; and antitrust law, 208–211, 215–216; Canadian attitudes toward, 126–129, 186; end of, 217–219, 223; in Muncie, 48–51, 219; regional patterns, 16, 57–59, 110–112, 114. *See also* dual service

Congress (U.S.), 65, 67, 218, 222
Congressional Record, 171
Connecticut, 111
Conservative Party, 177, 187
consumers, 55, 94, 96, 99, 101, 147–148, 263, 265, 272 n.8, 292 n.25
Cook, Frederick, 179
Cooke, Edward, 128, 161
cooperatives, 105, 109–110, 116, 136–141, 165, 190–191
corporations: "bigness," 6–8, 12, 63, 174, 244–245, 251; crown corporations, 189–191; legitimacy of, 10, 17, 29, 228, 242–243, 252–255, 260–262
courtship. *See* telephone, social uses
Crownover, William, 113, 117, 168
Cumberland Telephone and Telegraph Company, 29, 36–38, 100, 116–117, 239–241
Cushing, William Henry, 188
Cushman, Sylvanus D., 40, 106
Cushman Telephone Company, 40, 105, 154
Custer, George Armstrong, 8
Cuyahoga Telephone Company, 145, 168
Czolgosz, Leon, 240

Dagger, Francis, 123, 126, 128, 179, 182, 187–188, 190–191
Davis, Jefferson, 87
Davis, Thomas, 129
Davison, Henry Pomeroy, 203–205, 242
Delaware and Madison County Telephone Company, 12, 50–51, 164–165
Demers, Jacques, 191–192
Democratic Party, 72, 114, 134, 218
Department of Agriculture (U.S.), 151
Department of Justice (U.S.), 156, 207–212, 215–217, 222–223, 266
Detweiler, A.K., 118
Dewart, Hartley, 181
dial telephones. *See* automatic switching
Dickson, Frederick, 145, 168, 170–171
Dominion Telegraph Company, 87
Dorion, Antoine-Aimé, 33–34
Dougherty, Hugh, 171, 200–201
Drawbaugh, Daniel, 103–106
dual service, 12, 93, 160–164, 195–196, 199, 215–217, 304 n.91; *see also* competition
Dundas, Ontario, 44
Dunstan, Kenneth, 123–124

Eastman, George, 201
eavesdropping, 55, 152
economies of scale, 74–75, 93
Edison, Thomas, 71
Edmonton District Telephone Company (EdTel), 187, 190
Efficiency, 233
Electrical Review, 83
Electrical World, 80, 101
Ellsworth, James, 243–246, 248, 252
Emerson, Ralph Waldo, 72
Empire Subway Company, 202
Erickson, Charles, 154
Erickson, John, 154
Erie Railroad, 232, 234

farmers, 20, 30, 52, 105, 117
Farmers' Alliances, 67
Fay, Charles Norman, 36, 58, 73, 76, 81, 95–100, 129–130, 245, 249
Federal Telephone and Telegraph Company (Buffalo, N.Y.), 206, 215–216
Federal Telephone Company (Montreal), 43–44, 128
federalism, 14, 174–175, 225–226; American, 263; Canadian, 17, 33–34, 262–263, 279 n.40; and telephone, 25, 35, 194
Field, E.B., 237
Fight with an Octopus (Latzke), 1–2, 207–208
First World War, 156, 218–222, 230
Fish, Frederick P., 120–121, 144, 163
flat rate service, 55–56, 70, 82, 99, 146–153, 221; in Muncie, 38, 49; in Rochester, 97–99
Fleming, Sandford, 176
Forbes, John Murray, 72, 74
Forbes, William Hathaway, 71–78, 86; and Bell patents, 43, 101, 104–105; business strategy, 73–78, 82–83, 97; views on telephony, 37, 63, 73, 78, 90, 121
Ford, Henry, 233
Fort William, Ontario, 44
Fowler, James Alexander, 209–211, 213
France, Thomas, 100
franchise agreements. *See* municipal franchises
French Canadians, 87–88, 163–164, 191–192
French phone, 158–159

Garfield, James, 240
Garland, Augustus, 106

Gary, Theodore, 137, 193, 204, 223–224
Geist, James, 205
"general advantage of Canada" clause, 33–35, 48, 125, 177
General Telephone and Electronics (GTE), 137, 204
generativity, 264, 267–268
George, Henry, 35
Gherardi, Bancroft, 158
Gifford, Walter, 150, 159, 227–228, 245, 257
Gilded Age, 8, 273 n.15
Gilliland Electric Company, 27
Gompers, Samuel, 221
gossip. *See* telephone users: social uses
Gould, Jay, 66, 72, 87, 290 n.93
Grange, 67, 105, 126
Grant, George Monro, 13, 42, 175–176
Gray, Elisha, 71, 102–104
Great Southern Telephone and Telegraph Company, 107
Green, Norvin, 65, 75–76
Greenback-Labor Party, 72
Gregory, Thomas, 215
Guiteau, Charles, 240

Hall, Edward, 85–86, 98–100, 119, 155, 196, 236–238, 241, 245
Hall, Robert, 201
Hanly, Frank, 198
Harding, Warren, 218, 222
Harper's Weekly, 248
Harrison, Benjamin, 41, 107
Harrison, William Henry, 11. *See also* Kemper, General William Henry Harrison
Haultain, Frederick, 188
Hayes, Rutherford B., 8
"hello girls." *See* operators
Henderson, Thomas, 23, 27
Hibbard, Angus, 117, 119, 147, 235
Hill, Lysander, 103
History of the Telephone (Casson), 229–231, 244, 258
Hitchcock, William, 50
Home Telephone Company, 112
Home Telephone Company of San Francisco, 118
Howland, Oliver, 125
Hubbard, Elbert, 247
Hubbard, Gardiner Greene, 64–72; business strategy, 68–69, 146; and Bell, 67–72, 87, 103; and Vail, 78, 80; views on telephony, 63, 70–73, 90, 96–97, 108, 114, 246; and Western Union, 64–67, 69–71, 76–77
Hubbard, Mabel, 61, 67–68, 288 n.62
Hubbell, Bert, 145, 156, 206, 215–217
Hudson, John Elbridge, 84–86, 88, 115, 120–121, 155
Hutchinson, E.H., 216

Illinois Telegraph and Telephone Company, 58, 155–156
Independent Long Distance Telephone and Telegraph Syndicate, 202
Independent Telephone Association of America, 212–213
independent telephone movement. *See* independents
independents, 1–2, 47–48, 109–121, 132–173, 195, 223–224; advertising and rhetoric, 2, 64, 112–113, 142, 172; and AT&T, 17, 172–173, 199–207, 214, 223, 245–248; in Canada, 44–46, 48, 57, 126, 128, 191–192; in Chicago, 57–58, 119, 155–156; financing, 139, 144–145, 201; and government, 16–17, 48, 93–94, 109, 128, 205–209, 212–213; in Indiana, 15, 24–25, 30, 37, 39–40, 132, 166; and long distance, 165–171, 202–203, 214; manufacturers, 43, 47, 57, 107–109, 136–138, 158, 206; in New York City, 201–202; in Quebec, 163–164, 191–192; wartime control, 219–220; women, 135. *See also specific companies*
Indiana, 23, 47, 114, 132, 151, 166; compared to Ontario, 15–16, 24, 51–55, 57; rate regulation, 35–41; state legislature, 35, 37–38, 41
Indiana Bell Telephone Company, 219
Indiana District Telephone Company, 25
Indianapolis, 25, 36–41, 100, 156, 219
Indianapolis Daily Sentinel, 36, 38
Indianapolis Journal, 38, 40
Indianapolis Telephone Company, 144
Institute of Social and Religious Research, 22
interconnection, 93, 140–141, 160, 197, 199–200, 223
Internet, 261, 266–268
Interstate Commerce Commission (ICC), 210–211, 222
Interstate Independent Telephone Association, 132–134
Iowa, 47, 110–111, 114, 122

Iowa Telephone Company, 115, 117
"island communities," 9–10

Jackson, W.A., 118
Jamestown, New York, 216–217
Jamison, Leigh, 135
Jekyll Island Club, 257–258
Jewett, Frank, 159
Johnson, George, 150
Johnston, Alexander, 180
Jones, Samuel, 230
J.P. Morgan and Company, 144, 203–205, 208–209, 237–238, 259. *See also* Morgan, John Pierpont
Judicial Committee of the Privy Council (U.K.), 34, 125
Justice Department. *See* Department of Justice

Kansas, 47–48
Kansas City Long Distance Telephone Company, 206
Kansas City Telephone Company, 223
Keelyn, James, 138
Kellogg, Leroy DeWolf, 203
Kellogg, Milo Gifford, 107–109, 137, 158, 207, 295 n.55
Kellogg Switchboard and Supply Company, 108, 137, 158
Kelsey, J.C., 213
Kemper, Arthur, 163
Kemper, General William Henry Harrison, 11–12, 261
Keystone Telephone Company, 160, 223
Kingsbury, Nathan, 203, 209–213, 222, 242. *See also* "Kingsbury Commitment"
"Kingsbury Commitment," 212–215, 217, 219, 222, 242, 311 n.95, 312 n.98
Kingston, Ontario, 22–25; and Bell Canada, 27–28, 45–46; compared to Muncie, 15, 22–25, 27–28, 42, 52–54, 56, 58; as representative community, 15, 22–23
Kingston British Whig, 27, 179
Kinloch Telephone Company, 135, 214, 223
Kipling, Rudyard, 252
kitchen phones, 117
kitchen-to-farm service, 167
Knights of Labor, 35, 66, 95. *See also* "Telephone Subscribers as Knights of Labor" (Fay)
Kurtz, W.J., 48–49

Ladd, George, 117
La Porte, Indiana, 40, 154–155
Latzke, Paul, 1–2, 113, 137, 200–201, 207–208, 240, 263
Laurier, Wilfrid, 177–178, 182–183
Liberal Party (Canada), 177, 187
Leverett, George, 168
Lewis, David, 212
Lighthall, William, 125–128, 179
Lincoln Telephone and Telegraph Company, 136–137, 203, 224
Lindemuth, A.C., 113, 140, 161
localism, 4, 9, 12, 133, 139–140, 170–171, 206, 225
local operating companies. *See* Bell operating companies
local ownership, 12, 25, 29, 68–69, 139–140, 144, 206
local telephone service, 15, 21–22, 28, 33–34, 126, 168
Lockwood, Thomas, 155–156, 159
long distance telephone service, 28, 81–82, 84–86, 119, 165–170, 223–224; in Canada, 88, 176–177, 179–180, 192; and consolidation of Bell System, 235–239; transcontinental line, 168–170, 192–194, 238–239, 252, 255–258
long lines. *See* long distance telephone
Long, Milton, 26–28
Los Angeles, 156
Lynd, Robert and Helen, 11, 22, 167, 259–260, 276 n.9

Mackay, Clarence, 218, 220
Maclean, William Findlay, 178, 180, 182–183
MacMeal, Harry, 109, 137, 208
mail, 62, 67, 79–80, 234
Manitoba, 184, 186–190
Manitoba Telephone System (MTS), 189
Maritime Telephone and Telegraph Company, 193
Mason, John, 259
Massachusetts, 72, 84, 120
Mavor, James, 185, 307 n.25
McCallum, Daniel, 232, 234
McCann, Harry, 230
McCann Erickson, 230
McCormick, Cyrus, 231
McFarlane, Lewis, 127
McIntyre, Donald, 46

McKinley, William, 240
McReynolds, James Clark, 211–215, 242
measured service, 54–56, 82, 98, 147–148; in Muncie, 38, 49; in Rochester, 97–98
Mellett, J.E., 42
Merchants Association of New York, 162, 196
Merchants' Telephone Company, 164
mergers, 8, 74, 203–205, 208, 210, 216–219, 223
Methodist Church of Canada, 230
Metropolitan Telephone and Telegraph Company, 85, 95
Meucci, Antonio, 106
Microwave Communications, Inc. (MCI), 266
Middletown (Lynd and Lynd), 11, 22, 259, 275 n.39, 276 n.9. *See also* Muncie, Indiana
Middletown in Transition (Lynd and Lynd), 259–260
Midland Telephone Company, 28
Midwest (U.S.), 32, 35, 47–51, 109–111, 119, 122, 132–133, 172; compared to Central Canada, 5, 14–16, 24–25, 42, 51–60, 93–94, 167, 262–263. *See also specific states*
Mitchell, John Purroy, 256–257
Mock, E.J., 112, 161
Mohr, Sigismund, 33
monopoly. *See* antimonopolism; natural monopoly theory
Montreal, 20, 43–44, 87–88, 163–164
Montreal Telegraph Company, 87
Morgan, John Pierpont, 121, 136, 237–238, 242. *See also* J.P. Morgan and Company
Morgan, John Pierpont, Jr., 257–258
Morse, Samuel, 63, 79, 102
Morse code, 69, 79
Mulock, William, 178–183
Mulock Commission. *See* Select Committee on Telephone Systems
Mumford, John Kimberly, 248
Muncie, Indiana, 11, 22–25, 167, 259–261; and Central Union, 28, 32, 38, 49–50; independents in, 48–51, 140; compared to Kingston, 15, 22–25, 27–28, 42, 52–54, 56, 58; dual service in, 12, 163–165, 219; as representative community, 15, 22–23, 59, 275 n.39, 276 n.9. See also *Middletown*
Muncie Bell Telephone Company, 26–28
Muncie Electric Company, 49–50
Muncie Herald, 50
Muncie News, 27, 42, 48–50
municipal franchises, 48, 50, 111: in Canada, 44–47, 59; Chicago, 58; Indianapolis, 37–38; Kingston, 45–47; Muncie, 26, 48–49; Toronto, 45, 124–125
municipal governments: 16, 25, 58–60, 93–94, 267; in Canada, 33–34, 44–46, 124–128, 176–182, 186–187; in the United States, 25–26, 31–33, 35–38, 41, 48, 110–111, 197–198
municipal ownership, 48, 179–180, 186–187, 189–191
mutuals. *See* cooperatives

N.W. Ayer and Son, 244–245
Nate, J.J., 134
National Bell Telephone Company, 72–73, 75–77
National Board of Trade, 66
National Cash Register Company, 230
National Civic Federation, 197–198
National Independent Telephone Association (NITA), 132, 138, 140, 203–205, 207–208, 214
Nationaliste, Le (Quebec), 88
National Telegraph Act, 125
National Telephone Exchange Association (NTEA), 81–82, 235–236
national unity, telephone and, 13, 16, 175–177, 179, 193, 224–225, 262
natural monopoly theory, 92, 112, 114, 128–131, 186, 199, 222, 264
New Brunswick Telephone Company, 178, 193
New England Telephone and Telegraph Company, 142, 145, 150, 221
"New Era in Telephony" (Carty), 235–236
New Republic, 222
New York Associated Press, 66
New York Board of Trade and Transportation, 66, 196
New York Bureau of Labor, 96
New York City, 31, 84, 95, 99, 196, 201–202
New York State, 85, 120, 216–217; state legislature 31, 35, 99, 196, 201
New York Telephone Company, 196, 216, 230
New York Times, 31, 40, 43, 77, 95, 105–106, 221
nickel-in-the-slots, 118–119
Northwestern Telephone Company, 211
Northwest Mounted Police, 186
Northwest Rebellion, 9

Northwest Territories, 186
Norton, Charles, 112, 121

Ocean to Ocean (Grant), 176
Ochs, Anthony, 129
octopuses, 6–7, 174, 251, 255, 269. *See also* Bell octopus
Ohio, 47–48
Ohio State Telephone Company, 223
"one big system," 63, 78, 81, 289 n.74. *See also* Bell System; system idea
"One System, One Policy, Universal Service," 81, 232, 244. *See also* Bell System; "universal service"
Ontario, 16, 35, 44–45, 89, 179, 191, 193; compared to Indiana, 15–16, 24, 51–55, 57; provincial government, 34, 45
Ontario Municipal Association, 46
operating companies. *See* Bell operating companies
operators, 56, 153–156, 221, 235; in Kingston, 28; in Muncie, 27
Order of the Patrons of Husbandry. *See* Grange
Orthwein, William, 214–215
Orton, William, 65, 75
Outlook Magazine, 150–151

Pacific Bell Telephone Company, 117–118, 211
Pacific Telephone and Telegraph Company. *See* Pacific Bell Telephone Company
Paine, Albert, 79–80
Pan-Electric Telephone Company, 106, 280 n.54
Parliament (Canada), 33–34, 51, 94, 123, 176–178. *See also* Select Committee on Telephone Systems
patent cases, 30, 37, 40–41, 47, 101–108; Berliner suit, 107–108, 207; Drawbaugh suit, 103–106; Indiana cases, 37; Pan-Electric case, 106; Toronto Telephone Manufacturing suit, 43; Western Union suit, 71, 76–77, 102–103
patent rights: American, 1, 24, 26, 30, 43, 47, 92, 101–107; Canadian, 24, 35, 43, 86–87, 92; telegraph, 102
Patterson, John Henry, 230
Pennsylvania, 30
People's Mutual Company (Bigfoot, Ind.), 139
People's Party, 36, 66, 113–114, 142
people's telephone, 4–5, 63–64, 93, 108, 112, 133, 233, 248, 265, 268–269
People's Telephone Association (Rochester, N.Y.), 97
People's Telephone Company, 112
People's Telephone Company (New York City), 103–106, 108
People's Telephone Company (Winnipeg), 44
Perkins, Charles, 232–234
Peterborough, Ontario, 44
Philadelphia, 160, 223
Phillips, George, 40
Pickernell, Frank, 57, 144, 235
poles. *See* telephone, poles
political economy, 11, 60, 238, 263; and political culture, 16, 93, 114–115, 122, 172, 175
populism, 5, 10, 113–115; and political economy, 16, 93–94, 114–115, 172, 174–176; rhetoric, 64, 105–106, 112, 142, 245–246; *see also* civic populism, technological populism
Populists. *See* People's Party
postalization movement, 65–67, 212, 218
Postal Telegraph Company, 218, 220–221
Prairie Provinces, 184–191. *See also* Alberta; Manitoba; Saskatchewan
prank calls, 55, 152–153
Prouty, Charles, 210
provincial ownership, 189–191
Provincial Rights Party, 188
public telephones, 54
Pupin, Michael, 255

Quebec, 14–15, 35, 44, 87–89, 122, 164, 176, 179, 191–192; provincial government, 20, 33–34
Quebec City, 19–21, 33
Quebec Daily Telegraph, 19–20, 33
Queen's University, 13, 42

race, 23, 252, 254, 276 n.9, 297 n.97
railroads, 6–10, 13, 34, 44, 80. *See also specific companies*
rates, 35–38, 49, 76, 116, 118, 143–144, 162, 220, 287 n.54; rate regulation, 35–41, 55, 99, 182, 198–199, 227; rate structures, 54–56, 97, 146–153, 221. *See* flat rate service; measured service
regional operating companies. *See* Bell operating companies

Republican Party, 72, 114, 207, 220
Richmond, Virginia, 125
Riel, Louis, 9
Robinson, George W., 209
Roblin, Rodmond, 187–189
Rochester, Indiana, 132, 134–135
Rochester, New York, 96–99, 208, 216
Rochester Democrat and Chronicle, 97
Rochester Telephone Company, 132, 136
Rockefeller, John D., 230
Rockefeller, John D., Jr., 22, 242–243
Rockefeller, William, 257–258
Romance of the Machine (Pupin), 255
Rooker, Calvin, 37
Roosevelt, Theodore, 174
Ross, Charlie, 100, 293 n.28
Ruef, Abe, 118
rural telephones, 29–30, 54, 94, 123, 136, 139, 150–151, 165–167, 265
Ruskin Colonies, 230
Ryan, Edward, 45

Sabin, John, 117–119, 123, 147
Sales Management, 260
San Francisco, 31, 54, 117–119, 156, 163
Sanders, Thomas, 64, 68, 70–71
Saskatchewan, 184, 186–188, 190–191
Saskatchewan Government Telephones (SaskTel), 190
Saturday Evening Post, 259–260
scale, 17–18; economies of, 74–75, 93; politics of, 9–11, 174, 194
Scientific American, 106
scientific management, 230, 233–234
Scott, Richard, 128–129, 177
Scott, Walter, 188
Scott, William, 44
Select Committee on Telephone Systems (Canada), 51, 178–183, 187
Sennett, William, 135
Shanklin, George, 145
Shaw, Arch Wilkinson, 233
Sheldon, George R., 144
Sherman Antitrust Act, 208, 210
Sibley, Hiram, Jr., 201
Sise, Charles Fleetford, 87–89, 262; business strategy, 43–44, 46, 48, 177, 281 n.80; and French Canadians, 87–88, 191; and Mulock Commission, 180–183; and Prairie Provinces, 184–185, 188; views on telephony, 122–123, 149
Smith, Chauncey, 104
social construction of technology, 19, 272 n.8
Sound Waves, 112, 138, 152–153, 248
Southern Bell Telephone Company, 125
Southern New England Telephone Company, 81, 84, 111
Southwestern Bell Telephone Company, 223, 266
Sprint Nextel, 266
Standard Oil Company, 129, 212, 230, 242–243
state regulatory commissions, 195, 198–199, 217, 227
Steinmetz, Charles Proteus, 247 n.69
Storrow, James, 95, 104
strikes, 8, 96–99, 218, 221, 224. *See also* boycotts
Stromberg-Carlson Telephone Manufacturing Company, 138, 201–202
Strowger, Almon, 153–156
Supreme Court: Indiana, 37; United States, 41, 102, 104, 106, 107, 125, 215
Swedish-American Telephone Company, 138
system, 63, 78–80, 229–234, 241–242, 249–251
System (magazine), 233

Tarbell, Ida, 9
Tarte, Charles, 135
Taussig, Frederick, 234, 250
Taylor, Frederick Winslow, 233–234, 250
technological determinism, 130, 181, 193, 241, 265, 272 n.8
technological nationalism, 13, 175–176, 179, 185, 193, 262
technological populism, 176, 261–262
telegraph, 6–10, 13, 61–62, 65–67, 75–77
telephone: batteries, 117, 158–159; handsets, 158–159; invention of, 1, 40, 59, 61, 67–68, 77, 101–104; switchboards, 74–75, 156–157 (*see also* automatic switching); operators (*see* operators); party lines, 24, 55, 117, 119, 152; poles, 19–21, 31–32, 45; wires, 6, 20–21, 31, 45
"Telephone Poles" (Updike), 19
Telephone Protection Association, 138
"Telephone Subscribers as Knights of Labor" (Fay), 95

telephone users, 51–54, 94, 155, 157–158, 249; business users, 52–54, 76, 94–101, 162–163, 194–197; children, 54, 56, 148–149; cultures of use, 15, 24, 54–56, 148–153, 264; doctors, 42; druggists, 42, 100; farmers, 20, 30, 52, 117, 123, 140–141, 165–167, 180, 247–248; merchants, 100, 165, 167, 195–196; servants, 54, 148–149; social uses, 24, 55–56, 99, 148–153, 264; women, 54, 94, 135, 148–150, 247–248; working class, 24, 52–54, 56, 124
Telephony, 109, 137–138, 151, 161, 208, 212–213, 248
Telus Communications, 190
Thomas, James, 137
Todd, George Carroll, 216
Toronto, 124–125; city council, 34
Toronto Telephone Manufacturing Company, 43
Transmitter, 212–213
transnational history, 14–15, 275 n.37
Tri-State Telephone Company, 223
Tumulty, Joseph, 218, 221–222
Twain, Mark, 149
Tyler, Morris, 25, 32, 81–82, 235

Union of Canadian Municipalities, 125–126, 178–179, 187
Union Pacific Railroad, 79
United Independent Telephone Association, 205, 212–214
United States Independent Telephone Association, 214–215
United States Independent Telephone Company (Rochester, N.Y.), 201–202
United States Telegraph Company, 66
United States Telephone Company (Cleveland), 202–203, 205, 209, 211, 223, 311 n.92
universal service, 81, 124, 160, 199, 204, 232, 235, 244, 304 n.93
Updike, John, 19
Urquhart, Thomas, 179
U.S. Army, 156
U.S. Census Bureau, 30, 47, 110, 139
U.S. Patent Office, 102, 107
U.S. Postal Service, 62, 65, 67, 234
utility poles. *See* telephone, poles

Vail, Alfred, 79
Vail, Theodore Newton, 78–86, 121, 228–230, 237–245, 255–258; business strategy, 81–83, 99, 200, 203–206, 237–241; and long distance telephone, 81–86, 88–89, 168, 238–239, 255–257; political strategy, 195, 197–199, 210, 213–214, 242–245, 250; views on telephony, 63, 78–80, 90, 119, 148, 160, 163, 231–235, 248–250; and wartime control, 219–222
Veblen, Thorstein, 233
Verizon Communications, 137, 204, 224
Vincent, Walter, 160
"Visible Speech" (Bell), 61

War Labor Board (U.S.), 221
Ware, J. B., 57
Washington Star, 221
Watson, Thomas, 68, 255–257
Western Associated Press, 8
Western Electric Manufacturing Company, 107, 137–138, 158–159, 238
Western Electrician, 115
Western Union Telegraph Company, 7–8, 62–68, 87, 203; and telephone, 68–71, 75–77, 102–103; contract with American Bell, 76–77, 81, 85, 103, 214; takeover by AT&T, 203, 209, 212, 214; wartime control, 218–222
white telephone movies, 159
Wickersham, George Woodward, 207–211, 213
Wilcox, Delos Franklin, 229
Wilcoxon, Charles, 26–28
Wilcoxon, Lloyd, 26–28
wildcats, 30–31
Williams, Samuel, 35–37
Willis-Graham Act, 222
Wilson, A. F., 112, 142
Wilson, F. Page, 44–45, 57
Wilson, Woodrow, 211, 213, 218, 221–222, 249–250, 256
Winnipeg, Manitoba, 44, 184, 187
Wire Operating Board (U.S.), 219, 221
Wisconsin Independent Telephone Association, 148
Woods, Frank Henry, 136–137, 139, 203–205, 224, 257
Wright, John Henry, 206–209, 213, 215–217, 224, 232, 266

Yost, Casper, 115, 165

Zimmerman, Adam, 51, 54, 56, 182

Acknowledgments

Alexander Graham Bell remarked in 1901: "One would think I had never done anything worthwhile but the telephone." I know how he felt. I am sheepish about the time this book has taken to complete, but eager to express my gratitude to those who helped me along the way.

I thank my colleagues, students, and friends at the University of Western Ontario, the University of Utah, the American Academy of Arts and Sciences, and Harvard University for their patience, their impatience when warranted, and especially their friendship and support. Many of them improved this book with their insight; all of them improved my time writing it. Those who know they helped this project include Christopher Beauchamp, James Carroll, Lizabeth Cohen, Carolyn de la Peña, Rebecca Edwards, Walter Friedman, Peter Galison, Daniel Hamilton, Kristen Haring, Isadora Helfgott, Edward Jones-Imhotep, Michael Kimmage, Lisa Laskin, Chandra Manning, H. V. Nelles, Christopher Schmidt, Jonathan Schrag, Stephen Thernstrom, and Daniel Wadhwani. Others who might not know how indebted to them I am include Sven Beckert, Christopher Cappozzola, Greg Downey, Joshua Greenberg, Lisa Gitelman, Christopher Klemek, Sean Lawson, Ken Lipartito, Ralph Luker, Alan MacEachern, Eli Nathans, David Nye, Joy Parr, John Durham Peters, Robert Pike, Asif Siddiqi, Geoffrey Smith, Lisa Szefel, William Turkel, Fred Turner, Laurel Thatcher Ulrich, Robert Wardhaugh, and the late, great Richard VanDuzer. Thank you all.

I also thank all the archivists and librarians who made my research possible, especially George Henderson at the Queen's University Archives, Bruce Geelhoed at the Center for Middletown Studies, and William Caughlin and Sheldon Hochheiser at the AT&T Archives and History Centers in Texas and New Jersey. Devon Elliott, Heather Stephenson, and Anna Zuschlag were terrific research assistants and are fine scholars in their own right. This project received welcome financial assistance from the Center for Middletown Studies, the Charles Warren Center for American History, the American Academy of Arts and Sciences, and the Social Science and Humanities Research Council of Canada.

Bob Lockhart has been a terrific editor, wise and patient and encouraging exactly when I needed it. Series editors Richard R. John, Pamela Walker Laird, and Mark Rose have been great friends to this project and to me. I thank them for inviting me to join their fine series, for close readings of multiple drafts, and for many invaluable suggestions. Richard, by my lights the preeminent historian of American communications, inundated me with assistance, suggesting and sharing primary sources and offering crucial insight, encouragement, and advice. His enthusiasm may not have sped the completion of this book, but it has made it immeasurably better.

Finally, I thank my wonderful family. My children, Yuki and Eli, may not have sped the completion of this book either, but they made writing it, and everything else, worthwhile. My deepest thanks go to Lisa Faden, always, for her generosity and love.